D0421487

Sacral Kingship in Bourbon France

Sacral Kingship in Bourbon France

The Cult of Saint Louis, 1589–1830

Sean Heath

BLOOMSBURY ACADEMIC
LONDON • NEW YORK • OXFORD • NEW DELHI • SYDNEY

BLOOMSBURY ACADEMIC
Bloomsbury Publishing Plc
50 Bedford Square, London, WC1B 3DP, UK
1385 Broadway, New York, NY 10018, USA
29 Earlsfort Terrace, Dublin 2, Ireland

BLOOMSBURY, BLOOMSBURY ACADEMIC and the Diana logo are
trademarks of Bloomsbury Publishing Plc

First published in Great Britain 2021

Copyright © Sean Heath, 2021

Sean Heath has asserted his right under the Copyright, Designs and
Patents Act, 1988, to be identified as Author of this work.

For legal purposes the Acknowledgements on p. x constitute an extension
of this copyright page.

Cover Design: Ben Anslow
Cover image: 'Saint Louis recevant la couronne d'épines des mains du Christ' by
Michel Corneille l'Ancien (c.1601-1664) © The History Collection / Alamy Stock Photo

All rights reserved. No part of this publication may be reproduced or transmitted in any form or by any
means, electronic or mechanical, including photocopying, recording, or any information storage
or retrieval system, without prior permission in writing from the publishers.

Bloomsbury Publishing Plc does not have any control over, or responsibility for, any third-party
websites referred to or in this book. All internet addresses given in this book were correct at the
time of going to press. The author and publisher regret any inconvenience caused if addresses have
changed or sites have ceased to exist, but can accept no responsibility for any such changes.

Every effort has been made to trace copyright holders and to obtain their permissions for the use of
copyright material. The publisher apologises for any errors or omissions and would be grateful if notified
of any corrections that should be incorporated in future reprints or editions of this book.

A catalogue record for this book is available from the British Library.

Library of Congress Cataloging-in-Publication Data

Names: Heath, Sean, author.
Title: Sacral kingship in Bourbon France : the cult of Saint Louis,1589-1830 / Sean Heath.
Description: First edition. | London ; New York : Bloomsbury Academic, 2021. |
Includes bibliographical references and index. | Summary: "What does Saint Louis'
cult actually reveal about the Bourbon monarchy's
ability to foster a political culture of loyalty through all religious, political, and intellectual challenges
of this era? From manuscripts to paintings to music, Sean Heath skillfully engages with a vast array
of primary source material and modern debates on sacral kingship to provide an enlightening and
comprehensive analysis of the role of Saint Louis inearly modern France"– Provided by publisher.
Identifiers: LCCN 2020039282 (print) | LCCN 2020039283 (ebook) | ISBN
9781350173194 (hardback) | ISBN 9781350214644 (paperback) | ISBN 9781350173200 (ebook)
Subjects: LCSH: France–History–Bourbons, 1589-1789. | Divine right of
kings. | Louis IX, King of France, 1214-1270–Cult. | France–Kings and
rulers–Religious aspects. | France–Politics and government–1589-1789.| Monarchy–France–History.
Classification: LCC DC121.3 .H43 2021 (print) | LCC DC121.3 (ebook) | DDC944/.03–dc23
LC record available at https://lccn.loc.gov/2020039282
LC ebook record available at https://lccn.loc.gov/2020039283

ISBN: HB: 978-1-3501-7319-4
ePDF: 978-1-3501-7320-0
eBook: 978-1-3501-7321-7

Typeset by Deanta Global Publishing Services, Chennai, India

To find out more about our authors and books visit www.bloomsbury.com and
sign up for our newsletters.

Dedicated to my parents

Contents

Acknowledgements

Over the years that it has taken to write this book, I have become indebted to numerous colleagues. Madeleine Belin, Lucien Bély, John Condren, Kate Davison, Claire Fontijn, John-Paul Ghobrial, Bridget Heal, Peter Hicks, Marc Jaffré, Ana Kotarcic, Alistair Malcolm, Phil McCluskey, Eric Nelson, William O'Reilly, David Parrott, Giada Pizzoni, Julia Prest, Munro Price, Joan Redmond, Nicole Reinhardt, Graham Sadler, Martin Schaller, Mathieu da Vinha and Daniel Weiner gave invaluable help and advice. The book has profited immensely from the expertise, suggestions and criticisms of Megan Armstrong, Cecilia Gaposchkin, Tom Hamilton, Michael O'Sullivan and Julian Swann, as well as the anonymous reviewer.

Most of all I thank Professor Guy Rowlands. It would be hard to imagine a more generous and supportive PhD supervisor. This book owes a great deal to his encyclopaedic knowledge of early modern France and inexhaustible ability to develop new ideas about the period. My PhD examiners, Joseph Bergin and Emily Michelson, have also been exceptionally helpful, not least in commenting on the manuscript.

I would not have been able to do this research without the support of the Arts and Humanities Research Council and the Centre de recherche du château de Versailles, for which I am grateful. In addition, I am thankful to Oxford University Press for allowing me to publish an updated version of my article 'Consensus or Contestation? The Memory of Saint Louis during the Restoration, 1814-30' (*French History*, 33 (2019), 44–64) as Chapter 7 of this book. Lastly, I must thank my editors at Bloomsbury, Rhodri Mogford, Laura Reeves, Mohammed Raffi and James Tupper, whose professionalism has made the final stages of producing this book very simple. Of course, all remaining errors are entirely my own.

Note on proper names and translations

I have followed the most common conventions for well-known proper names rather than putting them all in their English or French forms, so I discuss Anne of Austria rather than Anne d'Autriche but Henri IV rather than Henry IV. In order to minimize confusion in a book that refers to many people called Louis, I have used the form 'Saint Louis' when referring to the person and 'Saint-Louis' when referring to an institution named after him (such as 'Order of Saint-Louis').

All translations are my own unless otherwise stated; although I have kept as closely as possible to the original text, I have occasionally modified capitalization and punctuation to make the extracts more readable in English. Despite the fact that it was unfortunately not possible to include all the original texts for prose quotations, I have done so for verse (excepting very brief quotations), where the distorting effects of translation are more pronounced.

Abbreviations

Archives and libraries

ALG	Archives départementales de Lot-et-Garonne, Agen
AN	Archives nationales de France, Paris
Ars	Bibliothèque de l'Arsenal (BnF), Paris
ASM	Archives départementales de Seine-Maritime, Rouen
BIC	Bibliothèque Inguimbertine, Carpentras
BMaz	Bibliothèque Mazarine, Paris
BmB	Bibliothèque municipale de Bordeaux
BmG	Bibliothèque municipale de Grenoble
BmL	Bibliothèque municipale de Lyon
BnF	Bibliothèque nationale de France, Paris
BSG	Bibliothèque Sainte-Geneviève, Paris
SHD	Service historique de la Défense, Vincennes

Periodicals

ADPAA	*Avis divers et petites affiches américaines*
AP	*L'Ami du Peuple, ou le Publiciste Parisien, Journal politique et impartial par M. Marat*
AR	*L'Ami du Roi, des François, de l'ordre, et sur-tout de la vérité, par les continuateurs de Fréron*
ARR	*L'Ami de la Religion et du Roi; Journal Ecclésiastique, Politique et Littéraire*
C	*Le Constitutionnel, Journal du Commerce, Politique et Littéraire*
DB	*Le Drapeau Blanc*
G	*Gazette de France*
GNF	*Gazette nationale de France*
JD	*Journal des débats politiques et littéraires*

JT	*Journal de Trévoux*
M	*Mercure*
MdF	*Mercure de France*
MF	*Mercure François*
MG	*Mercure Galant*
MinF	*La Minerve Française*
MU	*Moniteur Universel*
NE	*Nouvelles Ecclésiastiques*
NMG	*Nouveau Mercure Galant*
Q	*La Quotidienne*
RdP	*Révolutions de Paris, dédiées à la Nation*
VC	*Le Vieux Cordelier; Journal rédigé par Camille Desmoulins, député à la Convention, & Doyen des Jacobins*

Introduction

There is something supernatural about monarchy: it is an expression of God's empire, kings are his mortal images, and their subjects regard them with the same veneration as they would regard gods, if gods rendered themselves visible.[1]

Jean-François Senault, *The Monarch, or the Duties of the Sovereign* (1661)

It may indeed be the highest secret of monarchical rule, and utterly essential to it, to keep men deceived and to disguise the fear that retains them with the specious name of religion, so that they will fight for servitude as if they were fighting for their own welfare and will think it not shameful but supremely honourable to give their blood and lives for the vanity of a single man.[2]

Baruch Spinoza, *Theological-political treatise* (1670)

Jean-François Senault and Baruch Spinoza wrote from very different perspectives. The former was a famous preacher and Oratorian priest whose book arguing for the superiority of monarchy over other forms of government was appropriately published in the year that Louis XIV's personal rule began; the latter was a Dutch philosopher of Portuguese Jewish ancestry whose treatise advocating democracy was one of the most controversial texts of the period. Their opinions converged, however, on the idea that royal power was cloaked in religion, resulting in the perception of monarchs as quasi-divine rather than merely political figures. To Senault this revealed the fundamental nature of monarchy as an expression of divine order, whereas to Spinoza it was merely a deception. Nevertheless, both agreed that it augmented the king's subjects' veneration, obedience and desire to serve.

The nature of this 'supernatural' aspect of monarchy, the way it was fabricated and the extent of its ability to foster loyalty are the principal themes of this book, which analyses the rule of the Bourbon kings through the lens of the cult of their dynastic patron, Saint Louis IX. The fraught circumstances of Henri de Navarre's accession to the throne of France in 1589 made the resuscitation of the memory of his thirteenth-century ancestor Saint Louis an obvious means of consolidating dynastic and religious legitimacy for the Bourbons. Over the next two centuries, Louis XIII, Louis XIV, Louis XV and Louis XVI would promote the commemoration of the saint-king who was not coincidentally their namesake. In 1618, royal lobbying resulted in a papal order for the feast of Saint-Louis to be celebrated across France. This was intended to herald the beginning of a period in which the subjects of the Bourbon monarchs would unite in devotion to the dynastic saint now proclaimed 'patron and protector of France'. His feast day was marked with public festivities, concerts, fireworks and processions. Panegyric sermons, epic poems and paintings celebrated his link to the reigning kings. Churches, colleges, hospitals, fortresses and even islands were named after him across France and the French colonies. An army of historians, Jesuits, poets and preachers turned Saint Louis into a powerful image of ideal kingship – although the Bourbons would find that this could be used to undermine and criticize as well as to flatter and praise. This book provides the first detailed history of this important cult across the whole period from 1589 to the abolition of the monarchy in 1792, through the period of Bourbon exile in the 1790s and 1800s to the Restoration from 1814 to 1830, when Louis XVIII, Charles X and their supporters tried to rebuild loyalty to the Bourbon monarchy after the extraordinary years of the French Revolution and Napoleonic Empire.

Saint Louis's dual position as an historical king and canonized saint placed him at the nexus of the relationship between religion and politics. Who among the French monarchy's subjects took to his cult with enthusiasm? What does this tell us about the ideological and religious cohesion of the kingdom and the efficacy of monarchical symbols of religious legitimacy? Was devotion to the canonized king widespread and did it contribute to people regarding their present monarch with the same veneration as they would a 'visible god'? And how did this develop over the period from the end of the Religious Wars in the sixteenth century through the high point of Bourbon absolutism under Louis XIV to the changed cultural atmosphere of the Enlightenment, the onset of the Revolution and the Restoration? What can Saint Louis's cult tell us about the monarchy's ability to foster a culture of obedience, loyalty and veneration through all the twists and turns – religious, political, social and intellectual – of this complex period? Answering these questions requires the understanding of several themes: sacral kingship, the politics of historical memory and sanctity in the early modern period.

Sacral kingship

'Sacral' monarchy refers to a political and religious concept in which the ruler is seen as a manifestation or agent of the transcendent or supernatural realm. It has appeared in numerous cultures, with rulers in some contexts regarded and revered as gods.[3] In Christendom there was only one God and no king could claim actual divinity. Some historians thus criticize the use of the term 'sacrality' in a Christian context, arguing that sacred conceptions of monarchy were theoretically impossible because the prince was merely an intercessor between God and humankind rather than divinized himself.[4]

However, when we consider the actual exercise of kingship in early modern Europe it is clear that, even if Christian kings were not living gods, they were able to 'participate in the divine, in a manner of speaking'.[5] This was obvious in the case of the French monarchs, 'Most Christian kings' and 'eldest sons of the Church' who ruled by divine right. Royal lives were saturated with daily prayers and religious rituals conducted in palace chapels filled with the iconography of sacred kingship.[6] Such devotions had significant political implications: Louis XIV told his son that 'our submission to [God] is the rule and example of what is due to us'.[7] Prayers for the king were incorporated into the liturgy and the monarchy used church ceremonies such as the *Te Deum* to communicate news of military victories and happy events in the royal family to its people.[8]

The intertwined nature of church and state came with serious obligations for the ruler, who was expected to use his authority to enforce Christian morality and orthodoxy. In 1675, the preacher and bishop Jacques-Bénigne Bossuet reminded Louis XIV that he had to reign according to God's laws.[9] Answering to God alone meant being subject to his terrifying judgement, so French kings needed to anticipate his reaction to every action and policy as a means of evaluating its potential success (Damien Tricoire has called this the 'politico-religious calculation'). Of course, critics of royal policies might oppose the king with different 'calculations'.[10] In many ways, 'the more the position of the ruler was elevated to omnipotence or sacrality, the more it tended to circumscribe the person on the throne'.[11] As Jean-Baptiste Massillon observed in his funeral oration for Louis XIV, 'the holy anointing bestowed upon kings consecrates their personage but does not always sanctify their character'.[12] Sacralization in the Christian context could create unachievable expectations of royal piety and morality. It is in this light that Nicole Reinhardt has argued that 'although at first sight sacred monarchy appears to strengthen royal authority, it might have been a liability and even an Achilles heel'.[13]

It was not attendance at mass or expectations of pious behaviour that are considered to have sacralized the French monarchs – after all, these were required of all Catholics. The lives of the Spanish kings were also saturated in devotional practices, but their monarchy was not sacral; they received no anointing or coronation in ceremonies of succession and did not claim to possess healing powers.[14] In contrast, the development of the French monarchy went hand in hand with an emphasis on the miraculous.[15] Royal rituals such as the *sacre* marked out the French monarchs as distinctive mediators between the earthly and heavenly realms and signified special sacred powers.[16] French kings claimed to be able to cure scrofula through the thaumaturgic power of their touch in a ritual that underscored their special esteem in God's eyes. Making the sign of the cross on each cheek and uttering the words 'the king touches you and God heals you', Henri IV, Louis XIII and Louis XIV all touched thousands of subjects afflicted with scrofula.[17]

Another concept that has received attention is that of the king's 'two bodies' – his 'natural' body, mortal and subject to decay just like any other, and 'political' body, untouchable and exempt from mortal feebleness.[18] Ralph Giesey saw this as manifested and represented in the funeral ceremonies that marked the transition of the sacred political body from the mortal body of one king to another, particularly in the use of effigies from 1422 to 1610.[19] There are numerous problems with this theory, not least the use of funeral effigies by individuals other than the king. Most importantly, Alain Boureau found little evidence that people really *believed* in this element of sacralization in the same way that they believed in, say, transubstantiation – and 'what, in effect, is a sacralization without belief?' Instead, he argues that the royal body remained 'simple' and 'banal' despite the theory of the two bodies, and that the church tolerated sacralization but never granted it the status of true belief. The only area in which sacralization could be seen was the royal touch, but even this followed the king's state of grace, transmitted from the sacraments, rather than from the body itself.[20]

Boureau focuses our attention not on abstract theories of sacralization but on its ability to foster belief and devotion. The focus of this book is on an aspect of monarchical culture that, unlike the royal touch and funeral effigies, is not concerned with the sacralization of the king's body. The cult of the dynastic patron saint was, however, of huge importance for the monarchy's ability to penetrate the devotional lives of its subjects and install reverence for the king into their religious practices. This was particularly important at the beginning of the period. Following the nadir of the monarchy's reputation in the final decades of Valois rule, especially under Henri III, Ronald Asch has charted a 'resacralization of kingship in France' under the first Bourbon king, Henri IV, in which a reconstituted *religion royale*, drawing on Counter-Reformation Catholicism and theories of divine right monarchy, 'established an emotional regime conducive to obedience'. The political consequences were significant in terms of reaffirming royal authority during the seventeenth century. For example, for the crown to exercise effectively its power to disgrace ministers, nobles, clerics and jurists – a process fundamental to the functioning of the absolute monarchy – it helped that for much of the period victims viewed 'their punishment as an expression of God's will'.[21]

Asch argues that the monarchy found it difficult to adapt to changing religious circumstances around the turn of the eighteenth century, at which time 'the old fabric of sacral monarchy began . . . to unravel', thanks more to tensions within Catholicism than to a real secularization of politics.[22] The longer-term consequence of such changes is the idea that has been labelled 'desacralization', now a popular way of explaining apparent disenchantment with the monarchy from the latter part of Louis XV's reign. This theory holds that the traditional understandings of kingship as based on a conjunction of religion and politics broke down in mid-eighteenth-century France as the disjuncture between myth and reality became harder to maintain in a changed intellectual environment. The fundamental transition from a mental universe centred on a traditional cosmology in which the physical world had an intimate relationship with the supernatural to a Newtonian model that operated according to fixed and knowable laws meant that many thinkers 'came to view politics and society not as divine but as human institutions that one could alter and improve through rational intervention'.[23] Although this trajectory should not obscure the continued vibrancy of Catholicism in eighteenth-century France, it had obvious implications for the theoretical underpinnings of the French absolute monarchy.

Historians of desacralization such as Dale Van Kley and Jeffrey Merrick have emphasized the appearance of new attitudes towards royal authority and sacral monarchy during the damaging confrontations between crown, church and Parlements (sovereign courts) in Louis XV's reign,[24] as well as the ridiculing of the king's personal immorality in scurrilous publications.[25] Voltaire wrote that he had lost confidence in the miraculous power of the royal touch when he heard that one of Louis XIV's mistresses had died of scrofula despite being well-touched by the king![26] In any case, Louis XV was unable to take communion or touch for scrofula, not performing the latter task from 1739 to 1774 (except in 1744).[27] This broadcast 'in silence that the king was not in a state of grace', causing an asymmetry between practice and ideology that meant 'the ideological fiction as well as the practices became dysfunctional and vulnerable'.[28] Louis XVI revived the practice after his *sacre* in 1775, but a sense of doubt was reflected in the change in the words spoken by the king to 'the King touches you, *may* God heal you'.[29]

Looming behind historians' interest in desacralization is a concern to understand how the same monarch could be decapitated within twenty years of his *sacre*. The search for 'cultural origins' of the French Revolution caused historians to look for longer-term changes that prepared people for the momentous events of the 1790s. According to Van Kley, we must 'hearken to the popular ground tremors . . . which anticipate the seeming ease with which the French dispensed with their monarch in 1792'.[30] Similarly, Roger Chartier noted a 'shrinkage in the sacred nature of the person of the king' in the late eighteenth century – although he was also doubtful that the monarchy was really previously 'sacralized' when seen from the perspective of the broader populace.[31]

This last idea has been developed by critics of the desacralization thesis. William Doyle argued that 'nothing leads us to believe that the great majority of the subjects of Louis XV or the young Louis XVI had a deep or even superficial knowledge of the doctrinal elements of the king's "sacral" authority. . . . The reverence of most subjects was far simpler and more instinctive – yet at the same time more flexible'. Moreover, 'the idea of a desacralized monarchy looks poorly framed, and underpinned by questionable presuppositions', since it follows the dubious tenet that great events require long preparation, whereas in fact 'it was the dynamic of events [from 1789], and not some prior desacralization of monarchy, that led Louis XVI to the scaffold on 21 January 1793'.[32] Literature vehemently critical of the monarchy was not a creation of Louis XV's reign and historians should be careful not to mistake dissatisfaction with a particular king for disenchantment with the monarchy overall.[33] Jens Engels has used police records and clandestine literature to undermine teleological understandings of desacralization by arguing that the sacrality of the king's 'official image' – even the theory of the royal touch – was never accepted by the majority of ordinary people; 'the king did not play a large part in the religious beliefs of Frenchmen; nor was he a sacrosanct figure'. Put simply, 'the French monarch was not a sacral monarch'.[34]

Teleological narratives of secularization charting a change from medieval mystification to modern demystification of monarchy in the seventeenth and eighteenth centuries are clearly oversimplistic.[35] But should we reject the notion of sacrality overall? Was there really nothing in Senault's description of the 'supernatural' mystique of monarchy? Of course, kings have always been criticized and many of their subjects did not unquestioningly view them as sacrosanct, but on the other hand we should not entirely dismiss the ceremonies, writings, art and symbols that broadly represented the crown's own self-conception. Rather, we should see them as part of the process by which the mystique of royalty was created – successfully in some contexts, unsuccessfully in others. For all the critical material cited by Engels, there are the indications of the 'simpler and more instinctive' reverence noted by Doyle. This book highlights the fact that much of what seems to be 'official' culture actually originated as gestures of loyalty from the middle-up rather than being imposed as propaganda from the top-down. Therefore, the quasi-sacred legitimacy conferred on the monarchy by references to Saint Louis was a tool by which various groups in early modern France could express their devotion to the monarchy, making it part of the processes binding the crown to French elites – and the management of relations between monarchy and elites is recognized now as crucial to the operation of the 'absolute' monarchy.[36]

On the other hand, 'unofficial' use of Saint Louis to criticize the monarchy shows the ways in which sacral culture could be inverted against the king. This is because individual sanctity and royal sacrality were not synonymous, despite their close relationship. Louis IX's sanctity could bolster royal sacrality if constructed in a way that sanctified the office of the king and reflected on his descendants in general. But the significant tensions between the ideals of sanctity and the realities of rulership meant that there was a long tradition of seeing him as having achieved sanctity *in spite of* his royal status.[37] This meant that the royal saint could both bolster and undermine sacral kingship in different contexts. He was often conflated with the reigning king, casting a glow of holiness around their person and actions; at other times, however, devotion to a *saint* Louis was a way of expressing warmth for the ideal of monarchy despite a decline in the mystique of the reigning king.

My approach is to consider sacrality less in terms of the sacred nature of the royal body than the monarchy's ability to use religious symbolism and ceremony to foster a culture of loyalty and devotion. This reflects the criticisms of Boureau and Engels in that it focusses on the reception and dissemination of royalist culture as well as its creation. Paul Monod has observed that the monarchy did not possess many effective means of spreading its messages: state rituals were attended mostly by courtiers, proclamations might be read (or understood) by comparatively few people, and coronations and entries were rare and limited geographically. 'Perhaps the only sure way to disseminate a message of obedience was through the churches, which had branches in every parish. Religious propaganda, however, was dependent on the adherence of local elites and the acquiescence of ordinary believers. . . . The king's name might be read at prayers every Sunday but would that guarantee submission to him?'[38] This is the issue that this book explores. Was the cult of Saint Louis effective in creating a climate of loyalty to the monarch by imbuing French kingship with a sense of the sacred? In which contexts was it useful or harmful for the monarchy to promote the memory of a saint-king whose reign was regarded as one of the most glorious periods in the history of France?

The politics of memory

As noted by the great medievalist Jacques Le Goff, 'to make themselves the master of memory and forgetfulness is one of the great preoccupations of the classes, groups and individuals who have dominated and continue to dominate historical societies'.[39] The cult of a former king is inevitably linked to the 'politics of memory', the ways in which constructions of the past are entwined with power relations. Historians of modern French political culture have highlighted the importance of invocations of the past and conflicts over the meaning of historical events.[40] In early modern France there was a similar possibility for competing memories to have political implications. One important difference, however, was that before the great rupture of the 1790s people were more likely to look to bygone centuries for precedent and justification. Memory was political because saying something was customary and ancient was a way of legitimizing it; this meant that the past was a primary frame of political, social, religious, legal and moral reference and as such was frequently contested, reinvented and distorted.[41]

In this environment, the deeds of Saint Louis were used by French rulers 'as a means of contextualizing their own achievements' and considered to hold significant lessons for those living centuries later.[42] Such lessons were often contested, and the fact that it was possible to create multiple representations of the holy king meant both that his cultural memory 'remained powerfully alive for centuries' and that details of his reign could provide spaces in which debates and conflicts could be conducted.[43] He can thus be seen as a 'site of memory' (*lieu de mémoire*), the term coined by Pierre Nora to refer to an object, place or individual transformed by time and human agency into a 'symbolic element of the inherited touchstones of memory of a community'.[44] In the early modern period, Saint Louis was an important 'site', subjected to a constant process of reinterpretation in ways that reflected contemporary concerns and debates.

Early modern Europeans often looked to the past for analogies that would teach them something about the present. Did this view of the relationship between past and present change over the period? Reinhart Koselleck proposed that before roughly 1750 Europeans relied on an 'always-already guaranteed futurity of the past' in which history was a seemingly continuous space of experience from which it was possible to draw conclusions for the future. He saw this as dissolving during the Enlightenment and especially after the French Revolution; the philosophy of historical progress opened up a future that transcended the hitherto predictable, leading to a more 'modern' perception of temporal differences between historical periods and the expectation of novelty rather than repetition.[45]

This rather linear development has been criticized. Judith Pollmann argues that early modern people were highly aware of change but chose to think anachronistically because doing so provided an effective 'rhetorical technique for structuring a spin on the present' that could be used to persuade, do politics or pre-empt criticism.[46] In the case of Saint Louis, there was often an impulse to conflate the past with the present in ways that served political purposes – but at the same time this coexisted with a clear sense of the difference of the Middle Ages. There was no consistent attitude to the medieval period; early modern French people exhibited a spectrum of opinion ranging from utter contempt to nostalgic regret.[47]

This book is not the first to explore the memorialization of medieval events or rulers in early modern France.[48] Especially relevant is a work by Adrianna Bakos on the early modern reputation of Louis XI, the fifteenth-century monarch memorably labelled the 'universal spider' by his detractors. As Bakos shows, memories are often incomplete and selective, with past and present interpreted in relation to each other. Just as texts outlive the intentions of their authors to be reinvested with new meanings as the language of political discourse evolves, so actions outlive their agents and are reinterpreted in new political contexts. As such, Louis XI's memory was 'inextricably bound up in the debates characterizing political theory' and events of his reign were used to portray him as everything from a monstrous tyrant by sixteenth-century resistance theorists to an effective ruler by seventeenth-century royalists.[49] This highlights the importance of former monarchs to political discourse in early modern

France and the ways in which the memory of a distant king could be harnessed to make divergent arguments about the nature of government in the present. I do not intend simply to repeat Bakos's findings in this book and there are some important differences between the two examples. Saint Louis was far less controversial than Louis XI and his reputation did not fluctuate as wildly; instead, he was generally regarded as the ideal Christian ruler whose example his descendants should aspire to follow. As a saint, moreover, his memorialization was not limited to history books and political treatises but manifested in devotional practices, public ceremonies and a prominent place in religious iconography. Louis XI did not have a feast day and would have been quite literally less visible to early modern French people.

Many historians have explored the role of memories of traumatic events such as revolts, exiles and conflicts, and the ways in which they sustained group identities.[50] Perhaps surprisingly, given the general recognition that early modern people used the past as a source of legitimacy and precedent, there are fewer studies of the memorialization of periods perceived as 'golden ages'. Therefore, this analysis of the memory of Saint Louis offers something quite different from studies of the memory of a controversial monarch such as Louis XI or a traumatic period such as the Wars of Religion; an assessment of the role played by memories of a golden age and the ways in which they developed between the late sixteenth and early nineteenth centuries. There have been studies, of course, of the memorialization of other 'good' figures in early modern France, such as Jean-Marie Le Gall's book on the memory of Saint Denis.[51] However, whereas Louis XI was not a saint, Saint Denis was not a king. It was Saint Louis's singular position as dynastic ancestor, model of political virtue and saint of the church that makes him a unique figure through whose memory we can explore the relationship of early modern France to its past and the nature of religion and politics under the Bourbon monarchs.

It has been noted that memory studies can produce predictable conclusions – the past is constructed as a myth to serve the interests of a particular community – and that this is often because historians merely draw conclusions from one 'vehicle of memory' whose representation they have studied over a certain period. It can only be illuminating when linked to historical questions and problems, looking at not just how a past was represented but *why* it was received or rejected.[52] In this case, the historical problem is clear: the sacralization of the monarchy and its efficacy in using the dynastic saint to foster devotion and loyalty. This is, therefore, not just a study of the politics of memory but the study of a saintly cult.

Early modern sanctity

Saints have long been recognized as 'cultural indicators', reflecting the values of the society that elevated them.[53] Historians of early modern Catholicism often focus on the new saints of the period, but consideration should also be given to shifting attitudes towards those who were already canonized.[54] Moshe Sluhovsky compared saintly cults to organisms that are born, live, succeed or fail, and, in time, die. Unlike living organisms, however, they could also be reborn – resurrected or recharged with new importance after periods of neglect, as was certainly the case with Saint Louis's cult under the Bourbons. Saints are invoked because of their perceived relevance to living people with evolving hopes, pressures and ideals – a constant process of change.[55]

Central to any historical examination of a saint is an appreciation of their cult – the feast days, iconography, hagiography, miracles, shrines and relics through which worshippers accessed them.[56] From the perspective of the majority of 'consumers' of sanctity during the early modern period, 'the efficacy of a saint was measured above all by his or her capacity to deliver miraculous cures' through their intercession.[57] The challenge of Protestant rejections of miracle-working saints, manifested in iconoclastic attacks on statues and reliquaries and denunciations of idolatry, was answered with a continued emphasis on the thaumaturgic powers of saints by Catholics.[58] Enthusiasm for miracles was strong in early modern France, particularly during the thirty years after 1610 (the period when Saint Louis's cult was revived).[59]

However, the debate on saints sparked off by the Reformation led to efforts to purge their cults of elements considered idolatrous by the Tridentine church. As Bruno Restif has shown in a detailed study of religion in Brittany, the 'time of miracles' from 1620 to 1670 was accompanied by efforts to 'transform the pilgrim'.[60] Although ecclesiastical authorities attempted to regulate the validity of miracles and authenticity of relics with greater scrutiny, they were often unable to examine all manifestations of miraculous activity.[61] It is easier to establish the hierarchical church's view of saints than that of the mass of the population with its bewildering variety of cults; nevertheless, it is clear that it was hard for the authorities to create genuine popular enthusiasm for those saints that they promoted, in part because they were generally casting them more as models of virtue than as miracle-workers in the Christocentric era of Catholic Reform. The emphasis was moving from supernatural to intercessory power, at least in terms of the ideals of the church hierarchy, and there were attempts to move the focus from the cults of minor saints to Jesus himself.[62] However, across Catholic Europe ordinary people were seldom prone to accepting impositions from above passively, often preferring cults of local origin.[63]

How far did the cult of Saint Louis, promoted by the civil and ecclesiastical hierarchy rather than developing out of popular enthusiasm, lodge itself in the devotional and spiritual life of the subjects of the Bourbon kings? How widespread was it geographically and how deep socially? Such questions often lead to distinctions between 'elite' and 'popular' religion.[64] Michel Vovelle has argued that historians need to go beyond such simple dichotomies and instead provide more complex accounts of social groupings.[65] In this book I have taken account of various social and geographical sites of veneration for Saint Louis. Where and among whom did he become a popular saint and where was he ignored? Among those who did develop enthusiasm for his cult, was he valued primarily as a model of virtue or because miracles were attributed to his intercession?

Moreover, how did this change over time? Saints and miracles proved easy targets for eighteenth-century *philosophes*. Some historians have seen miracles as 'exceptional' after 1680, soon disappearing in many shrines, and a decline in pilgrimages over the course of the eighteenth century has been noted for both Paris and the French provinces.[66] However, the picture is more complex when viewed from below, especially taking a regional perspective. A decline in the official registration of miracles in Brittany after 1670 did not mean that they were any less present on the ground, indicating that we need to be sensitive to local realities and geographical variation.[67] Moreover, from around 1730 there was something of a rediscovery of the miraculous by hagiographers: 'when miracles were omnipresent in French society, they warned the public against the dangers of credulity; when miracles became rare, on the other hand, they stigmatized scepticism.'[68] There may have been a general decline in the procession of reliquaries in the eighteenth century and an increasing use of saints to moralize and provide models rather than work miracles, but up to the 1780s there was considerable interest in – even craze for – strange phenomena, inexplicable recoveries, levitations and prophecies.[69] Most notorious was the cult that developed after the death of François de Pâris in 1727, featuring miraculous cures and crowds of believers speaking in tongues and foaming at the mouth. This was associated with Jansenist opposition to the papal bull *Unigenitus* and as such condemned by royal and ecclesiastical authorities, a reminder that manifestations of the miraculous were often beyond official control.[70]

As the only king of France whose sanctity was officially recognized by the church and a saint whose cult was promoted from the top down, Saint Louis was at the opposite end of the spectrum. Any exploration of his cult needs to be sensitive to the functions peculiar to royal saints, such as ancestor and sanctifier of the reigning dynasty and model of good government and ideal kingship.[71] He was prominent in the chorus of praise that surrounded the French monarchs, material often described as 'representational culture', through which the king's authority was made visible through display, ceremony, art and entertainment. Such material cannot be taken at face value, as the royal image under the Bourbon monarchs was neither homogenous in its content nor received unquestioningly.[72] Laudatory royal culture was not just promoted from the top down but also by various interest groups seeking to position themselves in relation to the monarchy; Saint Louis's association with the Bourbons made him a powerful symbol that could be used by a wide range of constituencies. Therefore, we need to consider how the monarchy used his cult while being aware of 'the frequent inability of any single authority, however powerful, fully to control and appropriate the cult' of a saint.[73]

Another important question is whether Saint Louis's cult contributed to a sense of French national consciousness centred on sacral monarchy. Joseph Bergin has argued that the choice of 'national' saints 'was designed to enhance the monarchy and the unity of the nation'.[74] Seventeenth-century French patriotism was largely 'crown-centred', expressed in terms of loyalty to the prince and through the prism of France's dynastic history.[75] Discussion of concepts such as national identity and patriotism in early modern Europe is fraught with the danger of anachronism, but if 'nationalism' was a nineteenth-century phenomenon, forms of 'national consciousness' or 'national sentiment' were present in earlier periods. Whereas this has sometimes been seen as the preserve of elites, Pollmann argues that local memories – often focused on relationships between particular communities and their patron saints – were important in the early modern period as a means of asserting 'one's importance to the larger world of region, state, kingdom, and nation'.[76] Saint Louis was proclaimed 'patron and protector of France' in 1618; Michael Schaich has called this the 'religion of patriotism'.[77]

'Gallicanism', a compromise between Catholic universalism and early forms of French national consciousness, is an important part of this issue.[78] A complex set of tendencies associated particularly with the judicial elite of the Parlements and the episcopate, but also invoked by the kings when it suited them, Gallicanism never questioned the strong link between Catholicism and French identity but nevertheless emphasized France's independence from Rome in temporal affairs. Gallicans defended the 'liberties' of the Gallican church and displayed hostility to papal interference. The past was mined by all sides in the inevitable debates, with Saint Louis invoked (often anachronistically) by both Gallicans and Ultramontanes, who upheld papal authority.[79]

Alongside these religious and crown-centred forms of national consciousness, it is important to consider the relationship between the 'national' and 'French' aspect of Saint Louis's cult and the development of a new sense of *patrie* and nation in eighteenth-century France.[80] Robespierre's famous declaration in 1792 that 'Louis [XVI] must die because the *patrie* must live' is indicative of major conceptual developments in which ideas of citizenship and of sovereignty embodied in the nation ultimately prevailed over the older notion of sovereignty embodied in the king. To what extent did these processes affect and interact with the cult of Saint Louis in the eighteenth century? Was it possible to rebrand him as the 'father of the fatherland', as attempted by some panegyrists, or would his memory fall out of step with changing sensibilities?

The study of a saintly cult, therefore, needs to be sensitive to several issues: the broader context of attitudes to saints and miracles in which the details of any particular cult may prove either typical or exceptional; the differences between the intentions of the hierarchical church and the realities of popular devotion; the geographical variation in the intensity of a particular cult; the motivations of those who promoted it and their ability to keep control of it; the extent to which the cult contributed to identities, local or national; and the ever-changing social makeup and priorities of a particular saint's constituency of devotees. In doing so, a wide range of sources must be considered, for 'devotion to the cult of saints was a kinetic, multi-media experience, a mobile *Gesamtkunstwerk* in which art, architecture, sculpture, word, music, and print were deployed to move heart and soul through eye and ear'.[81] As the frequent discussion of visual, material and musical depictions of Saint Louis in this book makes clear, Catholic piety and spirituality cannot be understood with references to texts alone. This opens a vast range of possible material with which to explore Saint Louis's cult.

The historiography of the cult of Saint Louis

In his magisterial biography of Louis IX, Jacques Le Goff noted that 'writing the life of Saint Louis after Saint Louis, a history of the historical image of the sainted king, would be a fascinating subject'.[82] Numerous historians have made major contributions to this topic, most importantly Cecilia Gaposchkin in her study of the construction of Louis IX's sanctity up to the mid-fourteenth century. She expertly shows the ways in which Louis's memorialization was shaped to suit varying interests, noting that 'there was no single Saint Louis' as he represented different things to different constituencies. In discussing the use of Saint Louis to criticize Philip IV, she concludes that 'Louis was always going to represent a double-edged sword for the Capetians – symbolizing the legitimacy of their claim to being the *rex christianissimus* but also . . . providing a standard of behaviour and piety by which they would thereafter be judged'.[83] Gaposchkin is not the only scholar to have noted this essential ambiguity in Saint Louis's memory. Collette Beaune stressed that he was 'a political model more embarrassing than useful for the monarchy' in the fourteenth and fifteenth centuries.[84]

Another major work is Anja Rathmann-Lutz's study of late medieval representations of Saint Louis.[85] She focuses on the 'images' of Louis IX that were used to influence specific publics, presenting a set of concentric but porous circles which indicate the probable size of their audience. The smallest circle in the centre signifies objects and texts reserved for groups of elites, such as books of hours and the interiors of palace chapels, whereas further out are more public items such as monuments and spectacles that accompanied royal entries. It is not easy to say with certainty how such items were read or by whom, let alone with what result. This way of conceptualizing the problem is, however, extremely useful. Over the course of this book, many such 'images' will be considered. It is important constantly to consider not just for what kind of public each was destined but also the intentions of the patron and artist as well as the reaction of the intended audience, unanswerable as these questions are in many instances.

While such works are undoubtedly important to the subject of this book, they are not concerned with the early modern period. The 700th anniversary of Saint Louis's death in 1970 sparked some interest in this later era, notably an exhibition at the Musée de la Légion d'Honneur on the 'renaissance' of Saint Louis's cult as expressed in two important institutions founded by Louis XIV: the Military Order of Saint-Louis and the Maison de Saint-Louis at Saint-Cyr.[86] In the same year, Pierre Morel wrote an article on the spread of parishes dedicated to Saint Louis up to the nineteenth century, concluding that the cult was particularly centred on the Paris region and that the Bourbon centuries made up the period of its 'greatest diffusion'.[87] Such a large topic could hardly be covered comprehensively in a short article. Numerous questions remain, not least who decided on the dedications and why. More importantly, dedications are just one part of the cult and a much wider range of issues needs to be considered for its significance to be fully assessed.

Among the most important sources for the early modern cult are the panegyric sermons delivered year after year on 25 August. In addition to writing detailed analyses of individual panegyrics, some historians have examined them as a genre.[88] Pierre Zoberman has highlighted the ways in which Louis XIV was lauded through the praise of his ancestor in panegyrics delivered before the Académie Française.[89] Jean-Pierre Landry, on the other hand, has studied other panegyrics less concerned with the praise of Louis XIV and analysed what they can tell us about attitudes to important religious issues.[90] Such studies are useful but clearly leave possibilities for further research. Both Zoberman and Landry limit themselves to a handful of panegyrics (five and seven, respectively), which represent little more than the tip of the iceberg. Furthermore, the panegyrics in their articles cover roughly the same period, namely the decades on either side of 1700. A wider chronological frame is needed to understand the ways in which they evolved over time, for there were significant changes in the ways the panegyrists treated themes such as the crusades and the relationship of Saint Louis to the reigning king. To have a gallery of annual portraits of the same historical figure from the reigns of Louis XIII to Charles X is a unique curiosity in the history of French literature.[91] Analysis of this corpus over a longer period thus highlights broader contours.

Other texts relating to Saint Louis have received attention, particularly histories.[92] Daniel Weiner's admirable study of the 1688/9 biographies by Filleau de la Chaise and the Abbé de Choisy sees them as part of an ongoing struggle for 'custody of the memory of Saint Louis' and the 'effective climax' of the Bourbon exploitation of the life of Saint Louis. However, since his story stops there and does not consider the eighteenth century the point is by no means firmly established.[93] Indeed, such a statement is a result of limiting his source material to written histories.

Manfred Tietz noted 'Saint Louis's strong presence in the religious, intellectual and political life of the seventeenth century'.[94] The important historian of sanctity in early modern France, Éric Suire, has challenged this idea, stating that he had not found that Saint Louis had an important place in early modern religious sensibilities; along the same lines, Damien Tricoire argues that Saint Louis was primarily a dynastic patron and his broader popularity remained limited.[95] In this book I have assessed these judgements, taking care to account for varying levels of importance in different contexts and among different constituencies. Saint Louis clearly did have a strong presence in controversial contexts related to the three themes identified by Tietz. In terms of religion, Jansenists and Jesuits tried to appropriate his memory on both sides of their long struggle.[96] This was because identification with Saint Louis effectively meant identification with the monarchy, making his cult a useful tool which could be used by elites to position themselves in relation to the political centre.

In terms of politics, the strong identification of the Bourbon monarchs with Saint Louis's cult is best illustrated by Louis XIII's successful attempt to restore the feast day in 1618, an event first explored by Alain Boureau.[97] It is important to note the importance of the relationship of Saint Louis's memory to the practice of kingship by the Bourbon monarchs and the 'fabrication' of their image.[98] More recently, Géraldine Lavieille has made important contributions to the study of Saint Louis as a dynastic and national saint.[99] However, as far as the relationship between the saintly exemplar and the living king is concerned, there has been little consideration of the 'negative' side, namely the use of idealized presentations of the latter to criticize his descendants. The flip side of the political dimensions of Saint Louis's cult has been recognized for earlier periods by Gaposchkin and Beaune but needs exploration in the era of the Bourbon monarchs.

Numerous historians have, therefore, contributed an invaluable basis without which this book would have been impossible. However, some significant topics, such as the geographical spread of the feast day and the use of the relics, remain absent from the historiography, although they are immensely important if we are to take stock of the overall significance of the cult and the level of its success in embedding the imagery of sacred monarchy in devotional life. Indeed, the rather fragmentary understanding of the cult in the present historiography, spread as it is over several specialized articles, means that until now it has been impossible to assess its overall significance. The eighteenth century has been almost entirely unstudied, despite offering fertile ground for exploration of desacralization. Tietz noted that 'there has not been a synthesis on

dead than stained by mortal sin. Blanche succeeded in inculcating her son with great piety. Louis showed profound emotion in 1239 when, barefoot, he received the crown of thorns into France, having purchased it along with other relics of Christ's passion from the Byzantine emperor; the Sainte-Chapelle was constructed in Paris to house them. Most significant were the events of 1244 when, recovering from a serious illness, Louis took the cross.

What ensued was one of the best prepared of all the crusades. To assure the kingdom's purity, mendicant investigators were dispatched to redress injustices committed by royal officials. In June 1249, after years of preparation, the crusader army arrived in Egypt, quickly capturing Damietta – which Louis entered as a humble penitent rather than a victorious conqueror. However, the crusaders failed to capitalize on this initial success and were defeated by the Mamluks at Mansurah and Fariskur in 1250. Louis himself was captured.[5] He was later freed in exchange for a heavy ransom and the surrender of Damietta, but remained in the region for a few years, sending emissaries to the Mongols and attempting to bolster the remaining crusader strongholds. News of his mother's death caused him to return to France in 1254.

According to his confessor Geoffrey of Beaulieu, 'in much the same way that gold is even more precious than silver, the saintly and new comportment with which [Louis] returned from the Holy Land outshone his previous comportment'. Viewing his own sinfulness as the reason for the failure of the crusade, he remained penitent for the rest of his life, his piety manifested in self-flagellation, touching the diseased, eating with the poor and forsaking rich clothes. He even had to be told by Geoffrey – a Dominican – that his use of hair shirts was excessive. Unusually for a French king, he not only never took a mistress but also refrained from intimate relations with his wife, Marguerite de Provence, in Advent and Lent and on feast days and vigils; if he were with her at one of these times and felt 'an inordinate movement of the flesh, he would rise from the bed and stride about the room until his rebellious body had calmed down', according to Geoffrey.[6]

Louis IX's kingship was also shaped by his strict piety, according to the values of the time. He worked hard to eradicate blasphemy, dice games and prostitution. In addition, he took action against Jews, including burning the Talmud in 1242 and issuing fines against Jews found not wearing identifying badges in 1269. His attitude to rulership was set out in a French text that became known as the *Enseignements*, given to his son Philip towards the end of the reign. Existing in various versions, the essential points stressed that kings should avoid mortal sin, confess often, attend services and sermons frequently, be compassionate to the poor, act with justice (giving the benefit of doubt to the poor over the rich), respect property, take care in the granting of benefices, respect and obey the church and pope, remove sin and blasphemy from the realm and never start a war against another Christian ruler.[7]

Acquiring a reputation as an arbiter and devotee of intra-Christian peace, Louis tried to resolve long-standing conflicts. In the Treaty of Paris (1259), Henry III renounced his claims to Normandy and territories on the Loire while paying homage to Louis for Gascony and parts of Aquitaine. According to his crusading companion Jean de Joinville, Louis defended himself against accusations that he was needlessly throwing land away in this treaty by referring not just to ideals of peace and familial ties but also to the more practical advantage that '[Henry] is now my vassal, which he has never been before'.[8] Peace at home was not, however, enough for a king preoccupied by recent developments in the Holy Land, and in 1267 Louis announced his decision to depart once more on crusade. It was this expedition that arrived in Tunis in June 1270, the king dying soon afterwards.

In a letter to French prelates of September 1270, Philip III asked for masses to be said for his father's soul, 'though many believe it needs no outside intercession'.[9] With a view to initiating canonization proceedings, Pope Gregory X asked Geoffrey de Beaulieu to write an account of Louis's life. The resulting *vita*, structured around Louis's virtues rather than the chronology of his reign, stated that he had never knowingly committed a mortal sin and at one point even desired to give up the crown and become a mendicant. Geoffroy's rather limited discussion of Louis's kingship caused William of Chartres, another Dominican who had been in captivity with Louis, to write a supplementary work including more discussion of his acts as king. In 1282–3 an inquest was held at the abbey of Saint-Denis near Paris, where dozens of miracles were being reported at Louis's tomb.[10]

Louis was canonized in 1297 as a confessor (not a martyr, much to the anger of Joinville) with his feast day as 25 August. The first canonization of a king in over a century, and the last until that of Ferdinand III of Castile in 1671, this act was situated in a context of tension between the papacy and Philip IV.[11] In his canonization sermons, Pope Boniface VIII sought to use the new saint as a standard of royal behaviour against which Philip could be judged. Nevertheless, the canonization once achieved was to Philip's political advantage. He made frequent allusions to his grandfather and regularly reissued his ordinances, contributing to a process by which Louis IX's reign came to be perceived as a golden age. Philip also promoted the new cult by distributing relics and asking bishops to celebrate the feast day.[12] Foundations such as a new Dominican monastery at Poissy were dedicated to Saint Louis, and in 1299 Philip gave relics of his grandfather to the bastide at Lamontjoie near Agen that he had built the previous year.[13] He also sought to translate (move) Saint Louis's relics to the Sainte-Chapelle, though resistance from Saint-Denis meant that only the skull made the journey in 1306, alongside a rib given to Notre-Dame.[14] Through all this, Philip hoped to harness the lustre of Louis's sanctity to the glory of the Capetian dynasty.[15]

Despite the translation of the head, Saint-Denis remained central to Saint Louis's cult. A side chapel was dedicated to him in 1304 and collected substantial sums from offerings in the early years of his sanctity.[16] An altar dedicated to the saint-king by a burgher of Saint-Florentin in the late 1310s suggests that devotion was becoming more widespread geographically and socially.[17] Another mark of the saint's popularity at different levels of society was his patronage of confraternities and merchant guilds in the fourteenth and fifteenth centuries, ranging from the sergeants of the Châtelet to carpenters, anglers, lacemakers, upholsterers, ropemakers and dry-goods merchants, whose shops were near the Sainte-Chapelle and who claimed that their privileges came from Louis IX.[18]

The royal family's personal attachment to the new saint was manifested in devotional manuscripts and numerous *vitæ* commissioned in the fourteenth century. William of Saint-Pathus wrote one at the request of Louis's daughter Blanche in 1303. By far the most important in the long run was that written by Jean de Joinville, completed in 1309 and dedicated to the future Louis X. Whatever the distortions resulting from Joinville's tendency to place himself at the heart of the story, the text (part chivalric narrative, part personal memoir, part hagiography – and perhaps an amalgam of different texts written before and after the canonization) is remarkable for introducing a king who jokes, laughs and gets angry, as opposed to an idealized figure shaped by the traditions of hagiography. Joinville was capable of criticizing what he saw as Louis's flaws or bad decisions, such as excessive punishment of blasphemers or the second crusading expedition.[19]

Joinville's life was barely known outside the royal court until the sixteenth century. Instead, the liturgies written around 1300 are far more representative of medieval understandings of the saint. Reflecting the varied and sometimes competing interests of different institutions, they memorialized Louis in different ways. *Ludovicus decus*, used at the Sainte-Chapelle and Notre-Dame, was probably the office commissioned by Philip IV in 1298 and emphasized themes of sacred royalty; identifying Louis's sanctity with the language of kingship was to sacralize the office of the king. On the other hand, the Franciscan office *Francorum rex* emphasized Saint Louis as living up to Franciscan ideals and connected him to Saint Francis. The Franciscan lections included only two references to kingship, both of which mention Louis's desire to renounce it.[20]

One significant development of the early fourteenth century was the use of Saint Louis's memory against the monarchy; it began to hang heavily over later kings who could be criticized by comparison to their holy ancestor. After all, Joinville wrote that the canonization brought

> great honour to those of the good king's line who are like him in doing well, and equal dishonour to those descendants of his who will not follow him in good works . . . for men will point a finger at them and say that the saintly king, from whom they have sprung, would have shrunk from acting so ill.[21]

This was intended as a criticism of Philip IV (thus opposing his claim that Louis's sanctity reflected an inherent Capetian sanctity) as well as a warning to the future Louis X. Saint Louis became associated with freedom from excessive taxation, the preservation of local and noble customs and liberties, and a return to 'good money'. He was thus invoked by the noble leagues (in which Joinville participated) that opposed Philip IV and Louis X in the 1310s. Louis X confirmed Saint Louis's laws and promised to return to his sound coinage, but the myth of his fiscal freedoms became cumbersome for the monarchy.[22]

Saint Louis was invoked by both sides during the Hundred Years War, his reign often seen as a golden age to which kings or claimants to the throne could promise to return. Both Philip VI and Edward III recalled their descent from him and promised to restore his good laws. Jean sans Peur, Henry V and Charles VII all invoked his memory, and he even supposedly appeared to Joan of Arc before the assault on Orléans. A 'Pragmatic Sanction of Saint Louis', apparently dating from 1269, appeared in the 1450s. Demanding respect for the liberties of the French church and prohibiting the levy of taxes by the Holy See without the approval of the king and the French church, it was not exposed as a forgery until the nineteenth century. It is telling that the government of Charles VII appealed to the memory of the holy monarch to provide the historical pedigree for the Pragmatic Sanction of Bourges (1438).[23]

Nevertheless, Louis IX's military failures made him an increasingly awkward patron during the Hundred Years War. Other figures such as Charlemagne and Clovis (who were sometimes claimed as saints but were not officially recognized as such by the church) came to the fore.[24] Moreover, Saint Louis himself was increasingly coming in for criticism. A myth developed that his crusades and ransom money had bankrupted the kingdom to the point that leather had to be used as currency. Many criticized him for being under the excessive influence of mendicants and the Treaty of Paris was viewed as having precipitated the Hundred Years War by granting lands to the English king. Condemnation of the crusades became frequent from the fifteenth century; in a panegyric from 1516, Josse Clichthove noted that 'numerous are those who criticise those perilous and poorly-led operations'. Some defended Saint Louis by asserting incorrectly that his crusades were victorious, but in general it seems that the cult was in decline and his reputation falling. Even at Saint-Denis offerings to Saint Louis dwindled and his original chapel was used as a sacristy.[25] Of course, these signs of decline should not be overstated. Late-fifteenth-century prayers by Jehan Panier showed continued devotion to Saint Louis in certain constituencies, in this case the merchant haberdashers of Paris.[26]

Around the turn of the sixteenth century a number of works defending Saint Louis's reputation appeared, written by people such as the royal clerk Louis le Blanc, who argued against the myth of the leather money and the idea that Louis's crusades and ransom ruined France.[27] The Collège de Navarre, part of the University of Paris, played an important role in this re-evaluation. Masters and students of the university gathered in the college's spacious chapel on 25 August to celebrate the feast of Saint-Louis, a practice codified by Charles V, and to hear sermons by figures such as Jean Gerson.[28] Men associated with the college such as Clichtove and Louis Lasserre produced works on Saint Louis, and Lasserre was also responsible for the rediscovery and publication of Joinville. It is telling that one of the most common pictures of Saint Louis from the early modern period onwards – the king listening to the problems of his lowliest subjects and dispensing justice under an oak at Vincennes – was largely unknown in the Middle Ages because it depended on Joinville.[29] Lasserre mentioned his indebtedness to the Bourbons, who had close connections to the college and a strong sense of being 'closer to the line of Saint Louis than the Valois'.[30] The Guise also made claim to the work of their ancestor Joinville, commissioning manuscript copies in the 1540s to underline their crusading heritage.[31] The first publication of Joinville (dedicated to François Ier and with the archaic language 'improved' for modern tastes) appeared in 1547 and was reprinted in 1561, 1595, 1609 and 1666 (by which time it had been superseded by better editions). Joinville's journey to becoming the key source defining perceptions of Saint Louis began at this time – by the 1680s he was seen as 'the most credible of all the historians of Saint Louis' the style of whose work 'left no room for doubt that he reported things as they occurred'.[32]

The religious conflicts of the sixteenth century made Saint Louis a partisan figure. Jean Calvin mocked Louis's credulous devotion to relics even as Louis's own relics were mobilized by Catholics at moments of religious and political tension.[33] The head reliquary of the Sainte-Chapelle was processed through Paris in January 1535 following the 'Affair of the Placards' and in 1559 on behalf of the dying Henri II. In 1568, Charles IX organized a procession in Paris involving the relics of Saint Louis to thank the saints for having protected him from the Huguenot conspirators of the 'surprise of Meaux'. When the Catholic League held Paris it also deployed them in processions against the alliance of Henri III and Henri de Navarre in 1589, and against Henri IV in 1592 and 1593 (at the beginning of the Estates-General).[34]

References to Saint Louis started to appear more frequently in the 1560s, mainly from Catholics whose hostility to any compromise led them to revive the memory of the Albigensians from relative obscurity in order to encourage Charles IX to imitate Saint Louis by crushing the heretics of his day.[35] As Catherine de Médicis struggled to keep the peace with various compromise edicts, this was probably the reason why Saint Louis did not appear much in official propaganda. It is striking that he was hardly mentioned during the infamous massacres of 1572 even though St Bartholomew's day immediately precedes the feast of Saint-Louis. Of course, there were some isolated examples; in a panegyric of Saint Louis delivered on 25 August 1572 at the Collège de Navarre, Denis Hangard crowed triumphantly of the significance of the date on which 'yesterday's massacre of the enemies of religion and public tranquillity' had fallen, and Claude Nouvelet similarly lauded the events of 'the eve and day of Saint Louis'.[36] Louis continued sometimes to be invoked as a model of good government, for example, in the remonstrance of a 'good Catholic' to the Estates-General in 1576, and the *Enseignements* were recommended to Henri III.[37] Signs of more personal devotion to Saint Louis at this time are also occasionally visible. A 1583 stained glass window at the church of Saint-Patrice in Rouen shows scenes from Saint Louis's life with an inscription stating that it was paid for by 'Louis Sandres, bourgeois of this town'. Still, in general the Valois kings and their propagandists were reluctant to promote the memory of Saint Louis, scarcely mentioning him even when discussing crusading or ideal Christian kingship.[38] Louis XII was the preferred example of good kingship in sixteenth-century France – but even so, the name Louis was rarely given to royal heirs.[39]

By contrast, the cult was developing in Spain. Saint Louis – who was the grandson of a Castilian king – was invoked under the Emperor Charles V and in 1556 was the subject of a literary contest in Seville.[40] Confraternities were founded, he was painted by El Greco, Philip II's third wife Élisabeth de Valois funded a Spanish translation of Joinville, and the *Enseignements* were used in the education of Philip III.[41] Most worryingly from the perspective of the Bourbons, the cult was used to consolidate links between Philip II and the Catholic League.[42] The recovery of Saint Louis's memory for the Bourbon monarchs and renewal of his cult in their kingdom were thus important tasks that would receive attention under Henri IV and Louis XIII.

Henri IV and the establishment of Bourbon legitimacy

According to Jean-François Senault, the Bourbons were fortunate to have in Saint Louis 'the divine hero' from whom they were descended and 'the sacred knot' tying them to the previous kings of France. Senault presented their accession to the throne of their ancestors following Henri III's assassination in 1589 as heaven's response to centuries of patience.[43] Henri de Navarre depended on his status as 'a straight and green shoot from the stock of Saint Louis', as the jurist Pierre Pithou put it at the time, but few kings have come to their thrones in more difficult circumstances.[44] Excommunicated and still a Huguenot, Henri faced the opposition of the Catholic League, which prioritized the Catholicity of the French monarchy by choosing a religiously worthy successor to what was often called the 'throne' or 'crown' of Saint Louis, instead of Henri, the rightful heir according to the Salic Law.[45] In 1589, the majority of cities and towns in his new kingdom did not recognize Henri, who could not enter his capital until 1594, having been denounced from Parisian pulpits in the meantime as a heretic, demon and wolf in sheep's clothing.[46]

Despite this, he was able to establish his legitimacy as king over the coming years through both military success and a careful strategy of propaganda, patronage and reconciliation.[47] Legitimation of Henri's rule was difficult given that France had just experienced a sequence of weak kings and was now presented with a Protestant one. Recent political thinkers had questioned divine right and, in some cases, even advocated the overthrow of tyrants or heretics.[48] Henri had to establish his dynastic legitimacy and renew the close relationship between the Roman Catholic Church and the king of France.

The reconciliation of the Salic Law with Henri's Protestant faith had become a serious problem in 1584 when, as the senior agnatic descendant of Louis IX, he became heir to the French throne. In December 1586, Louis de Gonzague, duc de Nevers – a Catholic but also a royalist who refused to join the League – wrote to Henri III reporting a conversation in which he had told Henri de Navarre that the fate of France was in his hands and that he had only to do one thing to bring an end to civil war and restore royal authority:

> 'It is necessary, Sire . . . that you become a Catholic. You are of the line of Saint Louis. Be of his religion. Believe what he believed. Believe what you believed for a long time. Return to the church into which you were baptised . . .' The king of Navarre did not respond with the sharpness that I expected from the change in his expression. He merely said that there were too many aspects and consequences in what I had said for him to respond straight away.[49]

Nevers's appeal to the memory of Saint Louis was revealing. Louis IX was not just Henri's great-great-great-great-great-great-great-great-grandfather but the last king of France in his direct paternal ancestry. The house of Bourbon descended from Louis's youngest son Robert de Clermont; twenty-two degrees of cousinage separated Henri IV from Henri III, who descended from Louis's oldest son Philip III. This lineage was a powerful argument in Henri's favour. After the death in 1590 of Henri's uncle the Cardinal de Bourbon, who had been proclaimed king as 'Charles X' by Leaguers, Nevers rejected the League's ideas of designating a new king by election or resorting to a foreign candidate: it would be a grave mistake to abandon the 'true royal blood issued from Saint Louis'.[50]

the ridiculousness of the pretentions of the social-climbing Monsieur Jourdain, who has just rejected a request for his daughter's hand in marriage on the grounds that the suitor is not a gentleman, are exposed when his exasperated wife asks if they are also descended from Saint Louis.[67]

The figure of Saint Louis had a prominent place in the encomiastic culture surrounding Henri IV, partly because of this strong dynastic link but also because he was in tune with the spirit of Catholic Reform that Henri was promoting in the Gallican church.[68] In 1593, Sébastien Garnier, a moderate Catholic magistrate from Blois, published the first three books of his *Loyssée*, or poem on the history of Saint Louis. The poem focusses on the 1249 crusade and Louis's 'heroic' deeds against the Saracens, but he also emerges as a pacificator, living 'in peaceful concord' among the Cypriots as he prepared for the crusade and soothing discord between the Greek and Latin churches. Henri IV was, of course, the new Saint Louis, capable of establishing peace between Catholics and Protestants. Completion of the poem, dedicated to Henri's sister Catherine de Bourbon, was prevented by the poet's death in 1595. Still, the fact that a provincial official (*procureur général au bailliage de Blois*) who did not belong to the king's entourage chose to spend night and day describing the deeds 'of our great Henri and of his holy ancestor' reveals that Saint Louis was as much a symbol used by people to highlight their loyalty and devotion to the crown as one directly used by the king.[69] Abraham de Vermeil, who had fought for Henri against the League, wrote an epic poem in twenty-four books on the subject of Saint Louis in the early 1600s. The poem has not survived, but Vermeil's friend Nicolas Richelet, an advocate of the Parlement of Paris, wrote Latin verses proclaiming it to be a work worthy of Apollo.[70]

Another significant poem from the 1590s was by Jean Bertaut, a favourite of Henri III who rallied to Henri IV and was rewarded the diocese of Séez in 1611. Bertaut praised Saint Louis's deeds as those of 'some holy angel dressed in the body of a man to show mortals the steps of virtue' (*quelque Ange sainct d'un corps d'homme vestu/Pour monstrer aux mortels les pas de la vertu*).[71] Many of the themes which would become clichéd over the next two centuries were present here: Louis's maintenance of virtue in the corrupting environment of the court, love of justice and peace, chastity and charity, valour against mutinous vassals, clemency in victory, concern for law, hatred of blasphemy, and commitment to crusading. Bertaut advocated a kingship rooted in obedience to God's laws, saying that 'kings were made for the peoples of the world, not the peoples for them' (*les Rois furent faits pour les peuples du monde, / Non les peuples pour eux*).[72] The perfect model of this was of course Saint Louis. The Bourbons were praised for the fact that their blood derived from a king so just and good who could, moreover, obtain blessings from God for his progeny. The poem finishes with praise of its dedicatee, Henri de Bourbon, duc de Montpensier rather than Henri IV but is a clear example of how the idealized figure of Saint Louis (which was gaining ground over more critical opinions) was being used to praise the Bourbon house.[73] Nicolas Rapin's 1595 poem celebrating Henri II, prince de Condé, shows that other prominent Bourbons were highlighting their links to Saint Louis at this time.[74]

Henri IV's personal interest in his thirteenth-century ancestor was not limited to dynastic descent but also extended to the moral virtues praised by Bertaut. The former Leaguer turned royal historiographer Pierre Matthieu recorded that the king spoke to him about Saint Louis in Lent 1608, admiring Louis's austerity and use of hair shirts and asking if Matthieu had seen the portrait of him at the abbey of Royaumont. They went to see the image, which showed the saint in an act of repentance and humility being disciplined by his confessor.[75] The story was probably dressed up by Matthieu to make his biography of Saint Louis appeal to Louis XIII by signalling his father's admiration for the subject matter. Still, Henri gave several indications of his respect for the saint around this time, further linking Saint Louis's memory to the Bourbon dynasty. A monumental plague hospital outside the Porte du Temple in Paris (the present day Hôpital Saint-Louis) was constructed between 1607 and 1612. Its chapel dedicated to Saint Louis was opened on 25 August 1609 and projected directly into the public domain in order to collect donations; the chapel's need to draw a large following prompted Henri's request in 1608 that the pope grant full indulgences on the feast of Saint-Louis, granted later that year.[76] The decision to name the hospital after Saint Louis, taken by Henri himself according to the *Mercure*, underlined the foundation as an act of charity worthy of the successor to a saint-king associated with various hospitals including the Quinze Vingts and the Hôtel-Dieu.[77] It both indicated that Henri emulated Louis IX's concern for the poor and reiterated his legitimacy. This was the first of many royal foundations under the Bourbons named after Saint Louis, all seeking to reinforce the link between the dynasty and its patron saint as well as anchoring his cult in specific locations across the kingdom.

Henri IV also patronized an important new Parisian church dedicated to Saint Louis on the rue Saint-Antoine, linked to the Jesuit professed house. This owed its origins to Henri's uncle the Cardinal de Bourbon, who gave a property there to the Jesuits in 1580 in order for them to build a chapel dedicated to his saintly ancestor; the choice of Saint Louis was thus imposed on the Jesuits, but they would come to associate themselves strongly with his patronage as part of an effort to link themselves to the crown. It might be presumed that the association with the League's 'Charles X' was fatal for the Jesuit establishment once Henri had regained control of Paris, but instead both the Society and king used devotion to Saint Louis to consolidate a new relationship based on loyalty and obedience. When the Jesuits were allowed back to Paris following the Edict of Rouen in 1603, Henri reopened the church and the Jesuits celebrated the feast of Saint-Louis in his presence in a grand ceremony involving the royal musicians. He frequently attended masses at the church of Saint-Louis and touched for scrofula there in 1610, underlining his support for the Society.[78]

It is worth pausing here to consider the significance of Henri IV's patronage of the Jesuits. Since their formation by Saint Ignatius Loyola in 1534, the Jesuits were associated with ultramontanism on account of their oath of allegiance to the papacy. This would have been suspect enough in Gallican eyes even without the support expressed in numerous Jesuit publications for the papal power to depose kings and the legitimacy of assassinating heretical or tyrannical monarchs, not to mention the activities of Jesuits in Leaguer Paris who had called for the assassination of Henri IV. In the 1590s, the *parlementaire* Antoine Arnauld described the Jesuits as traitors, scoundrels and regicides. Following an attempted assassination of the king in 1594, and despite any direct evidence of a link between the Jesuits and the attack, the Parlement of Paris expelled them from its jurisdiction. Their return to the capital depended on

Henri IV, who in 1603 allowed them back but placed them under the royal courts and the French church hierarchy, requiring them both to be French and to take an oath of loyalty to the king. The circumstances of their readmission to France enhanced Henri's Catholic reputation and tied the French Jesuits closely to the monarchy, upon which they depended for support against their enemies. In 1604, Henri IV chose a Jesuit confessor. Members of the Society would play this role uninterrupted (except for a brief period early in Louis XV's reign) until their expulsion in 1764.[79]

The most important of Henri IV's efforts to associate the Bourbon family with Saint Louis was the baptism of the dauphin in September 1606. 'He was named Louis, at which the king showed on his face that he was overjoyed because of Saint Louis, the first of the Bourbon branch', according to the *Mercure*.[80] The next day Henri wrote to the duc de Montmorency, constable of France, saying that the name was chosen 'to renew the memory of Saint Louis, from whom our house is issued'.[81] According to a panegyric of Marie de Médicis by Pierre Matthieu, it was actually her idea, intended to foster Saint Louis's virtues in the boy and recall that 'the first nourishment that [Louis IX] had from his mother Queen Blanche having made him reign over men in justice and sanctity, he is today served by angels and invoked by kings'.[82] However, there is also evidence that Clement VIII, who was asked to be the dauphin's principal godfather, encouraged Henri IV to name his son 'Louis', the *Gazette* even stating that he 'imposed' the name.[83] The choice of name, in fact, suited all three figures: for Henri IV it reinforced the dynastic link with his Catholic ancestor in the aftermath of the controversial Edict of Nantes (1598); for Marie de Médicis the connection between Saint Louis and the dauphin also created an implicit link between their mothers, Blanche of Castile and Marie herself; for the pope, who died before the baptism, the name served to reinforce Henri's commitment to Catholicism. Saint Louis was now the dauphin's patron twice over, firstly as his dynastic ancestor and secondly as his namesake. This was significant, for 'to name a child after a saint created a permanent special bond between them'.[84] The name Louis, 'name of happiness, innocence [and] virtue' according to Rousselet, acquired a certain sacred quality of its own. According to a publication celebrating Louis XIII shortly after his death, the choice was 'an inspiration from above to mark the sanctity of his life'.[85]

A simple list of Bourbon kings and heirs to the throne over the coming two centuries reveals that it became effectively obligatory to name them 'Louis': Louis XIII; Louis XIV; Louis the Grand Dauphin; Louis, duc de Bourgogne; Louis, duc de Bretagne (1704–5); Louis, duc de Bretagne (1707–12) and Louis, duc d'Anjou (Louis XV), who were both baptized with the same name on Louis XIV's orders during a moment of dynastic crisis following Bourgogne's death in 1712, probably as an act of precaution to ensure that the next king would be called Louis;[86] the dauphin Louis; Louis-Joseph-Xavier; Louis-Auguste (Louis XVI); Louis-Joseph, who died in 1789; Louis-Charles, recognized by royalists as 'Louis XVII' after his father's execution; and Louis XVIII (Louis XVI's brother Louis-Stanislas-Xavier). It was only in 1824 that there was a change of name (Charles X). Although the 'legitimist' Bourbons would never return to power following the 1830 revolution, Charles's son Louis-Antoine would claim the throne as 'Louis XIX' from 1836. The preference for the name 'Louis' can only be explained by the importance of Saint Louis as the dynastic lynchpin and patron saint.

It had the effect of making his day the *fête du roi* for the entire period from 1610 to 1824 (although from 1792 to 1814 only recognized as such by royalists who rejected the revolutionary and Napoleonic regimes).

Henri IV's decision to name his son Louis therefore played an important role in establishing the dominance of the Saint Louis over his dynasty and thus over France for the next two centuries. He also took steps to have his ancestor's feast day celebrated more extensively. In November 1607 – attributing the graces and benedictions bestowed by God on his kingdom to Saint Louis in particular, stating that he had wanted the dauphin to inherit the saint's name in the hope that he would one day inherit his virtues, and remarking that his people's devotion to Saint Louis was remarkably large – Henri wrote to Pope Paul V, the new godfather, to request that 25 August be celebrated in France as a feast of obligation, meaning that people would be forbidden to work and required to attend services.[87] The Congregation of Rites responded positively in 1608, though Henri's death in 1610 delayed proceedings.[88] The letter reveals Henri's investment in promoting the memory of Saint Louis. Although this was based on an appreciation of his continued value as a symbol of dynastic legitimacy and Catholic faith, there is also an impression of genuine devotion. Henri's sense of his ancestor's intercession may have been further strengthened the following year when his son Gaston was born on the birthday of Saint Louis; the king apparently demonstrated great contentment at this new connection to the 'stem of the royal house of Bourbon'.[89]

The final link between the first Bourbon king and Saint Louis was the Jesuit college of La Flèche on the Loire, founded and funded by Henri IV following the Edict of Rouen. The chapel, built between 1607 and 1621 and consecrated in 1637 by the bishop of Angers, was dedicated to Saint Louis and chosen by Henri as the location where his heart would be interred after his death.[90] The Jesuits made much of La Flèche as a demonstration of their close relationship with the monarchy, claiming that in supporting the college Henri IV was 'like a good father'.[91] In 1610, they commissioned an engraving to commemorate Henri IV's gift of his heart and the new king Louis XIII's promise of protection. The Jesuits excelled at producing emblems – combinations of text and image whose whole was formed by the interaction of the component parts, conveying a message or moral lesson.[92] This image is rich in detail and revealing of the nexus between the Jesuits, the monarchy, and Saint Louis. With the buildings of La Flèche in the background, an angel presents the arms of France on the left hand side and a personification of France holds a medallion showing Henri IV's heart and the IHS of the Jesuits on the right accompanied by the text 'this is my light and pillar' (*hoc lumen columenque mihi*). The focus of the image, however, is the three kings of France dressed in coronation robes who occupy the central space. Henri IV and Louis XIII kneel on either side of a standing Saint Louis, whose crowned head emits a dazzling halo. Henri IV says to Saint Louis, 'O divine one, from your palm trees La Flèche hangs its ivy-vines. May you cherish it' (*Dive tuis hederas appendit Flexia palmis. tu foveas*). He simultaneously gestures towards a palm tree, symbol of victory, up which climbs the ivy that symbolizes the Jesuits. An accompanying text explains Henri's statement as 'marking that he places the college of La Flèche under the protection of this saint monarch whose palms, that is to say victories, were no less admirable than his virtues, and that the Jesuits and their students will attach themselves to his cult as much as the ivy to the palm tree that sustains it'. Saint Louis points to Louis XIII with his sceptre and says 'From now on, Louis, fasten the laurel tree to [my] palm trees' (*hinc daphnem palmis Lodoice marita*); needless to say, there is a laurel tree (another symbol of victory) growing at the foot of the palm tree between Saint Louis and Louis XIII. The young Louis XIII responds 'while I remain, it will flourish' (*me stante vigebit*). The image thus depicts the transfer of protection of the college from Henri IV to Louis XIII via Saint Louis. Thanks to the king's protection, the Jesuits will flourish, and as such they literally attach themselves to the cult of the royal patron saint (Figure 1.1).[93]

Despite presenting an image of orderly dynastic succession and secure royal patronage of the Jesuits, this engraving was produced at a time of real weakness for both the French monarchy and the Jesuits. Henri IV's assassination in May 1610 by a Catholic fanatic was a reminder of how precarious Bourbon legitimacy remained, and the Jesuit association with regicide made this an extremely dangerous moment for them given that they had only recently returned from exile thanks to the support of a king who had just been stabbed to death.

Figure 1.1 *Estampe que les Jésuites ont fait graver à l'honneur du Collège de La Flèche* (1610) by Jaspar Isaac (*c*.1585–1654). © Bibliothèque nationale de France.

The restoration of the cult in 1618

At this vulnerable juncture, it was important to continue reminding the kingdom of the Bourbons' descent from Louis IX. Unsurprisingly, he was the most frequently invoked model of kingship in the funeral orations for Henri IV, who was said to have inherited more than Louis's blood. The court preacher Jean Petriny stated that Saint Louis's clemency was hereditary among the Bourbons and had infused Henri IV. Other preachers compared their love of justice and valour, construction of churches and hospitals, and even the manner of their deaths. The Jesuit Jean Arnoux, who as Louis XIII's confessor would play an important role in the restoration of Saint Louis's feast day, noted that terrible deaths often fell 'on those whom God cherishes, and as much on our Henri the Great as on his forefather Saint Louis, who died in distant lands'. This recast Henri's assassination as a mark of divine favour comparable to Louis's death at Tunis. Arnoux stated that Saint Louis had interceded daily for Henri in heaven and even advised him on earth; in Toulouse, Pierre Louis de Catel called him 'the saintly protector of this kingdom'. Some orations prefigured the most laudatory panegyrics that would be delivered under Louis XIV by suggesting that Henri had *surpassed* the model of good kingship presented by Saint Louis. Referring to the creation of a Jesuit college in Constantinople, Philippe Cospéan compared the two monarchs' successes in the Holy Land:

> Saint Louis left his kingdom to go and make war against the common enemies of Christendom . . . spilt his blood there and won several victories; the king [Henri IV], at least as far as this issue was concerned, never left his Louvre, and did no more than write to them; and if at the end Saint Louis won nothing more for the service of God on earth than the loss of his army, then of his liberty and life, the king on the contrary found a way of making their towns flow with the faithful servants . . . of Jesus the true father of believers.[94]

Even during these funeral orations, attention was turning to the new king. The Jesuit Étienne Binet delivered one in Troyes in 1611 which addressed Louis XIII, telling him that he combined Henri's 'IV' and Saint Louis's 'IX' to make 'XIII', the 'golden number' which would cause the revival of the 'golden age in France'.[95] Numerical observations of this kind were a popular way of predicting the glories of Louis XIII. The historian Scipion Dupleix noted that twenty kings after Clovis came Charlemagne, after another twenty kings came Louis IX and after another twenty came Louis XIII. The implication was that Louis XIII was on a comparable level of piety and glory with these famous monarchs.[96] Soon after the assassination, another Jesuit Louis Richeome printed a 'consolation' for Queen Marie, telling her of her resemblance to Blanche; she could similarly make a 'Saint Louis' of her son.[97]

References to Saint Louis proliferated more generally in the first decade of Louis XIII's reign, as his example was endlessly recommended to the king and invoked by the queen regent, who revived memories of Blanche of Castile's regency in order to legitimate her own position. The president of the Parlement of Paris, addressing Louis soon after Henri IV's death, recalled the happiness and success that had resulted

intercede with the pope.[121] Bentivoglio advised Rome to satisfy the king in such a pious demand, mentioning his devotion to his ancestor and saying that 'the king . . . recites every day a particular prayer to this saint and, on Wednesdays, his entire office'.[122]

In June, Denis-Simon reported that the pope was happy to accord Louis XIII's request and that it was passing sufficiently quickly through the bureaucratic channels in Rome for the feast to be celebrated in August – though he noted that Rome was reluctant to make it a Double everywhere for fear of multiplying the number of feasts too much.[123] Paul V's brief, issued on 5 July, stated that that he had been made aware of 'the devotion [Louis XIII] has for Saint Louis' as well as the great veneration of the people; as such, the pontiff had been willing to grant 'the good and praiseworthy desires of the said king Louis' and instructed that 'from now on and in perpetuity the feast of the abovementioned Saint Louis be kept as [a feast of] obligation by the whole kingdom of France' and that the office be celebrated 'in the manner of Double feasts, conforming to the rubrics of the Roman Breviary'. The brief was soon printed in French by the bishop of Paris's printer, accompanied by a *mandement* of 18 August from the bishop, Cardinal Henri de Gondi. Gondi added his authority to that of the pope by ordering all deans, chapters, abbots, priors, convents, communities, parish priests and vicars in his diocese to celebrate 25 August, not just as before with particular services in churches, but publicly; work was prohibited and the people were instructed to devote themselves 'solely to the service of God and to works of piety and religion'. Gondi ordered the clerics to mark the feast with as much honour as possible and to exhort the people to celebrate it every year with devotion by attending divine service and visiting places dedicated to Saint Louis. They were to invoke the saint's intercession 'generally for the fortunate state of this kingdom his ancient patrimony, and particularly to obtain from his divine majesty an abundance of celestial benedictions, as much spiritual as corporal on the person of the king our sovereign lord'. The cardinal wrote that 'it is useful and necessary for this state, at such a dangerous time, to seek out more than ever the assistance and protection of holy friends and favourites of his divine majesty, principally those who have long been recognised as benefactors and protectors of this kingdom'. Saint Louis was clearly one of these: Gondi proclaimed him 'patron and protector of France'.[124]

These papal and episcopal instructions were supposed to be read from the pulpits and received further publicity by being printed in the *Mercure François*. On the day itself, the streets down which the Sainte-Chapelle was to process its relics were lined with tapestries early in the morning; the procession waited for Louis XIII, but, significantly, he chose instead to go with the queen to the Jesuit church of Saint-Louis. Accompanied by princes and courtiers, they took communion there in the morning, later hearing vespers and a sermon on the glories of Saint Louis by Arnoux. (The king's preference for the Jesuit church over the Sainte-Chapelle will be discussed in a later chapter.) A procession of all the city's parishes and monasteries drew huge crowds and the evening was marked joyfully with lanterns, illuminations, cannonades, bonfires and a firework display near the Louvre. Bentivoglio informed Rome that the king displayed great piety and religiosity.[125]

Louis was commended for his zeal in renewing and augmenting the praise of his ancestor in a panegyric by Étienne Molinier, who noted that France would deserve to be called ungrateful to Saint Louis for having delayed this honour for so long were it not clear that God had reserved the glory for Louis XIII. Molinier described Saint Louis's life as full of miracles – indeed, a continual miracle – thanks to his extraordinary virtues. 'He is the patron of princes, the model for nobles, the exemplar for judges, the mirror for the people, the rule for the clergy, the image of those in religious orders, the measure of each individual, and the prototype of all.' Emphasizing Saint Louis's patronage of France, Molinier stated that he was watching over his former kingdom and his current worthy successor with care, and finished by telling Louis XIII to continue emulating his ancestor and the French people to unite in prayer to their patron saint. Crucially, Molinier presented a mimetic relationship between Louis XIII and Saint Louis in which the homology between them was both innate (transmitted by royal blood) and acquired (through imitation). To the panegyric were appended twenty-five verses making up a prayer to Saint Louis for the king's prosperity, finishing: 'O star of the French, the honour of our provinces, support [Louis XIII's] designs, favour our wishes, O saint among princes, O prince among saints.' (*O Astre des François, l'honneur de nos Provinces, / Seconde ses desseins, / Favorise nos vœux, O sainct entre les Princes, / O Prince entre les Saincts.*)[126] According to a letter written by Molinier a few months later, he presented his work to the king at his *lever* at the Louvre on 25 August 1618. It was well-received and won him the patronage of Arnoux, who recommended it in his sermon before the king and cited some of the concluding prayers.[127]

Another publication that used the elevation of the feast to praise Louis XIII was a pamphlet with the self-explanatory title *The Triumphs of the Most Christian king of France and Navarre, Louis the Just, Worthy Heir and Successor of the King Saint Louis.* The author of this short text claimed to hate flattery but proceeded nevertheless with hyperbolic praise of Louis XIII. Following the obligatory observations on Louis XIII's descent from Saint Louis and inheritance of his virtues, the pamphleteer imagined the advantages that the recently restored cult would bring to the kingdom:

> We must not fear pernicious events in the future: Saint Louis will guide our ship better than ever. He will draw on us the benedictions from on high in the name of his son, of you, Sire, who will render the same advantages to posterity to the name of the good kings your successors, when you act like him; when you do so, I say, because your deportment assures us that it could not happen otherwise.[128]

This pamphlet not only praised the king for renewing the cult, which would accrue untold benefits to the kingdom thanks to Saint Louis's intercession, but also implied that Louis XIII would himself one day be able to give saintly assistance to France. It is hard to find a clearer example of propagandistic attempts to use the cult of Saint Louis to sacralize the Bourbon monarchy.

Historians have proposed various interpretations of the renewal of Saint Louis's cult in 1618. Alain Boureau saw it as marking Louis XIII's assumption of real power following the coup of 1617.[129] However, I have found no evidence that this is how it was perceived at the time. Instead, there was direct continuity from the efforts of Marie de Médicis to celebrate the cult to the successful renewal in 1618; Paul V's brief was a result of initiatives since Henri IV rather than something marking a new direction.

Fabien Montcher has argued that it was an attempt to re-appropriate the cult from Spain. If it was the case that 1618 helped consolidate a French 'monopoly' over the cult, it is worth noting that Marie also wrote to Philip III asking to have the feast celebrated at the Spanish court and that the diplomatic correspondence with Rome indicates the French monarchy's desire to have it promoted across the Catholic world.[130] It seems, therefore, that neither of these interpretations is correct, and we should take care not to over-interpret the meaning of the elevation of the feast. The events of 1618 were the culmination of the promotion of Saint Louis under Henri IV and Marie de Médicis, who used it to bolster the legitimacy of their accession and regency respectively, as well as Louis XIII's evident devotion to his namesake, which taken together led the French crown to lobby Rome to elevate the feast. But if it was a result of initiatives started under Henri IV, 1618 was also supposed to herald a new beginning and open a period in which the cult of the Bourbon patron saint would be inserted into the devotional lives of all French people. The renewed prominence of Saint Louis that was confirmed in 1618 would last for the rest of the *Ancien Régime*.

Conclusion

The development of Saint Louis's cult from 1297 to 1589 was marked by the vicissitudes of three centuries of war, dynastic change and religious upheaval. Having been promoted as an essential part of Philip IV's attempts to sacralize the Capetian dynasty, Saint Louis suffered criticism and neglect during the Hundred Years War. However, the Bourbons came to associate themselves strongly with him during the fifteenth and sixteenth centuries. The circumstances of their accession to the throne necessitated the promotion of Saint Louis to underline their dynastic and religious credentials as well as to recover the saint's memory for the monarchy as part of the recatholicization of the French crown following the nadir of the royal image during the last years of Valois rule. As Nicole Reinhardt has argued, 'the fragile foundations of the new dynasty, with a doubtful and contested conversion of its founder at the heart, go a long way to explain why [Henri IV's] successors, too, always felt compelled to promote the legacy of sacral monarchy and divine right with unprecedented intensity'.[131] Saint Louis's cult was part of this agenda which sought to sacralize the dynastic line, with Henri IV as the crucial figure in establishing the importance it would enjoy over the next two centuries. The naming of the dauphin and nurturing of a Jesuit cult of Saint Louis were both important, as well as the beginning of a tradition of royal foundations dedicated to the dynastic patron saint; moreover, although the elevation of the feast did not actually occur until 1618, it was the result of initiatives started at least a decade earlier.

The wider context was crucial. Following the violent struggles of the Wars of Religion, the early seventeenth century was a period of renewal and reform in French Catholicism, marked by the influence of the Council of Trent (if not its formal reception in France), the use of seminaries and visitations to ensure higher standards among the lower clergy, efforts to reform the old monastic orders and the attempt to purify popular religion of 'pagan' influences. New religious orders proliferated, often advocating intervention in the world through charity, teaching and missions, and frequently promoted by pious laypeople and Counter-Reformation bishops. Saint Louis chimed perfectly with the spirit of the times not just as a dynastic lynchpin but as a symbol of piety. A figure associated with devotion, charity, justice, zeal and almost all other religious virtues, he assumed the position of model of Christian kingship par excellence for the Catholic monarchy of the seventeenth century.

This model was often turned to the monarchy's advantage, casting a sacral aura around the current king by comparing him with his holy ancestor. As Anne de Lévis, duc de Ventadour wrote to Louis XIII on 19 January 1619, 'in the person of Your Majesty we see reborn the great, holy and generous actions of the good king Saint Louis which, by his prayers, will make the person and reign of Your Majesty prosper for an entire century'.[132] But, as Joseph Bergin has noted, the development of the 'royal religion' paid dividends until the monarchy failed to live up to it in moments of crisis.[133] As has been seen, the memory of Saint Louis was not the exclusive preserve of the monarchy. The elevation of his feast and crafting of his memory involved all sorts of people, from Jesuits to poets, historians to noblemen, each with their own motives. Often they sought to win favour from the monarchy or to highlight their loyalty to the king by writing about or celebrating Saint Louis, but a critical element would also become apparent in the seventeenth century. The resuscitation of Saint Louis's cult was an elite affair, driven by the interests of the monarchy and groups or individuals with proximity to the crown, and the promotion of his feast was ordered from the top down rather than growing out of enthusiasm from the lower levels of society. What remains to be seen is how successfully the cult was revived across a broader spectrum of early modern French people – and, ultimately, whether it was useful or harmful for the monarchy in the long run.

The saint of kings and the king of saints

Perceptions of Saint Louis, 1618–1715

How was Saint Louis perceived and remembered in the seventeenth century? What contexts shaped the production of written accounts of his reign? Before we examine political uses of his memory in subsequent chapters, it is important to establish what people knew and thought about him and where they got their information.

The first two sections of this chapter focus on two genres which transmitted knowledge of Saint Louis and shaped perceptions of his life and reign: histories and panegyric sermons. In these texts, the criticisms that had developed during the Hundred Years War were buried under an avalanche of praise as Saint Louis was established 'as the model of an ideal sovereign'.[1] Although there was therefore a general positive view of Saint Louis, with criticism of his actions becoming extremely unusual, all writers moulded his memory into a form that benefitted their ideology, patron or interest group. They could do so because there was scope for different presentations in the context of certain seventeenth-century debates. For example, Louis IX's dealings with the papacy were used by both Ultramontanes and Gallicans to argue that he represented their opinion. Jansenists tried to construct a version of Saint Louis that supported their views on grace and the frequency of communion; given his association with their enemies, the French monarchy and the Jesuits, this was unsurprisingly contested.

The third section addresses a particular theme in Saint Louis's kingship – the crusades. These had been frequently criticized in the previous period and would return as a point of controversy in the eighteenth century. For much of the seventeenth century, however, a broadly positive consensus was projected not just in histories and panegyrics but also in poetry and even music. The crusades were lauded as indicative of the saint-king's zeal and held up for his descendants to emulate.

Thanks to the confluence of the rise of the Bourbons and Catholic Reform, the seventeenth century was the zenith of the memory of Saint Louis. Almost everyone found it worthwhile to stake claim to the memory of a monarch who was considered to have been – to quote Pierre Matthieu's summary in 1618, which set the tone for the coming century – 'generous and magnanimous on all occasions, just in punishments and rewards, wise in all sorts of matters, holy in all aspects of his life'.[2]

Saint Louis in seventeenth-century historiography

The elevation of the feast in 1618 made Saint Louis a topical subject. As discussed in Chapter 1, numerous publications devoted to him appeared in the late 1610s, including Claude Médard's two volumes of sources and Pierre Matthieu's biography. The story of Louis IX's reign would be retold numerous times by seventeenth-century historians in biographies and general histories of France as well as in books of piety and analyses of texts such as the *Enseignements*.

One of the most important – and certainly the longest – of the publications exalting Saint Louis in the decades after 1618 was the Jesuit Georges-Étienne Rousselet's *Lys sacré* (1631). The work contributed to the establishment of Saint Louis's position as the primary model of Christian kingship under Louis XIII, casting a sacral glow over the monarchy as a whole. On the frontispiece engraving, Saint Louis occupies the central petal of the *fleur-de-lys*, symbol of the French monarchy, with Louis the Pious and Louis XIII kneeling and looking up reverently from either side. This clear representation of the saint-king's pre-eminence is developed over almost 1,500 pages of dense text in which Rousselet exalted the French monarchs from Clovis to Louis XIII as paragons of piety and Christian virtue. There is hardly a bad word to be said about any of them, even in the section on chastity (though Rousselet forgot to mention Henri IV there). Among all these paragons of virtue, the 'life of Saint Louis reveals to us all the perfections of the other Christian princes':

> He possessed Clovis's zeal against the Arians, Childebert's piety, Clotaire I's justice, Clotaire II's zeal, the holy generosity of Dagobert, Pepin's obedience to the sovereign pontiffs, Charlemagne's [use of] hair shirts, Louis the Debonnaire's leniency, [Hugh] Capet's prudence, Robert [the Pious]'s fasts, Philip Augustus's hatred of the Jews, Louis VIII's chastity, Charles V's good counsel, Charles VI's hope, Charles VIII's nocturnal prayers, Louis XI's devotion to the Virgin, Louis XII's kindness, Francis I's generosity, Henri III's eloquence, Henri IV's clemency and Louis XIII's royal justice.

All these attributes – including, most shockingly to modern eyes, 'hatred of the Jews' – were considered by Rousselet to be highly desirable in a ruler. They were united in Saint Louis, who was presented as superior to Solomon. By comparison to Saint Louis, the greatest classical rulers were mere 'shadows of justice'. Rousselet quite simply presented him as the most complete and perfect monarch in all biblical, ancient and modern history.[3]

Rousselet's intention to use the French monarchs to encourage piety is reflected in the book's structure, organized around virtues such as hope, faith, charity and prudence. Each is given an introductory chapter, a second discussing it with relation to French monarchs from Clovis to Louis XIII (excepting Saint Louis) and a third exclusively devoted to Saint Louis in which he was invariably presented as its ultimate exemplar. This structure elevated him above the others and was typical of the way French Jesuits promoted the saint. Another Jesuit, Joseph Filère, produced a work in 1641 filled with endless praise of the virtues of 'the most illustrious prince of this monarchy' and encouraging the French to pray to him and take communion once a month under his protection.[4] A later edition updated the original letter praising Louis XIII as a new Saint Louis by shifting the focus to Louis XIV. Filère stated that the Jesuits owed their establishment in France to princes descended from Saint Louis and wished to use their efforts to serve the king by devoting themselves to the cult of his patron saint.[5]

Jesuit authors thus participated in the idealization of Saint Louis that was a function of the monarchy's promotion of the cult after 1618. They also linked him to their various controversies, such as the debate between Gallicans and Ultramontanes. The great defender of Ultramontane claims of papal authority, the Jesuit Cardinal Robert Bellarmine, invoked Saint Louis to insist on the prince's duty to obey the pope.[6] Rousselet similarly emphasized Louis IX's reverence for the papacy; 'never did a prince kiss the feet of the Vicar of Jesus Christ with more reverence than did our incomparable monarch.'[7] On the other side of this debate were those such as Matthieu and the royal historiographer Scipion Dupleix who argued that Saint Louis was Gallican, emphasizing his disapproval of the misuse of excommunication and instances where he treated Rome firmly such as his impartial attitude to the conflict between Innocent IV and the Emperor Frederick II.[8] The most useful piece of evidence for those seeking to harness Saint Louis's memory to support the 'Gallican liberties' of the French church was the (forged) 'Pragmatic Sanction', frequently cited as an example of resistance to the overextension of papal authority.[9]

Alain Boureau has argued that such debates show that Saint Louis was still an ambivalent figure from the perspective of the monarchy, passing 'from hand to hand' in various polemical contexts. In his opinion, the crucial moment at which Saint Louis was recovered for the monarchy was the 1627 publication of the *Precepts of the king Saint Louis to Philip III* by Adam Théveneau, an advocate of the Parlement of Paris. Seeking to 'make Saint Louis and Louis the Just reign jointly', Théveneau's tome was a huge gloss on the *Enseignements,* lines from which were used to expand on the nature of government.[10] The *Enseignements* were problematic as various versions allowed different emphases and interpretations. The 'short' and 'interpolated' versions omitted the call for loyalty to the pope found in the 'long' version used by Théveneau.[11] The contrast can be seen in standalone publications of the period: the 'long' version published in 1617 and Joinville's shorter version printed under the confrontational title of 'remonstrance', which added a potentially 'anti-absolutist' injunctions to observe 'the good customs of your kingdom' and not to 'raise any *taille* without great necessity'.[12]

According to Boureau, Théveneau's presentation of the *Enseignements* places him 'close to Richelieu and to absolutist conceptions of the state'.[13] In fact, Théveneau emphasized the importance of limitations on royal power. He contrasted Saint Louis's 'royal' government, in which the king commanded by laws and justice, with seigneurial and tyrannical monarchy, which employed 'absolute power'. He also described it as impertinent to see the people as slaves of the king and him 'tyrant and absolute lord over them'. The ideal system was one in which the king commanded and the nobility served; nevertheless, the power of the king was tempered by God and by the clergy, nobility and Parlements, all of which had the duty to advise and even admonish. Crucially, kings had to observe the ancient laws and customs of the kingdom. Extended passages state that taxes had to be strictly necessary for the defence of religion and the kingdom, and that their legitimacy would be scrutinized by God.[14] Combined with the emphasis on the Parlement, this contrasted with absolutist theorists like Cardin Le Bret who cited Louis IX as founder of the *taille* to justify the argument that the right to raise taxes was an essential royal prerogative.[15] Boureau's argument that Théveneau's work marked the decisive point at which Saint Louis was remade for the absolute age, therefore, appears flawed; it was more of a *parlementaire* reading of the saint-king. As discussed in Chapter 3, the history of the Fronde would soon show that Saint Louis could be used by the Parlement to critique the overextension of royal power. What Théveneau's book *does* reflect is Saint Louis's return as the essential paradigm of good government. Other good kings – notably Louis XII – are discussed in the text, but the fact that its structure rests on the words of Saint Louis made him pre-eminent.

This pre-eminence was based on a perception of Saint Louis's superlative virtues as a man and ruler that was also projected in more general historical writing. An 'almost insatiable' interest in former kings created a market for reign-by-reign histories such as that by Dupleix, for whom Saint Louis was 'religious without superstition, magnanimous without ambition . . . humble without baseness, simple without feebleness', his life 'the true paragon of all royal and heroic virtues'.[16] In another reign-by-reign history of France by the royal historiographer François Eudes de Mézeray, Saint Louis was described as pious, humble and clement (though hard-headed against the enterprises of the papal curia), his life 'completely pure and with no passion other than to draw all to God'; through him, God had 'preordained this monarchy to be the most holy and illustrious there was in Christendom' – a striking example of Louis's holiness being used to enhance the monarchy's collective sacrality.[17] Mézeray's *History* was read to the young Louis XIV at bedtime, with the stories of his lazier predecessors said to have incensed the young king.[18] That Saint Louis was not one of those was reinforced by the card game devised for Louis XIV by Desmarets de Saint-Sorlin to illustrate the reigns, qualities and faults of France's monarchs. Saint Louis was 'pious, equitable, chaste, prudent, valiant, [the] true model of good kings'.[19]

Despite the general presentation of Saint Louis as an ideal monarch, old criticisms were occasionally expressed, particularly regarding the 1259 Treaty of Paris (in which Henry III had renounced his claims to territories lost by King John but retained Gascony and parts of Aquitaine, but only as a vassal of Louis IX). In 1661, Jean-François Senault stated that Louis's 'incomparable generosity caused him on this occasion to commit a fault against the state . . . This was a wound which bled for almost two hundred years'.[20] Louis Maimbourg – a Jesuit whose Gallicanism got him ejected from the Society in 1682 – similarly wrote that 'this treaty having placed the foreigners in France, gave birth to a war which lasted for almost two hundred years before they could be put outside'.[21] Responsibility for the Hundred Years War was a serious charge, but these authors still conformed to the general view that Saint Louis was a model of monarchy. Given that Senault advocated piety as the foundation of politics, he was unsurprisingly full of praise for the one he called 'the most just, valiant and pious of our kings'.[22] As for Maimbourg, criticism of Louis's English policy was followed by the observation that it was 'almost the only thing for which one could reproach Saint Louis, for having too much kindness on this occasion, against the advice of his council', thus portraying him as *too* generous and pious. Few praiseworthy qualities are missing from Maimbourg's assessment that Saint Louis possessed

> an admirable mixture of all royal and Christian virtues . . . austere, humble, modest, devout, respectful to the Holy See, zealous for the glory of God and for the salvation of souls . . . civil, affable, kind . . . loving his subjects, as he was reciprocally loved; firm and unmovable in asserting justice . . . jealous of the rights of his crown, and those of the Gallican church.[23]

Other authors went further and actually praised and defended the Treaty of Paris. In a 1662 biography of the saint-king, the Franciscan Jean-Marie de Vernon noted that 'critics find in Saint Louis's proceedings on this occasion more simplicity or scrupulousness than intelligence; as for me, I notice an uncommon wisdom and an admirable grandeur of spirit'. Vernon harnessed an idealized Saint Louis to the advantage of his order, never losing an opportunity to claim him as a supporter of the Franciscans, arguing he was a member of the Third Order of Saint Francis and mentioning the particular devotion of their convent in Paris.[24] Themes of pious conduct are prominent, particularly the Franciscan ideals of poverty and charity. There is also a notable focus on chastity. Vernon states that, had Louis not been aware that his marriage was essential for the kingdom, he 'would never have consented to deprive himself of virginal purity' – a line which might have been awkward reading for the young Louis XIV. Nevertheless, like most books concerning Saint Louis, Vernon's biography was dedicated to the king and prefaced with a laudatory letter. Like the Jesuits, the Franciscans produced material glorifying Saint Louis to flatter the king and positioned themselves close to the royal patron saint in order to highlight their loyalty to the monarchy.[25]

As well as being a period rich in printed histories of kings and reigns, the seventeenth century was a time of significant advances in medieval research. The great scholar Charles du Fresne, sieur du Cange, published a monumental tome on Saint Louis in 1668 comprising Joinville's life as well as numerous other primary sources, tables and genealogies, and his own detailed observations and dissertations, all covered with a thick coat of learned references.[26] Du Cange's painstaking erudition (he apparently studied for several hours on his wedding day) reflected a seriousness in medieval research that showed how things had changed since Matthieu's statement that he had removed 'everything that seemed to me to be superfluous and tedious' from Louis IX's letter from the Holy Land.[27] He was helped by Antoine Vyon d'Hérouval, a Parisian *érudit* who also found documents for another great scholar, Louis-Sébastien Le Nain de Tillemont, whose work (still consulted by medievalists) not just represents the pinnacle of seventeenth-century research on Louis IX but also reveals the pressures and corporate interests that lay behind biographies of the saint-king.[28]

Tillemont's *Life of Saint Louis*, composed between 1679 and 1684, had its origins at the abbey of Port-Royal-des-Champs. This was the centre of Jansenism, an austere theological movement emphasizing human sinfulness and the inefficacy of human actions in obtaining divine grace that caused enormous tension and controversy in seventeenth-century France. Like their sworn enemies the Jesuits, Jansenists tried to lay claim to the memory of Saint Louis, using the royal saint to legitimate their position. Saint Louis was regarded as a benefactor at Port-Royal and Saint François de Sales consecrated an altar to him there in 1619. The Jansenist bishop of Alet, Nicolas Pavillon, even invoked 'the example of the great Saint Louis' in his widely circulated letter of 25 August 1664 reproaching Louis XIV for his treatment of the Jansenists.[29] A long-term project at Port-Royal was to write a biography of Saint Louis that would present him according to Jansenist ideals. This was originally commissioned by the French-born Queen Marie-Louise Gonzaga of Poland, who was closely connected to the abbey. Angélique Arnauld, abbess of Port-Royal, mentioned the book frequently in letters to Marie-Louise, often expressing regret that it was being slowed down by the Fronde and the persecution of the Jansenists.[30] The project was given a new lease of life thanks to the decision to write histories of key monarchs for the education of the Grand Dauphin. Following the 1669 'Peace of the Church' (a temporary respite in the Jansenist controversy), the task of writing Saint Louis's biography was given to Louis-Isaac Le Maistre de Sacy, a priest at Port-Royal best known for his translation of the Bible, to whom the duc de Montausier, governor to the dauphin, wrote in January 1673 that

> Monseigneur the Dauphin awaits from your hand the model of a great, sage, just, brave and pious prince; you understand well that it is the life of Saint Louis of which I speak. . . . It is necessary to render virtuous a man whose good or bad qualities will make the happiness or misfortune of all Europe.[31]

The job of collecting materials for the biography fell to Tillemont, an ascetic and hard-working man who said his first mass on the feast of Saint-Louis after his ordination in 1676.[32] Establishing facts and dates through meticulous examination of the sources, he wrote a chapter for each year of Louis IX's reign as well as many more dealing with contextual information (including 115 preliminary chapters).[33]

The *History of Saint Louis* based on Tillemont's research did not appear until January 1688, long after the completion of the dauphin's education. Although it was printed with no author's name (which, like the fact that Tillemont was not acknowledged, reflected the spirit of humility of Port-Royal), it was known to be the work of Nicolas Filleau de la Chaise (an associate of Port-Royal) rather than Sacy, who had died in 1680.[34] In the dedicatory letter to the Grand Dauphin, Filleau said that in everything regarding human glory and military and diplomatic triumph, the dauphin needed to look no further than Louis XIV for a model; it was in the glory of sanctity that it was difficult to surpass or even equal Saint Louis. Therefore, he made religion the focal point of Saint Louis's value as a model of kingship, telling his dedicatee that 'you have so many aspects of Saint Louis that it can only be hoped that God sanctifies them in you, as he sanctified them in him'. Filleau celebrated the decline of the nobility's feudal independence in the face of 'royal power' during Louis IX's minority, praised his actions against duelling and defended the Treaty of Paris. By 1270, France was a land of justice, peace and prosperity. Filleau presented a Gallican Saint Louis who defended his right to the *régale* (the king's claim to the revenues of vacant bishoprics) in the diocese of Limoges in 1246, praising Louis IX's Pragmatic Sanction, of which that of Bourges was 'a mere extension'.[35] This was significant given Louis XIV's serious rift with the papacy in the 1680s, which had started with a dispute over the *régale*. In the famous 1681 General Assembly of the Clergy that issued the 'Four articles' of the Gallican church, Bossuet also recalled the Pragmatic Sanction of Saint Louis during his *Sermon on the unity of the church*.[36]

On the other hand, Filleau was more sympathetic to the Albigensians than was typical in the decade of the Revocation of the Edict of Nantes. Although he did not defend their beliefs, he mentioned the 'ravages' of their Catholic opponents and wrote with respect for the moral purity of the Cathar *perfecti*, described as 'sincere to the last exactitude and of a continence beyond suspicion'. This admiration for their rigorist morality probably stemmed from Filleau's Jansenism, as did his harsh words for those who were debauched and indulgent beneath an exterior of devotion. He similarly argued that Louis IX's captivity had the effect of making 'everything that the world regards as great and delicious seemed to him only more contemptible and bitter'.[37]

Filleau's Jansenism became controversial when he noted that Saint Louis 'communicated at least six times a year, but with such compunction, despite the innocence of his life, that the greatest penitents would have been happy to approach it'.[38] This statement was a contribution to the dispute over communion that had developed between the Jesuits, who advocated frequent communion, and the Jansenists, who saw it as requiring lengthy preparation. Jesuits such as Joseph Filère stated that Saint Louis took communion every week, whereas Filleau limited his communions to six times a year.[39] The prominent Jansenist Antoine Arnauld (son of the *parlementaire* mentioned in Chapter 1) praised Filleau for portraying Saint Louis 'according to his true virtues', but Louis XIV's Jesuit confessor, Père La Chaise, was scandalized.[40] According to Madame de Sévigné, the author was asked to produce his sources.[41] In a manuscript *mémoire*, Filleau argued that Saint Louis did not communicate every Friday, noting that 'had he done so . . . it is clear that we [Jansenists] would have lost much', a comment indicating the extent to which Saint Louis was a powerful symbol that both sides wished to harness to their cause.[42]

Late in 1688, royal permission was given for the publication of another biography of Saint Louis by the Abbé de Choisy. Daniel Weiner has described this volume and Filleau's as 'battling biographies': his argument is that the Jansenist element in Filleau's biography 'ruined' it, leading Choisy to be chosen quickly to write another, which eventually drove Filleau's into 'oblivion'. Choisy's statement that his biography had been commissioned by 'a superior authority' leads Weiner to propose that this may have been Madame de Maintenon or Père La Chaise. Weiner makes much of a speculative psychological motivation for Choisy, namely that replacing Filleau's biography was an act of revenge against the duc de Montausier for having humiliated him while dressed as a woman in the 1670s (although there is some debate as to whether this event was anything more than 'a fabricated plot device' in Choisy's *Memoirs*).[43] Choisy himself gave a less antagonistic reason for writing the biography, namely that he was inspired by Filleau's reference to Saint Louis's private life as 'matter for a second history'. Filleau had concentrated on the political issues of the period, whereas Choisy would focus on 'the particular and holy actions of Louis'. He was respectful of Filleau's work but said that he was writing a *life*, not a *history of the reign*; as a result, foreign affairs would only be discussed when necessary – his background history of the crusades, for example, is only two pages long.[44] Choisy appears not so much to be competing with Filleau, but producing a biography with a different focus.

Choisy wore his erudition lightly and the biography has a more easy-going feel than Filleau's. At times it borders on the gossipy, for example, in recounting rumours that the nineteen-year-old future saint was indulging in 'criminal pleasures' or the difficult and jealous relationship between Marguerite de Provence and Blanche of Castile. The biography is more attuned to aristocratic culture than Filleau's, depicting a king who loved hunting and physical exercise even if he would go on to lead 'a harder and more mortified life' after his return from the Holy Land. Crucially, Choisy argued that Louis IX took communion frequently, and presented Louis XIV as Saint Louis's equal in both military *and* religious accomplishments.[45]

Choisy's style and presentation was different but the reality seems to have been less confrontational than Weiner argues. Filleau's book also received a royal approbation and was never removed from circulation. Both works were cited by eighteenth-century panegyrists and the patronizing advice from a 1785 *Historical library for the use of ladies* indicated they were still read a hundred years later, even if Choisy's was the preferred option.[46]

> If the ladies could manage the reading of a book in old French, we recommend the *Mémoires* of Joinville . . . but that would perhaps demand too much of them : . . . but to make them aware of the affairs of this great reign, I recommend they read the *Life of Saint Louis* by the Abbé de Choisy, which is agreeably written, rather than that of M. de la Chaise, however much the latter is respected.[47]

A year later, Louis-Pierre Manuel similarly indicated that Filleau and Choisy were the 'go to' historians of Saint Louis during the eighteenth century: the former was commendable for his erudition if not for his cold, colourless style; the latter was more lively even if, written in only three weeks, less impressive intellectually.[48]

In a curious history of the minority of Saint Louis also dating from the 1680s, Antoine Varillas stated that no other Christian prince deserved as much praise, but also that none had been so poorly treated by historians. He denigrated both Protestant historians for misrepresenting Saint Louis as superstitious and Ultramontane Catholic ones for criticizing his defence of the rights of his crown against the papacy.[49] Although Varillas presented himself as a lone defender of Saint Louis, the evidence points overwhelmingly to the latter's status as an ideal monarch – indeed, *the* pre-eminent model of kingship – throughout the seventeenth century. To be sure, there were points of controversy; the Treaty of Paris could still be criticized, and Saint Louis was dragged into contemporary debates over Gallicanism and Jansenism. Other former points of criticism, however, had completely vanished. For example, the myth of 'leather money' was hardly mentioned at all except very occasionally to disprove it.[50] In the historiography of this period, Louis IX had become the ideal saint and king; this was only more so in the panegyrics that were delivered profusely under the Bourbons.

The panegyrics of Saint Louis

French sermons changed significantly in the seventeenth century as the overheated rhetoric of the Wars of Religion cooled and the focus shifted from polemic to eloquence.[51] A key genre was the panegyric, a type of sermon focused on the praise of a particular saint. Saint Louis dominated the printed panegyric literature during this period.[52] Resting largely on information provided in the histories already discussed, the panegyrics of Saint Louis formed an important sub-genre of devotional literature during the *Grand Siècle*.

Panegyrics could prove problematic if a preacher ventured into topics of political or theological controversy. Two notable examples occurred in the mid-seventeenth century. One is a panegyric delivered on the eve of the Fronde in 1648, which is discussed in Chapter 3. Another was delivered in Rome in 1650 by the controversial ex-Oratorian preacher Charles Hersent, who used Saint Louis to defend Jansenist theology. Because 'the saints as saints do not have true being and substance except for that which they receive from Jesus Christ by the gift of a purely free grace', Hersent's Saint Louis became a channel of grace rather than someone who chose to live piously through his own free will. The sermon was printed with a letter to Pope Innocent X stating that he could perform no greater service to the church than by protecting Augustinian notions of grace.[53] It was, therefore, an attempt to use the annual celebration of Saint Louis's feast in Rome to argue the Jansenist case to the papacy at a tense point during the controversy over Jansen's *Augustinus*, stirring up a brief storm of controversy that got Hersent into trouble with the Inquisition.[54]

From the 1660s, the panegyrics of Saint Louis became more uniform and less controversial. This was principally thanks to the establishment of a series delivered annually before the Académie Française, the literary institution established by Cardinal Richelieu in 1635, which chose to celebrate the king's patronage after passing under his protection in 1672 by establishing a ceremony on 25 August. From 1677, this involved mass at the Louvre followed by a panegyric of Saint Louis. In the afternoon new members were admitted and discourses read before illustrious assemblies that could barely fit into the hall. Nearly two hundred people were present in 1673, including the archbishop of Paris and Jean-Baptiste Colbert (although the king himself never attended).[55] Most years saw the awarding of two prizes, the first (for prose) rewarded with a medal depicting Saint Louis and the second (for poetry) with one depicting the king. In 1699, the Académie Royale des Sciences also took Saint Louis as its patron and established a tradition of annual masses and panegyrics at the nearby Oratory church, from 1701 celebrating together with the Académie des Inscriptions & des Medailles (later the Académie des Inscriptions et Belles-Lettres).[56] Praise of the royal saint served to ingratiate these institutions with the monarch but also to remind Louis XIV of his obligations. The occasion was often used to portray Saint Louis as supporting men of letters and himself establishing an 'academy' (the Sorbonne).[57] Members of the Académie Française reminded the king in 1690, when they felt they had not received certain customary honours, that Charlemagne and Saint Louis had apparently viewed men of letters as no less important than men of war.[58]

According to a popular eighteenth-century sermon manual,

> The most magnificent praise that one can make of Saint Louis is to say that he
> was king and saint together . . . on the one hand he had to overcome the greatest
> obstacles to sanctity, which are found in the condition of kings; and on the other
> he had to join what are called the advantages of royalty, namely riches, power,
> grandeur and magnificence, with Christian humility, detachment from earthly
> possessions, mortification and the other virtues that make great saints.[59]

The most common way of presenting Saint Louis in panegyrics was indeed to focus
on his position at the interface of kingship and sanctity, thus constructing his sanctity
in a way that would bolster sacral kingship. In Rome in 1648, the Carmelite Léon de
Saint-Jean (Jean Macé) called Saint Louis the 'saint of kings' and 'king of saints'.[60] Like
other sermons of the period, panegyrics were generally based on one or two verses of
scripture, quoted in Latin at the beginning and used to divide the discourse into two
or three parts.[61] The structure of the panegyrics normally reflected the division of king
and saint. In 1703 the Abbé Miton preached at the Louvre on *Magnificus in sanctitate*:
according to the *Mercure galant*, 'in the first section he showed the heroic virtues
sanctified by the Christian virtues; and in the second, the Christian virtues elevated
by the heroic'.[62] Most preachers structured their discourse directly around Louis IX's
titles of king and saint; in the words of Jean-Baptiste Massillon at the Oratory, 'Louis's
sanctity . . . made him a great king; royalty made him a great saint'.[63] Some clearly
thought that the title of saint was superior – as the Père de Saint Jacques noted in
1706 at the Louvre, Louis IX's titles of king and conqueror had all passed, but it was as
a saint that he was immortal.[64] In general, though, he was praised for combining royal
and saintly virtues.

Such themes allowed preachers to define a Christian model of politics and kingship.
The message was that kings could only be truly great when religion and devotion
formed the core of their rule.[65] The Jesuit Guillaume de Ségaud distinguished between
great kings and holy kings (Saint Louis was both) – the latter had to possess piety,
humility, charity and austerity.[66] Christian kingship in the hands of seventeenth-
century panegyrists necessitated harsh actions towards non-Catholics. At the Jesuit
church in Paris in 1681, the Abbé de la Chambre praised Saint Louis for implementing
'severe ordinances against blasphemers, against the heretic Albigensians, against the
Jews exterminated from the kingdom by his order'; with these acts, 'he showed well that
he was truly filled with the spirit of equity and justice'.[67] This was a message particularly
attuned to the spirit of the 1680s, the decade of the Revocation of the Edict of Nantes,
but the persecutory model of kingship was praised in panegyrics throughout Louis
XIV's reign. In 1710 the Abbé du Buisson, preaching before the Académie Française,
lauded Saint Louis's zeal to make religion flourish in France, reflected in vanquishing
the Albigensians, chasing Jews ('that odious nation') from his lands, and applying
harsh punishments for blasphemy ('this monster of impiety').[68]

Most panegyrists placed Saint Louis in the 'absolutist' model of kingship. In Rome
in 1674 Antoine de Bretagne spoke of a king who was absolute master of his kingdom,
esteemed and admired by foreigners – but at the same time humble and modest.[69] At

the Louvre in 1681, the Abbé Anselme opened with the dubious statement that 'never was there a sovereign more absolute than he'; Saint Louis's turbulent minority was an occasion for 'cowardly souls' to engage in factions and revolts and his achievement was to destroy the power of these semi-independent nobles in his kingdom.[70] The historical actions of the baronial rebels of Louis IX's minority, based on a range of feudal and personal motivations, were cast as the wicked treachery of pantomime villains. For the Abbé de Montelet at the Louvre in 1691, there was nothing 'so odious or detested than to see subjects rise against their legitimate prince'.[71] Nevertheless, the conflicts were interpreted in a providential light. For the Abbé Le Prévost at the Louvre in 1705, God actually took care to make the beginnings of the greatest reigns tumultuous 'as if he wanted to tell the universe to pay attention and not to miss any event'.[72] The intended parallels with Louis XIV's reign must have been obvious to those listening. Others such as the Abbé de Cambefort at the Louvre in 1707 saw the troubles of Louis IX's minority as God using adversity to teach him to be a king who could conquer himself 'and join the glory of pardon to that of triumph'.[73]

Such discussions led to depictions of Louis's victory at Taillebourg in 1242 and his subsequent clemency. The Abbé de la Chambre described Louis's forgiveness of the count and countess of La Marche after Taillebourg before calling clemency 'a hereditary virtue for our kings'.[74] This was situated in a discussion of what was seen as *the* defining quality of Saint Louis's kingship: justice. The panegyrics helped popularize the iconic image of Louis seated beneath an oak tree at Vincennes 'and receiving himself in person the petitions of widows and orphans, consoling the miserable and the distressed, listening to the poor, and rendering justice to everyone without distinction', in the words of the Jesuit Louis Bourdaloue.[75]

The panegyrists did not ignore Louis IX's military prowess; indeed, when considering Taillebourg and Damietta, de la Chambre asked who could dare to compare the valour of the ancients with that of Saint Louis (obviously superior).[76] Nevertheless, he was never bellicose for its own sake, but rather pursued the repose and tranquillity of his subjects and the advancement of religion.[77] According to Bourdaloue, Louis IX did not seek peace through laziness or war through a search for false glory.[78] The ultimate example of his desire for peace was the contentious 1259 treaty with Henry III, the old criticisms of which went unmentioned. According to the Jesuit preacher Charles de La Rue in 1704, the Treaty of Paris demonstrated wisdom and foresight. 'Louis, more perceptive and wise than his subjects . . . was strongly convinced that excessive justice pushed to the extreme is often an injustice; that war is only a remedy, but peace is the health of the state'.[79] He was, therefore, right to come to an agreement with the English rather than attempt to push all his claims as far as possible through war.

As a king, therefore, the Saint Louis of the panegyrics was absolute yet clement and just, valiant yet peaceful. These qualities were, of course, deepened by his saintly virtues, which were discussed at great length. Bourdaloue challenged his listeners to 'tell me a single vice that he tolerated'.[80] Most preachers emphasized the court as a place in which almost insurmountable difficulties were placed in the way of those seeking to live virtuously, making the achievement of Saint Louis even greater. He was, to quote Le Prévost, 'always more mortified than the court is voluptuous; and always humbler than it is arrogant'.[81] If the court was dangerous, the throne itself was one of the most perilous places to be from the perspective of salvation. As the Abbé du Buisson pointed out at the Louvre in 1710, a king was surrounded by flatterers and the temptations of pride and dissolute behaviour; Saint Louis actually regarded the eminence of his position as the greatest threat to his salvation according to this panegyrist.[82] There was some variation among the preachers. Those preaching before the Académie Française were more likely to praise grandeur and magnificence as a necessary part of royalty recognized by Saint Louis than those preaching elsewhere, such as Bourdaloue, who depicted the bodily mortification of a king dressed not in rich clothes but a 'frightful *cilice*'.[83] Some preachers at the Louvre did mention the cilice and Louis's mortifications, but generally it was less emphasized.[84] Nevertheless, the danger of the court and royal status was a constant theme, and Louis's holiness against the odds was proposed by many preachers to argue against the idea that sanctity could only be achieved in poverty.[85] At the Louvre in 1715, the Abbé Bion attacked the 'fanciful and detestable idea' of Machiavelli (to whom Saint Louis was often opposed) that Christianity was incompatible with kingship.[86]

Magnificent surroundings made princes vulnerable to the temptation of pride – but no prince was ever further from this than Saint Louis, according to the Abbé du Jarry's panegyric at Saint-Cyr in 1689.[87] For other preachers, his grandeur actually came from his humility.[88] It was almost obligatory to mention that he preferred the name 'Louis de Poissy' to any other title on account of its reference to the place of his baptism, which he regarded as more important than his coronation.[89] This demonstrated that the quality of being a Christian was greater for him than that of being a king.[90] Louis's constancy of faith in different situations, particularly during his imprisonment in Egypt, was another mark of devotion and humility. For Cambefort he was 'as humble in grandeur as he was in humiliation, and as submitted to God in prosperity as in adversity'.[91] Indeed, although he was humble in the proud surroundings of the court, he was great and courageous in adversity.[92]

The humble king's charity was another essential component of a panegyric of Saint Louis. Considering the poor, blind, leprous, sick, orphans and fallen women as his brothers and sisters, he was constantly visiting, consoling, instructing and helping them, according to Buisson – a point used to condemn the repugnance in which they were held by many of the *grands* according to the preachers.[93] Bourdaloue noted that the extent of his love for the poor (lodging them in his palace, feeding them with his own hands) would seem too much for a pagan king but could never be enough for a Christian king.[94] The construction of churches, monasteries and hospitals across the kingdom was a further sign of Louis's charity and faith. His devotion to relics and prayer was also lauded – the Abbé de Pézène in 1690 mentioned 'entire hours given to prayer, without removing anything from time devoted to the state'.[95] Some preachers also weighed in on the side of Choisy against Filleau by stating that Louis was devoted to frequenting the sacraments.[96]

Panegyrists agreed that Saint Louis was a Gallican monarch. His humility did not prevent a strong defence of the Gallican church against Rome, however much he respected the papacy.[97] The Pragmatic Sanction was 'one of the holiest monuments that [Saint Louis] left us' according to Bourdaloue – a striking expression of 'Jesuit Gallicanism'.[98] Louis's neutrality in and attempted arbitration of the conflict between pope and emperor as well as his refusal of the papal offer of the imperial crown for his brother Robert d'Artois (part of struggle between the papacy and Frederick II) were also often presented as demonstrating his independence from Roman intrigues and presumptions.[99]

All in all, Saint Louis's combination of royal and saintly virtues made him the ideal exemplar of Christian kingship in the hands of the panegyrists. At the Louvre in 1694 the Abbé Estor noted that 'God only makes kings depositaries of his power in order that they be zealots of his glory'.[100] Saint Louis had clearly carried this out to perfection as he had made God reign in his realm, defined as the first duty of kings by Montelet.[101] For, as Pézène put it, 'the more he recognised himself as above men, the more he regarded himself as below God'.[102] All of this was crucial because the thinking of the day was that when piety reigned in the heart of a king, it passed down to his subjects.[103] For Bourdaloue, France had never been more flourishing, abundant, cultivated and tranquil as under Saint Louis, and it all came from his piety.[104] This sense that the reign of Saint Louis was a golden age led some preachers to criticize the seventeenth century by comparison. For Léon de Saint-Jean it was a 'century of corruption and debauchery'.[105] This is the point at which there was the clearest divergence between the panegyrics for the Parisian academies and those elsewhere. Pierre Zoberman in his study of the former argues that their preachers were 'complete strangers to the nostalgia for a bygone perfection that the other preachers reflect' because of their general insistence that Louis XIV was equal to Saint Louis's example; on the other hand, Jean-Pierre Landry, who does not include the academicians in his study, sees the panegyrists' evocation of Saint Louis as 'tinged with melancholy' and condemnation of the depravation and corruption of modern times.[106] However, all preachers were united in their insistence on the centrality of piety to kingship and the alliance of throne and altar.

The panegyrics displayed relative unity of content. This is because as time went on panegyrists based their texts on the models of other panegyrics, creating a self-generating literature in which the same material was rearranged every year by each preacher. Sermon manuals not only mentioned medieval accounts of Saint Louis such as Geoffrey of Beaulieu and Joinville, as well as modern biographies such as Choisy and Filleau in their list of sources for a panegyric of Saint Louis, but also privileged lists of modern preachers who could be consulted, including pages of quotations from panegyrics and histories which could be used for information and inspiration.[107] Although some panegyrists included references to primary sources, they were not historians and relied more on other sermons and sermon manuals than original research. Their information being second- or third-hand, they instead sought to distinguish themselves through 'the ingenuity of their divisions and subdivisions, by the power, elegance and virtuosity of their writing'.[108]

It is impossible to reconstruct a complete picture of how these ideas were projected. Historians can only work with the printed text, but a great deal of the impact of a sermon depended on the oral delivery of the orator. As Hersent noted, 'it is very difficult to transmit to a discourse delivered by the pen, a mute instrument, the force and grace given to it by the mouth, which is an animated organ or instrument'.[109] Moreover, as discussed in Chapter 6, there is evidence that changes were sometimes made to the text between delivery and publication, especially in the case of controversial sermons, so we cannot always be sure that the words printed were the same as those spoken. Still, the printed texts were themselves important in diffusing the panegyric construct of Saint Louis. Académie Française panegyrics were printed annually, often by members of the Coignard family (printers to the king and to the Académie) or other royal printers such as Christophe Ballard (the king's music printer, who printed Le Prévost's panegyric in 1705). Even more important for their wider reception were the reports in the *Mercure galant*, a periodical containing literary news and endless flattery of Louis XIV.[110] In its first few decades from 1672, the *Mercure* included lengthy reports on panegyrics of Saint Louis, often at the very beginning of the September issue. In 1707, the analysis of Cambefort's panegyric ran for almost eighty pages and was immediately followed by a description of the panegyric and music at the Oratory church.[111] The editor, Jean Donneau de Visé, clearly thought his readership would find the panegyrics of Saint Louis interesting enough to merit almost hundred pages.

What listeners and readers actually thought is harder to reconstruct. The periodicals generally included positive comments. In 1706 the young Augustinian Père de Saint-Jacques preached 'to general applause' according to the *Mercure*, which also praised his 'beautiful moral reflections' and the 'moving air' with which he dealt with the disasters of Louis's first crusade.[112] The *Gazette* tended to report the names of preachers with terse and suspiciously formulaic reviews; from 1706 to 1713 the panegyrists at the Académie Française all preached 'with much eloquence'.[113] The repetitive content of the panegyrics of Saint Louis delivered before the Académie, which recycled very similar material, meant that reviewers had to focus on how it was being repackaged in their assessments of the panegyrists' quality. Nevertheless, the relative uniformity of content entrenched the idealized picture of Saint Louis as a model of Christian kingship.

Saint Louis and the crusading ideal

If we move the focus from the presentation of Saint Louis in printed and spoken word to changes in attitudes to a specific aspect of his kingship – the crusades – we can see clearly how he was remoulded as an ideal monarch in the seventeenth century. Late medieval criticisms of Louis IX's crusades as military and financial disasters had survived into the early Bourbon period. Henri IV's principal minister Sully saw the crusades as the calamitous result of Louis IX's 'ruinous devotion', destroying the glories of the first twenty years of his reign through their enormous expense and loss of life.[114] Such views would become uncommon under Louis XIII and Louis XIV, buried under a mountain of praise for Saint Louis's intentions, valour and conduct in the crusades.

The crusading ideal lasted long into the early modern period, manifested in anti-Ottoman projects such as the 'Christian militia'.[115] In France, commercial and diplomatic interaction with the Ottomans developed alongside growing intellectual curiosity about the Islamic world but also coexisted with negative stereotypes of Muslims and chivalric legends celebrating the crusades. The sentiment that France was destined to play a decisive role in Christendom's triumph over the 'infidel' played a lively part in prophetic literature.[116] Great plans to retake 'Constantinople' or liberate Greece were preached to Henri IV and Louis XIII, with Henri at one point declaring himself ready to join the league proposed by Clement VIII (who had invoked the example of Henri's ancestors).[117] At the same time, the Bourbon monarchy used the title of 'Protector of the Holy Places', granted by the Ottoman Sultan Ahmed I in the *Capitulations* of 1604, to expand French authority over the Franciscan-held Custody of the Holy Places and promote a larger role for French clerics in the Holy Land. As discussed by Megan Armstrong, this was a means of reassuring French critics of the Catholicity of the Bourbon house, challenging Spanish claims to universal Christian dominion and legitimating the controversial Ottoman alliance.[118]

Within this context, Saint Louis's crusades were re-evaluated and praised by seventeenth-century historians and panegyrists. Pierre Matthieu called the crusades the most just of wars and disputed the idea from people either 'malign, ignorant, or both' that they had impoverished the kingdom.[119] For Rousselet, Saint Louis's crusades were just because they were concerned with returning to Christianity its ancient patrimony: 'various objections to Saint Louis's voyage to the east are worth nothing.'[120] Panegyrists portrayed the crusader Louis as a liberator; in 1707, Cambefort evoked 'the cries of the children of Israel who were wailing under a harsh captivity' reaching the saint's ears and arousing his charity.[121] Many preachers still accepted the crusades on their own terms, praising Louis's intention to 'deliver the fatherland and tomb of the Lord from the dominion of the infidel' in the words of Charles de La Rue (though he also mentioned a more pragmatic reason – keeping France's turbulent barons occupied).[122] Antoine de Bretagne tied these justifications together when he imagined Saint Louis speaking to motivate his troops:

> My good friends, my dear children, my faithful subjects, be not afraid of anything, God will be on our side (*sera pour nous*), we are ready to fight for him with vigour and courage . . . what is at issue in our important enterprise is to recover the Holy Land, to stop the conquests of the infidels, to deliver the poor captives who groan in their chains, to remove from them these sacred treasures that they have usurped, to knock down the mosques of Muhammad, to exterminate the worshippers of this false prophet, to tame the pride and fury of these proud and cruel enemies of the faith.[123]

Bretagne clearly intended to use stirring language to remind his Roman audience of France's ancient role in the Holy Land, providing historical legitimacy for the Bourbon monarchy's current ambitions in the region.

However, the fact remained that Louis IX's crusades were military disasters. Many panegyrists, such as Estor, marvelled at the success that might have been expected from the extensive preparation and the divine favour accrued by Saint Louis's personal piety; but 'you did not wish it to be so, Divine Providence; I respect, I adore your eternal secrets'.[124] Objections to the crusades' failure were countered by passages proclaiming the triumph of Louis's fortitude in ruin and disaster; true Christians could see that God wished to purify him through adversity.[125] Joseph Filère argued that Saint Louis was never more glorious than when he was at the point of losing his life 'in the disastrous success of his enterprises, because it was there that heaven admired his virtue'. Filère repeated a common myth that Louis IX's Mamluk captors were so amazed by the extent of his virtue that they wanted him to rule them following the death of their sultan.[126]

Some writers presented crusading as a pious form of valour that deserved more respect and thus turned to verse to celebrate and promote it. Charles de La Rue regretted that his contemporaries praised pagan conquerors, motivated by glory and adventure, rather than their own old princes, motivated by the honour of religion.[127] In his Latin poem on Louis XIV's victories in 1667 (well-received at court in its French translation by Pierre Corneille), he praised the Sun King for supporting the Hungarians, hitherto 'groaning' under the Ottomans until they were saved thanks to French participation in the battle of Saint-Gotthard in 1664, actions worthy of 'the great Saint Louis, stem of the Bourbons' who fought 'the battalions of the sultan'.[128] At around the same time Jacques de La Fosse wrote a Latin poem celebrating Louis IX's second crusade, and in 1687 Nicolas de Bonnécamp published a sonnet addressing Saint Louis's successor with the hope that he would similarly 'plant the cross over the crescent'.[129]

It was Pierre Le Moyne who produced the grandest poetic celebration of Louis IX's crusades. Le Moyne was a Jesuit who lived and worked at the *maison professe* in Paris – a location devoted to the cult of Saint Louis.[130] His first version (*Saint Louis, or the Christian hero*) was over 7,000 lines long in 1653; by 1658 this had mushroomed into a massive work of 17,880 lines in eighteen books, now called *Saint Louis, or the Holy Crown reconquered* and printed with images. Critics would be divided in their assessments of the epic; Nicolas Boileau-Despréaux considered it 'too elevated' to criticize and 'too wayward' to praise, whereas Voltaire was less polite, remarking on the experience of reading Le Moyne that 'if ever anyone was punished for his indiscrete curiosity it was me, I swear'.[131] Nevertheless, its popularity during the early years of Louis XIV's personal rule is attested to by the fact that it had gone through three editions and eight publications by 1671.[132]

Le Moyne emphasized the familiar point that Saint Louis proved that Christian devotion was compatible with military bravery:

> I could not chose a more accomplished hero than [Saint Louis]: and, moreover, the choice that I have made is honourable to France, which brought him up; to our kings, who are born from him; to the royal house, which is of his race; to the nobility, which has him as patron and model; to the whole nation, to which God gave him as protector; [and] to the church, which has received him to the rank of the saints that it reveres.[133]

Le Moyne cast Saint Louis in proto-patriotic terms. He was not alone among the Jesuits in doing so; Bourdaloue said that most saints were given to the world by the church, but that Saint Louis was given by France to the church.[134] Such rhetoric sought to present the Jesuits as loyal Frenchmen. The aim of Le Moyne's poem was clearly to create a national epic for France; 'we will one day have our Saint Louis, as the Italians have their Godfrey and the Romans their Aeneas'.[135]

There was still the awkward fact that Louis IX's Egyptian crusade was a military disaster. Le Moyne dealt with this in his dissertation by saying that without experiencing misfortune a hero can only be mediocre. However, the poem itself simply avoided it, failing to bear out Le Moyne's insistence that the poet should build on truth drawn from history.[136] That he would not deal with the problem of defeat was evident in the first lines of the 1653 version: 'I sing the combats, I sing the victories/Of a saint reigning in Heaven, reigning in History'. (*Ie chante les combats, ie chante les victoires/ D'un Saint regnant au Ciel, regnant dans les Histoires.*) This was epic poetry, not history, and Le Moyne introduced a host of supernatural characters and episodes. Demons, monsters, the ghost of Saladin and enormous serpents all play their part, alongside a suit of poisoned armour that would have killed Louis had heaven not intervened with a lightning bolt. Moreover, the entire premise of the later versions of the poem (in 1653 Louis states that his aim is to draw the infidels to Christianity) – that Saint Louis went to Egypt to regain possession of the crown of thorns – was in itself entirely fictional.[137]

Unsurprisingly, the poem exalted the heroism of Saint Louis and the French while demonizing their enemies and Islam. Muhammad was a 'deceiver' who 'with a pestilent and fatal vapour/Has snuffed out the light of all the Orient' (*d'une pestilente & fatale vapeur/A de tout l'Orient étouffé la Lumiere*), and the Saracens were capable of enacting 'strange cruelties' on the Christians. Egypt was of course ruled by a tyrant who appeals to Hell for assistance against Louis: 'Proud and barbarous . . . he had made laws the slaves of power'. (*Orgueilleux & barbare . . . Il avoit fait les lois esclaves du pouvoir.*) The French, by contrast, are courageous and hardy. Louis himself was sublime and pure in his virtue, intelligent and courageous in his leadership and a great warrior who filled the sea with blood (a good thing). In the 1653 version, Louis inspired his troops in difficulty by telling them that the highest virtue for a Christian champion was to be submitted to God's designs and stay constant in adversity; 'the less courageous kindled their courage/From the noble and serene fire that emanated from his face'.[138] (*Les moins courageux allument leur courage, / Au feu noble & serain qui sort de son visage.*)

In book four of the 1653 version and eight of the later versions, Saint Louis is taken up to Heaven by Saint Michael, where he beholds Christ in majesty. Jesus promises success and shows the king his descendants down to Louis XIV, who is praised for defeating the Fronde and in whom is found 'the flower of age joined to the flowers of virtue'.[139] Opportunities to praise the Bourbons and Louis XIV are never missed – indeed, considerable attention is devoted to the adventures of his ancestor Archambaud IX de Bourbon, such as his visit to a desert hermit who tells him of his descendants down to 'Louis given by Heaven, after Louis the Just'.[140] Although there is a sense of impending trials to come in the extended version, the poem ends not with the disastrous battle of Mansurah but the defeat of the lion and giant who guard the holy crown, Louis's coronation, and the rendering of thanks to God.[141]

This triumphant version of Saint Louis's crusades was also expressed in music during the first decades of Louis XIV's personal reign, when royal iconography was dominated by the image of a 'king of war'.[142] Pierre Perrin's set of motet texts for the Chapelle Royale included one for Saint Louis, *Pulsate, pulsate tympana* ('Beat, beat the drums'), put to music by Henri du Mont in 1668–70.[143] Its triumphant presentation of Saint Louis's crusades is similar to three works by Marc-Antoine Charpentier – H320 (1677), H323 (1683–5) and H332 (1683).[144] The texts of *Pulsate* and the Charpentier motets begin by evoking the sound of trumpets and drums, common signifiers of war and military glory. The composers also probably chose the keys (C and D major) on account of their bellicose associations; Charpentier's composition treatise of the 1690s described these keys as 'happy and warlike' and 'joyous and very warlike', respectively.[145] The opening solo vocal lines use trumpet-like arpeggiated material and dotted rhythms to convey a celebratory tone, appropriate to the martial atmosphere of the text. In Perrin's text for *Pulsate*, Saint Louis is an invincible warrior prince fighting on behalf of Christ. The words refer to his death from disease, but there is no mention of the disastrous context in 1270. Instead, the crusades are portrayed as victories and the motet finishes with the triumphant saint in Heaven receiving the palm of victory. This exuberant mood is matched by du Mont's sumptuous music and dramatic use of the two five-part choirs to convey the chaos of battle in the polyphonic section setting the words 'the enemy falls to the ground and flees'. Charpentier's motets H323 and H332 are also musical celebrations of military glory. They both begin with exhortations to 'celebrate Louis with joy' and finish jubilantly with the whole ensemble singing of Louis's triumphs. In both the du Mont and Charpentier motets the name '*Ludovicus*' is not qualified by '*Sanctus*'. This probably assisted the potential conflation of Louis IX and Louis XIV, perhaps particularly at moments such as the massive cadence on 'Louis triumphs' in *Pulsate*.

These various evocations of victorious crusades by historians, preachers, poets and composers were produced in a context in which Saint Louis's crusades were not just praised but offered as models for imitation by his successors. There were numerous prophesies that Louis XIII would follow Saint Louis in carrying his arms to Palestine.[146] In his edition of Joinville, Claude Ménard predicted that Louis XIII would defeat the 'common enemy' and plant 'our lilies in the place of his crescents'.[147] The Capuchin friar Père Joseph, Richelieu's *éminence grise*, lobbied for holy war, citing the example of Saint Louis in an exhortation to the king in 1616/17 and in 1629 even dangling before Louis XIII the prospect of becoming 'a future Saint Louis' if he displayed similar enthusiasm for crusading.[148] Most striking is an engraving of 1639 (a few years into the war with Spain) by Grégoire Huret (Figure 2.1). It shows Saint Louis appearing on a cloud to Louis XIII, pointing his sceptre across the sea to a land of palm trees (representing victories) and buildings topped by crescent moons (representing Islam). His sword drawn, Louis XIII stands in front of an army flying the standard of France and Navarre. Saint Louis tells him that 'Europe is too small for you' (*Europa te non capit*). Contemporaries would have recognized this as a reference to Philip of Macedon's words to Alexander the Great (sometimes cited in Latin as '*alias tibi pete terras, Fili, nam te Europa nostra non capit*').[149] This connection implied that, if the son followed his forefather's advice, great victories would ensue. At times, such ideas seem to have rubbed off on Louis XIII: Jean Héroard, his physician when he was dauphin, recorded that the young prince boasted that 'one day, I will lead a great army into Hungary against the Turk'.[150]

This spirit was by no means universal. In 1617, the bishop of Mâcon addressed Louis XIII on behalf of the clergy saying that 'we are not asking that, in imitation of this holy king [Louis IX] . . . you cross and re-cross the seas in order to chase the enemy of Christianity from the Orient' but rather that he should restore Catholicism in Béarn, where Catholics were apparently treated worse than Christians under the infidel.[151] This suggested that crusading spirit was better directed against Protestants at home

Figure 2.1 *Saint Louis apparaissant à Louis XIII et l'excitant à aller combattre les Turcs* (1639) by Grégoire Huret (1606–70). © Bibliothèque nationale de France.

rather than Muslims abroad (and Louis XIII did indeed re-establish Catholicism in Béarn). Others were directly critical of crusading projects. In considering the life of Saint Louis in 1625, François Langlois lamented these disastrous voyages and criticized those advocating similar projects to Louis XIII.[152]

Calls for new crusades were one side of a debate in which the exhortations to holy war became merged with the opposition of the *dévots* to foreign policies that involved conflict with other Catholic powers. They, therefore, carried a critical dimension; behind praise of the king's smallest gesture against the infidel lurked exhortation, if not blame.[153] Sometimes this could spill into outright criticism, as seen in the next chapter, and such calls could take on an implicitly critical dimension during the Fronde. *The Bloody Naval Combat given between the Venetians and the Turks* (September 1651) praised the Venetians as the vanguard of Christendom for fighting the Ottomans during the siege of Candia at a time when other Christian nations were wasting their strength on each other. The French nobility was exhorted to show 'its courage in a legitimate war as it had done formerly among the Saracens under the most valiant and holy king in Europe' and, once he had secured peace in Europe, Louis XIV was predicted to march 'in the tracks of the great Saint Louis at the head of a plentiful Christian nobility to ruin entirely this great power'.[154] An underlying criticism here was the monarchy's focus on war with Catholic Spain rather than the Muslim Ottomans.

Mazarinade writers who hoped for action against the Ottoman Empire attached importance to a prophecy that a French king would liberate Greece and destroy Turkish power.[155] Many writers of the mid-seventeenth century held Louis XIV to be the monarch in question because of the apparently miraculous circumstances of his birth. A pamphlet of 1650 stated that 'the conquest of the holy land is infallibly reserved for a young French monarch, descended from the stem of Saint Louis'.[156] A 1649 pamphlet, celebrating the king's return to Paris, predicted that

> In imitation of Saint Louis, he will display the standard of the cross against the Mahometans and will be the sacred conductor of faithful troops for the conquest of the terrestrial Jerusalem, and for the accomplishment of the prophecy which causes the Turban and the Crescent moon to tremble with fear, that a king of the race of Saint Louis must destroy their empire.[157]

Such ideas would continue into the personal reign. Du Cange finished the letter dedicating his *History of Saint Louis* to Louis XIV by stating that the ruin of the Ottomans, 'signified to mankind by the stars, is reserved for Your Majesty'.[158]

Throughout the period, a number of crusading projects were conceived, often emphasizing the weakness of the Ottoman Empire.[159] The most comprehensive was drawn up by the philosopher and mathematician Gottfried Wilhelm Leibniz, who advocated a reorientation of Louis XIV's foreign policy away from inter-Christian warfare and towards the Ottoman Empire, specifically Egypt. Leibniz was sent to Paris in March 1672 by the archbishop-elector of Mainz with a document of his composition entitled *Consilium Aegypticum*.[160] In it he argued that for a ruler of Louis XIV's power, 'Egypt, at the present time, offers a conquest preferable to that of any other country in the world'. Leibniz made much of the precedent of Saint Louis, arguing that the job would be easier for Louis XIV than it had been for his ancestor because the seventeenth-century inhabitants of Egypt were much weaker and the French much stronger than their thirteenth-century predecessors. 'While Europe is at peace, the prosperity of France augments . . . on the contrary, an untimely war in Europe, particularly an enterprise against the maritime nations, could lead to the ruin of French commerce.' When writing of the glory and renown that Louis XIV would gain from this project, which would liberate the oppressed Christians of the orient, Leibniz even dangled before the monarch the possibility that 'pious posterity will honour two saints of the same name'. He also imagined Saint Louis appearing to Louis XIV in a dream to speak of God's designs, predict Louis XIV's success and instruct him to follow in his footsteps.

> Take pity on the unfortunate Orient, o my son! Be thus the honour of your country and obey the orders of Heaven. Therefore, this [Egyptian] soil, more fortunate for you than that of Holland, this soil which formerly gave birth to marvels of art and genius and which is now barbaric, will hand over to you the empire of the Levant and the immensity of the seas.[161]

In the context of Louis XIV's preparations for the Dutch War, Leibniz was using the memory of Saint Louis's crusades to advocate a very different policy from that which the king was pursuing. Over the previous decade Louis had flirted with the idea of participating in anti-Ottoman leagues, making the idea of an offensive credible to some extent.[162] He viewed the Turks as the 'common enemy', a sentiment that was expressed by sending French troops to Hungary and supporting the Venetians in Crete.[163] The duc de Beaufort invoked Saint Louis in his final rallying cry in a disastrous sortie in

Crete of late June 1669 following which he and eight hundred Frenchmen under his command lay dead.[164] During this period, the rhetoric and language of crusading was deployed by the French monarchy, though it would be neglected after 1669 as commerce was prioritized.[165]

It is not clear whether Leibniz presented his plan to Louis in person.[166] The correspondence between Simon Arnauld de Pomponne, Louis's foreign minister, and Leibniz's patron the baron von Boineburg shows that a copy of the document was placed in the *cabinet du roi*, but its effect was limited.[167] Pomponne wrote in a letter of 21 June 1672 to the French ambassador to the elector of Mainz, the marquis de Feuquières, that 'I say nothing to you of the projects for a holy war: but you know that they have ceased to be fashionable since Saint Louis'.[168] The sentiments expressed by Leibniz appear to have had no impact on the Sun King's foreign policy – he declared war on the Dutch soon after Leibniz's arrival in Paris. Over the coming years the Sun King would pursue aggressive policies on the continent rather than new crusades; the annexation of Strasbourg in 1681 would provoke Leibniz's critical pamphlet *Mars Christianissimus*. In 1683 Louis XIV's anti-Ottoman actions in the 1660s were not continued when the Ottomans reached the gates of Vienna. The perception that Louis was in league with them became a point of criticism, with the title 'Most Christian' proving particularly fruitful material for sarcasm.[169]

Towards the end of the century, the triumphant crusading rhetoric of earlier decades shifted somewhat, as can be seen by comparing Charpentier's two later motets for Saint Louis to the works already discussed.[170] H418 was probably the motet that 'charmed' the congregation at the Jesuit church in Paris on 25 August 1692.[171] Its opening evokes the *failure* of the crusade: an agonized instrumental prelude sets the scene for the narrator's introduction, which describes Louis languishing among the dead bodies of his crusading companions. This penitential mood is carried into an *air* sung by Louis himself, begging God to spare his people. From this dark beginning, a more positive atmosphere emerges. God himself addresses the king, noting his satisfaction with Louis's faith and conduct and announcing that the latter's seed shall reign forever, with the future birth of one who 'will destroy my enemies' also disclosed. Reminiscent of Le Moyne's poem, this is a clear reference to Louis XIV. The final section is similar to the endings of the earlier Charpentier motets; the crucial difference is that Saint Louis's triumph is now a result of his constant faith in the face of military disaster rather than military glory.

Charpentier's longest motet for Saint Louis, H365, begins with militaristic, overture-like music and a text evoking the noise of war.[172] God sings that he will 'spread fire in Egypt' and in an energetic chorus Saint Louis is instructed to gird his sword 'and wage the wars of the Lord'. This might sound like a return to the martial music of the earlier works, but this work follows the historical narrative of Louis IX's first crusade more closely, moving from victory at Damietta to defeat at Mansurah – although, like Le Moyne, it suggests that Louis brought the crown of thorns back from Egypt. At its heart is a penitential aria sung by a vanquished Louis in captivity. The most profound moment occurs when Louis begs for God's mercy, asking him to spare his people lest the proud ask 'where is their God?' The music then becomes more positive, closing with a chorus singing 'blessed are those whose king has faith in the Lord: their enemies shall not prevail against them'. As seen in the next chapter, the emphasis on Saint Louis's constancy in adversity was an increasingly prominent theme in the panegyrics in the latter part of Louis XIV's reign. Such ideas may have been of some comfort as France, now in no position to contemplate crusading projects, faced large coalitions of enemies in the wars of Louis XIV's later decades.

How should we interpret seventeenth-century invocations of the crusades? They were clearly more than mere rhetoric. Louis IX was an important part of the history that gave many Frenchmen a sense of France's providential role in the region. The Bourbon monarchy, with its shaky origins and dealing with constant religious problems in France, sometimes invoked crusader language. Yet at other times – for example, in the funeral orations for Henri IV, discussed in Chapter 1, and in the debate over *Mysteria politica*, discussed in Chapter 3 – royal propagandists defended the monarchy's practical cooperation with the Ottomans as having done more good for Christians in the Holy Land than the violent crusades of Louis IX. It was, after all, the Ottomans who accorded the status of Protector of the Holy Land in 1604 and gave permission for the 'ministerial chapel' of Saint-Louis in Istanbul, dedicated on 25 August 1674. It was within this context that French monks were able to operate in the Ottoman Empire and spread the name of Saint Louis.[173] The crusading spirit that flowed through French culture in the seventeenth century thus did not always align with the interests of the monarchy. For our purposes, however, what is important is that it allowed late medieval criticisms to be swept away. If the 1618 elevation of the cult were to work, it needed Saint Louis to be beyond reproach.

Conclusion

In the seventeenth century a highly laudatory view of Saint Louis was projected through histories and panegyric sermons. He was the ideal and virtuous Christian ruler, praised for his piety, charity and justice, and lauded as an absolute king who protected the interests of the crown from rebellious nobles and the Gallican church from the papacy. His crusades were mostly viewed as glorious, even when writers chose to acknowledge his defeat.

As we have seen throughout this chapter, all those who produced Saint Louis's memory shaped it to suit their group or patron. The very success in reviving Saint Louis as an idealized figure made his memory a valuable source of legitimacy that could be invoked to support one side or the other in several important debates and disputes. This made his memory hard to control from the perspective of the monarchy, although the Académie Française's panegyrists developed a more standardized interpretation under Louis XIV. The valorization of Louis IX's crusades was a mixed blessing for the monarchy. On the plus side, it invested Bourbon efforts to increase French standing in the Holy Land with historical pedigree as well as contributing to the military glory of the dynasty. On the other hand, exhortations to go on crusade could be problematic as they often contradicted the monarchy's continental and Ottoman foreign policy.

Much of the seventeenth-century consensus on Saint Louis would change in the eighteenth century, when the crusades would be strongly criticized. Before this is explored, however, we need to examine the political dimensions of his memory under Louis XIII and Louis XIV. In Le Moyne's poem, Jesus tells Saint Louis that he will leave other kings 'your virtues as an example and your life as a model'.[174] The next chapter explores the relationship between the memory and model of Saint Louis and the kingship and reputations of his seventeenth-century successors.

Ruling France under the shadow
of Saint Louis, 1610–1715

The memory of a saint-king who had been moulded into a paragon of ideal kingship had immense political significance in a kingdom strongly conscious of religious confession and dynastic tradition. This chapter examines how Saint Louis interacted with the kingship of Louis XIII and Louis XIV. Each king and heir was fêted as a new Saint Louis and encouraged to emulate his example, often under the tutelage of a mother compared to Blanche of Castile.[1] Once on the throne, they were praised for equalling or even surpassing their ancestor, although it was hard for any living king to live up to the example of perfection into which Saint Louis had been transformed.

The Bourbon monarchy was surrounded by a chorus of sycophantic praise. Much of it was less a product of top-down instructions than of efforts to flatter the king, often out of a mixture of genuine adulation and practical efforts to secure patronage or favour. Rather than seeing this 'representational culture' as a homogenous, propagandistic whole, we must, therefore, be sensitive to specific contexts and motives and the ways in which the royal image was appropriated and mediated by writers and artists. Just as scholars of *Ancien Régime* politics have drawn a distinction between theoretical claims of 'absolutism' and the reality of a political culture based on collaboration, so we can see that even idealized images of the king were often the product of cooperation rather than centralized propaganda.[2] In this context, references to Saint Louis always had a political edge when connected to the reigning king, but the 'meaning' of his idealized image was unstable and not always defined according to the monarchy's interests.

Saint Louis and Louis the Just

Of all the Bourbon kings, Louis XIII exhibited the most genuine devotion to Saint Louis. As discussed in Chapter 1, it was reported that the king prayed daily to his ancestor in 1618. His mother Marie de Médicis had encouraged this devotion and continued to do so even after their relationship became more difficult. In January 1622, during a temporary reconciliation following the death of Louis XIII's favourite, the duc de Luynes, she offered her son a golden image of Saint Louis enriched with diamonds and pearls.[3]

The king himself continued to signal his devotion by naming places and institutions after his holy ancestor. When the rebellious Huguenot stronghold of Saint-Jean-d'Angély near Saintes was defeated by Louis XIII in 1621 it was temporarily renamed the 'Bourg Saint-Louys' to highlight the return of royal authority and Catholicism.[4] The royal saint was also an obvious choice for charitable institutions like the Commandery of Saint-Louis at the Château de Bicêtre in Paris, founded to support the war wounded. At the king's demand, a richly decorated chapel dedicated to Saint Louis was erected in 1634. According to a short printed description of the ceremonies, Louis XIII's piety in founding this institution showed that he imitated the saint's charity, a sentiment echoed in the *Gazette*.[5] Dedications to Saint Louis thus both displayed royal devotion and provided opportunities to underline similarities.

In the heart of Paris, the development of the Île Notre-Dame and the Île aux Vaches involved the creation of the parish of Saint-Louis-en-l'Île in 1623. The first stone of a larger church was laid by the archbishop of Paris in 1664; numerous setbacks were overcome thanks to the generosity of benefactors wishing 'to contribute to the completion of a church that is dedicated to God under the name of Saint Louis, ancestor and patron of His Majesty' and the church was consecrated in 1726.[6] The island itself would come to be called the Île Saint-Louis. Such dedications helped to anchor Saint Louis in the Parisian landscape, as did statues on the Quai des Augustins and near the church of Saint-Eustache as well as the new 'rue Saint-Louis' (part of what is now the Quai des Orfèvres).[7]

The most important project anchoring the revived cult in the capital was the new and larger Jesuit church of Saint-Louis. Louis XIII was the principal funder and laid the first stone in 1627. The façade, paid for by Cardinal Richelieu, used saints to create a striking visualization of the relationship between the Jesuits and the crown. On the top level is a statue of Saint Louis with the Bourbon coat of arms; two Jesuit saints (Ignatius and Francis Xavier) occupied the niches to either side on the level below, sending a clear message that the Jesuits were the faithful servants of the French monarchy. The building was opened in 1641 in splendid ceremony: royals, nobles and foreign dignitaries processed through streets packed with spectators and Richelieu said the inaugural mass. Pierre Le Moyne wrote a poem in which Saint Louis addresses Louis XIII and praises the church's decoration as drawing the attention of all the saints; the Franciscan Jean-Marie de Vernon described the church as 'one of the most beautiful monuments that could be imagined', citing it alongside Saint-Louis-en-l'Île as evidence of strong faith in Saint Louis. In 1641, Louis XIII gave the church all the prerogatives of a royal foundation.[8] A set of canvases depicting Saint Louis were painted in the 1640s, including one from the workshop of Michel Corneille showing Louis XIII presenting a model of the church to Saint Louis, who descends on a cloud surrounded by angels, with the foreground occupied by courtiers and the black-robed figures of three Jesuit priests.[9]

It is important to consider the relationship between Louis XIII's devotion to Saint Louis and to the Virgin Mary, to whom he famously dedicated France in 1638. Damien Tricoire presents the promotion of dynastic saints in the early seventeenth century as a transitory stage towards a piety centred on the Virgin's pivotal place in a 'universal hierarchy of divine love'.[10] Her importance during the Catholic Reformation cannot be denied, but we should not assume that Saint Louis's significance simply melted away in the face of her supremacy. Their cults were by no means mutually exclusive; indeed, they were often linked. In 1602, François de Sales prayed for Henri IV to the Virgin in the name of Saint Louis and Rousselet later mentioned 'the devotion of Louis the Just with regard to . . . supremely Saint Louis his ancestor and the Queen mother of God'.[11] The chapel of Notre-Dame de Liesse at Maubranche in Picardy was dedicated to the Virgin on 25 August 1620; Bruno Maës notes that the Recollet friar Artur du Monstier, reflecting on this dedication in a publication of 1637, wrote of his particular devotion to the Virgin and to Saint Louis, 'as if these two devotions formed a couple'.[12]

More importantly, Saint Louis chimed with the attributes of kingship emphasized (if not always displayed) under Louis XIII – piety, humility and justice.[13] The idea that Louis XIII 'bears the name, possesses the crown and imitates the virtues' of Saint Louis was repeated endlessly after 1618.[14] Shortly after arriving in Paris in 1621, Dominique de Jésus-Marie, an Italian Discalced Carmelite regarded by many as a living saint, preached to (allegedly) twenty thousand people, telling them that Louis XIII had the same justice and piety as his ancestor.[15] Similarly, a thirty-verse poem printed in Rouen praised Louis XIII for inheriting Saint Louis's virtues, name and sceptre, and stated that they both faced comparable challenges in their minorities and combated heresy.[16]

The elevation of the feast day in 1618 gave those hoping for favour a theme that could be used to ingratiate themselves with the monarchy. A paraphrase for the feast of Saint-Louis of the hymn *Gaude Mater Ecclesia* was published in 1628 by P. Le Comte with a dedication to Claude Bouthillier, intendant of the Queen Mother's household. Le Comte mentioned Bouthillier's high rank and service to the king as making it likely that the mere sight of the name of Saint Louis would make him want to read this 'little present', which is 'a sample of my desire to bear witness to my good intentions'. The paraphrase lauds Saint Louis's faith, justice and charity, and cited him as a model for other kings. Naturally, this leads to praise of Louis XIII, particularly his zeal against the Huguenots. There are also verses berating the French for not celebrating with enough zeal a homegrown saint venerated by foreigners. How was it that France did not have 'the courage to adore him on its altars' and was in 'silence' on the feast of one of its children? Le Comte thus aligned himself with the king's project of spreading devotion to Saint Louis, encouraging Louis XIII's subjects to venerate a saint who was conflated with their reigning king.[17] Interestingly, his words suggest that many were ignoring the 1618 instructions to celebrate Saint Louis, a point to which we will return in Chapter 4.

These comparisons to Saint Louis contributed to the construction of a religious aura around Louis XIII.[18] However, not all of them were positive. In the 1620s there was a revealing dispute over whether the example of Saint Louis supported or condemned the French crown on a specific foreign policy issue, which was causing great scandal in France: the 'Valtelline crisis' in which France sided with Protestants against a Catholic population under papal and Spanish protection.[19] The pamphlet *Mysteria politica*, thought to be by the Jesuit Jacob Keller, appeared in 1624; advocating war against the Turks, it criticized the French policy from a Habsburg perspective as unjust and irreligious.[20] Saint Louis was deployed to point out Louis XIII's failings: 'The king Saint Louis set out for Syria in order to spread the [Catholic] religion; will our Louis, with his Catholic commanders, cardinals, bishops and priests, lead an army into Germany in order to restore heretics and drive out Catholics?'[21] This negative comparison, only a line long, was thought dangerous enough for a long rebuttal to be printed in the *Mercure François*, an organ of official opinion.[22] Drawing on Joinville and the *Enseignements*, the author likened Saint Louis's peace-making efforts to Louis XIII sending an ambassador to solve the problem of the Valtelline, with blame for the subsequent descent into hostilities placed firmly upon Spain. As for religion, there was Louis XIII's recent restoration of Catholicism in Béarn. The author argued that the crusades were unsuccessful, whereas the Bourbon kings had conserved the holy places even under Turkish domination by developing commerce and establishing freedoms for Christians under Ottoman rule; moreover, Louis XIII in 1620 had intervened with the sultan to ensure that Armenian Christians did not succeed in removing Catholics from Bethlehem and Jerusalem. This was a defence of the policy of cooperating with the Ottomans to secure protection for Christians against the model of violent crusades represented by Saint Louis (as discussed in Chapter 2).

Censured by the Sorbonne in November 1625, *Mysteria politica* revealed the danger that Saint Louis could be turned against the king.[23] He was often used to critique anti-Habsburg foreign policies by the *dévots* (the 'devout' faction, best seen as a 'constellation of groups' rather than a specific party).[24] Fearing the consequences of a French foreign policy that displeased God by allying with Protestants against Catholics, they used comparisons between Saint Louis and Louis XIII to suggest a preferred course of action in which religion played the central role in determining policy.[25] One example is Cardinal Pierre de Bérulle's letter dedicating his *Discourse on the State and Grandeurs of Jesus* (1623) to the king, whom he praised for possessing the name, innocence and sceptre of Saint Louis.

> Blessed be God, who honours Saint Louis on earth in the person of Your Majesty and wishes that his race ruins heresy inside and perhaps outside France. It is Your Majesty who gathers and carries on earth this benediction ordered by God on the posterity of Saint Louis, in honour and favour of Saint Louis.[26]

While praising Louis XIII, this also implicitly suggested that he should focus on combatting heresy. Bérulle was referring to campaigns against the Huguenots when he noted that the 'king's first wars were for the faith, like those of Saint Louis', but he became increasingly opposed to the course of French foreign policy in the 1620s, especially the intervention in the Mantuan succession war.[27] The Jesuit Nicolas Caussin also praised Saint Louis in his *Holy Court*, a large book which first appeared in 1624 and was intended to convince the nobility that honour and Christian morality were compatible rather than contradictory. Regarding Saint Louis as showing the way to Christian perfection, it is easy to imagine Caussin recommending the example directly to Louis XIII, to whom he was confessor for most of the year 1637.[28] Caussin was famously exiled in December after questioning Cardinal Richelieu's dominance and voicing concerns that the exile of Marie de Médicis and alliances with Protestant powers in the Thirty Years War were sinful.[29] Although we cannot penetrate the secrets of the confessional, it is plausible that Caussin referred to Louis IX's obedience to Blanche of Castile and abhorrence for intra-Christian warfare when he made these points to

Louis XIII. If so, it would be hard to argue, as Asch does, that Saint Louis's position as dynastic ancestor gave the king 'a mandate to pursue his policies regardless of clerical criticism' because it made them the policies of a king descended from a saint.[30] At this time Saint Louis was associated with *dévot* politics and, indeed, clerical criticism.

Exhortations for Louis XIII to follow Saint Louis by going on crusade were used to critique the wars in which he was actually engaged. A pamphlet of 1640 whose title evoked the 'groaning voices' of Christians and Catholics overwhelmed by the 'disasters and miseries' of the Thirty Years War is a good example of this position. Hostile to the war against the Habsburgs, the author was nevertheless absolutist and Gallican rather than Ultramontane, recognizing that the king of France drew his power directly from God and did not depend on any superior earthly power such as the pope. He praised Louis XIII's virtues and courage but expressed his frustration that, since France's declaration of war on Spain in 1635, these qualities had been employed in the service of unjust causes such as supporting 'the inhabitants of the North' (the Protestant Swedes), maintaining the Dutch in their rebellion against the Spanish, trying to extend French jurisdiction across the Alps and Pyrenees and trying to remove from the Empire that which Heaven had promised to protect – contravening 'divine laws' that prevented Louis XIII from possessing these territories.

> The lance of Achilles was in a good hand, but it was not used well: the point should have been turned towards the Orient, instead of towards the North, the Midi, and the Occident. The effusion of the blood of so many brave Frenchmen ought to have happened in a place that the Saviour of the world reddened with his own blood, in order not to give cause to regret it. The great Saint Louis urged you [Louis XIII] to go and take vengeance for the death of his most valorous soldiers and repair the failure that he received there, leading two hundred thousand men that you have lost in Italy, Germany, Holland, the Low Countries, at Fuenterrabía, in Piedmont and in Salses: you could have promised yourself great success in such a high intention.[31]

According to this pamphlet, the foreign policy pursued by Louis XIII and Richelieu risked the anger and displeasure of Heaven, whereas a crusading project in the tradition of Saint Louis would be certain to receive divine support.

Elsewhere, however, Saint Louis was presented in line with royal policies. According to the *Gazette*, Heaven itself responded to the king's enthusiasm for Saint Louis in a remarkable way on 26 August 1635. Louis XIII's hunting party was returning home when lightning struck, one bolt perilously close to the king; preservation from lightning was a clear mark of divine protection. Recalling an incident when one of Augustus' retinue was killed by lightning not long before the emperor triumphed in the Cantabrian war (in northern Spain), the report concludes:

> It was while marching against the same enemies that lightning surrounded these two Augustuses. But it is not with a lesser mystery that it was on the day after the feast of Saint-Louis, the celebration of which has just pushed the wishes and enthusiasm for the prosperity of our prince from earth to Heaven, that Heaven

wished to respond to earth by thus solemnising the feast of this saint with two *feux de joye* thrown innocently around his living image.[32]

Given that France had declared war on Spain earlier that year, this incident was used to highlight the nexus between God, the king and the cult of Saint Louis, as well as to suggest future victory over the Spanish.

Another example is the panegyric delivered in Rome in 1640 by Jean-Jacques Bouchard, a client of the pro-French Cardinal Barbarini. This was an emphatic assertion of French pre-eminence; in his dedicatory letter to Louis XIII, Bouchard stated that, since most of the audience was not French, he sought to persuade them of the superiority of the French nation. Saint Louis embodied more things worthy of praise than could be found in any other great person from history and the house descended from him was the most illustrious in the world. The kings of France possessed absolute command and independence from foreign powers (a significant point in Rome). Bouchard finished by asking for Saint Louis's intercession for France and especially for his pious, just and victorious successor.[33] This was Saint Louis as he was supposed to be used from the perspective of the Bourbon monarchy: a model of absolute monarchy and Catholic triumphalism, harnessed to the glorification of the current king and the French monarchy but *not* being used to criticize current foreign policy.

Saint Louis featured in funeral orations delivered after Louis XIII's death in 1643, just as after Henri IV's. Their names were, of course, a point of comparison. One preacher called the naming of Louis XIII 'a certain omen of his future sanctity'.[34] In Catalonia, which had been incorporated into the French monarchy in 1641, Louis XIII was presented as having inherited the virtues of his ancestor to an extent that made it possible to speak of a second Saint Louis.[35] One preacher in Paris even made the rather extraordinary claim that 'if metempsychosis [the transmigration of souls] passed into belief, it would be said that the soul of Saint Louis had returned in the body of Louis the Just'.[36]

The idea of Saint Louis reincarnated in his successors is evident in the practice of depicting him with the traits of subsequent kings. The absence of reliable representations of Louis IX from his lifetime meant that his face could be rendered in many ways. Some sought accuracy by using the head reliquary at the Sainte-Chapelle, as can be seen in the frontispiece engraving to Charles du Cange's edition of Joinville. Many artists derived their image of Saint Louis from such models, showing a clean-shaven figure with shoulder-length hair. It was also common, however, to depict the saint with the features of the reigning king, with seventeenth-century coiffures and facial hair resembling the Bourbon monarchs.[37] The Parisian church of Notre-Dame-de-Bonne-Nouvelle, constructed in the 1620s, contains a painting attributed to Louis Testelin that shows Saint Louis with the facial features of Louis XIII. The sumptuous altar of the chapel of the Trinity at the Château de Fontainebleau was flanked by statues of Charlemagne as Henri IV and Saint Louis as Louis XIII, sculpted by Francesco Bordoni in 1633. This common pairing, which went back to the fifteenth century, associated the Bourbons with two icons of French monarchy and would appear in the 1620s as far apart as Calais and Avignon[38] (Figure 3.1).

Figure 3.1 Statues of Henri IV as Charlemagne and Louis XIII as Saint Louis (1633) by Francesco Bordoni (1580–1654). Chapelle de la Trinité, Château de Fontainebleau. © Alamy Stock Photo.

An unusual example of a non-royal personage painted as Saint Louis is Philippe de Champaigne's mid-seventeenth-century portrait of the poet Vincent Voiture, depicted with the accoutrements of royalty and holding the crown of thorns (Saint Louis's standard relic accessory) in order to circumvent regulations at Voiture's daughter's convent that only permitted religious images.[39] However, it was more common to transplant the king's features onto the saint. A unique parallel depiction of two Bourbon kings *en saint Louis* survives in the chapel of the Jesuit College in Poitiers. Dedicated to Saint Louis at the behest of Louis XIII in 1615, it was decorated in the 1650s with two paintings of its patron above the altar. Saint Louis appears with the facial features of Louis XIII on the right-hand side, devoting himself to the crusade; on the other side, with the features of the young Louis XIV, he gives alms to the poor.[40] It is a striking visualization of dynastic legitimacy and the transmission of Saint Louis's virtues from one descendant to the next.

Saint Louis during the Fronde

The beginning of a new reign entailed a fresh round of comparisons to Saint Louis. As Louis XIV's confessor exclaimed, 'what felicity must not France expect, seeing its young monarch who, marching in the steps of his ancestor Saint Louis, begins so early to distinguish himself by his piety'.[41] A new regency began in 1643; Blanche of

Castile was cited as a precedent for Louis XIV's mother Anne of Austria both by Louis XIII shortly before his death and in the Parlement by the advocate-general Omer Talon.[42] In 1644 Charles de Combault Auteuil published a book on Blanche with a dedicatory letter to Anne filled with flattering parallels between the two regents.[43] Mézeray also told Anne that the French 'rightly say of Your Majesty that which was formerly said of the queen mother of Saint Louis, *that you are the wisdom with which all good things have come to us in abundance*' (emphasis in original). His chapter on Blanche herself made much of the fact that through her example and education she had turned a great monarch into a great saint.[44] Blanche's education of Louis IX was clearly a precedent for Anne's education of Louis XIV, who duly encouraged the publication in 1644 of a work by Antoine Godeau on princely education (including the *Enseignements*).[45]

However, Saint Louis's memory played a more problematic role in the Fronde revolts that shook France from 1648 to 1653. The survival of fourteenth-century perceptions that he was the protector of local and aristocratic liberties was evident in the harangue delivered at the end of the 1645 General Assembly of the Clergy by Paul de Gondi, coadjutor-archbishop of Paris and future cardinal de Retz. Gondi proclaimed that 'the kings of France have not always been absolute to the point that they are', and that the 'middle ground' by which their powers were tempered by the Estates-General and the Parlements 'was considered by the good and sage princes as a seasoning of their power, very useful to make their subjects taste it; it was regarded by the unskilful and ill-intentioned as an obstacle to their irregularities and caprices. The history of Joinville shows us clearly that Saint Louis knew and esteemed it'.[46] This was a clear attack on the overextension of royal power under Cardinals Richelieu and Mazarin and defence of the Parlements. Saint Louis had an important place in the self-conception of the Parlement of Paris, aided not least by the presence of his head reliquary at the Sainte-Chapelle. A fifteenth-century painting in the Grand Chambre of the Parlement depicted him with the features of Charles VII.

Considerable friction between the government and Parlement developed in 1648 when the sovereign courts started meeting in a collective body known as the 'Chambre Saint-Louis' after the room in which it met. This provided the tense background to a panegyric of Saint Louis delivered at the Jesuit church in Paris on 25 August by Gondi – an 'inflammatory and seditious' preacher – before a congregation that included the regent, her chief minister Cardinal Mazarin and the young Louis XIV himself.[47] Many of the themes from Gondi's harangue of 1645 reappeared in the panegyric, the overall message of which was clear and addressed directly to the king: 'Since your subjects are unfortunate enough to imitate their fathers in their crimes, will you not be just enough to imitate your glorious ancestor in his laws?'[48]

This sermon has been described as 'fraught with serious political implications' because of Gondi's use of an idealized past to criticize the present state of France.[49] He enumerated 'an infinite number of oppositions that meet to the dishonour of our century between the virtue of Saint Louis and our sins', and the cure was the *Enseignements*. Although Gondi stated that he was simply presenting them as Louis IX had to his son, it was this section, which concluded the panegyric, which contained the most implicit criticism of the current government.

Know that you are king to render justice, and that you owe it equally to the poor and to princes. . . . Comfort your people . . . listen to their complaints. . . . Do not enter into war against any other Christian prince, unless you are obliged by considerations of great urgency . . . be generous with your possessions and prudent with those of your subjects . . . maintain the good rules and ancient ordinances of your kingdom . . . conserve inviolably the privileges and immunities of the church.[50]

For a government running into serious opposition for the ever-increasing tax burden demanded by the war with Spain, Saint Louis's exhortations to peace and to respect the church and the realm's ancient ordinances (of which the *parlementaires* viewed themselves as custodians) took on a critical dimension. The *Gazette* reported drily on 29 August that Louis XIV had paid attention to the instructions given to him from the life and words of Saint Louis, giving the court 'a great hope to see flourish again during his reign the happy government of this holy monarch'.[51] That this report was a whitewash, however, is indicated by the fact that it hardly mentioned the dramatic events of 26 August, when Anne of Austria and Mazarin had the prominent magistrate Pierre Broussel and other *parlementaires* arrested, sparking the Parisians to erect barricades.[52] The writings of Gondi's associate Guy Joly, who helped get the sermon printed quickly, suggest that Anne of Austria thought Gondi insolent and that the courtiers found what he had to say seditious, even if Retz himself merely noted that on leaving the church Mazarin politely thanked him for recommending Saint Louis's example to the king.[53]

Gondi would soon be intriguing against Mazarin and he was profoundly moved when, at a meeting of Frondeurs in February 1651, Omer Talon went on bended knee and called on Saint Louis to safeguard France.[54] It was not just the *parlementaire* Frondeurs who invoked Saint Louis. The prince de Condé was also proud of his descent from Louis IX (as would be made clear in the symbolism of the decorations for his funeral in 1687), and used 'S. Louis' as a watchword for his supporters in 1651.[55] This had echoes of Louis XIII's password against Concini; perhaps Saint Louis's 'French' connotations made him once more a useful symbol to rally around against another foreign queen mother's Italian favourite.

In the 1648 panegyric, Gondi was careful to commend Saint Louis's respect for Blanche, to which he paralleled Louis XIV's obligations towards his own mother.[56] On receiving his cardinal's hat from the king in September 1652 he delivered a harangue stressing the church's duty to remind Louis of his duties, recommending the examples of Henri IV and Saint Louis, and – somewhat hypocritically, given his own recent intriguing – telling him that he should obey his mother, 'who animates, by virtues that are without comparison . . . the same blood which flowed in the veins of Blanche'.[57] Others, however, were not so positive about Blanche and Anne. In a controversial work of the Fronde period that argued for a monarchy limited by representative bodies, Claude Joly criticized Saint Louis for exposing the kingdom to perils by leaving its government in the hands of his mother, who 'had many enemies . . . because she was foreign and made use in her affairs of the counsel and advice of foreigners'. Opposed to Anne and Mazarin, he argued that because 'foreigners do not have the love for us that they could have for those of their own countries, thus we do not have the affection for them that we have for our compatriots'.[58] Unsurprisingly, his work was burned by order of the Châtelet de Paris.[59]

The royal family also used devotion to Saint Louis to assert its authority, continuing Louis XIII's habit of celebrating 25 August at the Jesuit church in Paris.[60] In 1649, following the suppression of the *parlementaire* Fronde earlier that year, the *Gazette* stated that they did so out of respect for Saint Louis – and that the magnificently dressed king went on horseback so that his people could see him.[61] Huge crowds watched the cavalcade of princes, nobles, officials and troops from the streets, windows and roofs; indeed, there were so many people that some of the specially constructed scaffolding collapsed.[62] The princes de Condé and Conti rode at the king's side. This procession, which concluded to the sound of trumpet fanfares when the Jesuits met the king on the steps of the church and was followed by fireworks after the service, was designed to highlight Louis XIV's power and status as a 'worthy successor of Saint Louis' as well as royal support for Mazarin (who sat in the coach next to the king).[63] Its efficacy is hard to assess: according to Guy Joly, the murmuring of the crowd caused Mazarin 'to repent of his rashness, in trusting himself amongst them', whereas the maréchal d'Estrées reported that there was 'no appearance of hatred against the cardinal'.[64] This display of royal authority and confidence in Mazarin was certainly not successful in retaining the loyalty of Condé and Conti, both of whom were soon rebelling against the government, but does show how the feast of Saint-Louis could be an opportunity for representation on a grand scale at moments of political tension.

Another notable incident occurred in 1651, when the abbey of Saint-Denis was ordered by the queen mother to expose the reliquary of Saint Louis during the period from his feast day to the birthday of Louis XIV in order to obtain extraordinary graces from God in the year of the king's majority.[65] Many masses were said in front of the relics, placed in the centre of the choir, and by royal command they were carried in procession, accompanied by great devotion from the people. On 5 September, Louis XIV's birthday, his brother Philippe visited Saint-Denis and showed great piety before the relics.[66] The precarious political situation gave this incident and its publication in the *Gazette* an important propaganda value, making visible the sacrality of royal power which went beyond the physical person of the sovereign – a fact underlined by the fact that Louis XIV did not go in person – at a tense moment when the crown's practical authority was compromised.[67]

In the same year, Grégoire Huret produced a print depicting Saint Louis's protection of the young king (Figure 3.2). Haloed and crowned, he stands behind a kneeling Louis XIV, whom he presents to the Virgin; it is the patron saint who establishes this communication between the king and the Queen of Heaven. The Virgin extends a laurel branch towards Louis XIV and a dove representing the Holy Spirit flies towards him carrying the holy ampulla. The accompanying prayers include one said by the king at his *sacre*, asking that Jesus 'remember my ancestor the king Saint Louis' and send the holy unction so that he might be filled with the wisdom and virtue to maintain his people in peace. Although Louis XIV's *sacre* would not actually occur until 1654, Huret used its symbolism to produce a strong visualization of the sacral authority accorded to Louis XIV. Basking in the support of his saintly ancestor

Figure 3.2 *Prière du roy* (1651) by Grégoire Huret (1606–70). © The British Library Board: 134.g.10 f23.

and the Queen of Heaven, Louis XIV is the only figure in the scene to gaze directly at the viewer, implying that to rebel against royal authority now that the king had reached his majority would be to act against religion.

This trio of figures were depicted together in another engraving, celebrating Louis XIV's victory over Spanish forces and the prince de Condé at Arras in 1654. The fact that this had occurred on 25 August was an additional sign of the efficacity of the royal patron.[68] If Saint Louis had been invoked by Frondeurs in the early stages of the revolts, the monarchy had subsequently sought to regain control of his memory. Both sides saw him as a political symbol of good government and a religious symbol of sacral monarchy. His importance should not be exaggerated, as he did not appear in most of the estimated 5,500 pamphlets printed during these years.[69] Nevertheless, the appeal by both sides to the memory of the saint-king is significant. Historians have tended to argue that religious content and passion were absent from the *parlementaire* and princely Frondes of 1648–52 (if not the 'Fronde' of the Parisian *curés* between 1652 and 1662).[70] Tricoire, however, has shown that this stems from the overidentification of 'religious' with 'theological' or 'confessional' but that during the Fronde the confrontation was not between two rival confessions or versions of Catholicism but two representations of what Heaven thought of French politics, and thus how to preserve the monarchy from divine displeasure.[71] In this context, different parties mobilized religious symbols, including saints; 'the exploitation of links and interactions with divine protectors and intermediaries was considered an important means of mobilisation and legitimation of political action'.[72] Saint Louis clearly fits into this use of saints, his memory serving to oppose Mazarin and Anne of Austria and his feast day and relics, conversely, to reaffirm the crown's sacral prestige.

Saint Louis and the Sun King

Louis IX was portrayed on one of the arches erected for the king and queen's triumphal entry into Paris on 26 August 1662 – although, given that he was shown alongside non-Christian figures such as Mercury, he was shown without the attributes of sanctity. Elsewhere he appeared as part of a quartet with Henri IV, Louis XIII and Louis XIV, underlining the Sun King's illustrious ancestry.[73] This was soon after the beginning of the Sun King's personal rule, a period in which Saint Louis would be harnessed more securely to the glorification of the monarchy and the mimetic relationship between saint and king pushed to its height.

The Fronde, once safely over, could be used to point out that both monarchs had overcome difficult and rebellious minorities. Charles du Cange told Louis XIV that 'the beginnings and progress of the life of this incomparable monarch [Saint Louis] have much in common with those of Your Majesty'.[74] He emphasized the similarity of their minorities, devotion to justice and zeal for the maintenance of the Catholic religion. Dedicatory letters such as this served as propaganda for their dedicatee and might also earn the writer a gift or *gratification*.[75] Du Cange received 2,000 *livres* in 1674 and 1682.[76] Although this may not have been a direct result of the Saint Louis volume, published in 1668, du Cange's flattery no doubt helped secure his place in royal patronage.

Parallel praise of Saint Louis and Louis XIV was an integral ingredient in panegyrics, especially those delivered before the academies. In a 1681 discourse at the Académie Française, Jean Doujat set the tone by speaking of the similarities between the minorities and reigns of Saint Louis and Louis XIV, both of whom placed piety at the centre of their kingship, especially in their dealings with 'heretics' and 'infidels'.[77] The panegyrics themselves firmly harnessed their idealized image of Saint Louis (discussed in Chapter 2) to the glorification of the reigning king. The idea that, in the words of the Abbé Le Prévost in 1705, 'in an exact picture of the reign of Saint Louis, it is difficult not to find the reign of Louis the Great' became a cliché repeated endlessly under the Sun King.[78] The *Mercure* remarked in 1698 that 'the rare virtues of [Louis XIV] are so in keeping with those of this holy king [Louis IX] that it is near impossible to speak of one without speaking of the other, so much the comparison between them presents itself as natural and just'.[79] Even panegyrists such as the Abbé de Montelet who said they did not want to confuse the two reigns ended up claiming to hear the history of Louis XIV when praising Saint Louis.[80] Some panegyrists even stated that the marvels of Saint Louis's reign were only believable because the same or greater could be seen under Louis XIV.[81]

Certain issues were particularly appropriate for comparison. Louis XIV's commitment to the destruction of Protestantism was regularly compared to the harsh suppression of the Albigensians during Louis IX's reign.[82] In 1686, the Abbé Robert told the Académie Française that he was sure they had already made the connection to Louis XIV themselves when he mentioned Saint Louis fighting heresy.[83] This obvious point of comparison in the decade of the Revocation of the Edict of Nantes in 1685, when persecution of Huguenots was at its height, was taken up by many royal flatterers. The Venetian composer Antonia Bembo wrote many pieces praising Louis XIV in gratitude for his patronage; in one cantata, the soprano soloist sings of Saint Louis's example being followed by a younger king destroying the heresy that had divided France.[84] Zeal against heresy was not, of course, the only similarity noted by panegyrists and flatterers. The kings' dissipation of factions during their minorities, efforts against duelling, and love of virtue and justice were all praised by Simon de la Vierge in a panegyric delivered in La Rochelle in 1689 in which he said he would weep at the death of Saint Louis if he did not see his virtues reborn in the admirable reign of Louis XIV.[85]

Central to this 'parasitic praise' was a sense that Saint Louis was the model of a perfect king that Louis XIV had equalled or surpassed.[86] On 25 August 1687 the Augustinian Louis Frotté preached a sermon in Blois, stating that

> Saint Louis leaves his kingdom to deliver the Christians [of the holy land] from captivity and remains with them in chains, Louis the Great without leaving his throne breaks the chains of all Christians by the mere reputation of his arms . . . Saint Louis conserves the limits of his states, Louis the Great imposes limits on all the states of Europe . . . Saint Louis relieves those whom the misfortunes of the time have made miserable, Louis the Great who causes the happiness of his peoples prevents them from falling into misery.[87]

The use of the present tense telescoped the centuries between the two kings to allow a direct comparison in which Saint Louis is well-meaning but ineffective, surpassed by Louis XIV's achievements on every point. The following year, the Abbé Cappeau included a similar passage in a panegyric delivered at Saint-Cyr, adding that just as Saint Louis merited the epithet 'great', so Louis the Great merits the title of 'saint' – presumably welcome news to Madame de Maintenon, who was present.[88]

During the Sun King's difficult later years, the emphasis shifted; Saint Louis's greatest triumph was now his constancy in adversity, which cast an aura of holiness around Louis XIV's similar fortitude. In 1707, the Abbé de Cambefort stated that disgraces were, for princes, like clouds that obscure the sun for some time only to reveal a new brightness in its rays.[89] The same year, Simon de la Vierge delivered a panegyric in Loudun evoking Saint Louis's fortitude in prison: 'The more kings are elevated above other men, the more they are exposed to the bitterness of tribulations.'[90] At the Oratory on 25 August 1709, the year that financial collapse and military disaster brought Louis XIV close to making drastic territorial concessions to his enemies in the War of the Spanish Succession, the Abbé Antoine Anselme praised Saint Louis for remaining great and holy in both prosperity and adversity, and stated that 'it is this which he seems to have transmitted to the one who has inherited his throne and who seeks to imitate his virtues'.[91]

Parallel praise of the two kings sometimes occupied only a small part of the text of a panegyric, just a few lines or a paragraph and normally near the end, as the comparison was only worth making once a positive image of Saint Louis had been constructed. The Abbé du Jarry only came to Louis XIV after hundred pages of text in the printed version, though he did then call him the most religious of Saint Louis's successors.[92] Still, the *Mercure* found it noteworthy in 1693 that the Abbé Nolet limited the customary praise of the king to one prayer at the end, suggesting that this was perceived as being more restrained than usual.[93] The lengthy reports of panegyrics at the Académie Française contained in the *Mercure galant* tended to privilege sections praising Louis XIV – an insight into what was deemed important and interesting by its editors and readership. Indeed, panegyrics which did not develop the comparison, such as the Abbé du Buisson's (which made little reference to Louis XIV before the very end) received reduced coverage.[94] Generally speaking, praise of Louis XIV was sufficiently integrated into the genre for the *Mercure* to remark in 1707 that preachers never forget to laud him for all he had in common with his patron saint.[95] These panegyrics were thus an important part of the king's 'representational culture', sacralizing Louis XIV with reference to his holy ancestor. Of course, the Sun King's image was composite and Saint Louis was one of many rulers used in its 'fabrication'; in a sermon of 1686, Bossuet called Louis XIV a new Constantine, Theodosius, Marcian and Charlemagne – not mentioning Saint Louis.[96] Still, Saint Louis was the only figure in the pantheon of heroes to receive annual praise linking him to Louis XIV.

Nevertheless, this praise was double-edged as it also implied expectations of good government to which the king should conform. Preaching before the king in Advent 1669, Bossuet denounced the vanity of ancient rulers to whom the Sun King enjoyed being compared, such as Alexander the Great; instead, 'let him be near Saint Louis, who extends his arm to him and shows him his place'.[97] Court sermons were exercises in counsel and advice rather than (or in addition to) mere flattery.[98] Beneath the laudatory surface remained the possibility that Saint Louis could be used to critique his successor on a spectrum from oblique chastisement to outright condemnation. A revealing example of the former is a panegyric delivered by Esprit Fléchier, the famous preacher and future bishop of Nîmes, at Saint-Louis-en-l'Île on 25 August 1681. Louis XIV was not part of the congregation but heard a summary later.[99]

Fléchier began by decrying kings who lose themselves in worldly pomp and indulge in passion and sin, contrasting them with those who turn to justice and religion. Saint Louis, of course, was one of the latter, and Fléchier proceeded to praise him at first not by listing his virtues but by discussing the three faults ordinary to kings that he avoided:

> A self-esteem which attaches them to their glory, interests and pleasures, and renders them indifferent to everything else; an impression of independence, which persuades them that everything that pleases them is permitted; a worldly spirit to which they hold on in many ways, which throws them into irreligion or at least apathy.[100]

Louis XIV was not mentioned. This cannot have been an oversight; instead, the Sun King may have been implicitly associated with those kings who had *not* avoided these faults. This analysis is supported by the rest of the text, in which Fléchier contrasted the ideal past of Saint Louis's reign with the debased present.

At the heart of this panegyric is the contradiction between grandeur and sanctity. Saint Louis showed that piety is not contrary to valour, but his courage was inspired by love of peace rather than desire for victory. When praising Louis IX's clemency, Fléchier pointedly asked 'where does one find sincere and magnanimous hearts today?' Few people can have missed the contrast with Louis XIV's continental policies when Fléchier praised Saint Louis for having conserved peace with his neighbours, or with the king's lavish court life when he said that Saint Louis 'changed the softness of the court into an austere and penitent life'. 'If [Saint Louis] overcame pride, he no less overcame sensual pleasure, and one saw him live with the austerity and mortification of an anchorite in the middle of his court.' Saint Louis was praised for 'wanting no other title than that of *Louis de Poissy*', perhaps in contrast to Louis XIV's recent assumption of the epithet 'the Great'.[101] Many of these points were commonly made in the panegyrics at the Académie Française, but when uncoupled from praise of Louis XIV they could take on a critical dimension. Although François-Xavier Cuche sees it as 'unthinkable' that Fléchier was thinking of Louis XIV when he said that the sin of some kings was to receive 'the incense and wishes of their subjects' like idols, it is not clear why, given the extraordinary culture of praise surrounding the Sun King.[102] Stating that Louis IX had banned spectacles and comedies – entertainments enjoyed by Louis XIV – Fléchier exhorted his contemporaries to follow Saint Louis's example: 'Let us conform to this holy King, in order that, practising the same virtues, we arrive at the same happy immortality.'[103]

The historian François Bluche called this panegyric a 'masterpiece' in its transformation of a eulogy of Louis IX into a lesson for the reigning monarch.[104] Of course, it was not directed at the king alone. Fléchier proposed Saint Louis as a model for general emulation, singling out groups such as magistrates, and the text reflected *dévot* preoccupations such as the struggle against misery and poverty. Unlike Bluche, Cuche argues that it was not a sermon on the duties of kings but rather a religious exemplum to all Christians emphasizing a severe morality and the importance of grace.[105] However, it could be both, and given that Fléchier opened the panegyric with faults specifically relating to kings, it would seem misguided to ignore the sermon's political connotations. The distant past was idealized and contrasted with a degenerate present, and the modes of representation used by the king's flatterers reflected back at him to remind him of what he should be and how he should act.

The sense in which Saint Louis could be turned against Louis XIV is also evident in princely education. The catechism prepared for the Grand Dauphin encouraged him to pray to 'Saint Louis, my patron and ancestor' and the *Abrégé* of French history that he wrote under his tutor Bossuet's direction referred to 'the most holy and just king who ever wore the crown'.[106] Bossuet set out his view of Saint Louis in a letter on the education of the Dauphin sent to Pope Innocent XI in March 1679:

> When we draw, from the whole history of our kings, examples for life and morals, then we propose only Saint Louis as the model of a complete king. We demonstrate not only the glory of his sanctity, with which no-one is unfamiliar, but also, by revealing the sources of his acts and counsels, praise him in his valour, fortitude, constancy, fairness, magnificence, and outstanding political intelligence. From this comes the glory of the house of France ... which, born from this founder, employs him as an example of morals, a tutor in the art of ruling, and most certainly an intercessor with God.[107]

He immediately followed this by observing that the living history of Louis XIV's reign was also a model of good kingship.

This double model was *not* employed when it came to the education of Louis XIV's grandson, the duc de Bourgogne, whose tutor François de Fénelon's *Survey of Conscience on the Duties of Royalty* exhorted him to be virtuous and frugal and to avoid the thirst for glory and conquest. That Fénelon associated such dangers with the Sun King is evident in his astonishingly frank letter accusing him of having turned France into 'a great hospital, desolate and without provisions'.[108] Fénelon hoped that his pupil would do better, exhorting him to imitate the virtues of Saint Louis, who was noble but without pomp or luxury. Describing the harmful moral effects of excessive magnificence, Fénelon told Bourgogne that

> The only way to stop luxury completely is yourself to give the example of great simplicity that Saint Louis gave. . . . It is insufficient to give it only in clothes. It must be done also in furniture, carriages, tables, and buildings. Know how the kings your predecessors were housed and furnished. . . . You will be astonished at the extravagances of luxury into which we have fallen. . . . Everyone wants to have gardens where all the earth is overturned, with jets of water, statues, parks without limits, houses whose upkeep surpasses the revenue of the lands in which they are situated. . . . Only [the prince] can, by his moderation, return his own peoples to good sense.[109]

Since everything hinges on the king's personal example, the blame for France's moral degeneracy rests with Louis XIV. It does not take much imagination to realize that Fénelon had Versailles in mind as the ultimate symbol of degeneracy; he even targeted the palace gardens, which Louis XIV cherished to the point of writing a guidebook.[110] Although the king is not mentioned directly, the critical implications are obvious enough. Whereas Bossuet had proposed Saint Louis *and* Louis XIV as models to the Dauphin, Saint Louis was here used by Fénelon to exhort Bourgogne *not* to behave like Louis XIV and an idealized, purer past was held up as a mirror to highlight the failings of the present and to offer remedies for the future.

Saint Louis was not the only historical king used by Fénelon; indeed, he expressed a view of Charlemagne as 'a more agreeable model than Saint Louis' in a letter to Bourgogne's governor, the duc de Beauvilliers, thanks to the fact that the Carolingian emperor was militarily successful as well as pious.[111] Nevertheless, some of Fénelon's notions of a purer past and the model of former kings including Louis IX rubbed off on his pupil. In the duc de Saint-Simon's discussion of introduction of the *dixième* tax in 1710, which he saw as deplorable on account of its lack of respect for noble privilege, he recorded that Bourgogne spoke against it and against the financiers with such anger as to recall 'the memory of Saint Louis, of Louis XII the *père du peuple* and of Louis the Just'.[112] This is revealing of the way in which aristocratic culture made the memory of the past an ideal against which innovation, however necessary given the perilous state of the monarchy's finances, could be judged negatively.

For all his criticism of the Sun King, Fénelon told Beauvilliers in 1697 that he had 'great compassion for so exposed a soul' as Louis XIV's when he prayed for the king on Saint Louis's day.[113] The same cannot be said of the polemicists who produced a vast body of critical literature during the later decades of the reign. Louis XIV had been so frequently compared to Saint Louis that rebuttal of the link was irresistible to hostile writers. A *Mirror of Princes* printed in Amsterdam in 1684 stated that 'it is not in wishing to give peace to his neighbours that [Louis XIV] carries the fire of a bloody war against their states . . . it is not as Augustus that he encourages subjects to rebel against their sovereign [in Hungary], nor as the imitator of Saint Louis that he condemns his holy maxims'.[114]

A particularly notable example of this use of Saint Louis was *The Koran of Louis XIV*, which appeared in 1695 and is generally attributed to Gatien de Courtilz de Sandras, soldier, writer and sometime prisoner of the Bastille.[115] It is an example of the popular genre of imaginary dialogues between the deceased, in this case Cardinal Mazarin and Innocent XI. The pope blames Mazarin for 'all the misfortunes that have occurred in the world in the space of 45 years through the poor education that you gave the eldest son of the church'. This education is the 'Koran' of Louis XIV, a catechistic lesson inculcating ruthlessness, dishonesty and bellicosity. Of course, this suggested that Louis XIV had learned virtues diametrically opposed to those associated with Saint Louis, and Innocent made exactly this point when he reproached the cardinal for not making the king read the examples 'of the sage princes who have reigned . . . like Solomon, Augustus, Saint Louis and a great number of others'. Instead, Louis XIV is painted as a bullying, duplicitous warmonger whose desire for universal monarchy leads him even into an alliance 'with the Muslim prince, the detestable enemy of all people who believe in Christ'. When Mazarin defends the king's ultimate aim as forcing Christianity on the Turks, reminding the pope that one of his predecessors had canonized Saint Louis who had similar intentions, Innocent dismisses the notion that Louis XIV's alliance with the Turks was aimed at anything other than reducing Germany to his power, clearly denying any link between the Sun King and Saint Louis's crusades. Innocent draws on Saint Louis to deliver a comprehensive summary of damning criticisms of Louis XIV:

> This great Prince [Saint Louis] . . . what reproaches would he not give to his successor? For daring to aspire to immorality as a reward for having grieved the Head of the Church during all the time of my Pontificate; for having allied himself with the Infidels in order to desolate Christendom; for having violated all the Treaties of Peace and declared war on all the Princes of Europe by a pure principle of ambition and an insatiable desire to increase his territory; for having reduced half of Christian Europe to ash by the infernal fire of his Bombs and his Shells; for having forced the Huguenots of his realm, torch in one hand and sword in the other, to return to the bosom of the Church; for having wanted to make himself Pope in his Kingdom, and threatening to assemble a new Council if I refused to obey him: *O! The great Saint! The Saint above all the Saints of Paradise!*[116]

This is a complete repudiation of the panegyric literature, arguing that in his warmongering and treatment of the church Louis XIV completely failed to emulate Saint Louis's pious kingship. The fact that the latter is 'above all the saints of paradise' only serves to heighten the contrast.

Louis XIV's death was the occasion for a flood of critical poems and songs lambasting his pride, high taxes and perceived submission to the Jesuits. Saint Louis plays a prominent role in one extraordinary poem from September 1715 which opens with the observation that Louis XIV had for the first time made his people happy – by dying.[117] His arrogant soul is surprised to find Saint Peter distinctly unfriendly. Responding to the accusation that he had treated the church badly, Louis confidently lists the 'exiles, betrayals, injustices, oppressions, frauds and tricks' that he had employed for the extermination of the 'wretched party' (the Jansenists) disliked by his final Jesuit confessor, Michel Le Tellier.[118] When Saint Peter condemns these acts, Louis cowardly tries to blame Le Tellier, calling on various saintly patrons in growing desperation. The strongly anti-Jesuit tone of the poem is clear when Louis calls on Saint Ignatius, only to be told by Saint Peter to forget him and his followers: 'These dangerous serpents, these odious monsters . . . their father can do nothing here.' Louis is told rather amusingly that Saint Denis will be of little use as he lacks a head, that no help can be expected from Saint Geneviève (as women have particularly strong reasons to dislike the king), and that Saint Matthew, whom the king invokes as the patron of tax-collectors, regards Louis and his favourites with horror. In disgust and fear, Louis XIV spurns the assistance of these 'little' saints and calls on his cousin, patron and predecessor, Saint Louis. Peter tells him that he scarcely imitates Saint Louis as king but that he will soon be admitted if the saint takes his side: 'He has power in these parts.'

Overjoyed, Louis XIV regards the case as closed but is rather thrown off course when Saint Louis tells him that Louis XIII was the last king of his descent – he sees before him not a Bourbon but the son of a *gentilhomme*. Even so,

If you had been wiser,	*Si vous aviez été plus Sage,*
I was your patron, I could have helped you:	*J'étois votre Patron, j'aurois pû vous servir:*
But what have you done except subjugate	*Mais qu'avez-vous fait qu'asservir*
Your timid subjects under the hardest of laws?	*Vos timides Sujets sous la Loy la plus dure?*
Feed on their Property, on their blood?	*De leurs Biens, de leur sang vous faire une pâture?*
Reign as a tyrant, not as a king?	*Regner en Tyran, non en Roy?*

After delivering this devastating indictment of the Sun King's reign and legitimacy, Saint Louis leaves without granting an opportunity to respond, the gates of Heaven barred in Louis XIV's face.

This poem repudiates the comparisons between Saint Louis and Louis XIV so frequently made by panegyrists. Not only does the Sun King not live up to the former's kingship, but his status as his descendant is rejected, drawing on conspiracy theories about his parentage. Anger over the persecution of the Jansenists clearly informed the poem, with war and finances mentioned only in the vaguest terms – although the somewhat irreverent references to Saint Denis and others perhaps mean that it was penned by a friend of any enemy of the Jesuits rather than someone of severe Augustinian theology. Notably, it is the saints themselves who control admission to Heaven, a relatively democratic organization that has been seen as a rejection of strong monarchy.[119] Needless to say, the idea of a king of France turned away at the gates of Heaven was a direct challenge to the idea of sacral monarchy.

It is impossible to say who wrote or read this unprinted poem and it cannot be taken as widespread except, perhaps, in certain Parisian circles. The funeral orations for Louis XIV delivered a far more typical message. Massillon's, delivered at the Sainte-Chapelle, declared that Louis XIV had died as a king, hero and saint. 'May the guardian angels of France come before you to lead you to the throne that is destined for you in Heaven, next to the holy kings your ancestors, Charlemagne and Saint Louis.'[120] A preacher in Toul compared Louis XIV advantageously to all the kings who had preceded him, with even Saint Louis incapable of equalling him.[121]

Royal devotion to Saint Louis

Louis XIV celebrated the feast of Saint-Louis wherever he happened to be, for example at Bordeaux in 1659 when, accompanied by his brother and the prince de Conti, he worshipped at the Feuillant and Franciscan churches and later watched fireworks and cannonades.[122] At Marly in 1699 the feast day was celebrated by the officers of the Régiment du Roy; after mass, there was a panegyric of Saint Louis in the presence of the commander, the marquis de Surville, and at the end of the day the king reviewed the soldiers.[123] Interestingly, Louis XIV did not hear the panegyric and likewise never attended the annual celebrations at the Académie Française.[124] Some panegyrics, such as the highly laudatory one by Nicolas Lefèvre d'Ormesson, were presumably delivered before him, judging by the frequent use of 'Sire', but the printed text gives no indication of when.[125] The feast provided occasions for flattery and gift-giving, such as when the papal nuncio complimented Louis XIV and presented two expensive reliquaries on 25 August 1668 before discussing business.[126] The *Gazette* took Louis XIV's departure from Paris for Lorraine on 25 August 1663 as a mark that 'this great saint, who was one of our greatest kings, takes care of the glory of a monarch who imitates him'.[127]

Other members of the royal family also signalled their devotion to Saint Louis through foundations and ostentatious celebrations of the feast day. Anne of Austria constructed a new chapel at the Louvre dedicated to Nôtre-Dame de Paix and Saint Louis in February 1659, and the painting she commissioned for the dome of Val-de-Grâce, completed by Pierre Mignard in 1666, showed her being presented to God by Saints Anne and Louis.[128] The *Gazette* reported her devotions at Fontainebleau on 25 August 1658 and Queen Marie-Thérèse's at Vincennes in 1664.[129] In 1671, the Dauphin attended the benediction of a bell named after Saint Louis at Saint-Germain-en-Laye.[130] Two years later he celebrated the feast by hearing the *24 violons* at dinner and watching a *divertissement* on the grand canal of Versailles in the evening, followed by fireworks and artillery.[131] Versailles was often the stage for secular celebrations on 25 August, including a 1691 ballet by Michel-Richard de Lalande.[132] Of course, it is doubtful that people were thinking about Saint Louis during such entertainments. In 1674 Primi Visconti watched the fireworks set off over the canal at Versailles to celebrate the feast while Madame de Louvois asked him – known as he was for his powers of prediction – for his views on when her husband's affair with Madame du Fresnoy might come to an end.[133]

Nevertheless, Saint Louis was important at the Chapel Royal, depicted at the top of the title-page of a richly decorated liturgical book for use at Versailles in 1686.[134] The Holy Sacrament was exhibited on his feast day, which was celebrated lavishly as a first-class feast with the full octave at Versailles – and in 1710 the chapel possessed hundred copies of the Office of Saint Louis.[135] In the 1682 chapel at Versailles, placed under his invocation, there was a painting by Bon Boulogne the Elder of Saint Louis offering the crown of thorns to God.[136] There were also many depictions of him in the final chapel, also under his invocation. It is modelled structurally on the Sainte-Chapelle and the inlaid marble flooring is dotted with 'SL' monograms. This chapel was completed between 1699 and 1710, the same period in which panegyrists focused on Saint Louis's triumph in defeat. This theme is displayed strikingly in Jean-Baptiste Jouvenet's altarpiece painting for Saint Louis's side chapel. It depicts the haloed saint, wearing gleaming armour and a dark blue drapery patterned with *fleurs-de-lys*, visiting the wounded after his disastrous defeat at Mansurah in 1250, shortly before his own capture.[137] Together with the paintings at Saint-Cyr, the parish church of Versailles, and Chambord (where a church dedicated to Saint Louis was built at Louis XIV's command) mentioned in the accounts of the *Bâtiments du roi* in the 1680s, these depictions indicate Saint Louis's prominence in the iconography of royal chapels.[138]

The most visible sign of Louis XIV's devotion to Saint Louis – or at least his awareness of his ancestor's symbolic value – were the institutions he founded and named after him. The Sun King showed enthusiasm for spreading the cult at France's frontiers – both territorial and religious. On his journey to Breisach in 1673, he stopped at Sainte-Marie-aux-Mines, where he gave 5,500 livres for a new church, dedicated to Saint Louis on 25 August 1674.[139] Following the annexation of Strasbourg in 1681 a policy of 'Catholic reconquest' developed in Alsace. In Strasbourg itself, two churches took on Saint Louis's patronage: one known as Saint-Louis-en-la-citadelle which formed part of Vauban's new military fortress and another known as Saint-Louis-en-ville, a former Carmelite church which was restored and reconsecrated in 1687.[140] Saint Louis's patronage was also given to two chapels and the Capuchin hospital at Fort-Louis on the Rhine, constructed after 1686, as well as the provisional church in the fortified new town of Neuf Brisach in 1699.[141] In the mid-1680s the village of Saint-Louis was built in Alsace, existing officially thanks to an ordinance of November 1684, with the church coming under Saint Louis's patronage as a royal parish. Lucien Pfleger mused that Catholics in the region became devoted to the saint in gratitude to Louis XIV for having restored their religion; from the monarchy's perspective, the use of Saint Louis was part of a strategy of implanting the sacral culture of French royalty in newly acquired and strategically important areas in order to unite people in these territories behind Catholicism and the French monarchy.

Elsewhere there was a particularly military slant to Louis XIV's dedications to Saint Louis. One of the four chapels he built for his soldiers at Dunkirk in 1671 was dedicated to Saint Louis, and Bordeaux was rewarded for its rebelliousness in 1675 with a Fort Saint-Louis on the west bank of the Garonne.[142] The most monumental of Louis XIV's foundations dedicated to his ancestor, combining military and charitable themes, is the military hospital of the Invalides in Paris. A flattering poem from 1702 cited it to show that Louis XIV's charity was even greater than that of Saint Louis.[143] The project began in 1670 and the large chapel dedicated to Saint Louis, at which daily attendance was required of the veterans, was finished in 1679. Its altarpiece by Louis Licherie de Beurie showed the saint caring for plague-ridden soldiers while looking up to Jesus and God.[144] The separate private royal chapel of the Dôme was built later and inaugurated in 1706.[145] As in the chapel at Versailles, Saint Louis was omnipresent. On the left hand side of the entrance is a large statue of him holding the crown of thorns, twinned with one of Charlemagne; Nicolas Cousteau was paid over 4,000 *livres* for this between 1701 and 1704.[146] 'SL' monograms are everywhere and the various side chapels contain bas-reliefs that use scenes from Saint Louis's life to display particular virtues: charity (bandaging the wounded and touching the sick); hope (his wedding, taking the cross and sending out missionaries); humility (having a vision of Christ, washing the feet of the poor and ordering the construction of the Quinze-Vingts) and religion (justice, ordering the veneration of the true cross and receiving extreme unction).[147] Most spectacular is the dome itself, painted by Charles de La Fosse in 1702 and showing a triumphant Saint Louis (with the features of Louis XIV) presenting his sword to Jesus.[148]

Equally important was the establishment of the Royal and Military Order of Saint-Louis in 1693. The edict of creation did not mention how the name was chosen, but the 1627 Assembly of Notables had requested such an institution as a means of rewarding poor nobles and encouraging them to embrace the soldiering life.[149] Louis XIV and his secretary of state for war, the marquis de Louvois, had tried to adapt the orders of Saint-Lazare and Notre-Dame du Mont-Carmel to such purposes, but various complications meant that after the latter's death in 1691 the king resolved to create a new order.[150] According to the *Mercure*, it was Louis's appreciation of the 'incomparable actions of valour and courage' by which his officers had distinguished themselves that caused him to search for 'new means to show them how content he is with their zeal and fidelity'. The Order was restricted to those who had shown distinction on the battlefield with at least ten years of service – and were firm Catholics.[151] Conversely, membership was sometimes removed from officers deemed to have misbehaved.[152] It was inaugurated on 8 May 1693 in a scene subsequently painted by François Marot. The king gathered with the dauphin and various dukes and princes to listen as the marquis de Barbezieux, Louvois's successor as secretary for war, read the oath, after which he took his sword and received them into the order with the words 'By Saint Louis, I knight you'.[153] Each one was given a cross featuring a golden Saint Louis holding a laurel wreath and the crown of thorns and nails of the Passion; on the reverse were the words 'reward of martial virtue' (*BELL.[ICÆ] VIRTUTIS PRÆM.[IUM]*).[154]

Louis XIV declared that he would wear this cross alongside that of the Order of the Holy Spirit and that all members were obliged to attend his person on Saint Louis's day, unless prevented from doing so by illness or active service.[155] The Order's articles laid down that he and his successors would act as grand masters and set the conditions, attire and pensions (which ranged from 6,000 *livres* for the grand crosses to 800 for the knights) for membership of its three internal levels.[156] Such matters were important in a society that placed great significance on distinctions of dress and honours. The fact that admission to the Order depended on merit rather than genealogy and the awarding of pensions marked a departure from traditional chivalric culture.[157] By using Saint Louis's name to reward his officers in his later wars, the Sun King was harnessing the memory of his pious and valiant predecessor to the legitimation and blessing of his own conflicts. One of Louis XIV's greatest generals, the maréchal de Luxembourg, told him that the hope of gaining the cross was having the intended effect of restoring morale among the officers and inspiring acts of valour.[158] Equally revealing is a comment that, during the Nine Years War, '[the Order] was a great resource at a time when finances were exhausted to the point where the officer did not receive the smallest sum of money from the king to find the means of retaining him through the hope of obtaining this honour'.[159]

There are enough examples of extensive parallels between Saint Louis and Louis XIV to show that Peter Burke's statement that the Order's foundation was 'the climax of an identification, or at any rate a parallel, between the kings' is misleading. Nevertheless, it was significant for showing how Louis XIV perceived his ancestor as a symbol of French royal valour and piety that could enhance the loyalty of his subjects.[160] Its creation was inscribed in the context of what Ronald Asch has termed the 'reconfessionalization' of the French monarchy in Louis XIV's later decades, in which the king reinforced the sacral and confessional elements in royal representation. 'Being the successor of Saint Louis was now more important to him than being a modern Alexander or a new incarnation of Emperor Augustus.'[161] The Order's oath would be sworn by Louis XV and Louis XVI at their coronations.[162] The fact that a cross depicting the royal patron would be one of the most sought-after honours in the military in the final century of the *Ancien Régime*, worn proudly by countless officers up to and beyond the Revolution, is indicative of the importance of Saint Louis to Louis XIV in his pious later years.

However, it perhaps reveals less about his own personal devotion than the Royal House of Saint-Louis at Saint-Cyr, a school for girls from impoverished noble families that had served the kingdom in war, constructed in 1685–6 at the behest of Madame de Maintenon.[163] Part of the girls' uniform, personally examined by the king before adoption, was a cross of gold or silver with an image of Saint Louis. Bruno Neveu wrote that Saint-Cyr was 'a royal foundation in all the force of the term'; born of the sovereign's will, growing under his eyes, and under the protection of the royal saint.[164] Louis XIV underlined its function as a dynastic institution by ordering masses for the souls of his predecessors and eventually himself to be said there.[165] In 1692 it was placed under the Augustinian rule. The girls rarely saw their parents and had to follow an austere and busy schedule of work and prayer.[166] Given that the ideal 'Damoiselle de Saint-Cyr' was pious and devoted to humility and patience, Saint Louis was particularly appropriate as a model.[167] In his panegyric of 1689, the Abbé du Jarry told the girls that they should emulate the royal saint.[168] Every year on 25 August the girls sang simple motets praising Saint Louis's justice, composed by Guillaume-Gabriel Nivers and Louis-Nicolas Clérambault.[169]

Saint-Cyr's status as 'a place of relaxation and more personal devotion' for Louis XIV means that it gives a glimpse into a more intimate side of his devotion to Saint Louis. Still, it remains the case that he left few indications of his attitude to his holy ancestor other than these institutional dedications, which may represent little more than his recognition of a powerful symbol of legitimacy and sacrality. When he told the dauphin in the 1661 memoirs that 'several of my ancestors waited until the end of their life to give similar exhortations to their children', he probably had the *Enseignements* in mind, here contrasted to with his own decision to give advice while still in the vigour of youth.[170] Elsewhere he indicated a desire to emulate Saint Louis. According to Jean Chapelain in 1667, Louis XIV intended to make himself accessible to his subjects, no matter their condition, in weekly audiences that imitated Louis IX dispensing justice under the oak at Vincennes.[171]

It may have been that the Sun King's appreciation for Saint Louis increased with age, particularly as he became increasingly devout. In 1708, when the king needed divine intervention more than ever, Saint Louis was not just a model but an object of prayer. On 25 August, a poetic prayer was presented to Louis XIV by 'M. de Messange' (probably the poet Étienne Mallemans de Messanges). He implored Saint Louis to:

Cast your gentlest glances	*Jettez vos regards les plus doux*
On the inheritor of your Empire,	*Sur l'heritier de vostre Empire,*
Of your virtues, and of your tastes.	*De vos vertus & de vos gouts.*

Inflamed by the same love as you,	*Brûlé du même amour que vous*
He has shown the same zeal;	*Il a fait voir le même zèle;*
You combated the infidel,	*Vous combatîtes l'infidele,*
The Heretic has felt his blows.	*L'Héretique a senti ses coups.*
Favour his just arms;	*Favourisez ses justes armes,*
Trouble with mortal alarms	*Troublez de mortelles alarmes,*
Anyone who attacks his repose;	*Quiconque attaque son repos.*
And to render the world happy,	*Et pour rendre la terre heureuse,*
Fill with a glorious peace	*Comblez d'une paix glorieuse*
The days of this perfect Hero.[172]	*Les jours de ce parfait Héros.*

It is tempting to see such texts as royal propaganda, and the poem fulfilled just such a role by being disseminated by the *Mercure galant*. Nevertheless, it was the initiative of someone hoping to flatter the king, and it may be that the subject was chosen because of greater devotion on the part of the king himself in the final years of his reign. It is notable that Messanges emphasised the two kings' zeal in combatting infidels and heretics; as will be discussed in Chapter 6, this language became increasingly uncomfortable in the eighteenth century.

Louis XIV's gangrene developed badly during the night preceding his final feast of Saint-Louis on 25 August 1715. 'Nevertheless, [the king] wanted expressly that nothing was changed from the accustomed order of that day, that is to say that the drums and oboes, arranged under the windows, played their usual music as soon as he woke up, and that the twenty-four violins likewise played in his antechamber during his dinner.'[173] Louis expressed his wish for his heart to be interred at the Jesuit church of Saint-Louis, as his father had done (and echoing Henri IV's decision to inter his heart at the Jesuit chapel of Saint-Louis at La Flèche). The Sun King received the last rites on the feast of his ancestor.[174]

Conclusion

According to Bossuet, Saint Louis was 'the holiest king ever seen among the Christians . . . it remains to me only to say to our princes: "If you are the children of Saint Louis, do the works of Saint Louis".'[175] The range and variety of invocations of Saint Louis's memory by Louis XIII and Louis XIV as well as their flatterers and critics illustrates his importance as a figure of ideal monarchy, the benchmark against which his successors were to be judged. The Bourbons strengthened their link to Saint Louis by founding institutions in his honour, with all the depictions and imagery that came with them. Although it is difficult to gauge the extent of the kings' personal devotion, there is no doubt that Saint Louis was a symbol used to enhance their political and religious prestige and the 'go to' patron saint for royal foundations. Young kings and heirs to the throne were encouraged to emulate him and subsequently praised for having equalled or even surpassed his example, but it was not easy to 'do the works of Saint Louis' and live up to the unrealistically perfect exemplar into which he had been transformed by historians and panegyrists. Saint

Louis, therefore, held a place in criticism of Louis XIII and Louis XIV as well as the encomiastic culture that generated endless flattery.

Saint Louis's iconography filled the palace chapels, indicating his place in royal devotion under the Bourbon kings. But in 1618, Paul V had ordered the whole kingdom to celebrate Saint Louis's feast and Louis XIII had sought to foster more extensive devotion to his patron saint across his realms. The following chapter explores how far the subjects of the Bourbon kings responded.

The spread of the cult, 1618–1789

Any assessment of the historical importance of a saintly cult needs to consider where, why and by whom it was celebrated. The public rituals associated with feast days often served to articulate communal identities; in 1618, Louis XIII clearly intended that Saint Louis's feast would do this for all his subjects.[1] Imposition from above rather than pressure from below resulted in the feast's elevation, leading to the question of how far it was accepted down the social scale and across France's regions. Although established quickly as an important event in Paris, the feast of Saint-Louis spread unevenly over the dioceses of the French church. Instead of being observed across the kingdom, it was celebrated in specific locations, mainly by social elites or specific corporate groups such as learned academies and trade guilds. Despite its geographical patchiness within France, however, Saint Louis's patronage was extended to locations across the globe in the French colonies and his feast day became 'the' occasion on which to celebrate the Bourbon monarchy in foreign capitals. Frequently, the secular nature of some of the festivities in France, the empire and abroad showed that what was being celebrated was not so much the saint as the reigning king.

The feast in Paris

The feast of Saint-Louis became an important event in the Parisian calendar after 1618. Up to the 1650s, the royal family often celebrated it at the Jesuit church of Saint-Louis. In 1653, the court went there to hear vespers, a sermon and excellent music provided by 'I know not how many choirs', followed the next evening by a firework display at the Louvre whose beauty hardly seems marred, in Jean Loret's account, by the fact that a hay boat was set on fire.[2] Although courtly attendance at the Jesuit church on Saint Louis's feast declined after the move to Versailles, several other routine celebrations developed during Louis XIV's reign.

The most important were the public sessions held by the Parisian academies, including mass at the Louvre and the Oratory church. As discussed in Chapter 2, the purpose of these events was to celebrate the king's patronage on his name day. In addition to the prizes and panegyrics, elaborate music performed at mass was also a highlight of these events. The composer Claude Oudot was paid 300 *livres* for his annual motet for the Académie Française (though he had to pay the other musicians out of this sum).[3] The music was generally a setting of psalms or verses assembled from psalms (a practice known as centonization) rather than a specifically composed text in praise of Saint Louis. In 1680, Oudot set a text stitched together by the academician François Charpentier, offering a propagandistic reading of the Dutch War by

> composing a prayer for the king . . . in which the most considerable events of our times are marked, such as the uprising of the principal powers of Europe against the king, the inconceivable rapidity of his victories, the peace so gloriously concluded and whose terms he prescribed the conditions to his enemies . . . and finally the wishes of all peoples for this great king.[4]

Printed translations were often available, though unfortunately no scores of these annual motets survive.[5]

It was, of course, the panegyrics that were the principal focus of the celebrations of Saint Louis by the academies. There were other series of panegyrics at the Jesuit church, Saint-Louis-du-Louvre, Saint-Louis-en-l'Île, the Franciscan church and Saint-Eustache, as well as Latin panegyrics at the Quinze-Vingts and the Collège de Navarre.[6] Some preachers delivered the same text annually in different churches. The Père de Saint-Hilaire was banned from the pulpit after delivering a panegyric at Saint-Louis-en-l'Île in 1742 despite having been preaching it for ten years (including at the Oratory in 1739, though the periodicals give no account of the content); according to the pro-Jansenist *Nouvelles Ecclésiastiques*, this decision was a 'chimeric accusation' related to Archbishop Vintimille's 'war' against the Jansenists.[7] Such controversies aside, it is clear that there were in any given year numerous panegyrics of Saint Louis delivered in churches across the capital. When making this point in his periodical the *Année littéraire* in 1772, Élie Fréron remarked that no prince received as much praise during his life as Saint Louis long after his death.[8]

The numerous craft guilds that took on Saint Louis's patronage also celebrated his feast. In 1653, a confraternity was formed in his name by wigmakers and hairdressers, claiming that Saint Louis had worn a wig made from locks of hair from his barons. The obligation to celebrate his feast (and contribute to the expense of the church ceremonies at Saint-Germain-l'Auxerrois) was written into their statutes.[9] Saint Louis was the most important of four patrons of the upholsterers, who decided in the eighteenth century to celebrate only his feast day; in contrast, they would not close their shops on the feasts of Saints Geneviève, Sebastian and Francis. Saint Louis's patronage was also claimed by fan makers from 1650 as well as tailors and engravers of fine stones. Each confraternity of craftsmen that took him as patron was associated with a different church where they celebrated his cult – the makers of gold and silver embroidered cloth at the Église des Blancs-Manteaux, the linen maids at their chapel at Saint-Eustache and craftsmen of *passementerie* and *boutonnière* at Saint-Martin-des-Champs.[10] Saint-Eustache also housed a Confraternity of the Virgin and Saint Louis that had been founded by the grain and flour porters of Les Halles during the reign of Charles VI. Louis XIII confirmed their privileges in 1611, charging them to celebrate three masses a week 'to the honour of God and the holy Virgin Mary, and to the memory of Saint Louis, and for the prosperity and health of the king of France.'[11] Although this institution was an ancient foundation, others were created in the period. A fascinating example of female piety is the Confraternity of Saint Louis of the 'mistress seamstresses' (one of only three guilds open to women), established at the church of Saint-Gervais-Saint-Protais in 1677. Documentation for this institution is scarce, but it was 'an association of sisters united in charity, solidarity and spiritual devotion'. Saint Louis must have been a particular focus of devotion.[12]

The company of merchant haberdashers and jewellers in Paris was particularly devoted to Saint Louis, printing his liturgical office in 1688, 1711, 1733 and 1749, as well as an edition of Louis Le Blanc's biography in 1666.[13] The introduction to the 1688 *Office* praised merchants as the channel by which Christianity reached the furthest corners of the world, declaring that Saint Louis was an appropriate patron because he had preferred the difficulties of long voyages at sea to the pleasures of court life.[14] In 1674, they commissioned an altarpiece painting from Charles Le Brun for their church of the Holy Sepulchre in Paris.[15] Colbert (in the bottom right-hand corner of the painting) had negotiated a loan from them for the Dutch War, and their reimbursement came with a supplementary sum to ornament their chapel. Saint Louis looks up at the resurrected Jesus, gesturing with his left hand to present Louis XIV, who offers a helmet to Christ. There is no hint of the institutional church mediating the relationship between the king and God; instead, Christ directly blesses the monarch's earthly sovereignty and the triumphs of Louis XIV are confuted with those of Resurrection.[16] This is an example of a corporate body using the cult of Saint Louis to emphasize its relationship with the monarchy and, in doing so, producing the iconography of sacral monarchy (Figure 4.1).

Few celebrations of Saint Louis's feast were unrelated to the fact that it was the *fête du roi*. Elaborate celebrations were sponsored to indicate loyalty to the king. After he was made *grand écuyer de France* in 1643, Henri de Lorraine, comte de Harcourt organized a grand procession on 25 August to the Augustinian Convent, where mass was said for the king's prosperity, all to the sound of oboes and drums. In doing so, he showed 'the respect, love and zeal by which his ardent and faithful heart is incessantly aroused to honour His Majesty'.[17] Another example is a mass at Saint-Hippolyte in Paris on 25 August 1679, organized by Charles Le Brun to glorify Louis XIV on his *fête*. The church was decorated with tapestries depicting the king and a motet by Marc-Antoine Charpentier was admired by all who attended, according to the *Mercure*.[18] Patricia Ranum has speculated that Charpentier's involvement was a calculated demonstration of loyalty by his Guise employers, who sought to honour the king at a significant moment in the Affair of the Poisons soon after one of their bodyguards had been arrested. Although her argument is confused – at different points she states that Madame de Guise both organized Charpentier's involvement and 'could scarcely have played a role' in doing so – one of the Guise princesses probably approved the composition of this motet.[19] As much as the work (discussed in Chapter 2) appears at first sight to be top-down propaganda celebrating Louis XIV's military prowess through Saint Louis, it can more accurately be seen as an upwards-looking expression of loyalty and flattery.

A notable tradition developed in the 1660s to give thanks for Louis XIV's recovery from a critical illness in 1658, attributed to Saint Roch, whose relics the Carmelites had brought to the king.[20] Every year on 25 August, town officials would assemble in their finery at the Hôtel de Ville and go to the Carmelite church at the Place Maubert.

Figure 4.1 *La Résurrection du Christ* (1674–6) by Charles Le Brun (1619–90), Musée des Beaux-Arts de Lyon. © Alamy Stock Photo.

Following mass, there was a procession to the Louvre involving officials, guards in livery, archers and relics to the sound of drums, cymbals, trumpets and oboes. Having paused to chant a De Profundis for Henri IV at the site of his assassination, the procession was followed by a grand mass in the same chapel where the Académie Française met immediately afterwards. Perhaps this caused some inconvenience, because from the beginning of Louis XV's reign the procession went to the chapel of the Tuileries.[21] A note from 1750 states that 'this procession was made for a dangerous illness of Louis XIV and has since been continued for the conservation of Louis XV'.[22] The discourses pronounced by Carmelites to invite the city officials presented a similar message, making no mention of Saint Louis.[23] It is tempting to wonder why the procession did not take place on the day of Saint Roch (16 August), which had become popular as an unofficial festival. The fact that it was eliminated from the table of Parisian feasts in 1666 probably had something to do with this, but more important was that the day of Saint Louis was frequently celebrated just for being the *fête du roi* rather than because of the saint himself.[24] In addition, the Carmelites claimed that Louis IX had established them in France after his first crusade, so the use of 25 August served to strengthen their link to him.[25]

If Saint Louis was marginal to this event – a religious procession – he was even less present in the secular manifestations of the *fête du roi*. The Académie Royale de Musique put on annual concerts in the garden of the Tuileries from the end of Louis XIV's reign, often on the evening of 24 August but sometimes as late as 29 August.[26] Louis XV's presence on the terrace in the 1710s occasioned passionate acclamations of *Vive le Roi* – sometimes interrupting the actual music.[27] These events were popular, with crowds of such size that in 1719 several women were suffocated or crushed to death.[28] The repertoire was dominated by Lully as late as the 1740s, but many were not just there for the music.[29] According to one account of the concert on 24 August 1790, a year into the Revolution, the concerts were 'handy for lovers unable to enter the dwellings of their ladies'. A young *abbé* was taking 'some small liberties' with a young lady known to him, but the two lovers were separated by the crowd. An 'ex-gentleman' quickly substituted himself in the *abbé*'s place, with the lady only noticing after a quarter of an hour. As she started to protest and yell, her assaulter mounted a chair to appeal to the people, saying that the *abbé* had been taking liberties 'without her taking offense; I took his place without her perceiving; I have just finished what M. the *abbé* had started; . . . I ask you if an ex-gentleman is not worth more than an ex-*abbé*'. With everyone laughing, the lady's only option was to slip into the crowd.[30] Quite apart from what it says about sexual harassment at this time, the story is a reminder that the huge crowds often mentioned in more official accounts of celebrations of Saint Louis's day (or eve) were by no means always there out of devotion to the saint or a desire to celebrate the monarchy – or even to hear the music.

Nevertheless, much of the crowd was probably drawn by the more innocent pleasure of viewing the fireworks. These were particularly magnificent in 1721, when a huge edifice covered in representations of Mars, Jupiter and Minerva was erected in the gardens. Anyone who did not immediately grasp the parallels to Louis XV could read printed explanations. The fireworks included dragons which 'vomited torrents of flame from their enormous mouths'.[31] Twenty years later, a group of the king's pyrotechnicians demonstrated their craft in a firework display on the river on Saint Louis's feast; once again, this involved an edifice covered in classical imagery and the erection of structures along the banks of the river to support the spectators.[32] That the *artificiers* conceived of their project as a *bouquet* for the king says much about the significance of the feast, used to celebrate the loyalty to and patronage by the monarch of this or that group (Carmelites, academies, *corps de ville*). The date of 25 August was both appropriate symbolically and convenient practically (thanks to the summer weather), so not all celebrations of 'la Saint-Louis' were focused on Saint Louis himself.

This is evident when the feast coincided with important events in the royal family. In 1682, the birth of the duc de Bourgogne occasioned expanded celebrations, including fireworks and games on the river, the illumination of the Louvre with ten thousand lamps, cannonades, concerts and *Te Deum* services.[33] Saint Louis was largely absent, except at the Jesuit Collège de Clermont, in whose courtyard a large statue of Apollo was placed on 25 August; the day afterwards this was changed to a statue of Saint Louis with the inscription 'we have no Apollo other than this saint'.[34] According to the *Gazette*, the Jesuits wanted to show that they wished to work only for the glory of the royal house, under the auspices of Saint Louis. Similar illuminations, fireworks and games featured in 1704 for the duc de Bretagne's birth, and Louis XVI ordered special illuminations for 25 August 1775 to celebrate the marriage of his sister to the prince of Piedmont.[35]

Political events could inject celebrations of *la Saint-Louis* in Paris with tremendous popular energy. For a few days from 24 August 1774, huge crowds converged on the Palais de Justice to celebrate the disgrace of Chancellor Maupeou. This was regarded as a gift from the new king to his people on his nameday; Siméon-Prosper Hardy noted that Louis XVI could not better celebrate 'the feast day of one of his most illustrious predecessors . . . than by spreading happiness and consolation in all hearts' by dismissing the hated chancellor. Nevertheless, there was an ominous edge to the sight of large crowds burning effigies of Maupeou, his feet tied with the *cordon bleu*.[36] Similarly, the resignation of Loménie de Brienne on 25 August 1788 at a point when royal authority was rapidly unravelling in France sparked a week of effigy burning and popular celebration on the Pont Neuf.[37]

Nevertheless, for most of the period 25 August was a date on which Parisians expressed loyalty and devotion to the king. Examples of Parisian institutions using Saint Louis's day to celebrate the monarchy by putting on special events could be repeated ad infinitum – the exhibitions of new works from the Académie Royale de Peinture et Sculpture that normally opened on this date at the Louvre, special performances and balls at the Opéra comique, the celebrations of the military pupils from the rue Saint-Dominique.[38] The 25th of August was an important date in the capital's year, but not necessarily because of devotion to Saint Louis. Ultimately it is impossible to separate veneration to the saint from celebration of the monarchy.

The feast in the dioceses

The feast of Saint-Louis was supposed to be celebrated across France. Paul V instructed the episcopate to enforce his brief and in 1619 the Assembly of the Clergy ordered letters to be sent to exhort all France prelates to celebrate it in their dioceses. It does not seem that this issue met with opposition or even discussion.[39] Presumably the clerics were aware of the recent elaborate celebrations in Paris in 1618 as well as the fact that both king and pope had backed the elevation of the feast with their authority. It must have seemed an obvious issue on which they could please Louis XIII.

Signs of enthusiasm soon appeared. A thirty-verse poem printed in Rouen exhorted the French to celebrate 'the sacred day of the great king Saint Louis'.[40] According to the *Mercure*, Paris was 'the model on which all the other towns of France set themselves' and the Parisian clergyman Christophe Petit wrote that all of France participated in the celebrations.[41] Some historians have similarly assumed that the feast became obligatory across France after 1618.[42] This interpretation is clearly wrong. Many parts of the kingdom were slow to follow the papal brief, if they did so at all, and the feast spread in a haphazard manner. When visiting the countryside near Pontoise in 1722, the Parisian jurist Mathieu Marais noted that 'in the diocese of Rouen, they celebrate neither the Saint-Bartholomew nor the Saint-Louis, even though Saint Louis made many foundations at Pontoise'.[43] His surprise is as noteworthy and revealing as the local lack of enthusiasm for the cult of Saint Louis, indicating a difference between the capital and the relatively nearby provinces.

Lists of *fêtes chômées* (on which there was an obligation to abstain from work) for each diocese – found in ritual books, collections of statutes printed after diocesan synods, and episcopal ordinances to regulate the number of feast days – show that the spread of Saint Louis's feast was far from uniform. In Paris it was *chômée* throughout the seventeenth and eighteenth centuries, surviving various decisions to decrease the number of feasts.[44] This is unsurprising for a cult centred on the monarchy – although a late-eighteenth-century organist noted that in most Parisian churches is was merely in the fourth rank of feasts, whereas at the abbey of Saint-Denis it was in the first rank.[45] In other dioceses, however, the feast did not make it onto any rank at all. Noah Shusterman has identified it as neither specifically local nor universal, estimating that it was celebrated in 35 per cent of French dioceses in the seventeenth century and 12 per cent in the eighteenth century – but the evidence is patchy both chronologically and geographically.[46]

In the early seventeenth century, Saint Louis's feast was listed in important dioceses near Paris such as Chartres and Troyes, in Maillezais, and the southern dioceses of Rieux and Cahors.[47] It is not always easy to say whether or not it was on the catalogue of feasts prior to 1618 or added afterwards in response to the papal brief. In a copy of the ordinances of Langres from 1629, Saint Louis was not in the printed list but handwritten in one copy consulted, suggesting that his feast was added around this time.[48] Thirty years later, the ordinances of Mâcon stated that 'we order [the Saint-Louis] to be celebrated according to the intentions of the church'; this suggests a recent addition, though if it was a response to 1618 it was rather delayed.[49] Newly conquered territories, on the other hand, often adopted it more quickly. Bar-le-Duc in Lorraine was taken over by Louis XIII in 1632; in 1633, after swearing fidelity to the king, who stayed there on 24 August, the townspeople celebrated the feast for the first time as a gesture of loyalty.[50] In 1642, a year after Catalonia was incorporated into the French monarchy, 25 August was instituted as a public festivity, integrating Catalonia into a 'dynastic space'.[51] However, in many places that were already part of this dynastic space, the feast seems not to have been added to the calendars at all. In the 1620s it did not feature in the catalogues of Saint-Malo in Brittany or Limoges, Clermont and Bordeaux further south, and in the next two decades it was also not listed for Beauvais, Rouen, Orléans or Périgueux.[52] The episcopate did not unanimously follow the lead of

Paris; for example, the Bordeaux ordinances of 1621 (and 1683) included a catalogue of feasts from 1603 that had not been changed in light of the events of 1618.[53]

Louis XIV's reign shows similarly mixed results. In northern and central France, 25 August was *chômée* in Mâcon in 1668, Angers in 1680, Vannes in 1693 and Chalons-sur-Saône in 1700.[54] In the south, it was celebrated in Aix and Nîmes in the 1670s, Tulle in the 1690s and Toulon in 1704.[55] Perhaps as part of Louis XIV's tendency to promote the cult in newly acquired eastern territories, the feast was added in 1679 to the calendar of Besançon, formally part of France following the 1678 Treaty of Nijmegen.[56] Nevertheless, this was an age in which the authorities were looking to eliminate feasts. In 1666, Louis XIV sent a letter asking the bishops to reduce the number; only a handful responded, but Saint Louis's feast survived the cull in the Saintes in 1667 and Luçon in 1668.[57] Other dioceses reformed their calendars in their own time, so that whereas 25 August was celebrated in Angers in 1680, it had been removed by 1693.[58] Although it is impossible to be precise because the information is not complete for any one point in time, it was probably the case that Saint Louis's feast was not celebrated in the majority of dioceses under Louis XIV: certainly this is the picture that emerges from dioceses as geographically wide-ranging as Lisieux and Uzès in the 1650s, Narbonne and Toulouse in the 1660s, Alet, Grasse, Rodez and Reims in the 1670s, Digne in the 1680s, Grenoble, Angers, Sens, Albi, Lisieux and Toulouse in the 1690s and Pamiers, Autun, La Rochelle, Sisteron, Oloron and Carcassonne from 1700 to 1715.[59] This included the Roman ritual prepared for the diocese of Alet by Nicolas Pavillon, which began with a letter of admiration and endorsement from almost thirty French archbishops and bishops.[60] Sometimes the feast appeared to have a rather ambiguous status, for instance in Noyon, whose bishop declared in 1705 that it should be *chômée* 'where this feast is observed' (presumably in churches dedicated to Saint Louis) but also that it should not be *chômée* when transferred to another day, such as the nearest Sunday.[61]

This would become more pronounced in the eighteenth century, when efforts to reduce the number of feast days gathered pace. Although the feast of Saint-Louis still made it onto a number of catalogues, such as those of Blois and Vienne in 1730 and Dijon in 1744, it was in clear decline.[62] In a number of dioceses, such as Auch and Soissons in 1701, Troyes in 1706, Lavaur in 1729 and Bourges in 1746, it was to be celebrated only in the principal town or in urban areas.[63] In Troyes it had been celebrated by the whole diocese in 1640, so this was a withdrawal of sorts. In other dioceses, the feast was transferred to the nearest Sunday, indicating a second-class status. This happened in Chartres (where it had been celebrated fully in 1640) in 1742, in Metz in 1744, and in Noyon in 1782.[64] Elsewhere, it was among the feasts to be completely suppressed, indicating that it had been celebrated before but was no longer deemed of sufficient importance to be retained, for example, in Bayonne in 1754 and Poitiers in 1766.[65] In Boulogne the feast was listed in 1746 but withdrawn in 1778 by the same long-lived bishop, François-Joseph-Gaston de Partz de Pressy.[66] In Luçon the feast had been listed in 1668 but did not feature in the calendar a century later.[67] There were, however, exceptions to the trend; in 1736 Étienne-Joseph de La Fare re-established the feast of Saint-Louis in Laon, although he did allow parish priests to accord dispensations if peasants needed to work.[68]

Most dioceses did not include 25 August on their calendars. This was the case in the Breton dioceses of Quimper and Saint-Brieuc in 1717 and 1726, the south-eastern dioceses of Valence in 1728 and Belley in 1759, the southern dioceses of Comminges in 1751 and Fréjus in 1779, and the northern diocese of Amiens in 1784.[69] Unsurprisingly, it did not appear in the late 1760s in places such as Rouen and Saint-Malo where it had not been celebrated before, nor in other places where the number of feast days was being reduced, such as Trier (part of which was French territory) in 1773 and Évreux in 1775.[70] In general, bishops were largely independent of their archbishop in deciding which feasts should be celebrated. In the province of Paris, for example, the feast was celebrated in Paris and Blois but only partially in Chartres and not at all in Meaux and Orléans in the eighteenth century; in the province of Lyon, the feast was not celebrated in Autun or Lyon itself but was in Langres, Chalons-sur-Saône and Mâcon.[71] Nevertheless, bishops often worked together by region or province to produce more unified catalogues in the late eighteenth century. This happened in 1781 in the large province of Tours, comprising the Breton dioceses of Tréguier, Saint-Brieuc, Saint-Malo, Dol, Rennes, Vannes, Quimper and Saint-Pol-de-Léon as well as Angers, Nantes, Le Mans and Tours itself: Saint Louis's feast was not on the new list.[72] In the same year, Toul also collaborated with the dioceses recently created from it, Saint-Dié and Nancy, in reducing the catalogue of feasts.[73] Saint Louis's feast is not found in the list of *fêtes chômées* or even (when included) in the list of feasts no longer to be celebrated.

This mass of evidence does not provide a snapshot of any single year, and enough examples have been given of dioceses adding or removing the feast of Saint-Louis to counsel against reading eighteenth-century ordinances back to the seventeenth century. Nevertheless, what is clear is that the feast of Saint-Louis was not celebrated as consistently across France as might have been expected following the 1618 brief or the 1619 letter from the Assembly of the Clergy. Some dioceses did indeed promptly follow the pope and the king, such as Rennes, whose bishops added the feasts of Saint-Louis in 1620 and Saint-Joseph in 1665.[74] Louis XIV's desire for the latter to be celebrated across his kingdom was made known in the 1660s, but he was not able simply to order the bishops to carry out his wishes.[75] He was far from successful in fostering celebration of the feast of Saint-Joseph, just as his father had not succeeded in imposing Saint Louis across the kingdom.[76] In the 1660s, this was partly because prevailing attitude during the ministry of Colbert was to remove feast days rather than add new ones.[77] However, the most important issue was authority. Bishops had the prerogative over which feasts should be obligatory in their dioceses and, as indicated by a *mémoire* of 1669 by Louis Bassompierre, bishop of Saintes, they did not appreciate attempts by pope or king to usurp it.[78] Since it was in their hands, bishops might decide to celebrate or remove the feast of Saint-Louis for their own reasons independent of the interests of the court. In 1719, a century after Louis XIII's efforts to elevate the feast, the new bishop of Nantes, Louis de Tressan, informed his priests that he wished Saint Louis to be celebrated, probably because he was Tressan's patron saint. This was largely obeyed even though the bishop had overstepped the mark in not securing letters patent from the king. One *curé* (parish priest), however, objected, saying that it was not a feast of commandment and that those without the desire to celebrate it could carry on working. A *mandement* was issued the following year ordering the diocese to refrain from work on the feast, but this did not last long as the subsequent bishop transferred it to the following Sunday in 1730.[79]

Analysis of which dioceses celebrated Saint Louis's feast reveals no geographic logic; there was no north–south divide and proximity to Paris did not guarantee celebration. Given that these decisions were in the hands of the episcopate, it could be instructive to see which bishops promoted the feast. Proximity to the court was not crucial. Augustin Potier, for example, was almoner to Anne of Austria from 1616, but Saint Louis was not celebrated in his diocese of Beauvais in 1637. Given the cult's associations with the monarchy, it is perhaps surprising that 25 August was not celebrated in Reims in 1677; the fact that the archbishop was Charles Maurice Le Tellier, brother of the marquis de Louvois and holder of the honorific title of *maître de musique* of the king's chapel, seems not to have changed this.[80] What seems likely is that a minority of dioceses responded to the brief of 1618 but that consistent pressure on the others was not maintained. There are no indications of royal desire for other dioceses to follow suit later in the period. Moreover, this was a period in which the number of feasts was being reduced.[81] When Urban VIII had set out the major feast days to be kept across the church, he added that each kingdom or province could also celebrate its own patrons:[82] French dioceses tended to emphasize their provincial saints over the 'national' Saint Louis – for example, Saint Jean de la Grille in his former diocese of Saint-Malo, Saints Martin and Gatien in Tours or Saint Nicolas, the patron of Lorraine, in Toul, Saint-Dié and Nancy.[83] Saintly cults thus became a strong expression of local and regional identity.[84] The monarchy struggled to graft celebration of its saint onto this highly regional patchwork of devotions.

In any case, official lists of feasts were only part of the story. There were many jurisdictional conflicts and examples of religious orders, *parlements* and shop-owners ignoring episcopal changes to the calendar. After the calendar reform in Paris in 1666 poems circulated criticizing the removal of certain saints ('Saint Mark cannot suffer this unheard-of abuse,/He wants to be celebrated just like Saint Louis') and pressure was such that five of the seventeen suppressed feasts had returned by 1669.[85] The calendar reform in Saintes around the same time also generated controversy and conflict between the bishop and the cathedral canons (it was in this context that Bassompierre wrote the *mémoire* mentioned earlier).[86] Moreover, the existence of repeated ordinances banning merchants and artisans from opening their shops on feasts of commandment indicates that some were indeed doing just that.[87] Most people under the *Ancien Régime* chose whether to observe feasts, as penalties were rarely enforced – although Jeanne Mourgue, a *dévote* in the Auvergne who kept a diary of her confessions and communions, did note that her parish priest refused to hear her confession in 1678 because she had allowed dancing in her house on the feast of Saint-Louis.[88] Given that bishops normally justified their decision to suppress feasts by invoking not only the need of the poor to work for their sustenance but also the fact that these days had become occasions for such debauched and irreligious activities as playing games and dancing, we cannot presume even when 25 August *was* celebrated in a certain diocese that everyone there spent their time in pious contemplation of the virtues of Saint Louis. As was noted in 1787, 'it is for religion that the number [of feasts] must be reduced. The worker commits more errors on one feast day than during a whole week'.[89]

The feast in the provinces

Wider diffusion of the cult depended on its adoption by provincial elites. Many provincial academies followed the Parisian ones in taking Saint Louis as their patron and celebrating his feast day. The Académie of Villefranche in the Beaujolais did so in 1681, wearing their ceremonial robes and hearing a panegyric of Saint Louis. In 1688, they used the feast as an opportunity to erect a bust of Louis XIV and they continued to celebrate 25 August with panegyrics and public sessions.[90] The Académie Royale des Belles-Lettres, Sciences et Arts of Bordeaux, established in 1712, held public sessions on Saint Louis's day (not *chômée* in Bordeaux), frequently with panegyrics and music.[91] Academies in Montauban, Amiens, Besançon and Béziers founded in the 1740s and 1750s, celebrated Saint Louis's feast with high mass and a panegyric in the morning and a public session in the afternoon.[92] The periodicals rarely mentioned more than the name of the preacher, forgoing the extensive discussion frequently granted to the Parisian panegyrics. However, those texts that are available, such as a widely praised example delivered before the Académie de Châlons-sur-Marne in 1777, reveal that the provincial panegyrics were written in a Parisian mould.[93] In addition to panegyrics, provincial academies also commissioned motets celebrating Saint Louis.[94] Widely recognized for their part in diffusing the Enlightenment in eighteenth-century France, many provincial academies also helped spread the cult of a medieval crusader saint.[95]

The periodicals allow us to glimpse other occasions on which the feast was promoted by provincial elites and the varied reasons for doing so. In 1678, a terrible storm caused major damage to the church of Saint-Solenne in Blois, but by 1687 the reconstruction had been almost finished thanks to the generosity of Louis XIV and Colbert. According to the *Mercure*, the parishioners could not wait for the church to be completed before giving public expression of their thanks to the king.

> For this reason, they have founded in perpetuity a solemn service and *salut* which must be said every year on the feast day of Saint-Louis for the prosperity of the king, the royal house and the state. This feast was celebrated for the first time on the 25th of the previous month [August] with all the magnificence possible, and the support of the nobility, of all the officers and of the principle people of the province who had been invited.[96]

This provided the occasion for Frotté's panegyric, discussed in Chapter 3. In the same year, the merchants of Poitiers used the feast of Saint-Louis to erect a statue of Louis XIV.[97] Several decades later, the nobility of lower Poitou celebrated the feast at Fontenay-le-Comte in 1758 with a *Te Deum*, cannonades, dinners, fireworks, illuminations and a ball that lasted until the next morning – all to signal their love for Louis XV.[98]

These celebrations were not established by the top-down instructions issued in 1618, but as expressions of gratitude and devotion to the monarchy from the bottom-up (or rather middle-up). Every provincial panegyric or celebration was embedded in a different context. Royal office holders naturally celebrated the king's feast, such as the *avocats aux conseils du roy* who were invited to a solemn mass on 25 August 1712 at Fontainebleau.[99] Another example is provided by the merchants of La Rochelle, many of whom had recently converted to Catholicism after the Revocation of the Edict of Nantes, who gathered in the Carmelite convent to hear a panegyric of Saint Louis in 1689. For the merchants, the report in the *Mercure* served to publicize their loyalty to the king and their new faith; for the government, it presented the Revocation as having borne fruit.[100]

Military officers often organized and participated in celebrations of the feast, particularly after the creation of the Order of Saint-Louis.[101] On 25 August 1711, M. de la Brulerie, a former officer and chevalier of Saint-Louis, gave a magnificent dinner at Joigny in Burgundy, attended by many important military figures and chevaliers of Saint-Louis and followed by a ball lasting the whole night.[102] At Bar-le-Duc in 1757 an officer organized a special celebration in honour of Louis XV, including a cantata that depicted Saint Louis looking down from Heaven.[103] The year 1778 saw the company of *canonniers* in Dieppe celebrating the feast day for the conservation of the king's 'precious days' as well as a mass to celebrate the queen's pregnancy in Paramé (Brittany), organized by the lieutenant-general and the comte de Lusace, commander of the army in the region, following which the officers and chevaliers of Saint-Louis were treated to dinner.[104] Most interesting was the decision by military officers in Champagne in 1779 to give money to the municipal officers in five local towns 'which will be used to marry the poorest and most virtuous girl of the area', on condition that the five couples celebrate a low mass each year on Saint Louis's day 'to pray to God for the conservation of the health of the king, queen and royal family'.[105]

Military celebrations of the feast were particularly notable in conquered territories. There was a cannonade on 24 August 1657 in Montmédy, which had been captured shortly before in the presence of Louis XIV; the following day, the Abbé d'Orval, whose brother was an enemy commander, celebrated mass in the presence of the marquis de Vandy, subsequently proclaiming his loyalty to Louis XIV by saying that 'this great monarch, in conquering this place, had likewise conquered his heart and his inclinations, which have always been Spanish'.[106] In 1673, during the Dutch War, the feast was celebrated in occupied Maastricht and Utrecht.[107] On one occasion, it even served a tactical purpose. A splendid festivity was organized for the feast of Saint-Louis in Bergues near Dunkirk in 1648 to make the enemy believe that the officers were simply enjoying themselves, while in fact the maréchal de Rantzau 'secretly sent various units to war'.[108]

Events in the royal family were frequently the occasion for provincial celebrations of Saint Louis's feast. The sieur de Launay du Mas, commander of the Ile de Ré, had a *Te Deum* sung in La Rochelle on 25 August 1658 to give thanks for the king's convalescence.[109] In 1668, there were special services to give thanks for the birth of the duc d'Anjou in Soissons and Metz, where a *Te Deum* was sung in the presence of the city's clergy, *parlement* and military as well as a large crowd – which the *Gazette* remarks was all the greater because it was the feast of Saint-Louis.[110] Louis XV's recovery from illness in 1721 caused the Abbé Gervaise to organize a ceremony on the feast day at Suèvres near Chambord as well as other special celebrations in Châlons-sur-Marne, Brest, Valognes and Vendôme.[111] Conversely, the feast could be used to pray for the royal family in times of illness, as when the abbess of Chelles prayed for the health of the ailing queen mother in 1665.[112]

The feast of Saint-Louis continued to provide opportunities for provincial elites to signal their devotion to the monarchy into the last years of the *Ancien Régime*. The Ordre de Saint-Hubert du Barrois celebrated a mass at Bar-le-Duc on 25 August 1785, praying for the royal family.[113] Many of these celebrations had little to do with Saint Louis; a one-act work presented in Bordeaux on 24 August 1785 to show 'the love of the French for their kings' did not mention him but included a statue of Louis XVI in the scenery.[114] The prize to be awarded on 25 August to the most pious, dutiful and charitable girl in Saint-Ferjeux, near Besançon, was set up in 1776 to honour Louis XVI rather than Saint Louis.[115]

Historians have called the feast day a *fête nationale* on account of its widespread observance in places ranging from the court and Paris to small towns and army camps, stating that Saint Louis was 'commemorated everywhere'.[116] The periodicals give many examples of such celebrations, but these were too sporadic for it to be seen in terms of the national holidays of later eras. The feast was certainly not an actual 'holiday' in most of the kingdom's dioceses, and the small flashes of illumination provided by reports of individual celebrations should not dazzle us into forgetting the much larger dark areas. Many *Gazette* reports from places around France from late August and early September do not mention '*la saint-Louis*' at all. The very fact that they were reported in this way shows that the feast day was *not* observed universally – although it is also probable that those incidents that made it into the periodical were just the tip of the iceberg, especially since celebration of the feast by those further down the social scale was unlikely to be mentioned. What emerges is less a holiday celebrated 'nationally' across France than one episodically promoted by regional elites intending to prove their loyalty upwards to the monarchy and to display their royal connections downwards to others in their region.

Dedications across France

Churches placed under the patronage of Saint Louis would have celebrated his feast day as their patronal festival even if it was not *chômée* in their diocese; in addition, pilgrimage processions to neighbouring parishes on the feast day of their dedicatory saint were common. The parishes, chapels and institutions dedicated to Saint Louis – and there were more under the Bourbons than during any other period – therefore offer another window into the geographical spread of his cult.

Numerous Jesuit institutions were associated with the royal saint. The college of Béziers, founded in 1598 with letters patent from Henri IV, had a chapel dedicated to Saint Louis, as did the noviciate in Avignon (still papal territory) from 1611, probably because it was built thanks to the generosity of Louis d'Ancezune.[117] In 1615, Marie de Médicis laid the first stone of the chapel of the Jesuit college in Rouen; the chapel was dedicated to Saint Louis in 1631 and Abraham Bosse produced an image of him appearing to Louis XIII with the college in the background.[118] The Jesuits were granted the buildings of the old college in Angoulême in 1622, pronouncing that it will be 'from now on named the collège Saint-Louis in honour of His Majesty'.[119] At around this time another Jesuit college was established in Vienne (Isère), although the church dedicated to Saint Louis was not constructed until between 1673 and 1725.[120] Such projects often took several decades. Construction of a chapel dedicated to Saint Louis at the Jesuit college of Blois lasted from 1634 to 1671 and was aided financially by Louis XIII, Gaston d'Orléans and the 'Grande Mademoiselle'.[121] These foundations would have contributed to the spread of Saint Louis's cult, as indicated by reports of the celebration of 25 August 1643 by the Jesuits in Angoulême and Béziers.[122] This is significant given the popularity of the Jesuit colleges as institutions of elite education.

Some of the Jesuit foundations dedicated to Saint Louis resulted from the monarchy's use of the Society to combat Protestantism. In 1622, the Jesuits founded a college dedicated to Saint Louis in Pau following the king's suppression of the Protestant university of Orthez, though the actual church was not constructed until the 1680s.[123] The rector of the college of Metz petitioned Louis XIII for the building of a church under the auspices of Saint Louis, 'who well deserves to be given some honour in a large city like Metz'.[124] They were given an old Protestant temple; with a statue of Saint Louis placed on the altar, the first mass was celebrated in 1643 and the first stone of a new church laid by the *premier president* of the Parlement of Metz in 1665 with a Latin dedication to Saint Louis.[125] Annexed to France in 1642, Sedan was another town on the northeastern frontier with a large Protestant population. On 25 August 1664, the church of the new Jesuit college, founded to combat the Protestant academy according to the wishes of Louis XIV, was dedicated to Saint Louis in great ceremony by the Abbé de Guiscard, brother of the governor of Sedan. The municipal officials, officers of the garrison and a great crowd of people were present, according to the *Gazette*. In 1681, Louis XIV suppressed the Protestant academy and gave its buildings to the Jesuits.[126] In the same year he annexed Strasbourg. The Jesuit college established there a few years later following the Revocation of the Edict of Nantes also had a chapel dedicated to Saint Louis. The royal saint was used to foster Catholic conversion and attachment to the king in Huguenot areas.

The choice of Saint Louis for the dedication sometimes came directly from the king. The church of the Jesuit college at Poitiers, initially dedicated to the Saint-Nom-de-Jésus in 1613, was rededicated to Saint Louis in 1615 on Louis XIII's orders.[127] On the other hand, when the same king laid the first stone of the Jesuit *maison professe* in Toulouse in 1621, 'the church, which was to be dedicated to Saint Louis, king, took the patronage of Saint Ignatius'.[128] Sometimes the Jesuits were given colleges with chapels already dedicated to Saint Louis, as at Aix-en-Provence, so were not responsible for the dedication; in 1627 the Parlement of Provence had to warn them not to remove the image of Saint Louis over the altar or replace it with one of Saint Ignatius, considering it unseemly that 'a Spaniard turn his back on Saint Louis and on a king of France'. Although the Jesuits protested that they covered the portrait of Saint Louis in Paris with one of Saint Ignatius when the king attended the Jesuit church in Paris on the latter's feast, the Parlement's opinion that a French king could not lose his place of honour to a Spaniard reveals an association between Saint Louis and national dignity among provincial *parlementaire* elites.[129]

Other religious orders also dedicated institutions to Saint Louis. On 21 August 1657, Louis XIV laid the first stone of a church in Sedan to be dedicated to Saint

Louis and Saint Anne (his mother's patron), part of the Convent of Irish Capuchins.[130] Another Capuchin church dedicated to Saint Louis in his birthplace of Poissy was consecrated by the bishop of Chartres in 1665.[131] In 1674, a Benedictine priory was founded under the double invocation of the Virgin and Saint Louis at Torcy in Brie by the Abbé Louis Berrier, a canon of Notre-Dame.[132] Saint Louis was presumably chosen as Berrier's patron saint. In 1755, the Collège Royal Saint-Louis-du-Fort was established in Metz, run by the *chanoines réguliers* of the Congrégation de Notre-Sauveur. Unsurprisingly, the Jesuits opposed this project as it challenged their own college, but it had the patronage of the maréchal de Belle-Isle.[133] In Paris, the growth of the Chaussée d'Antin caused the government to construct a convent 'to procure spiritual help for the inhabitants of this area'. In 1783, the Capuchins of the Faubourg Saint-Jacques were transferred to the new convent of Saint-Louis, which later became the parish church Saint-Louis-d'Antin.[134]

Urban expansion often provided the impetus for the creation of new parishes, as shown by two churches dedicated to saints associated with Louis XIV (Louis and Joseph) by Cardinal Le Camus in Grenoble. The Saint-Louis church was consecrated in 1699; 25 August was not *chômée* in Grenoble, but the new church anchored Saint Louis in the devotional landscape.[135] This also occurred in the port cities that developed under Louis XIV. On the Atlantic coast, the chapel at the château de Rochefort on the Charente estuary was rededicated to Saint Louis in 1686.[136] On the Mediterranean, the first stone of the Saint-Louis pier at Sète (the port of the Canal du Midi) was laid in 1666, followed by the Fort Saint-Louis in 1689. A provisional chapel consecrated to the saint in 1670 was replaced by a more permanent church in 1703. As the town's patronal festival, Saint Louis's feast was a major event in Sète, marked with days of celebrations including a canal jousting contest. From 1673 merchants were able to sell goods duty-free. All this took place under the name of Saint Louis but was not necessarily a mark of devotion to him. There was plenty of licentious behaviour and on 24 August 1745 the grand vicar of Agde did not hesitate to vilify the jousters' irreligiosity.[137]

The Tour Saint-Louis was erected in 1737 in the Rhône estuary at what became Port-Saint-Louis-du-Rhône.[138] Further east, the Fort des Vignettes was renamed Fort Saint-Louis after its reconstruction in 1708 following the siege of Toulon.[139] A Saint-Louis church was also built in Toulon according to a project proposed by the bishop in 1705, though it had a rather troubled history. The bishop wished to create a new parish to serve the west part of the city but wanted to use part of the Place d'Armes. The municipality was opposed to this and refused to contribute to the expense, making the project an object of conflict. Although Louis XIV gave some of the square for the construction of the church, which began in 1708, lack of funds, the death of the bishop in 1713 and the devastating plague that hit Toulon in 1720 ensured that the parish was long housed in the chapel of the Blue Penitents. It was almost finished when, following repeated complaints from the navy of its inconvenience on the Place d'Armes, Louis XVI revoked the gift made by Louis XIV and ordered the demolition of the church in 1780. A new church of Saint-Louis was finally completed in the 1788.[140]

Another maritime church of Saint-Louis with a complicated history was begun in 1686 in Brest. Louis XIV's decision to unite it to the Jesuit seminary in 1688 caused significant and lasting tension, not least over the choice of patron saints. Whereas the townspeople wanted the church to be dedicated exclusively to Saint Louis, the Jesuits were determined to add one of their own saints, Francis Xavier. When the church was consecrated in 1702 by the bishop of Léon to Saint Louis alone, the Jesuits were predictably displeased. Louis XIV's failure to maintain financial support created resentment at the fact that Brest was burdened with funding a church for the Jesuits. The Jesuits (who were the almoners of the fleet) eventually consented to abandon their rights to the church in the 1740s in return for a sum of money; the church of Saint-Louis, now out of their hands, was finally finished in 1785.[141]

Numerous other parish churches also took the name of the dynasty's patron saint. After the parish church of Villemomble near Paris was destroyed in 1670, a new church was dedicated in 1699 to Saint Genesius of Arles with Saint Louis as the second patron; 25 August is conveniently the feast of both of these saints.[142] On the frontier with Spain, a church dedicated to Saint Louis was built from 1733 to 1737 at Mont-Louis, a town based on a fort constructed by Vauban; as in Alsace, Saint Louis was a standard choice for the fortified towns constructed on France's frontiers.[143] New cathedrals also took his patronage; the Saint-Solenne church in Blois was rededicated to Saint Louis when it became the cathedral in 1697, and in 1784 the cathédrale Saint-Louis at La Rochelle, a long-standing project supported by Cardinal Fleury and Louis XV and under construction since 1742, was finally finished and dedicated.[144] Many of the priests who populated the French church would also have been trained in the new seminaries established in France in the wake of the Catholic Reformation; three were named after Saint Louis – in Toulouse in 1623, in Paris in 1696 and in Rouen in 1726.[145]

Given Saint Louis's reputation for charity, it was unsurprising that hospitals were named after him. Elisabethines staffed a Saint-Louis hospital founded at Louviers in 1616 and also founded the Hôpital Saint-Louis-Sainte-Elisabeth in Rouen in 1662.[146] This was shortly after the establishment of a 'double hospital', Saint-Louis and Saint-Roch, in Rouen in 1654; the former was for victims of infectious diseases, the latter for convalescents.[147] A 'salle Saint-Louis' was created at the Hôtel-Dieu of Beaune in 1668, named in honour of the benefactor, Louis Bétauld.[148] This was around the same time that Louis XIV ordered the establishment of general hospitals across his kingdom following the creation of one in Paris in 1656 'to contain poor beggars, instruct them in piety and divert them from libertinage'.[149] Part of the Parisian general hospital was the Salpêtrière, a female penal asylum where a church dedicated to Saint Louis was completed in the 1677 by Libéral Bruant; in the shape of a Greek cross with five baroque chapels, it could hold four thousand women and was 'a perfect liturgical setting for expiating female sin'.[150] Hospitals named after Saint Louis were established in Saintes in 1656 and at La Rochelle and Bordeaux in Louis XIV's later years.[151] At the Hôpital-général of Orléans the boys slept in the Saint-Louis dormitory.[152]

The naming of an institution after Saint Louis was very often an indication of royal involvement or approval, even if the project had initiated elsewhere. Shortly after the formal incorporation of Lorraine into France, two advocates of the sovereign court of Lorraine presented a request to Louis XV to found a glassworks at Müntzthal. This was approved in 1767; the king and the Conseil d'État granted 1,600 hectares of woodland for the project and gave the name 'Royal glassworks of Saint-Louis', specifying that the church or chapel that they proposed to construct ought to be placed under the patronage of Saint Louis. This location in the Moselle, known as Saint-Louis-lès-Bitche, would become famous for its crystal.[153]

Saint Louis's status as the royal patron saint clearly made him a popular choice for dedications under the Bourbon kings and brought his patronage to all these locations. This spread of institutional dedications makes it clear that the diocesan decisions to celebrate the feast or not are far from the whole story; many of the places dedicated to Saint Louis were in dioceses where the feast was not *chômée*, raising the likelihood that his cult was centred on particular locations or elite foundations.

Saint Louis in the French colonies

The cult of Saint Louis was also exported to the French colonies. A fort named Saint-Louis de Maragnan was built in 1612 as part of the short-lived project to found a colony on the north coast of Brazil.[154] The choice of Saint Louis honoured Louis XIII. Similarly, a fort named after Saint Louis was founded on an island also named after the saint at the mouth of the Senegal river in 1659, honouring both Louis XIV and his ancestor; it came to be the capital of French Senegal and occupied an important place in the slave trade.[155] In the West Indies, one of four former English churches on the island of Saint-Christophe (St Kitts) was consecrated to Catholicism under the name of Saint Louis in 1666.[156] In North America, the first bishop of Québec chose Saint Louis as the second patron of his cathedral (after the Virgin) in 1670, and his feast was celebrated in the diocese thereafter.[157]

All these examples attest to the fact that Saint Louis was a common choice for churches and settlements across South America, Africa, the Caribbean and Canada. As a saint associated with the reigning Bourbon kings, he was a natural choice as French rule was established in these locations. However, the choice of his name was often not imposed by the French government but chosen by people on the ground. A settlement on the western bank of the Mississippi River founded by the French fur traders Pierre Laclède and Auguste Chouteau in 1764 was also named after Saint Louis. Chouteau claimed that Laclède immediately christened it thus in honour of Louis XV, but this narrative has been recently challenged by Carl Ekberg and Sharon Person, who emphasize the figure of Louis St Ange de Bellerive, commandant of Upper Louisiana, and argue that he named the new outpost in honour of Saint Louis as his own patron saint in 1765.[158] The choice was probably intended to honour both Bellerive and the king, and the name survived subsequent Spanish and American regimes to become the city of St Louis, Missouri.

The feast of Saint-Louis was also promoted by elites in the colonies just as in France. On 25 August 1765 there were salvoes, fireworks, dinner and a ball at Cap-Français on Saint-Domingue, put on by the general; local periodicals also mention fireworks at the Place Saint-Louis in Cap in December.[159] Moreover, many of the ships that carried soldiers, people and goods around the world were named after Saint Louis. To take just three examples: the *Saint-Louis*, a new ship of 64 canons, was launched at Rochefort in 1722; in 1754 the Compagnie des Indes expected a vessel *Saint-Louis* to arrive from

Pondicherry laden with goods; and in 1757 an English ship was taken by the *Saint-Louis*, a corsair from Dunkirk, and brought to Boulogne.[160]

Saint Louis's name could also be given to natural features. The Mississippi river was referred to as the 'fleuve Saint-Louis' throughout the eighteenth century, though by 1751 it was being called the river 'Mississippi or Saint-Louis'; naturally, it flowed into the Saint-Louis bay.[161] Further north, there was the Saint-Louis lake at the confluence of the Saint Laurence and Ottawa rivers, named by Samuel de Champlain in 1611, probably to honour the king and in memory of a young 'Louys' who had died in what are now known as the Lachine rapids. These rapids on the Saint Lawrence river were called the 'Sault Saint-Louis', a name also used for the village of Kahnawake.[162] In 1680, the French crown granted the Jesuits the Seigneurie du Sault-Saint-Louis to 'protect' and 'nurture' Mohawks converted to Catholicism. The village gained its current location with the construction of a wooden Fort du Sault-Saint-Louis in 1725, replaced by a stone fortification in 1747.

Unsurprisingly, Jesuit missionaries spread Saint Louis's name in New France. In 1632, Paul le Ieune wrote to Barthelemy Iacquinot, the Jesuit provincial in France, saying that he had baptized an Iroquois infant on 25 August and named him Louis. Relations with the Iroquois were not always so friendly. In the 1640s the Jesuits gave the name Saint-Louis to the stockade village of the Ataronchronon tribe of the Huron-Wendat. On 16 March 1649, this village was attacked and burned down by the Five Nations Iroquois, who captured and killed two Jesuits. This was part of a devastating series of attacks that left the Huron nations 'weakened, divided, and demoralised'. The French decided to build three forts on the Iroquois river to assure free passage and the security of commerce. In 1665, it was recorded that 'the second fort was named Saint-Louis, because it was begun during the week that the feast of this great saint, protector of our kings and of France, was celebrated'. In June 1670, Père Millet, in charge of the mission of Saint-Jean-Baptiste at Onnontague, wrote to the superior general of the missions in New France, Le Mercier, saying that he used a world map and an image of Saint Louis as well as portraits of the king and dauphin and a luxurious Bible to spark the imagination of the 'savages' he was trying to convert.[163] It is not possible to say whether or not this was common across the French missions in New France, but it does attest to the fact that the cult was spread across the globe in this period even if its reach remained limited in metropolitan France.

Saint Louis in foreign capitals

If the feast of Saint-Louis was not a 'national day' across France, it did merit this title when French ambassadors and expatriates in foreign cities used it to celebrate their kingdom. In Rome, it provided an ideal focus for sumptuous ceremonies underlining the Catholic identity of the French monarchy, centred on mass at the 'French church', San Luigi dei Francesi. A Latin inscription above a stoup at the entrance to the church reads 'whoever prays for the king of France will have ten days of indulgence'. Saint Louis's side chapel, completed between 1664 and 1680 and surrounded by elaborate *fleur-de-lys* drapery, was the work of Plautilla Bricci. Her altarpiece shows Saint Louis standing between personifications of history and piety, wearing ecclesiastical vestments underneath a French coronation mantle – a clear depiction of sacral monarchy (Figure 4.2). In 1756, Charles-Joseph Natoire painted the apotheosis of Saint Louis on the ceiling of the nave; wearing armour under his royal mantle, he is taken up from the camp at Tunis and received by Jesus in glory.[164] Every year on 25 August, this lavish interior received additional decoration and the musical establishment was expanded, with multiple choirs and instruments performing elaborate polychoral music.[165]

This was to impress the important guest list, which normally included nobles, diplomats and, most importantly, cardinals, the number of whom attended was often reported in the *Gazette*. Such information was also conveyed along more private channels. In early September 1651, Henri d'Éstampes-Valençay, the French ambassador in Rome, reported to the comte de Brienne, secretary of state for foreign affairs, that on Saint Louis's feast day all the cardinals then in Rome had attended the high mass, excepting those indisposed by ill health or infirmity.[166] The French ambassador normally

Figure 4.2 *San Luigi tra la Fede e la Storia* by Plautilla Bricci (1616–90), San Luigi dei Francesi, Rome. © Alamy Stock Photo.

treated the cardinals to dinner and perhaps a concert at his residence (frequently decorated with illuminations).[167] However, the Sacred College was known for its division into factions such as those supporting the Spanish and French monarchies. In 1648, it was cardinals 'affectionate towards France' who attended, indicating that this was a celebration of the French party in Rome.[168] Similarly, in 1703 'all the Roman nobility affectionate towards France' was there for a panegyric in which Louis XIV's actions against heretics were praised in tandem with Saint Louis's enthusiasm to pierce the tongue of a blasphemer.[169]

As well as the dignitaries, the *Gazette* also mentioned large crowds of ordinary people, who were drawn in 1665 by the magnificent decorations over which the Cardinal de Retz had taken such care as well as by the plenary indulgences on offer. On this occasion, a vast amount of money, far exceeding the previous and the following years, was spent on the music, provided by eight choirs and numerous instrumentalists including seven organists. Retz reported to Hugues de Lionne, Brienne's successor, that most of the cardinals and the Spanish ambassador were present, to which the foreign minister replied that the king was pleased with the care the cardinal had taken over the celebrations. Retz had long been persona non grata at court due to his intrigues during the Fronde, but in 1665 was given a diplomatic mission in Rome where, shortly after the resolution of the Corsican Guards affair, a new dispute arose when the Sorbonne censured a Jesuit book defending papal infallibility. The lavish celebrations of Saint Louis celebrated the glory of the French monarchy in this context – but were directed more towards Paris than Rome, intended to demonstrate the former Frondeur's loyalty to Louis XIV as part of an image-making campaign which Retz hoped would cause the king to 'deign to forgive my weakness' and recognize 'an inviolable loyalty and a most ardent and sincere zeal'. This did not work. Although the Rome mission ended in success, Louis XIV continued to treat Retz with considerable reservation.[170]

Celebrations in other cities were also reported in the periodicals, albeit less regularly than those in Rome. In Genoa, the feast was celebrated by the French representative and French expatriates with cannonades, concerts and prayers for the royal family. According to the *Gazette*, it was marked in 1749 with the zeal and magnificence typical of those occasions on which the French proved their attachment and loyalty to the king.[171] Similarly, French ambassadors organized religious ceremonies, concerts, dinners and balls (often attended by other diplomats, nobles and dignitaries) in Venice, Florence, Turin and Parma.[172] This was also the case beyond Italy. From Frankfurt to The Hague, from Copenhagen to Warsaw and from Bonn to Lisbon, French diplomats celebrated the feast with various combinations of masses, balls, concerts, fireworks, dinners and illuminations.[173] The *Gazette*'s reports from these cities are more sporadic than from Rome; however, although celebrations in Lisbon were not recorded for much of the first part of Louis XIV's reign, in 1698 the *Gazette* says they were 'according to custom', suggesting that they were annual and routine.[174] In other cases, celebrations of the feast may were used occasionally to celebrate an event depending on specific circumstances. For example, the one reference to masses, dinners and balls in Solothurn is in 1749, when the feast of Saint-Louis fell two days after the new French ambassador's entry into the city.[175] Generally, though, 25 August was used by French ambassadors to celebrate their king and dazzle foreign rulers with magnificent ceremonies. Such occasions were also opportunities for French expatriates to come together – in 1777, the high mass for Saint Louis was attended not just by the ambassador and consul of France but all the French people in Lisbon.[176] There was also a 'National Confraternity of Saint Louis' for members of the 'French nation' in eighteenth-century Lisbon.[177]

Sometimes it was the foreign ruler who organized the celebrations in honour of the king of France, as in Warsaw in 1726 when Augustus the Strong laid on a dinner to which he invited the French ambassador and other dignitaries.[178] Such events could also be used to celebrate diplomatic closeness to France, as by John IV of Portugal following his kingdom's secession from Spain in 1640. In 1643, he gave flags won from the Spanish to the French church of Saint-Louis in Lisbon in order to show his friendship and in 1646 used the feast day as an occasion on which to name a new ship after the medieval king.[179]

In some places, the feast was celebrated independently of its associations with the French monarchy, normally because Saint Louis was also the patron of local royalty.[180] Independent celebration was most significant in the Spanish monarchy. To be sure, following the end of war between France and Spain in 1659, French ambassadors in Madrid frequently celebrated 25 August as they did elsewhere, and in 1698 Louis XIV's ambassador extraordinary made his formal entry into Madrid on that date.[181] Nevertheless, there was an independent Spanish cult of Saint Louis, as discussed in Chapter 1. The Spanish named ships and locations after him, such as San Luis Potosí in Mexico. As in France, the Jesuits played an important role in promoting the cult, for example, constructing the church of San Luis de los Franceses in Seville.[182]

The Spanish monarchy organized its own celebrations of the feast thanks to the absorption of members of the Bourbon house. The marriage of Marie-Louise d'Orléans to Charles II of Spain in 1679 would make the feast day an occasion for celebrations in Madrid and Naples during her unhappy decade as queen of Spain.[183] The accession of Philip V brought a Bourbon descendant of Saint Louis onto the Spanish throne and the feast became an occasion on which the Spanish monarchy received the compliments of the court and foreign ministers and enjoyed other celebrations and entertainments.[184] In 1701, soon after Philip's accession, it was celebrated in Cádiz with illuminations and fireworks the night before and, on the feast itself, a high mass sung by multiple choirs, a magnificent dinner and a ballet; all this was accompanied by cries of *Viva el Rey* and *Vive le Roi* 'which made known the perfect union of the two nations', according to the *Gazette*.[185] Saint Louis was also a model of pious kingship in Spain. When he (briefly) abdicated in 1724, Philip V told Luis I (born on 25 August 1707) to 'have always before your eyes the two saint-kings who are the glory of Spain and France, Saint Ferdinand & Saint Louis'.[186]

During the War of the Spanish Succession the feast sometimes acted as a rallying point for the French and Bourbon Spanish forces. The Franciscans in occupied Modena in 1703 turned the portico of their church into a gallery of portraits of the French and Bourbon Spanish royal families and celebrated the mass (attended by all the French officers and a large crowd) with all possible ceremonial and musical magnificence. They received a large French donation, which they used to erect a new altar – dedicated, of course, to Saint Louis.[187] In 1711 in Gerona, the marquis de Brancas (French governor of Gerona and a commander of the Order of Saint-Louis) organized celebrations to show his loyalty to Louis XIV and Philip V including a triumphal arch decorated with the arms of the Spanish and French royal families and topped by an equestrian statue of Saint Louis.[188]

Conclusion

Saint Louis's feast day was not a national holiday in early modern France. The monarchy did not maintain pressure on bishops to add the feast to their calendars, meaning that many simply never followed the instructions of 1618, particularly as they were also being encouraged to decrease the number of feasts in their dioceses. Although it was a major event in Paris, the feast spread very unevenly over the rest of France, depending principally on the enthusiasm of local elites, who might choose to celebrate more as a means of demonstrating loyalty to the crown than out of devotion to the saint. It did become one of the main days in the year in which the reigning king could be celebrated in a mixture of religious and secular festivities, but this depended on specific contexts. Similarly, the dedication of churches and institutions to Saint Louis shows another layer in the patchwork geography of his cult across early modern France and the French colonies, highlighting once more the initiative of corporate groups and local interests. Elites could choose to celebrate Saint Louis's feast or name a hospital or church after him in order to highlight their loyalty to the monarchy or out of gratitude for royal support, thus binding them to the crown in a celebration of sacral monarchy.

Patterns of devotion

O God, who transferred your confessor Saint Louis from the earthly realm to the glory of the kingdom of Heaven, we pray that, by his merits and through the interces- sion of your son Jesus Christ the king of kings, we may share in the same kingdom.[1]

This was the most common prayer for the feast of Saint-Louis and must have been intoned countless times under the Bourbons. It is a reminder that, for all his importance as a political symbol, he was primarily a saint, considered to be watching over his former kingdom from Heaven and therefore a potential object of devotion. Rousselet encouraged the faithful to 'go to the altars of this divine monarch' to solicit his intercession.[2] The primary places where we can assess how many people responded are Saint Louis's relic shrines: the abbey of Saint-Denis, the Sainte-Chapelle and Lamontjoie. In assessing how far he resonated with different levels of French society, it is equally important, given that saints were emphasized as models of virtue during the Catholic Reformation, to consider the aspects of Saint Louis that were presented for emulation in liturgical and devotional texts and visual depictions.

There is little evidence that the cult of Saint Louis was adopted by the majority of the subjects of the Bourbon kings. Just as his feast day was mainly spread by corporate bodies and social elites, he principally appealed to and was explicitly constructed for the higher members of society. The broader population, who did not need to worry about how to reconcile piety with elite status – let alone how to be a good king – did not generally turn to Saint Louis for miracles or solutions to their problems.

Relics and miracles

The stock of relics of Saint Louis at Saint-Denis was slowly chipped away over the centuries, as discussed in Chapter 1. Louis XIV ordered the abbey to relinquish a tooth and part of the jaw to give to one of his allies in the War of the Spanish Succession, Archbishop-Elector Joseph Clemens of Bavaria, in 1707, as well as a relic for his own chapel at Versailles in 1710, as did Louis XV for a new chapel at Versailles in 1768.[3] Nevertheless, the treasury of Saint-Denis still contained Saint Louis's crown, ring, sword and jaw, the latter housed in an ornate reliquary of crystal and silver. The principal *châsse* (reliquary), dating from the sixteenth century, was an ornate object made of gold, silver, enamel and precious stones; in the shape of a church, it was supported by four lions and decorated with *fleurs-de-lys*.[4] The Sainte-Chapelle meanwhile held various objects including Saint Louis's cilice and linen shirt, both contained in small boxes decorated with ivory.[5] Louis XIII offered a casket for the shirt in 1627, and the cilice was described as 'more precious to us than gold and rare stones' in one of the readings for the Office as celebrated at Versailles.[6] Most important was the skull, housed in an enormously elaborate reliquary dating from Philip IV's reign – a golden model of Louis's head covered in precious stones and supported by four angels.[7]

There were thus numerous relics of Saint Louis in the Paris region. Given his renewed importance, it might be expected that the relics once again became the centre of a miracle cult, but in fact they were rarely used. Overall interest in Saint Louis increased after Henri IV came to the throne, yet interest in the relics declined in relation to previous periods. The reliquaries of Saint Louis had featured in processions in Paris at important moments in the sixteenth century, as discussed in Chapter 1. From 1594 they were once more under the monarchy's control and featured prominently in a procession on 29 March, attended by Henri IV, to celebrate the capital's return to obedience a week earlier.[8] Similar processions at significant moments became less frequent over the course of the Bourbon period. In May 1628, to pray for Louis XIII as he besieged the Huguenot stronghold of La Rochelle, the Sainte-Chapelle organized a procession over the Pont Saint-Michel that included the head of Saint Louis (which required six people to carry it).[9] As discussed in Chapter 3, the relics at Saint-Denis were used in 1651 in order to display royal sacrality in the tense context of the Fronde. They were also brought out in procession to pray for the royal family at moments such as Anne of Austria's illness in 1664 and the birth of the dauphin in 1781.[10]

However, these were all extraordinary events. The sources are frustratingly obscure about the use of the relics in 'normal' years. At the Sainte-Chapelle, the feasts of Saint-Louis and the translation of his head were celebrated with importance, as may be expected. Meetings of the chapter were moved from the normal Wednesday or Saturday if 25 August fell on one of these days and canons who requested leave around that time were told they could not depart before 'the Saint-Louis'.[11] An ancient confraternity of boy-messengers of the merchants of Paris (*Garçons-Facteurs des Marchands*) founded by Louis IX and known in the early modern period as the 'Confraternity of Saint-Louis' performed ceremonies in the lower chapel on 25 August to honour and thank its founder. They made contributions for the lower chapel's decoration but there is no indication that their devotions involved the relics of Saint Louis.[12]

A view of how the relics in the upper chapel were used is normally available only when there was a problem or dispute. On 25 August 1659, the scandalized canons held an emergency meeting to deal with a small crisis that had come to their attention just as they were about to set off on the annual procession. Undertaking unilaterally 'an enterprise that cannot be allowed', the Treasurer had decided to include the head reliquary in the procession, an action which went against the chapel's usual customs.[13] The canons did not want to prevent an action which might contribute to public devotion, but objected strongly to the Treasurer's decision to make such an innovation unilaterally. This conflict of authority reveals that the head was *not* normally carried in procession on Saint Louis's feast. In fact, the procession seems to have varied. In

1671 and 1672, it took place within the Palace of Justice, but in 1673 it moved outside, meaning that the inhabitants of the streets along which it would pass had to be warned to hang tapestries in front of their houses. The chapter was concerned not to let slip its prerogative to demand the hanging of tapestries on 25 August, which was shared only with Notre-Dame. A change from 1659 was indicated when the records state 'that the head of Saint Louis will be carried as usual with as much devotion as possible to ask God by the intercession of this great saint that he may conserve the king's person'.[14] This time, it was the Treasurer who objected, asking that the procession be kept within the palace. It is not clear exactly what happened on the feast itself. It may be that the procession of the head had become a regular event, as indicated in 1689 when the canons made arrangements for it to be brought out of the treasury a few days before – but, if so, it did not attract wider interest and was never mentioned in the periodicals.[15] The head was displayed on the altar between the procession and the end of Vespers, as was the case when the exiled James II (also a descendant of Saint Louis) made his devotions at the Sainte-Chapelle on 25 August 1698.[16]

The Sainte-Chapelle exploited its founder's memory in its dealings with the monarchy; in 1674 the canons complained to Louis XIV of the chapel's deplorable state, reminding him 'that the great Saint Louis, founder of this holy church, charged all his successors to maintain and conserve its revenues and privileges'.[17] The message was clearly that the king should follow his ancestor in maintaining the chapel. Nevertheless, the relics of Saint Louis there were frequently overshadowed by those of Christ's Passion, perhaps unsurprisingly given the Christocentrism of early modern Catholicism. It was a fragment of the true cross that Queen Marie-Thérèse sought for the duc d'Anjou in 1672, a gift which the canons unsuccessfully tried to resist by mentioning that Saint Louis had requested his successors not to remove any relics from the Sainte-Chapelle.[18] The relics of Saint Louis never created scenes similar to the cries and convulsions associated with the annual exposition of the true cross on Good Friday.[19] It was the relics of the Passion, not the head of Saint Louis, that Louis XIV ordered to be exposed for the 1690 jubilee and in 1706 (during the octave of the feast of Saint-Louis) to pray for the success of his armies, and it was the fragment of the true cross that Louis XV venerated in 1729 in thanks for the dauphin's birth.[20] There is no indication that any member of the royal family visited or venerated the head of Saint Louis.

On the other hand, at Saint-Denis the relics of Saint Louis were on an equal footing with those of Saint Denis himself. On 26 August 1653, Louis XIV visited, praying before the relics of Saint Louis and receiving a collation in the refectory to the immense pleasure of the monks, pleased to offer it to him in a place formerly honoured by the presence of Louis IX. The *châsse* was placed on the altar of Reims cathedral during Louis XIV's *sacre* in 1654.[21] Louis XV also prayed before the relics of both saints during shortly before his coronation in 1722, as did Queen Marie Leszczyńska during various visits between 1739 and 1767.[22]

When not being carried in procession or venerated on specific occasions, the relics were largely inaccessible to ordinary worshippers from the 1630s. After a fire in 1630, the head reliquary was moved from its home behind the high altar of the Sainte-Chapelle into the sacristy and brought out only for the feast of Saint-Louis. There is no indication whatsoever that it was the focus of a wider devotional cult or pilgrimages.[23] At Saint-Denis the *châsse* had been placed at the high altar until 1633 when the abbey joined the Congregation of Saint-Maur; moved to the treasury until a more fitting location had been prepared, it was brought out only on occasion for the rest of the early modern period.[24] The monks envisaged a more worthy and public solution and drew up proposals for a monument to Saint Louis which would serve also as the mausoleum of the Bourbon house during Louis XIV's reign. Advocating a marble structure including various representations of scenes from Saint Louis's life as well as effigies of all the kings from Hugh Capet to the seventeenth century, this monument would have celebrated Bourbon legitimacy on a scale that would have challenged the grandeur of the Valois tombs. Saint Louis's *châsse* would have been incorporated into the structure, which the writer envisaged placing in the very centre of the church, a focal point where it would be 'in full view of everyone in all its magnificence'.[25]

It was never built. Indeed, in the eighteenth century the monks were still complaining to the monarch that 'some relics, principally those of the glorious Saint Louis, have no location worthy for them to be placed according to their dignity'.[26] This fits into a wider context of requests for greater financial support for the dilapidated abbey; in 1776, the prior wrote to the director of royal buildings recalling the work carried out at the abbey under Louis IX and implying that Louis XVI should do the same.[27] Such appeals were never followed up, however, revealing a certain lack of interest or inclination on the part of successive Bourbon monarchs to make more of Saint Louis's relics or to create funerary monuments as grand as those of earlier kings. Given the immense resources poured into other building projects, it seems unlikely that this was simply a result of budgetary constraints. The Bourbon practice of burying monarchs and their families in the crypt without monuments may have been designed to highlight the unity of the dynasty more strongly than with various tombs for individual rulers.[28] It also reflected a complex relationship between the Bourbon monarchy and the abbey and its patron saint.[29] In the early 1690s Louis XIV signalled a demotion of the abbey by suppressing the title of abbot and transferring its huge revenues to the Maison de Saint-Louis at Saint-Cyr.[30] However, although the lack of interest in Saint Denis may partially explain why the monarchy ignored repeated calls to devote resources to building work at his abbey, it does not explain the apparent lack of enthusiasm for the relics of Saint Louis there or at the Sainte-Chapelle. There was little interest in fostering popular devotion to them, as an effort would otherwise presumably have been made to make them more accessible to pilgrims and miracle seekers or publicize processions.

The monarchy perhaps did not want to encourage this side of the cult because of the uncomfortable gulf between the saint-king and all the other non-canonized French monarchs that might have been opened. Some royal propagandists were clearly aware of the need to minimize potential discrepancies. Charles du Cange wrote that 'Joinville said that Saint Louis was *the greatest king of the Christians*. This is praise which is not particular to this great prince, but common to all the kings of France.'[31] However, Jean-Marie de Vernon developed a clear sense of contrast when he described his feelings seeing the *châsse* of Saint Louis placed on the high altar of Saint-Denis. He denied that Louis IX was being celebrated for having held the sceptre of France for forty-four years, since over sixty other kings were buried and reduced to dust whereas he alone was elevated in a magnificent reliquary. The difference was in the way they had conducted themselves in life:

> If the other Princes had been as humble as he when they lived, they would shine as brightly after their death. The same crown gives the same authority to those who wear it, but it does not lead to the same results for those who have worn it. If royalty found hearts similar to that of Saint Louis, it would make the same number of saints, not because they had been kings but because they had been humble, religious and charitable princes; may they never avoid following in the practice of his piety under the false pretext that it would damage their courage or prevent them from being good rulers.[32]

Rather than sacralizing the monarchy as a whole, Saint Louis's relics and miracles here highlight the contrast between his individual sanctity and the other kings' failure to achieve canonization. If this was the kind of view inspired by contact with the relics, it is perhaps unsurprising that the Bourbons were not keen to encourage it.

Even if the relics were not the focus of pilgrimages and miracles, they could serve as the focus of other kinds of devotion reflecting the elite nature of the cult and Saint Louis's role as an example of virtue for those in positions of power and responsibility. The Sainte-Chapelle was embedded in the Parlement of Paris. Liturgical texts spoke of the importance of the proximity of the head reliquary to the lawyers of the Parlement. Saint Louis's example taught the magistrates

> zeal for the faith, enthusiasm for religion, prudence in government, integrity in conduct, constancy in virtue and everything known to be beneficial for kings and their ministers. For on that account Saint Louis was considered fitting to be present in his palace after death, in order that he might both enlighten the place by his great example and become the protector and advocate of those called there by their affairs.[33]

Saint Louis was so associated with justice that it is hardly surprising the presence of his head so close to the Parlement was seen as appropriate, for example by Vernon, who wrote that 'the memory of the equity of the judgements formerly given by this just and equitable monarch oblige all those who exercise justice to imitate his inviolable integrity'.[34] Even if it was not at the centre of a flourishing miracle cult, the head reliquary still held great meaning as an object symbolizing the nexus of religion and temporal authority and offering a model of exemplary conduct for the *parlementaires*.

At the Leaguer Estates-General of 1593 the deputies of different estates carried the relics of saintly patrons in procession; '*messieurs* of the court of Parlement, [carried] that of Saint Louis, as they are accustomed.'[35] It may be that the association with the magistrates discouraged the crown from making more use of the head of Saint Louis. Instead, the centre of gravity in the royal cult of Saint Louis shifted from Saint-Denis and the Sainte-Chapelle to the Jesuit church of Saint-Louis. The inscription on the foundation stone revealed the royal intention to make this the centre of the new cult: 'Louis XIII built this church in order that France, which revered [Saint Louis] as king and loved him as a father, might venerate him here as an inhabitant of Heaven.'[36] The altarpiece was a painting by Simon Vouet depicting the apotheosis of Saint Louis (a theme favoured by the Jesuits) in which two cherubim present him with the crown of thorns while symbols of his earthly kingship rest at the bottom of the painting.[37] Barbara Gaehtgens has noted that Saint Louis in this image is dressed in a long white vestment – probably the linen shirt conserved at the Sainte-Chapelle. Normally inaccessible to ordinary people, here it was incorporated into a painting prominently displayed above the main altar (Figure 5.1). This she sees as an effort to establish a new centre of Saint Louis's cult which would symbolize the nexus between monarch, saint and Jesuits and, in contrast to the Sainte-Chapelle, would be presented to the widest possible range of people.[38] The Jesuit interest in identifying themselves with the cult of Saint Louis has been noted many times. They were among the few people in the early modern period who publicized contemporary miracles secured by Saint Louis's intercession.

There is a strong contrast between the vibrant miracle cult that flourished in the decades after Louis IX's death and the paucity of recorded miracles in the early modern period. Early hagiographers writing in the late thirteenth century took care to record his miracles, and their texts were made available in printed publications centuries later under the Bourbons. William of Chartres recounted seventeen miracles in which Louis's intercession cured the disabled, mainly fairly lowly people who had travelled to Saint-Denis.[39] William's *vita* was printed in 1617 alongside a 1299 list of twenty-five miracles involving the healing of unwell or infirm people such as the teenager Gillotus Cato who was able to walk after having spent his whole life crawling around on the ground 'like a brutish animal'.[40] Both accounts were also printed in 1649.[41] William of Saint-Pathus's *vita* finished with a detailed list of almost seventy miracles that had been performed thanks to Louis's intercession, solicited by all sorts of people (young and old, men and women, humble and wealthy) at his tomb. This was included in the 1761 edition of Joinville published under the patronage of Louis XV.[42] Miracle accounts such as these had served an obvious purpose in the period between Saint Louis's death and his formal canonization in 1297, namely proving his sanctity and creating enthusiasm for the cult: William of Chartres called them 'a demonstration of the worth and holiness of our aforesaid king'.[43]

The medieval miracles of Saint Louis were remembered in the Bourbon period and invoked in efforts to convert Huguenots. In 1620, a conference was held at Moissac near Toulouse between a Capuchin missionary, Père Hilaire, and the local minister. One of those present, the local *seigneur*, was a Huguenot apparently anxious to uncover the truth of religion. According to a one-sided account printed in Paris, the Capuchin defeated the minister with overwhelmingly superior arguments, at one point producing 'the miracles of Saint Louis, reckoning that the minister would not have the insolence to contradict so many French historians who report them as being true and worthy of memory'. Such stories as those of the child only cured of a mortal illness because his mother was present as the body of Saint Louis was taken to Saint-Denis in 1270, or the girl with a tumour the size of an egg on her ear who was healed when her parents visited the tomb were apparently impossible for the minister to refute and enough to secure the *seigneur*'s conversion to Catholicism.[44]

Figure 5.1 *Saint Louis enlevé au ciel* (1642–3) by Simon Vouet (1590–1649), Musée des Beaux-Arts de Rouen. © Alamy Stock Photo.

It is telling that the Capuchin had to use miracles from the late 1200s to make his case. There were few examples of more recent pilgrims making their way to Saint-Denis to secure Saint Louis's intercession through contact with the *châsse*. Instead, the few seventeenth-century miracles found in printed sources did not centre on relics or involve lowly people but instead concerned Saint Louis's patronage of the religious orders, most notably the Jesuits. After listing Saint Louis's medieval miracles, Rousselet lamented that people often placed more faith in medicine than in the saints, going on to argue that 'this miraculous king is as powerful to help us now as he has ever been'. To prove this, he recounted two stories. The first concerned a Jesuit who fell seriously ill in 1618, deteriorating to the point where in 1625 he barely resembled a living man. Several doctors proved to be of no assistance, but after he read of the miracles of Saint Louis, he started to recite the saint's collect every day and had recovered fully by 25 August 1626. The second miracle was centred on the town of Pontarlier in the Franche-Comté, ravaged by plague in the summer of 1629. A virtuous widow told her Jesuit confessor that when praying before the altar of Saint Louis she had realized that if nine masses were said in his honour, God would save the town. The municipal authorities arranged this and lo, Pontarlier was cured of the plague. The miracle led to masses being said for Saint Louis every year, his image redecorated and his feast celebrated (when people were not occupied with the harvest). Pontarlier was not yet part of France, causing Rousselet to comment excitedly that if *foreigners* were able to receive so much help from this miraculous king, his own subjects could expect no less if only their piety matched that of the Burgundians.[45] In the first of Rousselet's miracles, Saint Louis intervenes on behalf of a sick Jesuit, clearly showing his concern for and patronage of the controversial religious order. In the second, the Jesuit presence in Pontarlier and a pious individual connected to the fathers are crucial to the town being saved from the plague. The fact that the royal saint was intervening in Heaven on behalf of the Society of Jesus fits into a broader context of the Jesuit use of Saint Louis to strengthen their position.

Nevertheless, there is little evidence that anyone took up Rousselet's call to seek miracles from Saint Louis, and his examples are unusual even in the extensive Jesuit literature on Saint Louis. The early modern miracles for which evidence does survive were few and far between. Vernon recounted the recovery of Elizabeth Merault at the Franciscan convent of the Faubourg Saint-Marcel in Paris. The fevers, lethargy and paralysis of this 23-year-old nun were incurable by doctors and her only recourse was to the saints. Saint Louis was popular in the convent and she asked the abbess to make the procession on his feast day pass near her chamber and to have the saint's tunic, held as a relic there, placed on her legs. Praying to Saint Louis as the priest elevated the host during mass on 25 August 1656, 'she felt an extraordinary excitement across her whole body' and began to recover her movement and health. Everyone was amazed when she sprang out of bed and found she could walk with relative ease. The miracle was officially verified in 1657 and her grateful parents paid for the chapel to be decorated with images of Saint Louis.[46]

Interesting as such stories are, they stand as relatively isolated examples and appear in publications attempting to display the royal saint's protection of the religious order in question. Of course, this may be a problem of source survival: common people who prayed to Saint Louis and believed him to have interceded for them were less likely to leave evidence than religious orders with the resources to produce printed accounts. There are some indications of other miracles, including a man in Lyon whose son was cured of scrofula (thus linking the saint's cult to royal sacrality) after touching relics of Saint Louis at the church of the Third Order of Saint Francis at La Guillotière in 1659.[47] One place where it is possible to assess a more popular cult centred on relics of Saint Louis is Lamontjoie in Aquitaine. This was also mediated by the Franciscans, whose convent there was founded by the seigneur de Marin in 1623. The relics were put under the care of the Franciscans, who would keep them at their altar on the condition that they were not transported out of the village and that a quarter of any gifts and offerings made would be given to the local *curé*.[48] In 1646, the *curé* and the Franciscans agreed that the parish would pay for new reliquaries which would then be returned to the care of the convent; on the feast of Saint-Louis, the *curé* was to relinquish the church to the friars for the sum of thirty *livres*.[49] These arrangements left plenty of room for conflict. In 1688 a lawyer in Agen advised that the relics should never have been handed over to the Franciscans and in August 1716 there was an investigation into a dispute between the *curé*, who was demanding his thirty *livres*, and the Franciscans, who argued that the offerings made before the relics at the feast of Saint-Louis belonged to them in entirety.[50]

Such conflict indicates that there was something worth fighting over, and the accounts of the Franciscan convent indeed indicate a steady income. They took 200 *livres* on the feast of Saint-Louis in 1687, 120 in 1689, 105 in 1694, 146 in 1695, 186 *livres* 12 *sous* 6 *deniers* in 1705, 123 *livres* in 1706, 138 in 1709 and 152 *livres* 17 *sous* 3 *deniers* in 1716. The records are not complete enough to chart this income over the whole period, but the consistent taking of 100–200 *livres* on a single day each year in the latter part of Louis XIV's reign was relatively high when set in the context of the convent's income for the rest of the year. Between 8 December 1709 and 24 February 1710, takings were just above 31 *livres*; from then to 17 June, they were just above 142 *livres*; from then to 8 October, they were 245 *livres* 12 *sous* 9 *deniers*, including 117 *livres* for the feast of Saint-Louis.[51]

These financial takings seem to support the statement of a nineteenth-century historian that the relics at Lamontjoie were the focus of popular pilgrimage in the seventeenth century. He observed that numerous miracles were recorded, particularly healing people with ulcers, and that the pilgrims were mainly from local towns but also from Bordeaux, Toulouse, Pau, Tarbes and Marseilles, although unfortunately I found no record of specific miracles or pilgrims.[52] Nevertheless, the offerings do indicate that people were coming to see the seven relics *enchâssées* in gold, including a bust of Saint Louis, as well as a smaller eighth relic that was always kept in the sacristy 'for the commodity of pilgrims and the sick', who were allowed to touch it.[53] The relics were normally brought out on 24 August to be placed on a marble table, with the bust then carried in procession by four men after which it was kissed by the people before being transported to the sacristy, to be brought once more into the church on 25 August. On the feast day it was rubbed with oil to give it more lustre; pilgrims apparently believed that this oil was holy sweat. The *curé* in 1764 reported that the occasion was increasingly marked by irreverent behaviour; men and women were entering the sanctuary, rubbing the bust with their linen, touching it with hats and turning their backs on the Holy Sacrament as they prayed. 'When I wished to oppose myself to these profanations, the religious were the first to spread among the public that I wished to abolish the feast.'[54]

These relics had an important place in the parish identity of Lamontjoie. A concern for their safety was expressed in the decisions to build an iron gate in 1646 and to place them in a niche in the middle of the high altar in 1661, as well as regular inspections up to 1789 by local officials to ensure that they had not suffered any damage under the care of the Franciscans. Repairs to the reliquaries were normally undertaken at the expense of the village rather than the convent, perhaps to underline that they may be under the care of the latter but were still owned by the former.[55] There offerings on the feast day and the presence of a 'confraternity of Saint-Louis and the Virgin' indicate devotion to the saint in this small village far from the centre of the cult in Paris.[56] However, this devotion originated with the foundation of Lamontjoie by Philip IV rather than the restoration of Saint Louis's cult in 1618. Lamontjoie was never mentioned in the printed literature and panegyrics concerning Saint Louis, even in works by Franciscan authors such as Vernon. Either the custodians of the cult in Paris had no interest in acknowledging or promoting this local devotion or they were simply unaware of its existence. When viewed from the perspective of France as a whole, the devotion at Lamontjoie appears to be an exception based on a pre-existing devotion rather than an indication of popular responses to the restoration of the cult in 1618.

Another relic much closer to Paris but still never mentioned in panegyrics was the font at which Saint Louis had been baptized at Notre-Dame-de-Poissy, associated with the curing of fevers. It was so sought out by pilgrims that it was raised on a corbel to conserve it, and in 1685 the walls were decorated with *fleurs-de-lys*.[57] A cartouche of stone and marble surmounted by a statue of Saint Louis contained the text of a Latin inscription written in 1650 as a votive offering by Nicolas Mercier of Poissy, a member of the Collège de Navarre. This proclaimed that if someone burning with fever were to take a shaving of dust in a small cup, their sickness would soon be alleviated. 'O nature, admire: the order of things is overthrown, now stone extinguishes flames just like a wave (*O Natura stupe; Rerum pervertitur ordo:/ Extinguit flammas nunc, velut unda lapis*).' It is impossible to say how many people sought such a miracle, but according to an eighteenth-century source it happened several times.[58] Poissy prided itself as the birthplace of Louis IX. The municipal authorities wrote to Louis XIV of their devotion to his ancestor while reminding him of tax privileges granted by Henri III in honour of Poissy's link to Louis IX, a striking example of how a local community could mix devotion to their patron with more practical concerns.[59] The town's enormous Dominican monastery housed a relic of Saint Louis given in 1351.[60] The common belief was that its high altar was on the exact site of the bed in which Blanche of Castile had given birth to Saint Louis.[61] However, a vicious argument erupted in the periodicals after a 1735 dissertation by the Parisian advocate Maillart argued that Saint Louis was not born in Poissy but rather in La Neuville-en-Hez near Beauvais, which was met with a sharp rebuttal by the Dominican Matthieu Texte. Texte made much of the fact that Saint Louis liked to style himself 'Louis de Poissy', but as his opponents pointed out, 'Jesus of Nazareth' was born in Bethlehem. The importance of the acrimonious and erudite debate that ensued was not just that the barrage of arcane evidence held interest for the readership of the *Mercure*.[62] The debate over Louis IX's birthplace seemed to rouse real passion and it does seem that designation as the birthplace of Saint Louis carried immense prestige. One possible (though unstated) concern may have been that the possible demotion of the monastery would bring a decline in visitors and revenue.

Liturgy

The themes emphasized in liturgical texts are revealing of perceptions of Louis's sanctity and the types of devotion directed towards him. Readings and hymns for the canonical hours emphasized his combination of personal piety with royal status, valour and excellence of government, themes that chimed particularly well with the monarchy and other elites. Except for his concern for the poor and sick, which mostly served as an example of charity for elites, much of the focus on kingship probably held little of relevance for most ordinary people.

Condensed summaries of Louis's life appeared as lessons or readings in the office. In the Paris Breviary of 1640, the first of three readings emphasized the religiosity of Louis's rule: governing with custom and dignity, 'he was praised as parent of the people, prince of the nobles, guardian of the laws and true king of France'. The whole of the next lesson narrated his first crusade and stay in the Holy Land. The third began with his return to France, where he devoted himself to pious works such as building monasteries and hospitals. 'He frequently visited the poor, to whom he not only made available all his wealth but even . . . ministered with his hands.' After mentioning his austere dress and self-mortification, the lesson finished with his death and mentioned that his remains were at Saint-Denis ('not far from the city').[63] Appearing in other office texts that followed the usage of Paris,[64] though sometimes condensed into one reading,[65] the readings had changed by the 1720s. Into the first reading were inserted lines on the defeat of the Albigensians, the eradication of duelling and Louis's love of justice and concern only to appoint virtuous people to office, themes common in panegyrics. The third included the story of Louis saving his boat from shipwreck on the way back from the crusade by praying before the Eucharist and also mentioned his abstinence from conjugal relations during periods of penitence and on feast days.[66] Thus the lessons gave not only a condensed narrative of his life but also emphasized some common themes: the centrality of piety and justice to Louis IX's kingship, resulting from his education by Blanche and manifested in his zeal on crusade and concern for the poor, and the rigour of his own personal piety. These themes were expanded in some of the lections for the octave of his feast, which gave more detail on his personal piety and often also included a reading of the complete *Enseignements* over six lessons.[67] The combination of piety with an active life in the lay world (and particularly the elite lay world) would be the major theme of Louis's sanctity in this period.

Hymns also conveyed the narrative of Saint Louis's life. *Rex summe regum* was the most popular, appearing in Vespers and Matins in numerous sources.[68] It included many of the themes from the readings. The second stanza dealt with his high birth, early accession and pious education. The third listed the characteristics of his rule: 'Strict cultivator of justice, he governs his towns with laws, his subjects with love and his enemies with fear (*Justi severus cultor, urbes legibus,/Amore cives continens, hostes metu*).'[69] *O qui prona hominum vota capessitis* and *Templa nunc dument*, both sung at Vespers, had verses on Louis's good government, absolute devotion to God and military triumphs.[70] References to the crusades and a strongly militaristic spirit are prevalent in other hymns. *Te sancte rursus Ludovice prælia*, sung at Lauds, begins with God calling Louis to fight, which he did for the sake of Christ; Heaven took away victory on earth but gave it to him in the stars. The third verse mentioned Louis's relics protecting the kingdom and imagined the saint looking down from Heaven.[71] It is hard to know how such verses were perceived, particularly in terms of what connections may have been made to the reigning king. Normally unstated but perhaps implicitly understood, such connections were sometimes made more explicit. In a manuscript collection of hymns translated by Charles Perrault, an extra verse to *Rex summe regum* was added asking God to 'make that this holy king live in his successors'.[72] In 1701, Louis XIV was presented with a verse translation of the Office of Saint Louis; the translator made clear in his dedicatory poem that 'When I render homage to [Saint Louis's] immortal glory/I render homage to your virtue'.[73]

The bulk of the canonical hours consisted of the chanting of psalms, but a host of antiphons surrounded them with references to the royal saint. As can be seen in the antiphons for the first Vespers in a liturgy from 1688, these could be either explicit (the antiphon for psalm 109 began 'Louis accepted the rod of virtue sent from Sion') or implicit (the antiphon for psalm 111 stated 'he gave to the poor, his justice remains forever').[74] When Saint Louis was not explicitly named it is easy to imagine that there was a certain amount of perceived overlap between liturgical praise of the saint and praise of the reigning king, as was the case in other media. This is evident in many of the antiphons used at Versailles, which praised the ruler's justice and virtue.[75] However, other prayers expressed faith specifically in Saint Louis, sometimes addressing him directly: 'Saint Louis, glory of kings, pray for us that we might be gathered into the splendours of the saints in Heaven'.[76]

For all the importance of the liturgical offices, it was, however, mass that people were obliged to attend when Saint Louis's feast was *chômée*. Important saints had prayers and readings dedicated to them in the variable part of the mass, the proper (introit, gradual, alleluia/tract, sequence, offertory and communion), as well as the 'minor proper', namely the priests' prayers of collect, secret and postcommunion. Several prayers specifically addressing Saint Louis were inserted into the standard structure of the ordinary, beseeching God for the same virtues that he had shown so that those praying might ultimately follow him to Heaven. A common 'secret' prayer (said by the priest in a low voice at the end of the Offertory) began 'O Lord, grant your servants, who offer you these gifts, the same firmness of spirit that you gave to Saint Louis'.[77] The hope that, 'as Saint Louis your confessor denied the pleasures of the world and sought only to please Christ the King, we might be made more acceptable to you through his prayers', found in another Secret, includes the idea of Saint Louis's intercession as well as the example of his piety.[78] This prayer was used at the Chapel Royal on 25 August.

The most substantial piece of text devoted to Saint Louis during the mass was the Prose or Sequence, a liturgical hymn sung between the Gradual and the Gospel. *Christe Regum Imperator* consists of twenty-six verses covering the life and virtues of Saint Louis, including his crusades, pious foundations, justice and concern for the poor as well as an exhortation for the former king, now in Heaven, to look down on France.[79] Militaristic imagery was predominant in other Prose texts. *Quotquot Dei militae* told Louis that as an 'excellent prince in peace, you establish the maxims of law; as a great leader in war, you flee from no dangers' (*Tu pace Princeps optimus,/Legum firmas oracula:/Tu bello Dux magnanimus,/Nulla fugis pericula*).[80] It went on to praise him for his bravery, concern for his soldiers, and desire to combat the enemies of the faith. The Prose in the liturgy used at the Salpêtrière, printed in 1767, began 'the enemy rises up in vain: Louis reigns in Heaven' before expanding on his concern for the poor and devotion to the service of the lowliest of his subjects. These were expanded along the lines of late-eighteenth century paternalistic imagery in the accompanying French translation to include lines proclaiming that, in his tenderness, Louis 'believed he had found a son' in the lowliest of his subjects.[81]

Surviving standalone editions of the office include copies for the diocese of Paris,[82] the royal court at Versailles,[83] the Invalides[84] and the Salpêtrière,[85] to which can be added the most devoted publishers of the Office of Saint Louis, the Parisian company of merchant haberdashers and jewellers.[86] Magnificent and richly decorated manuscript copies of the chants for Saint Louis's feast were created for royal institutions such as the Invalides, for which an enormous volume filled with illuminations of Saint Louis was made in 1719.[87] Copies of the Office of Saint Louis often included French translations that helped people follow the mass. A slim volume containing the Office in Latin and French according to the usage of Paris was beautifully written in red and black ink in 1728, with a dedication to the duchesse de Noailles enumerating the qualities of Saint Louis (humility among success, patience and penitence in misfortune, 'tender and compassionate charity which went as far as serving the poor with his own hands') all of which were little known to the '*grands du monde*' but which were visible in the duchess's own conduct and in that of her husband the duke and their offspring.[88] Here we see Saint Louis used as a model of elite piety; the surviving copies of the Office reflect the geographical and social limitations of the cult in Bourbon France.

A saint for the *grands*

The compatibility of piety with an active life in lay society was a key concern in seventeenth-century French Catholicism. In his immensely influential *Introduction to the devout life* (1608), François de Sales (bishop of Geneva, future saint himself and a hugely important figure in the French Catholic Reformation) presented 'the great Saint Louis' as an example of someone who maintained devotion in a situation very different to that of the monastic life, saying he could not admire enough the saint-king's fondness for visiting hospitals and serving the poor.[89] De Sales also used Saint Louis's example to show that innocent and joyful recreations were compatible with devotion, even invoking him in a discussion of the 'caresses truly amorous but chaste, tender but sincere' that can preserve conjugal love. The extent to which de Sales was prepared to incorporate piety into secular life did have some limits. Music and hunting were harmless but dancing and betting potentially dangerous, and he mentioned approvingly the story of Louis IX throwing dice and money into the sea when he found his brother gambling. Although far from the only saint discussed in this work, Saint Louis was prominent; his life was recommended reading as it was one of those 'which give more light for the conduct of our life than others'. De Sales told his reader to pray to Louis, whom he described as watching and encouraging from Heaven alongside the Virgin and other important saints. Anticipating the complaint that people would not be able to fit devout practices into their lives, he countered with the example of a saint who with unequalled care administered justice, handled affairs, heard two masses a day . . . visited hospitals every Friday, confessed and received discipline, heard sermons very frequently . . . and with all that there never was a single occasion for the external public good that he did not do and perform diligently.[90]

Given that he viewed Saint Louis as 'worthy of being followed in the art of successfully leading courtiers to the devout life', as he wrote in the *Treatise on the Love of God*, it is unsurprising that de Sales gave Saint Louis as a model for emulation to specific individuals. In October 1604 he wrote to another future saint, Jeanne de Chantal, telling her to admire Saint Louis, who did not commit a mortal sin during his four decades as king and was constant in faith to the end despite the circumstances of his death. 'I give you this saint as your special patron for all of this year.'[91] In 1610 he wrote to Chantal's teenage son Celse-Bénigne (future father of Madame de Sévigné), asking him to

imagine that you were a courtier of Saint Louis: he loved, this saint-king . . . when people were brave, courageous, generous . . . and nevertheless, he especially loved when they were good Christians. And if you had been near him, you would have seen him laugh amiably on occasions, speak boldly when necessary, take care that all surrounding him was in lustre, like another Solomon, to maintain royal dignity; and, one moment later, serve the poor in hospitals, and finally marry civil with Christian virtues, and majesty with humility. This, in one word, is what you must undertake, to be no less brave for being Christian, no less Christian for being brave.[92]

These words show just how much Joinville's account had become embedded in perceptions of the saint since its rediscovery in the sixteenth century. Saint Louis clearly provided a strong precedent showing successful combination of devotion with life in the temporal sphere. Many such statements can be found in the pious literature of the age, particularly among the Jesuits. In *Easy Devotion*, Pierre Le Moyne used Saint Louis to show the harmlessness of hunting in a section proving that '*divertissements*' were not at all contrary to devotion.[93] For Bourdaloue, 'Saint Louis was on earth a great king and a great saint; one can therefore be a saint in all the states and conditions of the world'.[94] The idea clearly rubbed off on some people. James II was presumably thinking of Saint Louis and Edward the Confessor in 1690 when, in a letter to the abbot of La Trappe, he wrote that the history of France and England showed it was possible 'to be saint and king at the same time'.[95]

This of course meant that people could not use their condition as an excuse for living impiously. Rousselet asked Saint Louis 'what excuse can those excessive spirits have to cover up the intemperance of their pleasures, seeing you live amid the delights of the court like an archangel in the celestial court'.[96] Such ideas would be repeated endlessly by panegyrists. The preacher at the Jesuit church of Saint-Louis on 25 August 1681 aimed to show that 'the secret mortifications of penitence can be made to accord with the exterior pomp of royalty, that one can be chaste and restrained amidst pleasures', regarding this primarily as a lesson for the *grands*.[97] Life in elite society and especially the court was regarded as dangerous to salvation, making Saint Louis's achievement all the more remarkable, and the attention of preachers was often focused on the top of society. The poor do appear, but mainly as objects of the charity that should be demonstrated by the *grands*. Ségaud told the poor and afflicted that 'the imitators of Saint Louis must not only love you like him, but also, by his example, seem similar to you, that is, devout, humble, patient, mortified, simple, innocent'; the rich and powerful, however, would come to recognize 'that you are wrong to complain of the oppositions between your state and sanctity' when they considered the example of Saint Louis.[98]

Saint Louis was commonly associated with charity and devotion to the poor, prominent themes in seventeenth-century piety (as reflected, for example, in the activities of the Company of the Holy Sacrament).[99] His one appearance in a massive work from 1614 by a Parisian Capuchin was in the section on humility; his washing the feet of the poor was something 'that all Frenchmen can read, and kings imitate'.[100] He was also an inspiration for Vincent de Paul, who co-founded the Daughters of Charity with Louise de Marillac in 1633.[101] In de Paul's letters to Marillac in the early 1630s he emphasized that Saint Louis found interior peace even after failing to achieve what he had hoped on crusade; seeking to conquer the Holy Land, he instead conquered himself. The remarkable thing about Saint Louis's life was 'the tranquillity with which he returned from the Holy Land without having succeeded according to his design'. On various occasions from the 1630s to 1650s Vincent also recommended the example of Saint Louis to the Daughters, saying they should take him as an intercessor and dangling before them the possible ultimate rewards of their charity with such lines as 'my daughters, did not Saint Louis serve the poor at the Hôtel-Dieu in Paris with such great humility that it contributed to his sanctification?' In a sermon delivered on 25 August 1655 he prayed that God might 'make us participants in the spirit of Saint Louis, this great king who so loved the poor, this great king who had so disciplined a spirit'.[102] Pierre de Bérulle, an important influence on Vincent and responsible for introducing the Oratorians to France, used the charitable foundations and activities of Saint Louis to show his priests that good works speak in a more animated way than actual words.[103] For these key figures in the French Catholic Reformation, Saint Louis was an inspiring model of action and charity.

The focus on charity to the poor is also prominent in one of the first works on Saint Louis to appear after the elevation of the feast, the poetic version of his life by the Franciscan François de Sarcé, given its approbation in December 1618. Sarcé privileged the austerities and charity of Saint Louis, themes that would appeal to a mendicant.

This devout king and charitable prince	*Ce Roy devotieux & Prince charitable*
Invited every evening three poor people to his table,	*Invitoit tous les soirs trois pauvres à sa table,*
To whom, most often by his royal hand,	*Ausquels le plus souvent de sa Royalle main*

He gave meat and broke bread:	*Il donnoit la viande, & leur rompoit le pain:*
In what the worldly would be ashamed to do,	*En ce que les mondains auroient honte de faire*
This great king presents to them a perfect example.	*Ce grand Roy leur presente un parfaict exemplaire.*

Going on to describe Saint Louis washing the feet of the poor and building hospitals, Sarcé argued that actions of humility in serving the lowly did not in any way demean royal birth but was in fact required by it. This could apply equally to other elites. Unsurprisingly, he also privileged discussion of the 'two luminous torches' that established themselves in France during Louis IX's reign – the Dominicans and Franciscans – taking care to note Louis's patronage and support for the mendicants against their critics.[104] As usual, writers linked Saint Louis to their own interest groups.

For Sarcé, Saint Louis's devotion to the poor was foremost an example of the importance of charity and humility most relevant to those at the top of society. The same is true of *The holy and glorious monarch*, published early in Louis XIV's reign by Louis Forget, a canon of the cathedral of Tours. His dedicatory letter to Anne of Austria stated that the virtues of Saint Louis were so perfect as to be incomprehensible for those not in his position of merit and dignity. 'These are matters proper to the thought of princes to whom the eminence and glory of royalty gives notions above the spirit of inferior people.' The insistence that the regent was, by virtue of her position, better able to understand the significance of Saint Louis and more worthy of praising him than ordinary people was no doubt a mixture of genuine belief in the superiority of royal persons and the laudatory fawning typical of dedicatory letters. But it does suggest that Forget conceived Saint Louis principally as a model of ideal royal behaviour, of most relevance for the elites. Most of the book is concerned with the importance of charity. Saint Louis resolved to help the poor all his life, and of course the example of the prince was critical in inspiring similar actions from his subjects. Forget noted that Louis imitated Jesus in washing the feet of the poor and argued against the notion that by eating daily with three paupers at his table the saint-king was somehow contravening a natural order in which he should have dined with great lords. Service to the poor should clearly be more admirable than high status according to Forget; whereas Agrippina was admired for being mother, daughter, sister and wife of emperors, France had more reason to admire a king who was 'the father and servant of the poor'.[105]

Although Saint Louis in his piety and charity was generally constructed as a model for elites, some writers and preachers were more inclusive. The Jesuit Jacques Vignier published a life of Saint Louis in 1642 arguing that 'everyone can profit from this history'; not just the *grands* and the *mondains* but the common people, who would be encouraged in their miseries by the companionship of such a king.[106] Some preachers tried to make Saint Louis relevant to a wider constituency. In his 1694 panegyric, the Abbé Estor described him as 'leaving examples of humility to the great, submission to the ordinary, moderation to soldiers, contemplation to recluses, equity to judges, constancy to the misfortuned, perhaps a model of sanctification to everyone'.[107] The Abbé Cappeau described Louis in his charitable foundations 'where the poor find a father, the blind a guide, the ignorant a master . . . and virgins a defender'.[108] The idea that he had something to offer the lowly and misfortunate was also evident in the prayers that ended Clovis Eve's publication of 1610, which stated that Louis was the light of the blind, defender of the oppressed, scourge of the wicked: 'O Saint Louis . . . have pity on your people.'[109]

Nevertheless, the main focus of the prayers that typically concluded a panegyric of Saint Louis was the monarchy; panegyrics of saints traditionally finished with an exhortation for all to follow a Christian life but those to Saint Louis turned into a prayer for the king.[110] In Rome in 1648 Léon de Saint-Jean (Jean Macé) prayed for peace, for the church and pope and then 'particularly' for France, the royal family and the king.[111] In 1691, Montelet prayed that Saint Louis would live in everyone's hearts but singled out that of Louis the Great, whom he said the saint loved and watched over from Heaven.[112] The panegyrics played an important role in the public affirmation of the king's link to his patron saint, so it is unsurprising that this theme was generally favoured in the prayers, and that the body of the text was used to exhort those in elite positions to follow the saint in his piety.

As an example of the compatibility between life in the temporal sphere and active piety, Saint Louis chimed with the spirit of Catholic Reform. Tricoire has identified the transition from the eschatological anguish of the sixteenth century, when there was great emphasis on condemnation of worldly life, to a more optimistic piety centred on the universal hierarchy of divine love in the seventeenth century as a key development in the spirituality of this period.[113] It is worth remembering, however, that other strands of devotion were far less willing to accommodate piety with active life in the world. The Jansenists were the greatest opponents of the project of reconciling devotion with normal life in society, arguing that the conditions that were easiest to live in according to the world (wealth, power) were most difficult according to God, and on the contrary the religious life was easiest according to God but the hardest according to the world. Charles Hersent's controversial 'Jansenist' panegyric presented an ascetic and unworldly Saint Louis. He noted that Louis 'was touched by a very strong desire to abstain entirely by leaving worldly life and changing his royal purple into a religious habit'.[114] This drew on Geoffrey of Beaulieu's remark that Louis IX wished to become a mendicant, an awkward point for those presenting him as a model of saintly living in lay society.

However, in practice Jansenists also used Saint Louis to encourage piety in laypeople of high social status. The letters of Mère Angélique Arnauld of Port-Royal to Marie-Louise of Poland are revealing in this regard. Since the pronoun Marie was reserved for the Virgin in Poland, the queen took Louise to signal her descent from the saint and her French origins.[115] As her patron and ancestor as well as a model of royal behaviour, Saint Louis appears regularly in the letters. In June 1646, Angélique encouraged the queen to show charity to the poor, which would allow her to pass 'like your ancestor the very great Saint Louis, from the terrestrial to celestial realms'. On 23 August 1652 Angélique told Marie-Louise that the nuns of Port-Royal would pray for her on Saint Louis's day; elsewhere she called him 'your father in bodily birth and spiritual regeneration' and repeated several times that François de Sales and the Abbé de Saint-Cyran, a leading early Jansenist, had regarded Louis as one of the greatest saints. Such statements often provided opportunities to exhort the queen to emulate the saint's charity, justice and humility. As Angélique wrote in late August 1653,

Saint Louis sacrificed all his grandeur to God so perfectly that his life cannot be read without astonishment, and it is so admirable and convincing for the *grands* that one would not dare to write it in this time when corruption is so horrible that one can only see the truth when disguised. However, Madame, God never changes, and he judges those who die at this time as he did in past centuries.

For Angélique, therefore, Saint Louis was a light showing the *grands* how to behave in a dark and corrupt century. In 1655 she told Marie-Louise that God was preparing her to emulate him. Alluding to the Swedish invasion of that year, Angélique stated that God tested his 'elect' with hardship and adversity, for example rewarding the crusades of Saint Louis not with success but with the defeat and imprisonment that only served to make him more holy.[116] In this context, the Jansenist Saint Louis was not dissimilar to the standard presentation of a model of exemplary piety and charity particularly applicable to the *grands*.

Uncovering the extent to which less elevated people took note of the example of Saint Louis is hard. He was not a major figure in the popular publications known as the *bibliothèque bleue*. Robert Mandrou's study of this literature does not mention him even in sections considering the lives of saints and tales of the crusades.[117] Where he does appear it is as the royal patron. A prayer in a mid-eighteenth-century devotional publication asked God to conserve 'the house of Saint Louis . . . and ensure that his children imitate his faith and all his virtues'.[118] In the sixteenth century Saints Denis and Geneviève were invoked for the monarchy and Paris but did not inspire much individual or personal devotion.[119] Saint Louis seems in many ways a similar case: none of these three 'national' saints figure in Pierre Chaunu's list of saints commonly invoked in Parisian testaments of the period.[120] Where Saint Louis does appear (as in the testaments of Jeanne Pastoureau in 1693 and Nicolas Paris in 1720) it is merely as the patron of their parish church.[121] Both of these cases come from Saint-Louis-en-l'Île; even there, there was no mention of specific devotion to Saint Louis in a long list of foundations and mass endowments from 1642 to 1749.[122] Michel Vovelle's exhaustive study of wills and testaments in eighteenth-century Provence threw up one isolated invocation of Saint Louis from a sample of testaments of confraternity members from the 'notable' class between 1680 and 1720.[123]

People named Louis had a bond to Saint Louis, and the periodicals printed a number of *bouquets* celebrating those whose *fête* was 25 August.[124] In 1748 the chevalier d'Andigné, captain of the regiment of Piedmont, received a poem mentioning his zeal for the feast and the fact that he desired membership of the Order of Saint-Louis ('You desire to wear the cross of your pious patron, the holiest of our kings').[125] Jean-Philippe Rameau's *Cantata for Saint Louis's day*, probably composed in the 1730s for someone at the prince of Carignano's residence (perhaps his son Louis Victor), celebrates the 'beautiful name of Louis, a name given by Heaven to virtue'. The text, possibly by Voltaire, invokes Flore and Cloris rather than Saint Louis. Celebration of 25 August with such pagan themes is a reminder that it was not exclusively a festival of sacralized monarchy and could be entirely divorced from the saint himself.[126] In any case, only a small number of people were personally linked to Saint Louis by name. 'Louis' accounted for only 4 per cent of the Provence testaments studied by Vovelle and was, in general, not a popular choice in eighteenth-century France, limiting the extent to which the royal saint was invoked as a personal saintly patron.[127]

Individuals named Louis also had an obvious interest in commissioning images of the saint. Statues of Saint Louis were made for the family chapel of Cardinal Louis-Antoine de Noailles at Notre-Dame and the château of Louis Sextius Jarente de La Bruyère, bishop of Orléans. In the 1770s, Jean-Joseph Foucou made bas-reliefs of scenes from Saint Louis's life for the chapel of Château Borély in Marseilles, owned by the businessman Louis-Joseph Borély.[128] Poorer people obviously did not have the resources to commission iconographic cycles for their private chapels, but they might have purchased the cheaper images of saints that were common in the period. A print produced by Jean-Baptiste Letourmy (a specialist in woodblock prints and chapbooks) in Orléans in the 1770s or 1780s shows Saint Louis in royal robes and eighteenth-century breeches, with a prayer imploring this 'glorious friend of God' to 'pray for us'.[129]

It is the images in churches and hospitals which offer the clearest window into how the saint was represented to, and perhaps perceived by, ordinary people. Images of Saint Louis were relatively common in early modern French churches.[130] They sometimes appear in locations geographically and culturally far removed from the court and Paris. The baptistery of the church of Guimiliau in Brittany, dating from 1675, possesses a wooden statue of Saint Louis with the features of Louis XIV. Such images of royal iconography were often not court commissions produced as a result of the 'politics of glory' developed under Louis XIV but rather produced in an environment not controlled by the state, as shown by Géraldine Lavieille's detailed analysis of an altarpiece at La Forêt-Fouesnant, Brittany, dating from the 1680s. Painted for the Confraternity of the Rosary instituted by the Dominicans in 1683, it includes Saint Louis who, holding the crown of thorns, precedes Louis XIV; facing members of the ecclesiastical hierarchy in a way that suggests equality before God rather than the mediation of the clergy, they kneel in adoration of the Virgin. Lavieille shows that there was collective responsibility for this iconography, involving the Dominicans, the bishop of Quimper (who may have requested the inclusion of the king to emphasize his loyalty and connections to the royal family), and the *fabrique* of the church; the incorporation of the imagery of royal sacrality was a result of their initiative rather than royal power. She links Saint Louis's presence to his association with the rosary and notes that the painting was for the predominantly rural public who joined the confraternity[131].

Saint Louis was almost invariably depicted draped in blue coronation robes decorated with *fleurs-de-lys* and holding his accessories, the crown of thorns and the nails that had pinned Jesus to the cross. His devotion to the crown of thorns was a regular theme and associated him (and the French monarchy) with the kingship of Christ. Charles Le Brun painted a much-reproduced image of the saint kneeling before it, his eyes closed in deep contemplation (Figure 5.2). An engraving of this (now lost) painting, presented to the king, was accompanied with the comment 'he elevated himself in abasing himself thus': in other words, the profound piety of Saint Louis was entirely compatible with his dignity as king. It is worth noting that the Le Brun original hung in the chapel of the château of Villeneuve-le-Roi, home of Louis XIV's minister Claude Le Peletier. Once again, devotion to Saint Louis served to reinforce and express a relationship of loyalty and dependence between

Figure 5.2 *Qu'il s'élevoit en s'abaissant ainsy* by Gérard Edelinck (1640–1707) after Charles Le Brun (1619–90). © Alamy Stock Photo.

the crown and its elites. Similarly, Saint Louis was represented at the church in the marquis de Vauban's seigneurie of Bazoches in Bourgogne, perhaps as a recognition of royal patronage. In this painting, Saint Louis and the titular saint of the church, Saint Hilaire, stand on either side of Jesus on the cross. Churches as far and wide as Saint-Saturnin of Sos (Lot-et-Garonne), Saint-Geniès of Cesseras (Hérault) and Saint-Martin of Jaleyrac (Cantal) also contain crucifixion scenes featuring Saint Louis alongside the titular of the church. He may have been included as a 'national' saint, especially when there was no benefactor named Louis or a double dedication of a church, although, as we have seen, his cult was far too patchy for these examples to be viewed as representing a trend.[132]

Saint Louis was frequently depicted demonstrating charity. Paintings at Saint-Nicolas-des-Champs, Paris, and Sainte-Savine, Champagne, show him dispensing alms and washing the feet of the poor. Eustache Le Sueur painted a particularly magnificent canvas on this theme in 1654–5 for the altar of Saint Louis at the Benedictine abbey of Marmoutiers near Tours, drawing on the Salesian theme of serving the poor and

Figure 5.3 *Saint Louis pansant les malades* (1654) by Eustache Le Sueur (1616–55). © Musée des Beaux-Arts de Tours.

sick. The king is draped in his coronation robe and has his crown and sceptre held in the background. Despite these symbols of royal authority, Saint Louis is shown in a position of total humility, kneeling before a Christ-like sick man whose foot he washes.[133] His face thin and sallow, he regards the man's foot with the same expression of devotion, humility and piety that he displayed to the crown of thorns in Le Brun's painting (Figure 5.3).

How were such paintings viewed in the seventeenth century? Were they primarily visual reminders to the *grands* and wealthy of their obligation to charity and humility, as enunciated in the panegyrics and other literature concerning Saint Louis? Or did they foster a sense of affinity with the saint among those who either needed or received this charity? The panegyrist Guillaume de Saint-Martin called it glorious and admirable that a great king could serve the poor at his table, sometimes eat their leftovers, and wash, dry and

factors motivating recourse to the saints, it is perhaps unsurprising that a figure who exemplified ideal royal conduct was of less relevance than one who removed tumours from peoples' ears, a service Louis had formerly provided.[145] Thus the limited interest in relics and miracles is revealing both in terms of tensions in the cult as an effective vehicle for royal representation and sacralization and in terms of the limitations of the ability of the symbols of Bourbon monarchy to foster loyalty among the majority of people living under the *Ancien Régime*.

A genuinely popular cult did not develop around Saint Louis and in general he was constructed as a saint whose example held most relevance for those trying to combine pious activity with life in high society. His political resonances made him a useful saint for religious orders and other interest groups to align with but not necessarily a saint who sparked fervent devotion across French society. Yet whatever the weaknesses of Saint Louis's cult, this was the period in which he was promoted most strongly as an object of emulation and veneration. He did resonate with elites in the period, earning him a significant niche in the devotional life of Catholic Reformation France. What remains to be seen is how he fared during the intellectual, religious and political transformations of the eighteenth century.

Saint Louis in the age of Enlightenment and Revolution, 1715–92

By 1715, celebration of Saint Louis had become a routine part of the culture of the Bourbon monarchy. Over the following decades he continued to receive regular praise, new foundations bearing his name and a prime place in princely education. Although the contrast between his virtue and the behaviour of Louis XV made the panegyrics increasingly awkward, Saint Louis was still the patron of the monarchy and exemplar of kingship. However, from the 1750s the consensus around Saint Louis started to break down.

Although the idea of a secular Enlightenment has long dominated interpretations of this period, Catholicism remained a vibrant force in eighteenth-century France.[1] As 'enemies of the *philosophes*' took to the public sphere to defend religion, Saint Louis became a focus of argument.[2] The crusades, so lauded in the seventeenth century, became harder to justify, let alone praise, for people imbued with eighteenth-century sensibilities. However, as panegyrists wrestled with that very challenge, turning their sermons into a battlefield between *philosophes* and anti-*philosophes*, fewer people in wider society were taking any notice at all. Henri IV emerged to take the place of the ideal monarch as Saint Louis's cult lost some of its power to glorify the monarchy and bind elites to their king, contributing to the disintegration of the shared sympathies that held the *Ancien Régime* together.

Patron of the monarchy

Dynastic continuity continued to loom large in references to Saint Louis under Louis XV. Perhaps surprisingly, one of the most notable expressions of this theme was penned by none other than Voltaire in his *Henriade*, an epic poem about Henri IV that first appeared in 1723 and regularly revised and reprinted in the eighteenth century. While besieging Paris in 1589, Henri orders his soldiers to bring iron and fire to the proud walls of the city. At this moment appears a 'bright spirit' with eyes filled with tenderness and horror, telling Henri not to pillage the heritage of his ancestors or cut the throats of his subjects. With a voice louder than thunder, the spirit introduces himself:

I am that fortunate king that France reveres,	*Je suis cet heureux roi que la France révère,*
The father of the Bourbons, your protector, your father;	*Le père des Bourbons, ton protecteur, ton père;*
The Louis who formerly fought like you,	*Ce Louis qui jadis combattit comme toi,*
The Louis whose faith your heart has neglected,	*Ce Louis dont ton cœur a négligé la foi,*
The Louis who pities you, admires you and loves you.[3]	*Ce Louis qui te plaint, qui t'admire et qui t'aime.*

Saint Louis says that Henri will enter Paris as a victor – but that he needed to display clemency rather than valour. It is thus Louis's saintly intervention that transforms Henri from a bloodthirsty conqueror into a tolerant and magnanimous king. Struck by this awesome encounter, Henri retires to Vincennes to the oak tree where Louis formerly dispensed justice.

In a scene reminiscent of Pierre Le Moyne's poem, Voltaire describes Saint Louis showing Henri his posterity down to Louis XV, providing the opportunity for many platitudes on the morality of kingship: 'It is not much to be a hero, a conqueror, a king;/If Heaven does not enlighten you, it has done nothing for you' (*C'est peu d'être un Héros, un Conquérant, un Roi,/Si le Ciel ne t'éclaire, il n'a rien fait pour toi*). The point is reinforced in Hell, where Louis shows Henri tyrants being punished for their crimes, and Heaven, where great monarchs from Charlemagne to Louis XII live in joy. Saint Louis points out that the primary virtue of these kings was their love for the church. 'Their religion was mine; why have you left it?' (*Leur culte était le mien; pourquoi l'as-tu quitté?*)[4] He also intervenes during various other episodes leading to Henri's eventual triumph over the Catholic League, including an appearance before God himself to argue on Henri's behalf. God listens and sends Truth to help Henri denounce heresy; Louis himself leads his descendant into Paris. This is far from the better-known Voltaire of '*ecrasez l'infâme*'. Like many poets who wrote about Saint Louis, Voltaire hoped to win royal favour with this work. Although the dedication to Louis XV was not accepted in the end because the poem was suspected of containing heresy, it is notable that, even for a writer so associated later with criticism of religion, Saint Louis was still the dynastic patron and model of kingship par excellence in the early eighteenth century.

At one point, Voltaire's Saint Louis addresses André-Hercule de Fleury, preceptor to the young Louis XV: 'Lead his first steps, cultivate under your eyes/The precious store of the purest of my blood!' (*Conduis ses premiers pas, cultive sous tes yeux/Du plus pur de mon sang le dépôt précieux.*)[5] Fleury regarded Saint Louis as someone who 'knew that royalty was not destined to pleasure and rest; that it demands great work and serious application'. Part of his education for Louis XV involved copying and translating Latin sentences concerning Saint Louis.[6] 'One can admire in Saint Louis examples of all the virtues, piety, justice and force. The kings of France must always have him in view as the true model of kings.' This was an exercise in learning the art of kingship as well as acquiring proficiency in Latin, as is evident from the final translation, completed in May 1720: 'as Joinville said very well . . . [Saint Louis] will always be the glory of those who seek to imitate him, as he will be the shame and condemnation of those who distance themselves from him.[7]

As usual, the accession of a new king brought the hope that he could be shaped in the mould of Saint Louis. A poem from 1721 by the Jesuit Père de Blainville imagined Saint Louis counselling his descendant to make sure he was always guided by religion and peace.[8] The following year, Pierre-Charles Roy presented Louis with a poem describing his similarities to Saint Louis and stating that the altar that had received Louis IX's oaths 'is prepared for you', a reference to the upcoming *sacre* and a clear evocation of monarchical continuity.[9] Before the *sacre*, the archbishop of Paris gave instruction to pray 'that at the example of Saint Louis we see grow daily in [Louis XV] . . . a holy respect for religion'.[10]

Hopes for Louis XV to follow his ancestor were frequently delivered as prayers at the end of panegyrics. In 1725 the Abbé Descors stated that 'your intercession, great saint, will cause the happy days of your reign to be reborn'.[11] A year later, preaching at the Louvre before the Académie Française, the Abbé Guichon asked Saint Louis to ensure 'that the one who succeeds to your crown succeeds also to your virtues'.[12] Although this final prayer was sometimes the panegyrist's only allusion to Louis XV, as at Saint-Eustache in 1730 when the Abbé Letour addressed Saint Louis saying 'you still reign here in the person of the monarch who governs us', most panegyrists continued to include parallel praise in the main text.[13] In 1736, the Abbé Billiard noted at the Louvre that both Saint Louis and Louis XV ruled with the same piety and wisdom, while the preacher before the Académie Royale des Sciences and the Académie Royale des Inscriptions et Belles-Lettres at the Oratory even stated that the king resembled his holy ancestor in his vanquishing of pleasure and temptation.[14] Other preachers proclaimed that the happy days of Saint Louis were being renewed under his descendant.[15]

In June 1744 Louis XV fell seriously ill while on campaign near Metz; after years of avoiding confession, he was forced to renounce his disorderly private life in order to receive absolution. At the Jesuit church in Metz on 25 August 1744, following the king's recovery, the Abbé Josset concluded a panegyric of Saint Louis with a prayer for Louis XV in which he gave him the epithet 'the Beloved', which would soon be adopted widely.[16] The Jesuit historian Paul-François Velly compared Louis XV's illness in 1744 to Louis IX's in 1244, remarking that good kings arouse the same feelings across the centuries.[17] In 1745, the court painter Charles-Antoine Coypel painted Saint Louis with the features of Louis XV kneeling before the crown of thorns. Showing the saint in full armour, the painting conflated Louis XV with his ancestor in the aftermath of his recovery at Metz and much celebrated victory at Fontenoy in 1745 (Figure 6.1).

However, Louis XV's conversion to virtue did not last long and the 1740s have been seen as the crucial decade in which he lost control of the presentation of his image.[18] The return of the mistresses and his inability to take communion year after year made it hard for panegyrists to present him as a new Saint Louis. Some panegyrists from the later 1740s to the 1760s made no effort to connect the two kings, even in the prayers.[19] Others mentioned Louis XV only very briefly or omitted him at crucial moments. At the Louvre in 1751, the Abbé de la Tour du Pin declared that the 'tomb [of Saint Louis] is the school where all monarchs must educate themselves. Happy the nations governed by princes formed on the examples of Saint Louis!' He did not state whether

Figure 6.1 *Saint Louis sous les traits de Louis XV recevant la couronne d'épines* (1745) by Charles-Antoine Coypel (1694–1752). © RMN-Grand Palais / Gérard Blot.

Louis XV was one such monarch.[20] Such omissions cannot have been unintentional. In a *mandement* of the same year, the archbishop of Paris, Christophe de Beaumont, prayed that the new duc de Bourgogne be granted 'piety and the horror of vice', which alone were capable of bringing true happiness to rulers and assuring them glorious memory in centuries to come. 'The memory of the holiest of our kings will always be the most revered among us, and our monarchs always glorify themselves more that the blood of this Christian hero flows in their veins than that they descend from other heroes whose principal merit is to have made conquests and won victories.'[21] The historian Émile Régnault regarded this as an indirect lesson to Louis XV, and it is telling that the example of Saint Louis occupied a pivotal place in this condemnation of the king's immorality.[22]

Louis XV was still sometimes praised in the panegyrics. In 1750 at the Louvre, soon after the much-criticized Peace of Aix-la-Chapelle in 1748, the Abbé de Boismont described Louis IX's distaste for meaningless conflict and love of peace before asking if it was 'the soul of Saint Louis or that of the monarch who governs us that I offer to you here, Messieurs?'[23] Nevertheless, examples of the 'parasitic praise' of Louis XIV's personal rule are much less prominent in the second half of Louis XV's reign. This may partly reflect a changing sensibility in which overt flattery lost ground to more subtle references. After all, some orators merely stated that they did not need to make the comparison explicitly.[24] However, it was significant that Saint Louis's annual praise was uncoupled from the reigning monarch. Implied criticism is evident in panegyrics such as the Canon Bernard's at the Oratory in 1756.[25] He praised Louis XV for founding the École Militaire and the church of Sainte-Geneviève, but not for his virtues. Instead, he asked whether his contemporaries could believe possible Saint Louis's example of 'a prince always distant from those voluptuous routes that led David astray, lost Solomon and blackened the memory of so many otherwise recommendable kings; a prince as chaste as Job who made a severe pact with his senses never to even think of illegitimate objects'.[26] Given how well-known Louis XV's infidelities had become, it is hard to imagine that no one noticed the contrast. This was, in fact, recognized after Louis XV's death. In 1779 the Abbé Talbert remarked that under a less worthy prince than Louis XVI, 'the panegyric of Saint Louis becomes a satire: but today the orator need not fear the malignancy of contrasts'.[27] Louis XV was not mentioned, but it is hard to see whom else Talbert might have in mind. Catholic kings tend to be found 'wanting by comparison with the ideal of truly saintly kingship'; this seems particularly clear under Louis XV, when Saint Louis not only failed to confer sacral legitimacy on his successor but actually highlighted his failings.[28]

Nevertheless, away from the panegyrics, the *fête du roi* remained an occasion on which the king and the dauphin were praised and flattered with poems and medals.[29] A 1755 poem for the king mentioned 'this day on which everyone recalls/The virtues of Louis, the glory of the Bourbons'.[30] Each year, Louis XV received compliments from the court and listened to the royal musicians.[31] In the 1760s and 1770s the royal family celebrated the feast at Compiègne; the king presented the parish church with an image of Saint Louis in 1770.[32] Louis XV left little indication of his opinion of Saint Louis, though he apparently took a 'lively interest' in a new edition of Joinville published in 1761 and cited 'a particular devotion' to the saint when ordering Saint-Denis to grant him relics in 1768.[33]

However, Saint Louis was not the only royal patron. Indeed, it was Saint Geneviève's intercession that was credited with the king's recovery in 1744, hence the building of what would become the Pantheon, part of a royal appropriation of her cult in the eighteenth century.[34] Nevertheless, Saint Louis remained a natural choice for new royal foundations. The collapse of Saint-Thomas-du-Louvre in 1739, killing several canons, allowed a pre-existing project to unite it with Saint-Nicolas-du-Louvre to be pushed ahead. The chapel of the new united chapter of Saint-Louis-du-Louvre, named in grateful thanks to Louis XV, was completed in 1744.[35] The Parc-aux-Cerfs near Versailles (infamously associated with Louis XV's mistresses) gained a provisional chapel dedicated to Saint Louis. Its altarpiece by François Lemoyne, first shown to the king in 1727, showed Saint Louis surrounded by angels adoring the crown of thorns.[36] In 1743, the king laid the first stone of the church itself, designed by Jacques-Hardouin Mansard and dedicated on 25 August 1754.[37]

The chapel of the École Militaire in Paris, started in 1769, was dedicated to Saint Louis. A cycle of eleven paintings for the chapel, all depicting scenes from his life, were shown at the exhibition at the Louvre in 1773. An extensive review in the *Mercure* indicated what was prized in representations of Saint Louis by the end of Louis XV's reign.[38] Historical exactitude and simplicity were praised in Joseph-Marie Vien's painting of a young Louis remitting the government to Blanche, but it was to be regretted that facial features had not been kept consistent between this and Charles Amédée Philippe van Loo's painting of the *sacre*. The criteria ranged from the overall colour scheme to the artists' closeness to sources such as Joinville. Nicolas-Guy Brenet's painting of the reception of ambassadors from the 'Old Man of the Mountain' in 1238 was particularly praised: 'One notices here an artist who has informed himself about his subject . . . the spectator believes himself to be present at the scene he has painted . . . The facial features of Saint Louis seem to us to conform enough to the remaining portraits in relief of this prince' (Figure 6.2).

As well as these foundations, there is evidence of devotion to Saint Louis in the wider royal family. The dauphin Louis, whose birth in 1729 prompted speeches highlighting his descent from Saint Louis as well as the erection of a golden statue of the latter in Rome, took far more readily than his father to their ancestor's patronage and example.[39] Pious and devout, the dauphin told his preceptor that he wanted most to resemble Louis IX and become a saint like him. Every day he prayed that, in recognition of the merits of Saint Louis, God might accord 'that his descendants and all your people be the imitators of the virtues that he practiced'.[40] A copy of the Office of Saint Louis as celebrated at Versailles printed in 1760 with a dedicatory letter to the princesses included numerous meditations on his life that offer a window into his place in royal piety. The meditations used Saint Louis to illustrate that 'sanctity never had more splendour than when it was united to grandeur'. The compatibility of piety and sanctity with an active life in government and the world was emphasized, as well as the importance of charity. 'What would be the use of knowing the needs of the misfortunate if one did not sympathise with their fate . . . [the poor] are our brothers and they suffer. Louis loved them to the point of lodging them in his palace.' The meditations indicated the glory of Saint Louis, placing him above François I, Louis XII and Henri IV, and stressed his role as intercessor and model for the volume's royal dedicatees.[41]

One of the princesses took her saintly ancestor very seriously as a patron: Louis XV's daughter Madame Louise, who gave up life at court to become a Carmelite at Saint-Denis in 1770. This made her worthy of comparison both to Louis IX's holy sister Isabelle and to the saint-king himself.[42] At the end of his panegyric in 1772, the Abbé Pleuvri reserved all the parallel praise for Madame Louise, making no mention of

Figure 6.2 *Saint Louis, roi de France, recevant les ambassadeurs du Prince des Assassins* (1773) by Nicolas-Guy Brenet (1728–92), Chapelle saint-Louis, École Militaire, Paris. © Alamy Stock Photo.

Louis XV.[43] Louise herself saw in Saint Louis 'a model of wisdom amidst the grandeurs of the world', viewing his assiduousness in prayer as a reproach to her. She admired his dedication to religion, humility and charity. Considering him an active patron and attempting to have his feast celebrated with greater solemnity, she prayed to him regularly. When the dauphin caught smallpox in 1752, Louise prayed to Saint Louis to protect 'a brother all the dearer to my tenderness as he is worthy of a family that invokes you either as patron or as protector. You see all that our hearts desire in this moment . . . what must not the offspring hope under the shelter of the powerful and supporting stem who protects them in the heavens?'[44]

It is unsurprising that a princess turned nun was devoted to Saint Louis, but Louise's piety was probably not unusual among members of the royal family who had a genuine belief in their holy ancestor. Saint Louis continued to play the role of saintly patron, model of kingship and dynastic patriarch to the Bourbon monarchy under Louis XV.

The legislator king

For much of the eighteenth century, Saint Louis's memory hung over debates concerning the exercise of power in France, appropriated by proponents and opponents of royal authority and the Parlements. Such debates often focused on the baronial revolts of Louis IX's minority and his treatment of representative institutions and the church.

Among the last works penned by Henri de Boulainvilliers, an 'aristocratic reactionary' who advocated noble participation in politics and opposed absolute monarchy, was a critical commentary on the Parisian lawyer Antoine Aubery's history of Louis IX.[45] Boulainvilliers was damning of Aubery's royalist interpretation of Saint Louis, instead criticizing the lack of noble consent at Louis IX's accession and the despotism of Blanche's regency. Seeing minorities as periods from which royal power emerged augmented, he approved of the rebellious barons. Writing of the 'innovations' in France's government since the thirteenth century, he remarked that

> I will not accuse this good prince of having introduced them by ambition, nor with the view of preparing unlimited power for his successors. . . . But it does not follow that these novelties should be accepted without repugnance by the French lords, nor that those who opposed them should be regarded by posterity as rebels and seditious, especially compared to a regent who, far from having the right to make such ordinances, ought not to have involved herself in government.

Boulainvilliers criticized Louis IX for his crusading, arbitration in England in 1262 (when he supported Henry III against the English barons), and generally paving the way to despotism.[46] This unusual interpretation circulated in manuscript. Mathieu Marais read it in the early 1720s, calling it 'marvellous' but remarking that 'the authorities ought to act and prevent the circulation of these manuscripts which teach things so curious and contrary to sovereignty that one is almost criminal in reading them'.[47]

Boulainvilliers's volume appeared in the massive library of the *parlementaire* Jean-Baptiste François Durey de Meinières, a collector of historical materials that supported the Parlement's claims to check the power of church and crown.[48] Durey de Meinières's colleague Louis-Adrien Le Paige argued that the Parlement was the crucial institutional link between the king and his subjects, possessing an unbroken continuity going back to the Franks.[49] Praising Saint Louis for respecting the ancient laws of his kingdom and the Parlement's role in government, Le Paige cited approvingly an incident of 1263 in which a judgement banishing someone from the town of Seri was upheld over a contrary order of Louis IX. Instead of trying to resist the judgement, 'this sage prince' preferred the law to be given priority over his orders. This meant that the Parlement was cooperative, finding a way to satisfy him by allowing the banished person to return a few days after having been chased from the town. Louis IX thus showed the happy cooperation that could follow when a king respected the decisions of the Parlement. 'May kings imitate this prince; by taking this route, they will always be assured to see their subjects and judges even anticipate their desires.'[50]

For Boulainvilliers, Louis IX paved the way for the absolute monarchy; for Le Paige, he held it back by respecting the authority of the Parlement. What united these views was opposition to what they perceived as unrestrained royal power, but this was not shared by much of the eighteenth-century historical and panegyric literature on Saint Louis. New historical accounts of his reign such as those by Jacques Hardion and Richard de Bury broadly continued to portray him as a perfect model of justice and valour, the baronial rebels as villains.[51] Velly painted the rebels as conspiratorial and murderous, contrasting them with a young king devoted 'entirely to his people and thinking of nothing but ways of rendering them happy'.[52] The panegyrists shared this interpretation, casting Louis IX's minority as a tragic period of division, with the heroic king eventually triumphing at Taillebourg in 1242.[53] For the panegyrist at the Jesuit church of Saint-Louis in 1748, the 1220s to 1240s were 'dark days' when 'the great lived in independence and intended to escape from the supreme authority'.[54] This was an absolutist reading of Louis IX (he was called an 'absolute monarch' in another 1748 panegyric) that would have infuriated Boulainvilliers.[55]

Panegyrists continued to praise Saint Louis for his Christian kingship. The Abbé de la Pause noted in 1728 that he was far from 'worldly politics which make governments resort to disguise, dissimulation and artifice'.[56] Justice was a constant theme, normally illustrated by describing Saint Louis under the tree at Vincennes; in 1736 the Abbé Billiard conjured a 'rural site' in which 'he listened attentively to the small and the great, the rich and the poor . . . king, judge and father all together'.[57] Thirty years later the Abbé Vammalle asked 'who is the good citizen who can go along these solitary paths [at Vincennes] without quivering with joy and tenderness at every instant; it's doubtless here, he must cry, it's on this humble grass, it's under this ancient oak that the good king Louis sat to judge his people'.[58] Saint Louis's personal morality and pious qualities also continued to be praised. 'Was there ever a more humble king?' asked the Abbé de Saint-Vincent in 1739.[59] As in the seventeenth century, his example was used to berate the inadequate piety and humility of the *grands* and *mondains*.[60] In 1746, the Abbé Cousturier warned that elevated social rank and flattery were dangers but that by Saint Louis's example the *grands* could turn them into the 'means of sanctification and salvation'.[61]

As before, Saint Louis was depicted as a Gallican monarch. In 1744, the Abbé de l'Ecluse Desloges evoked a king who defended the prerogatives of his crown with the Pragmatic Sanction.[62] Jansenist opponents of the papal bull *Unigenitus* also used Saint Louis as a model of resistance to 'the innovations of the Jesuits' in the *Nouvelles Ecclésiastiques*, though preachers with pro-Jansenist leanings were prevented from delivering panegyrics of Saint Louis.[63] There was some debate over the authenticity of the Pragmatic, building on doubts first expressed in the seventeenth century.[64] A 1740 edition of the Jesuit Père Daniel's history referred to three schools of thought on the document (that it was entirely real or faked, or a mixture) in arguing against the Bollandist argument that it should be rejected entirely.[65] However, such arguments made little impact generally; in 1782, the Abbé Boulogne still referred to it as the 'sacred defence of the liberties of our church and the independence of our kings' and the *Nouvelles Ecclésiastiques* defended it from 'Roman journalists' who questioned its authenticity 'seemingly more by malice than ignorance'.[66]

New themes were appearing. From the 1750s many panegyrists emphasized Louis IX's interest in commerce, finance, agriculture and industry in a way that said more about eighteenth-century ideals than medieval kingship – as did new celebrations of the feast day, such as the *Feast of valiant and frank labourers* instituted by the sieur de la Peiriere in Cépède (Aiguillon), which included lectures on agriculture as well as church services and dancing.[67] The rhetoric of national identity started to appear in panegyrics with lines such as 'where can we find a more accomplished model of the ancient virtues which formerly formed the character of the French nation?'[68] Saint Louis had always been praised for his justice but from the 1750s this was increasingly discussed with reference to impersonal lawgiving as well as the oak of Vincennes. Velly's Saint Louis was a legislator busy establishing archives of laws and ordinances.[69] In particular, the so-called *Établissements of Saint Louis* (today considered to be a compilation made in the 1270s, comprising nine ordinances of Louis IX alongside customary laws from Anjou, Touraine and Orléanais) took on a cultish status under Louis XV.[70]

In *The Spirit of the Laws*, Montesquieu saw in the judicial changes of Louis IX's reign, such as the abolition of judicial conduct, 'a manner of proceeding that was more natural, reasonable, in conformity with morality, religion, public tranquillity, the security of people and goods'. However, he also noted that the manner of judgement established by Saint Louis was an example to be followed rather than a general law for the whole kingdom. On the authenticity of the 'obscure, confused and ambiguous' collection known as the *Établissements*, Montesquieu argued that they were a compilation of different codes rather than given by Saint Louis before his departure for Tunis.[71] Jean-Jacques Rousseau also touched on the *Établissements* in *The Social Contract*, deploring the fact that they authorized private wars and duels, abuses of the 'absurd system' known as feudal government, 'contrary to the principals of natural law and all good political organization'.[72]

For the panegyrists, however, the *Établissements* were the personal work of Saint Louis, a 'sacred code of laws and ordinances'.[73] In a celebrated panegyric of 1772 the Abbé Maury lauded them with rhetorical panache while implying that they could be used to hold subsequent kings to account:

> When our fathers were unfortunate under the following reigns, when they publicly reproached Philip IV for the alteration of money, what did they demand? *The Établissments of Saint Louis.* When they murmured against Louis X auctioning judicial offices, what did they demand? *The Établissements of Saint Louis.* . . . They knew of no other resource to escape from vexations and repeated, while shedding tears, these simple and touching words: *it was not thus that the holy king governed us; may his laws be followed!*[74]

In direct contradiction of Rousseau, praise of the *Établissements* often appeared in the context of describing Saint Louis as legislator replacing anarchy with law and bringing order out of chaos, part of a wider culture of criticizing feudal and seigneurial rights.[75] Preachers tended to reference 'the deplorable state of France' at the time of Louis IX's accession.[76] Vammalle argued that Louis IX's divine mission was to correct legislation and remove feudalism, his reign becoming 'the cradle of our sage and praised constitution, which renders France as tranquil as she is formidable, our kings as moderate as powerful and their people as happy as faithful'.[77] Panegyrists such as the Abbé Le Cousturier, preaching at the Louvre in 1769, agreed with Boulainvilliers's narrative of Saint Louis's role in the development of French absolutism, but from the opposite perspective, praising the triumph of legislation over aristocratic anarchy, a trajectory that would be completed with the affirmation of an all-powerful master under Louis XIV.[78]

The legislator king here was commendable for replacing cruel seigneurial justice with fairer royal justice. There was ambiguity, however, on where he stood on the boundaries of authority. In some contentious political contexts, Saint Louis had been invoked on the side of strong royal authority against the Parlement. The year 1770 saw acute tension between crown and Parlement over the trial of the duc d'Aiguillon, the former royal commandant in Brittany.[79] In October, a satirical poem entitled *Remonstrances of Saint Louis to the Parlement* caused great controversy (according to the gossipy 'secret memoirs' associated with Louis Petit de Bachaumont). The title itself was provocative, as it was normally the Parlement that remonstrated to the king. It was part of a corpus of anti-*parlementaire* material encouraged by Chancellor Maupeou, no doubt written by 'some *Aiguilloniste*, that is to say an extreme partisan of despotism'. The poem had Saint Louis inform the insubordinate lawyers that it was not customary in France for subjects to perform acts of disobedience while 'reclaiming the law' from the king, shameful for them to disrespect the 'silence imposed by authority' and dangerous to dare to participate in supreme power. Their rebelliousness would shock even the English and the best remedy was to imprison all those involved in stirring up these troubles. This reprove to the Parlement from 'the greatest king France ever had' was, therefore, a strong statement in favour of the line taken by Louis XV and his chancellor in what was to develop into the 'Maupeou Revolution'.[80]

The defence of absolute monarchy was not the only possible deployment of Saint Louis. The Parlement of Paris invoked his memory in its remonstrances. Christophe de Beaumont's decision in the 1750s to refuse the sacraments to those who did not adhere to *Unigenitus* sparked another Jansenist-related controversy pitting archbishop and king against the Parlement. In remonstrances of 1751 and 1753, the Parlement cited Louis IX's resistance to the false use of excommunication and interdict by the church; he provided 'a striking example' of combining 'respect for the church with the defence of the rights of the crown'. In February 1766, the Parlement of Paris finished a remonstrance in support of the Parlement of Brittany, then involved in a protracted struggle with the king, with a long quote from the *Enseignements* of Saint Louis, cited from Théveneau. This tactic cleverly used the saint-king's own words to tell Louis XV to maintain the liberties and customs of his kingdom and to warn him 'not to think, my son, that the French are the slaves of kings, but rather of the laws of the kingdom'.[81] Far from being the preserve of the monarchy, the 'Gallican' and 'legislator' Saint Louis could be turned against the king at moments of crisis.

Controversial crusades

In the 1730s a sense that justifying the crusades of Saint Louis was becoming difficult and a 'pitfall' for panegyrists emerged.[82] Preachers started to defend themselves pre-emptively from potential criticism. As the Abbé Poulle remarked in 1748 after having described Louis IX's love of peace, 'here, I anticipate that you are secretly countering me with those holy wars against which the malignity of the century rails with such licence'.[83] He went on to present the crusades as just, and up to the 1750s Saint Louis's crusades generally tended to be praised, with a particular focus on his period in captivity. In 1745, the Jesuit Père Lombard won a poetry prize from the Académie des Belles-Lettres of Marseilles with *The Heroism of Saint Louis*, which lauded his victories over the Muslims and the even greater triumph of his constancy in imprisonment.[84] The latter was also the theme of a Latin play by the Jesuit Joseph de Baudory, 'Saint Louis in chains'.[85]

However, a negative view was gaining ground. Velly noted that in the age of Saint Louis 'crusades were always in fashion, less from religious zeal than from a kind of sickness of the time, from anxiety and brigandage'.[86] In a panegyric of 1761 at the Louvre the Abbé Beauvais referred to the crusaders as 'Christian fanatics, who, under armour decorated with the cross, carried a heart perhaps as barbarous as the enemy they went to fight', but tried to contrast them to the virtuous king who led them.[87] Some preachers sought to defend Saint Louis less by contrasting him with his fanatical soldiers than by placing him in historical context. In 1767 at the Oratory, the Abbé Gayet de Sansale warned his listeners not to judge Saint Louis by the standards of Louis XV's reign. After all, was it really surprising that he chose to go on crusade given that 'the authority of the pontiffs, the example of his ancestors, the entreaties of the Greeks, all carried Louis there, his piety made him undertake them for the salvation of Palestine, and his wisdom took advantage of them for the repose of France' (for the absence of many difficult nobles gave France itself some much needed peace)?[88]

Others, however, adopted a more critical line. In his history of the crusades, Voltaire praised Louis IX's lawgiving but regretted his dedication to crusading and its negative consequences for France, both in terms of the tremendous human and financial cost and the harm caused by the king's absence for several years.[89] Elsewhere, he was much more critical. A section in his controversial poem about Joan of Arc presents a very different image of Saint Louis to that of the *Henriade*. The king is seen suffering in Hell, largely as a result of having gone 'to Turkish Syria to assassinate the poor Saracen':

This sanctimonious king, insane knight,	*Ce roi bigot, insensé paladin,*
Who would have had a good place in Heaven	*Qui dans le ciel aurait eu belle place,*
If he had simply been Christian,	*S'il eût été tout simplement chrétien,*
Burned down there and well deserved it.	*Grillait là-bas, & le méritait bien.*
[. . .]	
He impoverished, he devastated France,	*Il appauvrit, il dévasta la France,*
He filled it with widows and orphans.	*Il la remplit de veuves, d'orphelins.*
What devil did more harm to humans?[90]	*Quel diable eut fait plus de mal aux humains?*

Even if this was an extreme manifestation, criticism of the crusades was becoming common. Nevertheless, it could cause great scandal when presented in the panegyrics in too forthright a manner. No panegyric was more controversial than the Abbé Bassinet's, delivered before the Académie Française at the Louvre in 1767 and criticized for turning the event into a 'absolutely profane ceremony'. Bassinet included no citations from scripture and attacked the crusades as absurd, cruel and unjust. 'All the *dévots* are alarmed and treat this ecclesiastic as an atheist, and it is feared that they will stop the printing of the *Panegyric*.' On 4 September Bachaumont noted that 'this clash is regarded as a new attack by the Encyclopedist party against religion'.[91] The key problems seemed to have been Bassinet's criticism of the crusade and his consideration of Louis IX as man rather than saint. (Strangely, his praise of the Pragmatic Sanction was also cited as objectionable, even though it was such a common theme in the panegyrics; perhaps he had gone too far in criticizing Rome.) In the end, Bassinet did publish a copy of his sermon, but whereas preachers were normally given permission within two months of their delivery on 25 August, Bassinet was not given permission until 29 March 1768. Also unusual is the fact that the text was headed by a letter in which he defended his sermon as Christian, saying that those who accused him of irreligion had probably not actually heard it (he asserted that the printed text was identical to that which he had delivered, though this is impossible to verify).

> I condemned the crusades: yes, other panegyrists without doubt condemned them before me. But I searched in history for the causes of these prodigious emigrations which had devastated Europe . . . ambition and self-interest appeared to me to be their true motives, religion the means.. . . Among these two million crusaders who perished in Asia, only a small number were led by zeal; all the rest were drawn by a taste for dissipation and licence, by avarice and plundering. Among the princes, I see only Saint Louis who was led by his piety. . . . He abandoned his subjects to satisfy a vow, while the first vow of a king, and that which he must occupy himself with fulfilling, is to work for their happiness. That was doubtless a fault, and I did not seek to excuse it.

Although he regarded Saint Louis's motives as more pious than those of other crusaders, Bassinet clearly felt he had no need to defend him and even portrayed him as selfish. In the panegyric itself there is plenty of praise for other aspects of Saint Louis, but Bassinet did not pull his punches on the crusades. 'Holy religion! No, you have never recommended murder, usurpation or injustice.'[92]

Bassinet's panegyric would have been unthinkable in the previous generation. Yet in 1769 a similar controversy was stirred up by Le Cousturier's panegyric, which referred to the crusades as a 'mixture of superstition and debauchery, cruelty and religion'.[93] Once again, accusations that the preacher was part of the 'Encyclopedist party' were reported by Bachaumont, who also noted that 'even the praises that the orator received from spectators and the hand-clapping that are used only in profane assemblies, theatres and bars are being turned against him'. Le Cousturier was denounced before Christophe de Beaumont and banned from preaching in Advent, though the Académie Française had already managed to print the panegyric and present a copy to the king.

In 1777, perhaps tiring of such controversies, the archbishop had the Abbé d'Espagnac read him his panegyric on 24 August; but after Beaumont 'mutilated' his sermon, the abbé was able to remember and deliver his original version the next day.[94]

As these episodes show, the panegyrics were becoming a battleground between those loosely labelled *philosophes* and *dévots*. Criticism of the crusades by the former was matched by a counter-offensive defending them by those who saw perfect coherence between Louis IX's political reforms and crusades and defended him from irreligion.[95] As Père Bernard noted in 1756, 'I know that in this century of false philosophy, and thus errors, piety is regarded as a veil of feebleness . . . O saint-king, destroy these prejudices equally injurious to reason and religion'.[96] This was a reformulation of previous debates about the role of piety in active life for the intellectual climate of Enlightenment Paris. Other preachers, however, came down strongly on the *philosophe* side – though preaching too 'philosophical' a panegyric could ruin their chances of preferment.[97] This perhaps explains the modifications that were sometimes made before publication. In 1761, it is said that Beauvais defended the theatre and praised philosophy in his panegyric, but that these passages were changed in the printed version.[98]

In 1862, the conservative Abbé de Rosné wrote an article lamenting what he saw as a decline in religious inspiration in the eighteenth-century panegyrics of Saint Louis, manifested in their lack of enthusiasm for the crusades. He saw the turning point as the panegyric of 1749 preached by the Abbé d'Arty – but written by none other than Voltaire. Apparently the young abbé had sought the great man's opinion of his sermon but Voltaire burned it, either accidentally or in bad humour provoked by reading it; the *philosophe* then had to write a new one the week before 25 August, producing a work that Rosné saw as the model of subsequent eighteenth-century panegyrics.[99] According to Madame de Graffigny, everyone knew that the sermon was by Voltaire.[100] The attitude taken to the crusades in this text is different to that expressed by Voltaire elsewhere. Although he noted negative aspects of the crusades, Voltaire argued that they would be viewed more favourably had they been more successful; in addition, Saint Louis had good motives and did as much as possible to assure their success.[101]

In general, the way in which the panegyrist treated the crusades became the interesting focus of this otherwise formulaic genre. As the *Mercure* noted in 1774, the crusades were a 'reef where one waits for the panegyrist with a sort of anxiety to see how he can save himself and his hero from a step where the wisdom and all the glory of this prince have been more than once said to have been shipwrecked'.[102] A successful sermon would mix modest criticism with a defence that chimed well with eighteenth-century concerns. In 1743 the Abbé Griffet mentioned the stimulus the crusades provided to shipbuilding, navigation and commerce.[103] In 1774, the Abbé Fauchet defended the crusades as 'just and useful' in that they stemmed a Muslim tide threatening to engulf western Europe and occupied France's warlike lords.[104] One of the most successful preachers was the Abbé Maury in 1772, who painted a Saint Louis full of concern for the peace of France and the defence of oppressed Christians in the Holy Land by actually imagining how he might defend himself before the Académie Française:

Transport yourselves to the century in which I lived. . . . You are Christians. Well!
The holy city was the prey of the infidel, the tomb of Jesus Christ was desecrated

every day. . . . You are French. Well! There was no Frenchman who did not have parents captured by the Saracens. . . . These Christian groaning in iron were my subjects; they invoked me as the only liberator they could expect. . . . Could I refuse my help to these misfortunate people to whom nothing was offered except apostasy and martyrdom?[105]

Voltaire wrote that Maury *almost* made him wish to see another crusade – before launching into another criticism of Saint Louis for following the prejudices of his time: 'if he had better employed his great virtues, he would have been more of a saint and hero.'[106]

It is worth considering the social function and broader reception of these sermons, which did not result from a desire to study Louis IX but played a role in the career advancement of 'literary abbés' for whom a successful panegyric formed part of a *cursus honorum* that could bring benefices or mark an important step towards a chair in the Académie Française.[107] Previous recipients of prizes were often chosen (such as the Abbé de l'Ecluse des Loges in 1744, having won the prize for eloquence in 1743), as were those who had had some other involvement in the Académie; Maury delivered an *éloge de Fénelon* the year before he gave the panegyric.[108] Connections were important in being selected to preach, as indicated by a letter recommending a preacher to the president of the Académie des Sciences of Bordeaux in 1758.[109] The Parisian panegyrics were the most prestigious, and it is noteworthy who was *not* chosen. The Jesuits were not popular among the Parisian intelligentsia and the panegyric at the Académie Française only fell to them four times under Louis XV.[110]

For those who acquitted themselves well the rewards could be significant. In terms of reputation, the *Mercure* noted in 1717 that the Abbé Bion was well-known for his panegyric of Saint Louis two years earlier.[111] The rewards could also be more material. Fauchet was awarded a pension of 1,200 *livres* for his panegyric.[112] The Abbé de Ségui was also lucky. The Académie was so pleased with his panegyric that, knowing he was not wealthy, it wrote to Cardinal Fleury as early as 27 August to obtain a benefice for the preacher; three months later, Ségui was rewarded with the abbey of Genlis.[113] Poulle's successful panegyric of 1748 caused the Académie to recommend him to the bishop of Mirepoix (Fleury's successor as holder of the all-important *feuille des bénéfices*, controlling church appointments).[114] Although the response was that he was young, already had a pension, and 'we cannot extend graces on all preachers', Poulle was eventually given an abbey.[115] It was perhaps in the hope of such reward that the preachers normally made sure to flatter their audience.[116] Whereas under Louis XIV the Académie used the panegyrics to tie itself closer to the king's patronage through flattery, by the mid-eighteenth century praise of the Académie itself was being used by panegyrists to secure their own advancement.

As to wider reception, panegyrics were regularly reported in the periodicals. The *Mercure* often included reviews, normally focussing on points of literary style rather than content, perhaps because the material was so well-known and often rather similar from one panegyric to the next.[117] Regretting that it was not possible to print the whole sermon, the *Mercure* wrote of Poulle's panegyric that 'the style of his discourse is ornate without being affected or mannered'.[118] On the other hand, Fauchet received a more mixed response. 'There was more talent than taste in this panegyric . . . written in a very uneven style'.[119] Other writings offer alternative perspectives. Graffigny's letters indicate an interest in the panegyrics in Parisian literary society, stating that Boismont's sermon 'won all Paris' in 1750 and that the second part of the Jesuit Neuville's 1752 panegyric was 'very beautiful'.[120] The latter view was not shared by the author of a short verse parallel between the main panegyrics of 1752: Renaud's sermon at the Oratory was 'noble, touching and beautiful', Neuville's at the Louvre was rich in adornment and colour but lacking in substance.[121]

Also revealing is Bachaumont's account of the Abbé de Boulogne's panegyric at the Oratory in 1782. When he began, an elderly veteran of the Académie des Sciences shouted '*Voilà* a fool' but by the end was noting that 'it is I who am the fool'; the academicians, including d'Alembert, applauded the preacher as though they were in the theatre. Bachaumont noted Boulogne's elegant style and reconciliation of religion and philosophy as indicative of the quality of his panegyric, but also gave a clue as to the normal reception of these sermons:

> The habitude of only seeing mediocre panegyrics on so well-worn a subject normally drives the great writers away from this assembly, so that there is scarcely anyone other than the academicians obliged to be there, the friends of the author, and seminarians, monks, devout women and the idle, not having anything better to do.[122]

This is a reminder that what Montesquieu called the 'eternal babble' of the Académie Française probably held marginal interest for most people.[123]

By the mid-1700s Saint Louis was being subjected to something arguably even worse than criticism: ridicule. A nine-verse song from 1748 joked that he exhibited every virtue and combated vice, guarding his virginity – at least until the age of twenty:

And if he had not had eleven children	*Et s'il n'eût pas fait onze enfants*
With Marguerite in less than fourteen years,	*A Marguerite en moins de quatorze ans*
He would have been placed among the ranks of virgins	*On l'aurait mis au rang des vierges*
In paradise with a candle.	*En paradis avec un cierge.*

Louis IX's lack of mistresses and chastity outside marriage, so tirelessly praised by panegyrists, looked less impressive when set aside the fact that he and his wife were a veritable baby factory. His penitential practices were also fair game for comedy. When dancing, he sometime put nutshells in his shoes to 'earn his way to Heaven in rhythm' (*gagner le ciel en cadence*). It is not hard to imagine the song circulating in witty and sceptical circles; that its author viewed Saint Louis as a laughable figure whose ascetic virtues held little relevance is indicated by the last line: 'Christian people, it's your business' (*Peuple chrétien, c'est votre affaire*).[124]

The decline and fall of Saint Louis

What a king Louis IX was! . . . What a saint! . . . May you walk in his footsteps! May I, like Queen Blanche, see germinate the pious sentiments that I shall not cease to inspire in you.[125]

With these words, the dauphine Marie-Josèphe encouraged the duc de Berry to emulate his saintly ancestor. Given the traditions of Bourbon princely education, it is unsurprising that Saint Louis was prominent in the education of her three sons who would wear the crown – Berry (Louis XVI), the comte de Provence (Louis XVIII), and the comte d'Artois (Charles X).[126] Saint Louis was presented as 'the best of our kings' and 'the most just man of his century, because he was the most religious' in materials written for Berry's education by Jacob-Nicolas Moreau, whose opposition to 'philosophical' ideas was evident in his praise for the fact that 'Christianity was [Louis IX's] philosophy'.[127]

If the later years of Louis XV had seen a decline in the use of Saint Louis to sanctify the king, Louis XVI's accession in 1774 provided a return to normal with an abundance of flattering comparisons. The monarchy had not been mortally damaged or permanently desacralized by the misdeeds of Louis XV, and Nigel Aston has suggested that it was to some extent resacralized under Louis XVI.[128] Fauchet prayed that Louis XVI and Marie-Antoinette 'renew by their good deeds the reign of Louis IX and Marguerite de Provence', and other panegyrists were soon praising Louis XVI as the inheritor of Saint Louis's virtues.[129] The Abbé de Saint-Martin in 1784 pronounced that 'it is with Louis XVI that this long change of prosperities that will extend over the French empire will begin'.[130] The subsequent decade was probably not quite what he had in mind.

The king himself continued to perform the usual royal devotions to his ancestor at Versailles. On 25 August 1786 he listened to music at his *lever*, named a new grand cross of the Order of Saint-Louis and received compliments from the courtiers and the *corps de ville* of Paris.[131] He also attended the 'Mass of the *Cordons Rouges*', named after the red sash worn by commanders of the Order of Saint-Louis. In 1779, the prince de Montbarrey, secretary of state for war, encouraged the king to celebrate this mass in full military dress as part of a reform in which Montbarrey increased the number of grand crosses and commanders and reduced the number of *chevaliers*, which had mushroomed to more than 16,000. There was a perception that the Order had become divorced from its original military purpose, with membership granted to people who had not distinguished themselves in war or who left military service as soon as they were awarded it, as well as the cross being worn by people who had not even received it. Montbarrey's decision to limit nominations to once every three years in peace was unpopular with soldiers who were waiting to retire with their cross after twenty-five years of service.[132] This suggests that the cross was being awarded routinely rather than for 'incomparable actions of valour and courage' as instructed by Louis XIV. Still, it was apparently deemed prestigious enough for a 32-year-old officer to die of pleasure on receiving it in 1779.[133] Soldiers who according to the Abbé de Véri might have been fed up with military service after fifteen or twenty years considered it worth waiting for. A poem thanking the comte d'Argenson for awarding the cross of Saint-Louis in 1753 indicates the feelings of pride and loyalty to the monarchy that it could invoke:

I will wear the image of the father of the Bourbons,	*Du Père des Bourbons je porterai l'image,*
My breast will be marked with the stamp of valour:	*Mon sein sera marqué du sceau de la valeur:*
Like so many heroes, such a precious token	*Comme tant de Héros, un si précieux gage*
Almost unites me with my king . . .[134]	*M'unit presque à mon Roi. . .*

The cross was valued as a symbol of social distinction as well as for the pensions accorded. In 1785, harsh punishments were proscribed for those found wearing it illegally: nobles could expect twenty years' imprisonment, commoners the even harsher prospect of perpetual galley service. Curiously, those trafficking the insignia escaped with only a fine and six months in prison.[135] That thousands proudly wore a cross depicting Saint Louis throughout the eighteenth century – many illegally – probably says more about the importance of marks of distinction in a society that placed enormous importance on status than specific devotion to the royal saint. Nevertheless, it did strengthen the nexus between the military and Saint Louis.

Under Louis XVI, the feast of Saint-Louis remained an occasion on which panegyrists idealized the saint-king and negotiated the tricky waters of defending his crusades. Late-eighteenth-century sermons emphasized Louis IX's role in the history of legislation. The Abbé du Temps spoke of a king 'himself drawing up a new jurisprudence'; 'we owe all our legislation to that of Louis IX'.[136] Paternalistic and even nationalistic language started to feature more notably from the 1770s. The Oratorian Père Mandar called Saint Louis 'father of the fatherland' after describing the positive effects of his rule ('the nobility subdued, faithful subjects, civilized towns, the whole people happy, and royal authority finally resting on the foundation of the law') and before expanding on how 'at his voice, agriculture is restored, industry wakes up, commerce flowers again'. Mandar also tried to paint a more tolerant picture of Louis IX's attitude to the Jews than had been common in panegyrics in the seventeenth and early eighteenth centuries (as discussed in Chapter 2). Arguing that they had been previously persecuted, he stated that Louis's attitude was more 'human'; 'he at least made them citizens, if he could not turn them into disciples of the Gospel'.[137]

Despite this rather ahistorical repackaging of Saint Louis to suit late-eighteenth-century concerns by presenting a less persecutory image and injecting the language of patriotism and citizenship, people were losing interest in the panegyrics. Back in 1715 it had been possible to remark that the unchanging historical facts of Louis IX's reign 'will take an infinity of new forms, handled by men of genius'.[138] Throughout the eighteenth century, however, emerged the notion that the subject matter had become exhausted.[139] The frequency of statements – even in official organs such as the *Mercure* – that 'the orators have said successively everything that there was to say' suggested that the tradition of annual panegyrics was in decline, less as a result of 'desacralization' than of simple boredom.[140] The *Mercure*, which probably had the widest readership of the periodicals with around 1,600 subscribers in 1763, seemed decreasingly interested in the panegyrics.[141] In 1764, the Abbé Varé delivered one before the Académie Française, but the report on the Académie's proceedings did not mention it.[142] In the 1680s panegyrics had been on the first page and received reams of detailed analysis, but a century later it was rare to get more than a cursory mention far into the publication. Either the readership was bored with panegyrics of Saint Louis, or the editors thought they were bored, or the editors were bored themselves – or all three. In January 1785, the Académie Française ended the tradition by giving the preachers an open choice of subject, allowing them to deliver 'a sermon of Christian morality with or without mention of Saint Louis'.[143] This was seen as 'an innovation desired for too long' which would not necessarily prevent praise of Saint Louis but freed the orator to refer to him without delivering a full panegyric.[144]

When a panegyrist in 1777 asked the Académie de Châlons if there had ever been a more perfect model than Saint Louis, some may have actually answered 'yes'.[145] Louis IX was increasingly having to share his position as the pre-eminent model of kingship with others untainted by his reputation for excessive religiosity and persecution. As Saint Louis's prominence diminished, Henri IV's rose. The *vert galant* was the subject of endless articles in the *Mercure*, appeared frequently on the Parisian stage and started to intrude on Louis IX's role as dynastic touchstone.[146] And if Saint Louis's cult had had limited popularity in the lower rungs of society, Henri IV's was not so constrained; according to Bachaumont, he was 'the only monarch whose memory has been kept by the poor'.[147] It was not just Henri: Louis XII was also re-emerging as an ideal French monarch in the period before the Revolution.[148] Of course, neither had an annual *fête*, but their praise started to compete with that of Louis IX even on the latter's; there is no mention of a panegyric of Saint Louis being delivered before the Académie d'Amiens on 25 August 1772, but there was a speech in praise of Henri IV.[149] The blue penitents of Toulouse organized festivities on 25 August 1775 to celebrate Louis XVI's *sacre*; Saint Louis was not mentioned in the sermon delivered by the Père Rouaix to a congregation including members of the Parlement, even in sections on justice and legislation. Instead, Rouaix stated that 'Henri IV comes to reign again over France'.[150] People were searching for new models of monarchy. After mentioning the lengthy discussion of the relative merits of Charlemagne, Louis IX and Louis XIV in the Abbé Lambert's panegyric of 1783 and 1787,[151] the *Mercure* noted that everything about Louis IX had been praised a hundred times.

> Perhaps it is time to leave it there, to leave Louis IX in all his glory and offer another model. Always Louis IX, say the foreigners; did the French not have any other king who was great and good? We understand that Louis, placed among the saints, is the only king whose praise can be undertaken in the pulpit . . . but this is a panegyric offered by a learned company, which gives laymen the right to speak of a good king.[152]

Although Louis IX was safe in the exclusivity of religious praise accorded by his canonization, the position of exemplary monarch was becoming a more crowded field. Of course, the trend should not be exaggerated. New poetry celebrating the crusades was still being published in 1779, the year that M. Jourdain, an enemy of the 'philosophic spirit', released his *Louiseïde*, which began by praising Saint Louis heroically going to brave the tyrants of Africa.[153]

In general, though, it was the lawgiver rather than the crusader who received the most praise in the 1780s. The Abbé de Saint-Martin was unhappy to 'see weaken the solemn homage rendered each year by the premier literary body to the virtues of Louis IX'.[154] He compensated by producing a massive edition of the *Établissements*. The premise of the work was that dark periods of history were marked by the decadence of laws, glorious periods by legislator monarchs who gave and maintained good laws. Whereas Boulainvilliers imagined an increasingly absolutist monarchy annexing power from formerly independent nobles, Saint-Martin described seigneurs usurping sovereignty after Hugues Capet, rendering corrupt the good laws of Charlemagne; Louis IX swept away the anarchy of feudalism by reforming laws, replacing trial by combat with examination of evidence. Occasional references to Louis XVI paint him as a king in this mould (thus prefiguring his rebranding as the 'restorer of liberty' during the early revolution), for example, abolishing serfdom in the royal domain in 1779. Saint-Martin noted that, similarly, 'the wisdom and humanity of Saint Louis seized every occasion to bring some easing to the unfortunate condition of the serfs'.[155]

Another work that supported this interpretation of Saint Louis was published by the future revolutionary Louis-Pierre Manuel. He saw feudal society as chaotic and cruel, drawing connections between persecuted medieval Jews and the black slaves of his own time. Manuel saw some unexpected positive developments as having emerged from the crusades (including the appearance of an order that wished to make a brotherhood of all peoples – the Freemasons), but in general they were condemned as 'unjust, barbarous, ridiculous' ventures that resulted in thousands dead, money wasted and the arts languishing. Given this picture of 'a reign in which all crimes, follies and misfortunes of the world were united', it is unsurprising that he did not see Louis IX as exempt from faults or errors. Nevertheless, Louis was a virtuous king whose great achievement was to give the first signal of liberty. 'His greatest miracles, which assured him the worship of posterity, were the *Établissements*.' By fixing rules of procedure and ending trial by duel, he struck the first blow against the rule by the strongest that was inevitable in feudalism.[156]

Perhaps as a result of the increasing emphasis on Saint Louis as legislator, a 'constitutionalist' Saint Louis emerged in the lead-up to the Revolution. In 1788, an anonymous poem imagining his advice to Louis XVI appeared in Rennes: 'The law is the only master' and 'your hand is bound by her'. The notes that follow the poem in this publication make it clear that the author was arguing for national assemblies to be convoked at fixed intervals. 'If the convocation of Estates-Generals depends only on the will of the prince, despotism will have time to put down deep roots.' There is no doubt that the author thought that this was exactly what had happened, although the end of the poem imagined a happy scenario in which Louis XVI followed the advice of his saintly ancestor to the joy of his adoring subjects.[157] Many of the *cahiers de doléances* assembled once the Estates-General was finally called in 1789 confirm that, in the eyes of many Frenchmen, Louis IX was, along with Louis XII and Henri IV, part of the holy trinity of good kingship to be recommended to Louis XVI. The people of Caussade near Montauban evoked 'the good and prompt justice' that Joinville recorded and the *cahier* of Lauris called Louis XVI the 'heir to the sceptre and virtues of Louis IX, Louis XII and Henri IV'.[158] It is worth noting, though, that there are examples of references to Louis XII and Henri IV without Saint Louis – and that many of the *cahiers* referred to none of them.[159]

On the surface there was little about Saint Louis's cult that changed significantly in the first years of the Revolution. A lawyer from Le Havre, Jean-Baptiste-Jacques Laignel, erected a bust of Louis XVI in his garden on 25 August 1789, saying the king was 'adopting the justice' of Saint Louis by calling the Estates-General to discuss 'the abuses of an arbitrary regime'. Laignel came to the point in the letter to Louis XVI's chief minister Jacques Necker, to whom the poem was dedicated: He hoped to publish and address to the National Assembly a dissertation on interest. Over a month after the fall of the Bastille, Saint Louis's feast was still an opportunity to praise the king and seek favours from the government, even if there was a new desire to contribute 'to the great work of regeneration'.[160]

Supporters of the constitutional monarchy such as the comte de Mirabeau could still call France the empire 'of Louis IX, Louis XII and Henri IV' in July 1789.[161] The National Constituent Assembly did not sit on 25 August 1789 because it was still respected as the king's *fête*. Indeed, the Assembly sent forty-eight deputies to congratulate Louis XVI, who went to mass wearing the cross of Saint-Louis and later heard acclamations of *Vive le Roi* from the balcony at Versailles, the only ominous element in hindsight being the presence of a large contingent of *poissardes* (fishwives/market women) from the market of Les Halles.[162] This was the very day before the adoption of the Declaration of the Rights of Man and of the Citizen by the Assembly. About six weeks later occurred the dramatic and violent events of 5 October 1789, when the market women compelled the royal family to leave Versailles. However, fourteen days after that famous night, Louis XVI was still addressed in the Assembly as 'the heir of Louis IX and Henri IV'.[163] In 1790 the Assembly *did* sit on 25 August, a subtle but revealing change from the previous year, but even so, its president delivered a discourse in honour of the king's feast that praised Saint Louis for delivering the first blows against the feudal regime, work only being completed under Louis XVI.[164] Radicals were already criticizing this obsequiousness to the monarchy; the following day, an article by Jean-Paul Marat lambasted it as appropriate for despotic regimes rather than places where liberty reigns and argued that it was ridiculous to think that either Louis IX or Louis XVI had wanted to overthrow feudalism.[165]

Such views were still not mainstream. Saint Louis's continued status as a model of kingship was demonstrated on 15 June 1790, when *Louis IX in Egypt*, a three-act opera with words by Nicolas-François Guillard and François-Guillaume Andrieux and music by Jean-Baptiste Lemoyne, opened at the Académie Royale de Musique in Paris.[166] Performed ten times in 1790, this work is a fascinating exploration of the legitimacy of kingship in the years of the constitutional monarchy.[167] The preface to the libretto mentioned that the more obvious historical topic, Henri IV, had already been exhausted in the theatre, but that the period of Louis IX showed France groaning under feudalism, featuring a good monarch comparable to Louis XVI working to restore liberty. The libretto drew on two popular stories – that the Assassins had been sent on an unsuccessful attempt to kill Louis IX by the 'Old Man of the Mountain' and that Louis had been offered rule over Egypt following the murder of the sultan in recognition of his exceptional virtue – to create a strong statement of the virtues of constitutional monarchy.[168]

The story unfolds after Louis has conquered Damietta and much of the plot revolves around the jealous sultan's attempts to have him assassinated, and a pastoral love story between Almodan, the sultan's long-lost son, and Adele, daughter of Badouin de Boutillon. There are plenty of opportunities for Louis IX, the blameless hero, to expound a view of idealized kingship based on service to the people and respect for laws. He tells Joinville that 'My life is for my people and must be of use to them' and warns the sultan not to take 'our [kings'] whims for laws. Cherish our subjects and respect their rights'. The sultan responds by denying that these 'slaves' have rights at all, which Louis rebuts by emphasizing the necessity of laws and governing with love. Following the sultan's own assassination and the accession of the virtuous Almodan to his rightful throne, Louis advises him to free his subjects from the yoke of slavery and at every instant render liberty.[169] Throughout the work the chorus sing the praises of their 'good father' and his exemplary virtues and justice. Here we see how the increasing emphasis on lawgiving evident in the late eighteenth century allowed for Saint Louis's transformation into a constitutional, paternalistic monarch in the early years of the Revolution. The debates over his crusades were sidestepped in this opera by portraying him as bringing liberty and good government to Egypt (prefiguring later justifications of imperialism). Here the primary duties of the monarch lie in securing liberty and just laws for his people rather than serving God; the saint-king was still an epitome of the exemplary enactment of royal duties, but in a manner quite different from the sacralized, absolutist model that had been advanced for most of the Bourbon period.

The opera had respectable gross takings of 30,512 *livres*, 14 *sous* but Mark Darlow has suggested that the subject matter was ill-timed, coming just a month before the passage of the Civil Constitution of the Clergy by the National Assembly on 12 July 1790.[170] There was criticism from more left-wing publications such as the *Révolutions de Paris*, which called the text 'absurd' and accused it of seeking to foster adoration for Louis XVI, 'which could retard the progress of the spirit of liberty'.[171]

More positive reviews, however, praised the opera for focussing on national history.[172] This was in the vein of the sermon delivered by the Abbé Vigneras before the Académie Française on 25 August 1790. By now, the traditional panegyric of Saint Louis had been replaced by a discourse 'on the love of the fatherland'. Nevertheless, Vigneras mentioned Saint Louis, stating that his virtues and *Établissements* indicated that 'love of the fatherland was first among his sentiments' and ominously adding that this would be to the shame of any of his descendants whose love of the fatherland might weaken.[173] He finished the introduction by stating that 'in celebrating the feast of the best and wisest of kings, we celebrate the feast of French patriotism', and the rest of the sermon focused on serving the fatherland.

These operatic and panegyric presentations of an updated Saint Louis were designed to bring him in line with the new patriotic era of the constitutional monarchy. Nevertheless, a more traditional image of Saint Louis was weighing on Louis XVI's mind as he deliberated over whether to sign the Civil Constitution of the Clergy. Unlike his contemporary, the Emperor Joseph II, Louis XVI was unwilling to approve radical reform of the church in the face of papal opposition. Instead, he indicated his desire to respect the traditions of sacral kingship (if not Gallicanism) by presenting himself as 'the grandson of Saint Louis, submissive to the legitimate successor of Saint Peter' in a letter of 2 July 1790 begging Pope Pius VI not just for advice but for 'orders'. Although – reluctantly and under pressure – the king did eventually grant his assent despite the pontiff's objections, a disinclination to act in a manner contrary to that of his holy ancestor may have contributed to his hesitation, as well as causing later regret. In a letter to the archbishop of Arles of 29 June 1791, Louis XVI worried that God was punishing him for having preferred 'insolent philosophy' to the religion of his ancestors, 'so dear to Saint Louis, from whom I glory in descending'.[174]

Traditional modes of royal representation and court pageantry persisted in 1790, including the rituals of the Order of Saint-Louis. Only in 1791 did the Assembly interfere with the Order, deciding that all officers, regardless of rank, would be awarded the cross of Saint-Louis after twenty-four years, including the time served as an ordinary soldier for those who had been elevated from the rank and file. This was retrospective so resulted in huge numbers being admitted. There seems to have been no mention that Saint Louis was an inappropriate patron for such an important institution under the new order, though the exclusively Catholic nature of the Order was removed in September 1791.[175]

This occured in the context of increased hostility to the monarchy following the flight to Varennes in June 1791.[176] Two months after the failure of that ill-fated attempt to escape, there were no public celebrations on 25 August in Paris for the first time since the 1610s. A sense of eerie quiet is palpable in the *Gazette*'s report that 'the Saint-Louis, feast of His Majesty, passed without any of the festivities and ceremonies usual at this time. The Tuileries are closed and deserted as on ordinary days. The Académie de Musique did not give the *bouquet du Roi* following the old custom'.[177] This was not the case everywhere: the feast was celebrated with pomp in 1790 and 1791 in Avignon – not yet formally part of France – as part of the efforts of the 'patriot' regime there to redirect urban identity from the papacy towards France.[178] Nevertheless, the silence in Paris in 1791 was significant, part of broader developments which led to the abolition of the monarchy in 1792.

The marquis de Sade's *Aline and Valcour*, written in the Bastille in 1789, criticized the 'extravagant mania' with which 'this cruel and imbecilic king' (Saint Louis) had been praised, arguing that 'all his actions were false, ridiculous or barbaric' and that there were few kings from the history of France 'more suited to contempt and indignation'.[179] Political upheaval would ensure that in a few years this went from a fringe view expressed by radical libertines to the new consensus. Louis La Vicomterie's *Crimes of the kings of France*, first published in 1791, is a litany of cruelty, corruption and oppression from Clovis to Louis XVI (in some ways the inverse of Rousselet's *Lys sacré*). 'Louis IX, called Saint Louis' did not escape damning criticism, particularly for the crusades, 'projects which, in the eyes of enlightened people, would have sufficed for him to be at least deposed'. Louis's cruelty to heretics and blasphemers provided fertile ground for condemnation, and the shadow of old criticisms is palpable in the assertion that his ransom impoverished the kingdom. 'I will say that he was one of the kings who did the most harm to France through the senseless projects to which his empty and fanatical head gave birth.'[180] This complete reversal of the way Louis IX had been presented until very recently was indicative of a sea-change in the way the monarchy was perceived.

Following Louis XVI's execution, an attempt was made to purge France of Saint Louis, alongside other symbols of royalty. Institutions dedicated to him were suppressed, such as the Maison de Saint-Cyr in March 1793.[181] The cross of Saint-Louis had been abolished in October 1792 when it was deemed a 'mark by which the kings noted their slaves' that was incompatible with the new republic; Louis-Pierre Manuel was instrumental in this decision.[182] In July 1793 it was decreed that former members of the Order should surrender their insignia to their local municipalities.[183] On 23 August 1793 Joseph Delauny d'Angers addressed the National Convention stating that, although everyone should be able to celebrate the dead as appropriate, 'French republicans cannot allow the people to suspend their work to celebrate the memory of one of their ancient despots. The feast of Louis IX approaches; I ask that it be suppressed, and the merchants obliged to open their shops like on ordinary days.' His motion was passed.[184] Two days later, by order of the National Convention, the sale of furniture at Versailles began; it was surely not a coincidence that this was the feast of Saint-Louis, adding to the symbolic value of the event.[185] The citizens of Saint-Louis-en-l'Ile in the Dordogne showed they were moving with the times when, describing themselves as 'true *sans-culottes*', they wrote to the National Convention requesting permission to rename their town Montagne-Libre-sur-l'Ile.[186] Such changes were part of an effort to redefine public space by replacing names associated with monarchy with revolutionary ideals. The rue Saint-Louis in Sète was similarly renamed rue de la Liberté, and in Paris in 1793 the rue Saint-Louis-en-l'isle-Notre-Dame was renamed rue de la Fraternité.[187]

Louis IX's images, especially statues which could not be hidden away, were vulnerable to the iconoclasm through which republican France purged its royal and Catholic past during the dechristianization campaign.[188] The crown was ripped from a statue of Saint Louis at Saint-Eustache in Paris in July 1793 and another at Saint-Sulpice attacked in early 1794.[189] When the church of Saint-Louis in Brest was converted into a Temple of Reason, the statue of Saint Louis was smashed to pieces.[190] On 11 October 1793, following the suppression of the Girondin politician François Buzot's efforts to make Évreux a centre of opposition to the National Convention, the revolutionary authorities organized for an effigy of Saint Louis to be burned alongside other emblems of royalty and religion 'while the citizens danced'.[191]

The relics of Saint Louis were also vulnerable. The treasury of the Sainte-Chapelle, including the head of Saint Louis, was moved in 1791 to Saint-Denis, where the royal tombs were systematically desecrated between August 1793 and January 1794.[192] The windows depicting Saint Louis and his *châsse* were destroyed and the relics disappeared.[193] On 11 November 1793 the treasuries of both institutions, now disdained as symbols of a fanatical and oppressive past, were taken to the National Convention by the municipality of 'Franciade' (formerly Saint-Denis).[194] Many reliquaries were sent to be melted down, presumably including those of Saint Louis, although a *mémoire* from 1817 discovered by Philippe Boiry suggests that part of the skull was actually saved by one of the inspectors.[195] Although the reliquaries at Lamontjoie were successfully hidden away, the great Parisian reliquaries of Saint Louis did not survive the destruction of 1793.

Conclusion

'Saint Louis was not a prophet when he developed a great passion for the Jacobins and Cordeliers. . . . The good sire never predicted that they would give their names to two slightly different orders who would dethrone his race and become the founders of the French Republic.'[196] Speaking at the Jacobins on 25 December 1793, the revolutionary journalist and politician Camille Desmoulins took delight in the fact that the words Jacobin and Cordelier, formerly linked to the patronage of Louis IX, were now associated with the radicals who had destroyed the French monarchy. By this point the cult of Saint Louis had been swept away, his feast suppressed, his Order abolished, his reputation reduced to tatters, many of his images defaced and his relics destroyed.

Although these dramatic changes were a consequence of the Revolution, the cult had been in decline for some time. From the middle of Louis XV's reign, the very qualities that had assured Saint Louis such pre-eminence in the seventeenth century – piety and crusading – made him awkward for the elite strata of society most concerned with his cult. The fact that this was combined with Louis XV's worsening reputation meant that Saint Louis's efficacy in sacralizing the French monarchy was losing power. The panegyrics turned from being an effective vehicle of royal representation to an Enlightenment battleground between *philosophes* and *dévots*; moreover, wider interest in the panegyrics evaporated and the Académie Française ended its tradition of hearing them in 1785. The other corporate group that had played a major role in promoting Saint Louis, the Jesuits, had been expelled from France in 1764. Efforts to recast Saint Louis as a legislator king were not enough to make up for the fact that his promoters were disappearing and his cult's ability to bind elites to the crown was decreasing.

Nevertheless, these developments do not indicate the desacralization of a monarchy sliding inexorably towards revolution. If anything, the advent of Henri IV showed the adaptability of royal culture, which was able to dust down a new monarchical hero better suited to the mood of the times, even as it retained the old. Both Henri and Louis IX remained popular for some time after 14 July 1789. Furthermore, the destruction of Saint Louis in 1792–3 was not permanent. The Revolution recharged interest in a flagging cult among royalists, turning the saint into a figure of counter-revolution and giving renewed importance to his pivotal place in the Bourbons' conception of their legitimacy.

Saint Louis from exile to restoration, 1792–1830[1]

'Paris awoke with an air of celebration' on the morning of 25 August 1814. The royal colours flew from almost every window and Louis XVIII appeared on the balcony of the Tuileries to the delight of a huge crowd crying '*Vive le Roi*'. All in all, wrote the general Marie-Antoine de Reiset, the capital 'seems finally to have rediscovered its old love for its kings'.[2] The occasion, of course, was the feast of Saint-Louis, and the *Gazette*'s report indicated that many saw its revival in 1814 as the reassuring return of a tradition that had been cruelly interrupted by the Revolution.[3] A year later, however, having recently returned to Paris after Napoleon's defeat at Waterloo, Louis XVIII decided that official celebrations of Saint Louis's feast were inappropriate and forbade expensive festivities.[4] Although this did not stop a crowd assembling at the Tuileries to sing, dance and doff their hats to the king, Napoleon's return during the 'Hundred Days' had revealed that such expressions of loyalty could not be relied upon from all quarters and that the Bourbons faced serious challenges if their Restoration was to last.[5]

Most importantly, as during Henri IV's reign, the Bourbon monarchy needed to create a governing consensus by winning the support of its erstwhile opponents. This was particularly important in the bureaucracy and military. One means of doing so was through the liberal distribution of honours. Reiset, who had served in the revolutionary and imperial armies, was one of many to be admitted into the Order of Saint-Louis, an institution immediately revived by Louis XVIII in 1814.[6] However, following two-and-a-half decades of constitutional upheaval in which France had lurched from absolute to constitutional monarchy to republic before ending up in the Napoleonic Empire, this alone could not resolve some fundamental questions. How could the Bourbons win the allegiance of former supporters of the Revolution and the Empire while at the same time persuading their own partisans to accept the idea of a 'limited monarchy'?[7] How far could they revive the close alliance with the Catholic Church and the old language of sacral kingship? Could traditional monarchical culture recover the loyalty and affection of the people of France or would it alienate them? Would aspects of that culture, such as the cult of Saint Louis, create consensus around the Restoration settlement or provide fuel for contestation between different groups?

The essential problem of a restoration is the reconciliation of the recent and distant past, in this case the post-1789 period and the *Ancien Régime*.[8] Although the famous *Charte constitutionnelle* (1814) promised to 're-forge the chain of time', the Bourbon

Restoration was far from being a simple return to the past.[9] Many achievements of the Revolution were confirmed by the *Charte*, which established a representative political system as well as rights such as equality before the law and freedom of the press. At the same time, however, the monarchy made efforts to glorify the memory of the *Ancien Régime*, referring to several former kings (including Saint Louis) in the *Charte*'s preface. The tensions between this new situation and the old memory were a feature of this period and a problem for the monarchy. The *Charte* made Catholicism the state religion but also guaranteed freedom of religion. How did this relate to the Catholic monarchy associated with the *Ancien Régime* as symbolized by Saint Louis? Although this period is sometimes described as one of simple union between throne and altar, there were often serious tensions between the regime and the church over the nature of the Restoration settlement and whether the Revolution should be forgotten or expiated.[10] Discussion of Saint Louis's example became a revealing point of controversy and contestation between different factions in this fractured political landscape, from those among the ultra-royalists who advocated traditional conceptions of Catholic monarchy to the anticlerical or secular liberals who defended the *Charte* and the incorporation of Revolutionary achievements into the Bourbon monarchy.

In a society that mixed partisans of the *Ancien Régime*, Revolution and Empire, was it possible, as Françoise Waquet has asked, to 'create a union or communion through festivities?'[11] The feast of Saint-Louis was widely celebrated and often effective in providing an opportunity for royalists to demonstrate their allegiance, although it could also serve as an opportunity for those with different political loyalties to subvert Bourbon culture. However, the nature of the celebrations on 25 August organized by departmental and municipal authorities across France shows a clear preference for non-religious festivities that minimized the focus on Saint Louis himself. This secularization of a saint's feast day was perhaps due to the ultimately divisive nature of Saint Louis's memory during the Restoration and, indeed, to the broader context in which religion was 'the single greatest source of national discord', at the heart of a culture war between *les deux France* throughout the nineteenth century.[12]

Analysis of the revival of the cult of Saint Louis allows historians to view the problems at the heart of the Bourbon Restoration's attempt to craft a model of kingship that would create political consensus around the new regime. These problems came from the desire to create a sense of continuity with the past. Saint Louis typified the Catholic nature of the *Ancien Régime*, and the celebration of his memory revealed the deep divisions between advocates of the Restoration settlement and those who harked back to the sacralized ethos of the pre-Revolutionary monarchy. Fabian Rausch has argued that, although it convinced some on the left for a certain period that a Bourbon constitutional monarchy was conceivable, the *Charte* was 'not a means of integration between the great political camps of Restoration France'.[13] Much the same can be said of Saint Louis who, like other aspects of Restoration representation, served to encourage contestation and to entrench rather than overcome differences of opinion. Despite attempts by liberals to attach his memory to the *Charte* and the secularized nature of many celebrations on 25 August, he remained a figure associated with the reactionary right. As such, his memory served to consolidate a sense of partisan solidarity among ultras and royalists, therefore deepening rather than weakening wider political divisions and failing to create consensus around the restored Bourbons.

A counter-revolutionary saint

In an extraordinary passage in Jacques Necker's reflections on the French Revolution, first published in 1796, Louis XVI's former minister noted that virtuous and magnanimous conduct would have served all sides much better than the terrible policies they actually pursued. His thoughts went to the French monarch who had most captured his respect and admiration, Louis IX. Necker imagined Saint Louis addressing the French, declaring that he would not wish to trouble France with internal wars while they were seeking liberty, even if it was in the form of a republic in a land formerly ruled by his family. If the government they had chosen made them happy, he would prefer to renounce his rights than to form new divisions: 'I make this sacrifice with courage.' However, should the French decide that their current system is not what they had hoped for or if oppression succeeded liberty, he would race to join 'the citizen soldiers who wished to combat tyrants and tyranny, and to unite myself unto death to their cause and the defence of their rights'.[14]

The idea of Saint Louis, the dynastic lynchpin, renouncing the Bourbon claim to rule France in the interests of national harmony would have seemed utterly heretical to most royalists in the 1790s and early 1800s. Instead, they turned him into a figure of counter-revolution almost immediately following the downfall of the monarchy. When Barnabé Darosoy, author of the *Gazette de Paris*, was condemned to death for his contact with royalist *émigrés* in August 1792, he proudly announced that 'a royalist like me ought to die on the feast of Saint-Louis'.[15] Indeed, while the feast was abolished in France itself, it was celebrated with magnificence by *émigrés* in the Austrian Low Countries, who held a solemn mass to pray for the royal family.[16] In Rome, the feast, lavishly celebrated at San Luigi dei Francesi, was preceded by days of public prayers for France, with the pope himself celebrating mass in the chapel of Saint Louis there. The recently rebranded *Gazette nationale* showed how much it had changed with the times in its dismissal of the Roman celebrations: 'it would be impossible to make those who do not know the august farce of this country understand the wretched importance of this festival.'[17]

When Louis Capet (as Louis XVI was now known) was guillotined on 21 January 1793, his confessor the Abbé Edgeworth is said to have uttered the words 'son of Saint Louis, ascend to Heaven'.[18] Although this line has become a famous part of the *tableau* of the king's execution, Edgeworth himself 'could neither deny nor affirm that he had spoken the words'.[19] Whatever the truth of the matter, that the words quickly became part of the mythology of the execution says much about the importance of Saint Louis in the dynastic identity of the Bourbons. The story would be frequently cited in royalist literature commemorating the 'martyr king'.[20] Royalist iconography also associated Saint Louis with the moment of Louis XVI's death and apotheosis, such as the engraving presented to the comte d'Artois that showed the saint-king at the head of a welcoming committee (also including Louis XIV, Louis XV, Henri IV and Louis XII) that received the guillotined monarch into Heaven (Figure 7.1).

Back in France, Saint Louis was invoked by the counter-revolutionaries who rose in rebellion in the Vendée in the months following the 'crime' of Louis XVI's execution. As a *Declaration of Frenchmen faithful to the king* put it in May 1793, the Vendéens would stand firm as they had on their side 'the God of Clovis and of Saint Louis'.[21] Their 'Catholic and Royal Army' was motivated to oppose the revolution both by the execution of the king and by religious changes since the introduction of the Civil Constitution of the Clergy in 1790. In the words of a proclamation to the French people in 1794, 'it is for [the king] that we fight, it is to establish the altars of the true God ... it is to restore the throne of Saint Louis and Henri IV that we voluntarily risk our lives'.[22] The 'throne' or 'sceptre' of Saint Louis remained a powerful symbol of Bourbon legitimacy for royalists.[23] In January 1796 the Vendéen general Charles Sapinaud de La Rairie wrote to the comte d'Artois, discussing his devotion to the cause of throne and altar and describing himself as 'a faithful subject who has no other ambition than to contribute to the reestablishment of the throne of Saint Louis, or to die while fighting for God and his king. I share these sentiments with all my soldiers'.[24] Such sentiment was no doubt strengthened by the generous distribution of the cross of Saint-Louis

Figure 7.1 *Apothéose de Louis XVI* by Dulompré and Chasselat. © Bibliothèque nationale de France.

in the Vendéen armies – over 1,000 were awarded in the 1790s.[25] When Saumur was captured in June 1793, supposedly loyalist republicans suddenly appeared wearing the white cockade and the cross of Saint-Louis, showing a general appreciation that it was a symbol of counter-revolutionary royalism.[26]

In August 1793, Louis d'Elbée wrote to the comte d'Artois asking him to come and join the loyal armies in the Vendée. 'A descendant of Saint Louis at our head will be for us and our soldiers the presage of new successes and new victories.'[27] Although Artois did not take up this suggestion, the exiled Bourbons did appreciate Saint Louis's symbolic value. In February 1795, claiming to be 'regent' of France from exile in Verona, the comte de Provence wrote to the royalist general François de Charette, speaking of his desire to join him and 'share your perils and your glory'. In the meantime, he asked Charette to use 'Saint-Louis' as his watchword and 'the king and the regency' as a rallying cry.[28] Later that year, it was reported to the Committee of Public Safety in Paris that Charette had celebrated the feast of Saint-Louis with pomp at Saint-Christophe-du-Ligneron.[29]

In July 1795, Provence issued the Declaration of Verona, claiming the throne under the title 'Louis XVIII' following the death of his nephew and promising that 'the God of Saint Louis' would be his guide.[30] During his twenty-three years in exile after fleeing Paris in June 1791, chased across Europe from one insecure residence to the next, the comte de Provence regularly cited Saint Louis as both a model of fortitude in adversity and a symbol of his legitimacy even when it seemed highly unlikely he would ever be restored. On 22 March 1801 he wrote from Warsaw to the Abbé de Montesquiou, responding to General Bonaparte's request that he 'sacrifice what he calls my interests for that which he calls the good of my country'. Provence doubted that this would quash royalist sentiment: 'while there remained a descendant of Saint Louis, would the royalists forget these rights [of my family]?'[31] In fact, Napoleon allowed *émigrés* to return to France from 1802 in an effort to isolate the Bourbon pretender. With the First Consul acquiring legitimacy through conquest and agreeing the Concordat with the papacy, the chances of a Bourbon restoration seemed slim. Louis nevertheless resisted Napoleon's offer of 'great advantages' if he renounced his claim to the throne.[32] Stating that he would fulfil his obligations to God to his last breath, he declared that 'as descendant of Saint Louis, I shall try to imitate his example by respecting myself even in captivity'.[33] Any residual hope that General Bonaparte would play the role of General Monck, restoring Louis XVIII as the latter had restored Charles II of England, was of course gone by the time of Napoleon's coronation as emperor of the French in 1804. Louis responded with outrage: 'Never will we abandon our rights. Frenchmen! We take as witness to this oath the God of Saint Louis, he who judges the judges!'[34]

This grandiloquent language aside, Louis often had to keep a low profile in exile. Lewis Goldsmith, one of Napoleon's spies (at this point), reported from Warsaw in 1803 that 'the comte de Lille [Louis] lives very withdrawn here; he sees no-one'. Nevertheless,

> last Friday, Saint Louis's day, all the notable people of Warsaw were at his residence, Prince Joseph, the governor, and several others dined with him, and the servants of the guests were equally treated. This act of munificence on his part has been much

spoken of, because for the whole time he has been here he has not given a penny to the poor.[35]

On the same date, exiled royalists in London including the comte d'Artois, duc de Berry, duc d'Orléans and prince de Condé celebrated the feast at the French chapel on King Street.[36] Where it was possible to celebrate it, the feast of Saint-Louis remained an occasion for royalist celebration; where this was impossible, it remained a focus of hope. As an anonymous 'Regi-Phile' put it, 'although it is scarcely likely that we will be able to proclaim Your Majesty on the feast of Saint-Louis, I nevertheless implore you not to give yourself up to despair, and I swear to you on my head that, in a few centuries at the latest, we will head towards Reims in pomp'.[37]

The period's most important royalist writer, François-René de Chateaubriand, frequently invoked Saint Louis during the years of Bourbon exile.[38] In his *Genius of Christianity* (1801), Chateaubriand spoke of a monarch who was 'arbiter of kings, revered even by the infidels'.[39] His account of a journey to Jerusalem from 1806 to 1807, particularly the return to France via Tunis, included nostalgic reflections on Saint Louis: 'France, which could not console herself for having lost such a monarch on earth, declared him her protector in heaven. Louis, placed among the saints, thus became a kind of eternal king for the fatherland'.[40] This idealized image was put to the service of those whom he invariably called 'the sons of Saint Louis'. In writings, speeches and pamphlets such as the influential *De Buonaparte et des Bourbons* (1814), Chateaubriand never lost an opportunity to highlight the Bourbons' descent from Louis IX as evidence of the antiquity of their claim to the French crown as well as Napoleon's status as a usurper of the 'throne of Saint Louis'.[41]

Following the Concordat, Napoleon created his own equivalent patron by persuading Rome to canonize a saint for his new imperial dynasty.[42] Between 1806 and 1813, 15 August was celebrated as the feast of 'Saint-Napoleon'. Despite Napoleon's personal enthusiasm, it generated little popular fervour and 'essentially provided local officials with opportunities to sing the praises of the emperor'.[43] It remained to be seen whether Saint Louis could do any better for Louis XVIII after the Bourbons were restored to the throne.

Saint Louis and the *Charte*

O Saint Louis! from your fatherland
Welcome the pious harmonies;
It is to your dear posterity
That we owe these emotions:
For too long the days of turbulence
Had exiled this homage,
This veneration that we give you:
The hymn of recognition
Strikes up, and proclaims to France
Your feast, and that of the Bourbons.[44]

In this ode, which appeared at the beginning of the Restoration, a former musketeer named Clément-Joseph Pays d'Alissac, made a chevalier of Saint-Louis in 1814, tried to associate Saint Louis with the *patrie*, that new source of political legitimacy and focus of loyalty which had emerged in the eighteenth century and displaced the monarchy in the Revolution. In doing so, he was participating in a broader trope that used Saint Louis to re-establish the legitimacy of the restored monarchy. An image of Saint Louis was placed above the throne in Notre-Dame for Louis XVIII's formal entry into Paris in 1814 and the king would continue to honour his ancestor, for example, founding the Lycée Saint-Louis in Paris in 1820.[45] In 1822 he had the throne room at the Tuileries redecorated with scenes from the lives of Saint Louis, François I and Henri IV.[46] For Catholics, of course, Louis IX was not just an historical figure but also a saint who was watching over the kingdom from Heaven. This was clearly expressed in d'Alissac's poem, and in a *bouquet* addressed to Louis XVIII in 1815 which invoked a saint looking down on him and applauding his generous efforts to reunite his people.[47] For those with less impeccable royalist credentials, perhaps compromised by involvement with the various regimes since Louis XVI, Saint Louis could be a useful symbol of rediscovered loyalty to the Bourbons. Edouard-Thomas Simon, an octogenarian who had been 'a revolutionary of whatever stripe required by the regime in power', quickly produced an abridged version of Pierre Le Moyne's epic poem with a preface cheering the happy reestablishment of the Bourbons.[48]

Saint Louis's status as dynastic ancestor was thus important to Bourbon royalists, but which qualities of kingship did he represent for them? Their key source was Joinville, reprinted several times in the period (sometimes in editions intended for children).[49] Joinville was acknowledged as a principal 'guide' to the reign of Saint Louis by one of the Restoration's most important historians, Joseph-François Michaud. Given that his monumental *History of the Crusades* presented those conflicts as a source of French national pride, it is unsurprising that he treated Saint Louis as a beacon of justice, virtue and chivalric heroism, attributes also visible in 'the descendants of such a good prince'. Such selfless and humble acts as Louis descending from his horse to bury the putrefying bodies of dead crusaders with his own hands provided opportunities for contrasts with the 'hero of modern times' who poisoned the wounded on the battlefield (a reference to the story that Napoleon did so when retreating from Jaffa in 1799). Michaud noted Louis's pious devotion to the 'sacred cause' of crusading but also offered up to date justifications, making connections between the king's concern for Christian suffering under Muslim oppression to the Greek war of independence in the 1820s as well as arguing that Louis intended to found a colony in order to further 'the interests of commerce'.[50] The crusades were the most controversial part of Louis's record by the early 1800s and a spectrum of opinion from reactionary to liberal was marked by whether the writer in question praised, merely justified, gently criticized or outright condemned them.

Those not inclined to pore through weighty tomes of medieval history might have encountered Saint Louis in other media, notably theatre – part of a broader context in which idealized sovereigns from France's medieval history proved common topics on the Parisian stage during the Restoration.[51] Jacques-François Ancelot's *Louis IX* (premiered in November 1819) demonstrated the twin ideals of absolute loyalty to the monarchy and to Catholicism. Ancelot was a partisan of the regime and dedicated his work to Louis XVIII, noting that 'under Your Majesty's rule, it was easy for me to recount the virtues of the father of the Bourbons'.[52] The play caused controversy as it was perceived as a royalist response to Casimir Delavigne's 'liberal' play *Les Sicilian Vespers*, which focused on the overthrow of Saint Louis's oppressive brother Charles d'Anjou in Sicily.[53] The ultra-royalist *Conservateur littéraire* remarked patronizingly that 'the little shopkeeper elector (*petit marchand électeur*) is going to hiss at Louis IX' because 'his *Constitutionnel* has revealed to him that Louis IX is called Saint Louis and the merchant elector is a *philosophe*'.[54] This rather disdainful dismissal of the mere merchants brought into the franchise by the *Charte* and their 'philosophical' views (read Enlightened and anticlerical – and, of course, critical of the crusades) was an indication that Saint Louis's model of Christian kingship was likely to create contestation between partisan groups rather than consensus around the Restoration.

Another route into royalist constructions of Saint Louis is offered by the panegyrics. The feeling of exhaustion with the genre that had resulted in the Académie Française abandoning it in 1785 was completely changed by the events of 1789–1814, creating an immediate interest in resurrecting this pre-Revolutionary tradition. Panegyrics dating back over a century were rapidly reprinted in 1814.[55] Corinne Legoy has shown that royalist encomium during this period had a combative and polemical tone in its focus on the identification of adversaries of the monarchy and Catholicism.[56] This is visible in the triumphant and confrontational attitude of many Restoration panegyrists of Saint Louis. As the Abbé Guillon declared in 1818, 'religion is avenged'. A former opponent of the Civil Constitution of the Clergy, he used the panegyric to avenge the secularizing crimes of the Revolution and to put Catholicism back at the heart of the exercise of government in France. Presenting Saint Louis as a model of Christian kingship whose greatest glory was to have been canonized, Guillon divided the sermon into sections showing Louis's imitation of God on the throne by wisdom and goodness and then by justice and force. He praised the crusades – which, as discussed in Chapter 6, had become a focus of criticism in late-eighteenth-century panegyrics – on the grounds of honour, religion, patriotism and even humanity. There were, of course, implicit parallels between Saint Louis's genius as a lawgiver who secured royal power in the chaotic context of 'the monster of feudalism' and Louis XVIII's reestablishment of monarchy after years of upheaval. The panegyric finished by addressing Saint Louis directly, citing his 'powerful intercession' as the reason for the restoration of the Bourbons, imitators of his virtues as well as inheritors of his blood, to the throne of France.[57]

This unambiguous defence of the traditional model of Catholic kingship was typical of the opinion normally projected by Restoration panegyrists. According to the Abbé Béraud, preaching before the Académie Française in 1823, royalty was a sacrament instituted to channel divine kindness and justice to the nations.[58] The Abbé Montès in 1819 began by arguing the case for divine providence; God decides the fate of kingdoms, and when 'his justice is satisfied' he grants good kings who are able to heal the wounds of difficult times and cause them to be succeeded by pure and serene days.[59] Louis IX is the example, but the resonances with Louis XVIII were no doubt intended. Saint Louis was great in peace and war, but only because of his intense piety. His legislation, particularly the *Établissements*, was praised for bringing order to a

France racked with feudal chaos, but so was his devotion to the personal rendering of justice. Most preachers illustrated the last point by describing him doing so under an oak tree at Vincennes, a famous incident from Joinville frequently depicted by artists during the Restoration, including Georges Rouget in a painting commissioned in 1825 for the *Conseil d'État* where it was no doubt intended to serve as an example of justice.[60] Panegyrists were likely to emphasize that Saint Louis loved peace and did not fight out of a desire for glory.[61] However, the crusades were normally viewed positively, with preachers citing advantages mentioned by Michaud such as the opening of new commercial relations with the east. Some went further: Béraud called the crusades 'useful, just and necessary' and noted their success 'in holding back the Asiatic hordes, enemies of civilisation as well as of the Gospel'.[62]

This emphasis on religion became only more important with the accession of Charles X, whose desire to resurrect the traditional culture of sacral monarchy was displayed by his *sacre* at Reims. A preacher at the cathedral of Ajaccio praised the new king as a worthy descendant of Saint Louis who would govern in the interests of religion and voiced his hope that 'the France of Clovis and Saint Louis will reappear in the France of our century'.[63] Not everyone relished the prospect, particularly after the controversial Anti-Sacrilege law (1825).[64] In this context some panegyrists, such as the Abbé Gaudreau in 1829, discussed Louis IX's rigorous punishment of blasphemers with sympathy, making connections with 'our modern legislation'. Gaudreau argued that religion had raised Saint Louis to the height of virtue and his great achievements as king, legislator and warrior.[65] By drawing a line between the actions of Saint Louis and Charles X, Gaudreau was highlighting the continuity not just of legitimacy but also of religious kingship.

The implication was that the modern Bourbons should follow in the footsteps of their ancestor. Indeed, the preface to an edition of pre-Revolutionary panegyrics said this '*Manuel des Rois*' could encourage Louis XVIII to take Saint Louis as a model.[66] To what extent, however, was this compatible with the actual exercise of kingship during the Restoration? How could the Catholic monarchy represented by Saint Louis and advocated by the church and diehard ultras be reconciled with the toleration written into the *Charte* and the newer, secularized political culture of the Restoration? Under Louis XVIII there were efforts to minimize the discrepancy by remoulding Saint Louis's memory to the support of the new constitutional arrangements. These drew on the image of the lawgiver king that had been developed in the eighteenth century. In Necker's daughter Germaine de Staël's *Considerations on the principal events of the French Revolution*, published posthumously in 1818, Saint Louis is cited as one of the four best French kings, alongside Charles V, Louis XII and Henri IV. Each had wanted to establish the supremacy of law. Saint Louis made regulations to assure the independence and regularity of justice; he also advised Henry III to respect the Magna Carta when he was called to arbitrate between the English king and his barons in 1258.[67]

Although de Staël did not make a direct link between Saint Louis and the *Charte*, many did (Figure 7.2). Jean-François Heim's 1814 image of the king at work on the *Charte*, looking to busts of Saint Louis and Henri IV for inspiration, implies continuity and conformity between these models of kingship and the *Charte*. Odes printed for

Figure 7.2 *Louis XVIII consultant St-Louis et Henri IV pour la Charte Constitutionnelle* by François-Joseph Heim (1787–1865). © Bibliothèque nationale de France.

the feast of Saint-Louis sometimes reconciled Catholic kingship with the *Charte*. One example from 1817 contrasted warlike kings such as 'the fierce conqueror on his murderous march' (Napoleon) with monarchs devoted to justice and peace, such as Saint Louis and Louis XVIII. Having discussed the oak at Vincennes and defended the crusades, the poet had a message for the French:

Revere this law, present of wisdom;	*Révérez cette loi, present de la sagesse;*
This Charte which was the object of so many wishes;	*Cette Charte qui fut l'objet de tant de vœux;*
The spirit pondered it, reason professes it;	*L'esprit la médita, la raison la professe;*
May it go as far as our last nephews!	*Qu'elle aille à nos derniers neveux!*

[...]

In chains, Saint Louis contemplated sage laws;	*Saint-Louis, dans les fers,* *médita des lois sages;*
From the gardens of Sidon, he brought back flowers,	*Des jardins de Sidon, il* *apporta des fleurs,*
His son, in the fields of Holland, and in the middle of storms,	*Son fils, aux champs* *d'Holland, et du sein des* *orages,*
Announced the glimmers of the most beautiful dawn.[68]	*De la plus belle aurore* *annonça les lueurs.*

This poem clearly invoked Saint Louis to legitimate the Restoration settlement. By drawing a connection between the revered *Établissements* and the *Charte*, it created a sense of continuity that downplayed those elements of the new situation that consolidated innovations in government since the Revolution. There is also an implied connection between Louis IX's period of captivity during his first crusade and Louis XVIII's exile during the revolutionary and Napoleonic periods, both of which were followed by exemplary lawgiving .

However, invoking Saint Louis to legitimate the *Charte* merely sparked disagreements between ultras and liberals, revealing its limited efficacy in creating consensus around the Restoration settlement. A telling example is the controversy caused by a panegyric delivered before the Académie Française at Saint-Germain-l'Auxerrois in 1824 by Jean Labouderie, a literary abbé known for his 'philosophical' and Gallican views. Labouderie praised Saint Louis's laws as having struck the first blow against feudalism but recognized that they had been supplanted and surpassed over the intervening centuries as circumstances changed; 'if it is far from the drafts (*ébauches*) of Saint Louis to the institutions of Louis-le-Désiré, that is because the latter are appropriate *to the ever-increasing progress of Enlightenment*'.[69] The last phrase, italicized in the original, was a quotation from the preamble to the *Charte*, thus presenting the Restoration settlement as something that had grown naturally from – and represented an improvement of – the good laws of Louis IX. But ultras preferred to invoke Saint Louis against the philosophy of the Enlightenment.[70] Labouderie's panegyric was poorly received in the right-leaning royalist and Catholic *L'Ami de la Religion et du Roi*.[71] The reviewer noted that the section just quoted was well-received by 'admirers of modern ideas' (not a compliment) who liked the idea of placing 'a great gap between the *drafts* of Saint Louis and the *Charte*. They were particularly pleased to hear the *ever-increasing progress of Enlightenment* celebrated in the pulpit – a progress which has announced itself with such successful results over the past thirty years.' At a stroke, the upheavals of the Revolution were blamed on the ideas of Enlightenment. The reviewer was also severely critical of Labouderie's portrayal of a Gallican Saint Louis resisting the corruption of the papal court and disapproved of his comments on the 'horrors' of the Albigensian crusade and lukewarm assessment of Louis IX's crusading expeditions to Palestine.[72]

The *Journal des débats* (at this point conservative but not reactionary) gave Labouderie's panegyric a more positive review, noting that his view of the crusades 'showed the study of politics as well as the wisdom of the moralist'.[73] It was exactly this political rather than religious interpretation of the crusades that ensured Labouderie a highly favourable review in the liberal and anticlerical *Constitutionnel* (associated with the 'independents'), which praised him for treating Saint Louis impartially, producing 'a tolerant and moderate' discourse.[74] In January 1825, the periodical expressed its surprise on hearing that Labouderie had been stripped of some of his titles, until it recalled how his panegyric had angered certain groups – the kinds of people who read *L'Ami de la Religion*.[75] It noted that 'since the Restoration, the noble task of praising Louis IX was too often granted to ultramontane clerics' but that Labouderie had dared to praise aspects of Saint Louis that displayed a spirit of independence from Rome, such as the 'Pragmatic Sanction' and his resistance to the improper use of excommunication, both of which were here seen as anticipated criticism of the 'Jesuitism' of the ultras. Labouderie's panegyric therefore added further fuel to divisions between conservatives and liberals rather than rallying them behind the *Charte*.

In fact, liberals generally viewed Saint Louis with ambivalence. In a review of Népomucène-Louis Lemercier's tragedy *Louis IX in Egypt* (1821), a work described by William Jordan as 'a vehicle for the expression of opposition both to the legacy of Bonapartism and to the renewed pretensions of Bourbon absolutism' (so perhaps relatively attractive to liberals), *Le Constitutionnel* noted that Louis IX's life 'was exempt neither from faults nor weaknesses, and certainly not from fanaticism', as seen particularly in his bloody and wasteful crusades.[76] Although it praised Saint Louis for his charity and lawgiving, this passage showed that the more Catholic elements, those generally praised by ultras and panegyrists, were sufficient cause for liberals to have, at best, a rather mixed view of his kingship. *La Minerve Française*, a liberal publication favourable to the *Charte* and often suspected of Bonapartist or republican sympathies, went further in critiquing the institutionalized practice of delivering panegyrics of Saint Louis. It asked why it was necessary for the Académie to laud individuals who were inevitably imperfect rather than discuss their strengths and weaknesses. 'All in all, it was the spirit of adulation, a particular vice of arbitrary monarchies, and not public spirit, the creation and support of representative monarchies, which had presided at the foundation of the old academies'.[77] The very practice of institutionalized praise of Saint Louis, let alone the content, smacked too strongly of despotism to be much use in rallying those on the moderate left to the monarchy.

Saint Louis was not, of course, the only figure invoked by the new regime. Indeed, the importance of '*le bon roi*' Henri IV has been noted more frequently by historians.[78] As discussed in Chapter 6, the first Bourbon king had been gradually displacing Saint Louis in the decades before the Revolution. Henri's reputation as a pragmatic and conciliatory figure who reunified the kingdom after a period of fanaticism and upheaval was particularly appropriate during the Restoration. The celebration of his memory sometimes overshadowed that of Saint Louis even on the latter's feast day, most notably on 25 August 1818, when Louis XVIII inaugurated Henri's statue on the Pont-Neuf.[79] Many of the poems and songs printed for Saint Louis's day made no mention of Saint Louis but referred to Henri IV.[80] Although Francis Démier points out that references to ideal models of monarchy were confused in the Restoration, with too many different models for any to prevail, it seems that Henri IV had more reconciliatory power than Saint Louis as he was more appealing to moderate royalists and liberals; the latter remained a partisan figure around whom ultra-royalists and ultramontanes could gather but who, for this very reason, could not create broader consensus.[81]

Nevertheless, there were some for whom neither model was convincing and who saw the lauding of good kings as doing little more than highlighting the failings of all the others. The revolutionary politician Jean-Baptiste Robert Lindet – who had voted for Louis XVI's execution without appeal and been a member of the Committee of Public Safety – noted in a letter of 20 April 1814, shortly after the Restoration, that

> I don't know why people always cite Saint Louis or Henri IV: you need to go back 24 kings to find Saint Louis, who had great qualities [but], with the desire and intention to do good, caused tragedy for France because he was dominated by the spirit of his century, the passion for the crusades. They go back to Henri IV, already remote from us, whom the Protestants accuse of ingratitude, the Catholics regard as highly suspect, [and] who loved women and gambling more than was appropriate. . . . It is regrettable that among 32 kings, only two who are so distant from one another are cited. It goes to show that there would be nothing good to say about the thirty others.[82]

The feast of Saint-Louis during the Restoration

In 1819, new members of the Order of the Holy Sepulchre were encouraged to pray to 'the great Saint [Louis] . . . to re-establish union and peace among us'.[83] As has been shown, however, the memory of Louis IX could not create broader political consensus because of his identification with a style of Catholic kingship that was unacceptable to many liberals. Nevertheless, despite the partisan nature of his memory he was the only figure among the monarchical heroes of French history who had an official day in the calendar on which the government and its supporters could at least attempt to use spectacles and festivities to create consensus round the Restoration.[84] What form did the celebrations on 25 August take and were they predominantly religious or secular? How much of the focus of the celebrations on the feast was on the potentially divisive figure and Christian kingship of Saint Louis himself? Who participated and who abstained or even disrupted proceedings? Answers to these questions help us to understand the extent of the monarchy's popularity and the efficacy of its celebrations and historical symbolism.

Celebrations on 25 August were often the occasion for such language celebrating and professing loyalty to the king. Needless to say, celebration of the Saint-Napoleon was impossible after the Restoration. Louis XVIII instead re-established the Saint-Louis as a national holiday – but was it any more popular?[85] Sheryl Kroen has drawn our attention to subversion of the celebrations as an example of 'practicing politics' in this period as part of an argument that the broader population never accepted the Bourbon monarchy as a legitimate political authority.[86] Sudhir Hazareesingh has argued that 25 August had only a 'modest profile', with no special events to mark it across most of the kingdom and celebrations that were religious rather than festive or joyful.[87]

In fact, these accounts downplay the successful promotion of the Saint-Louis across much of the kingdom and overplay the extent to which it was religious rather than festive in tone. There were, of course, religious ceremonies, for example, at Savigny near Lyon, where the feast was celebrated with a solemn mass and religious procession involving all the confraternities and local authorities, carrying a statue of Saint Louis.[88] Such occasions were often opportunities for the expression of confrontational sentiments from those who wanted religion to be at the heart of government. Preachers used their Saint Louis sermons to defend religion against the pernicious influence of 'false philosophy' and even German-speaking Protestant pastors gave sermons noting the close resemblance of Louis XVIII to Saint Louis, in that they both revered religion.[89] It was perhaps because of this confrontational attitude that religious ceremonies were not the focus of the official celebrations in many places. In Paris itself they took second place to official banquets at the Hôtel de Ville, public concerts (put on at considerable expense in the Tuileries gardens), games, recreations, fireworks, an all-night ball and even public scientific experiments. Louis IX himself might have approved of the distribution of food to the poor but probably not the fountains of wine or the comic plays.[90]

According to the *Gazette*, the festivities in 1814 were not limited to the capital; 'the peasants shared the general joy, and the smallest hamlet had its bonfire on Saint Louis's day'.[91] Royalist papers often included gushing reports of joyful celebrations of the Saint-Louis from around the kingdom.[92] Often this came with a confrontational message. After attacking 'the so-called liberal journals' and those 'false, stubborn and corrupt spirits who believe in the anarchic dogma of popular sovereignty' in a report of 1820, the *Journal des débats* reported that the king's *fête* was celebrated with enthusiasm across France: 'in each [*département*], the authorities, [and] the constitutional bodies, veritable organs of public opinion, manifested their indignation against the enemies of paternal government, under whose shelter France has found peace and liberty, for which it long searched in vain'.[93] This polemical deployment of the feast should caution us against accepting such reports at face value and it may be that 'the smallest hamlet' is an exaggeration, but there is nevertheless evidence that the Saint-Louis was celebrated much more widely across the kingdom after 1814 than it had been before 1789, thanks to the centralization of such matters in the intervening years.[94]

Provincial officials were obliged to organize celebrations, a job they often took seriously. In 1818, the comte de Lezay-Marnésia, prefect of the Rhône *département* since 1817, wrote to Baron Rambaud, mayor of Lyon, asking for more *éclat* to be added to the Saint-Louis celebrations – in other words, salvoes of artillery, public *divertissements*, illuminations of public buildings and a distribution of food to the poor in addition to religious ceremonies. He received a respectful but not entirely cooperative response, in which the mayor discussed the prohibitive cost of the prefect's proposals. Lezay-Marnésia responded saying that, while he appreciated the mayor's inclination to economize,

> considerations of a more elevated order make me feel the indispensable necessity and political utility for the town of Lyon to give this year's feast of Saint-Louis not all the splendour that one might expect from the kingdom's second city but at least enough pomp that it does not remain below what is done in towns of the third rank.

This reveals an element of competition between towns to show they were celebrating the king's day, as well as conflict within the provincial hierarchy. In the case of Lyon, the prefect noted that recent disturbances had cast the city in a bad light, making an exuberant celebration particularly appropriate. In short, the mayor needed to spend more. Accounts show that the following year 6,370 francs were spent on the Saint-Louis in Lyon, including 3,000 on fireworks.[95] In 1823, a mock battle on land and water around the Ile-Barbe were added to the festivities there in honour of France's intervention in Spain on behalf of Ferdinand VII, in which the French army had come to be known as the 'Hundred Thousand Sons of Saint Louis' thanks to the invocation of Saint Louis in a speech by Louis XVIII.[96]

Programmes of events that were posted in public places give an indication of how municipalities organized their celebrations. In Orléans in 1822, the municipal authorities went to mass at the cathedral and the day finished with games and fireworks.[97] Sometimes descriptions were printed after the event to highlight a town's loyalty. In 1816, the celebrations in Reims included mass with a sermon linking the qualities of Saint Louis to those of Louis XVIII, loyal speeches, processions and a banquet, while at Morlaix the festivities were focused on the 'sacred person' of Louis XVIII.[98] Contrary to Hazareesingh's characterization of Restoration celebrations of Saint Louis's day as religious, most municipalities organized games, balls, fireworks and other secular entertainments, with the religious ceremonies sometimes appearing as a mere prelude – as in Cambrai in 1816, where 'before throwing ourselves in full security into these pleasures, we all feel the need to reunite in the Lord's temple in order to demand the conservation of our august Sovereign'.[99]

Numerous individuals and groups used the feast to highlight their devotion to the restored monarchy, often through publications. These could be serious in tone, such as the *Discours* pronounced in Lille in 1815 by a former member of the municipal council, lauding both 'our good king' and his 'glorious ancestor' as well as praising the troops in Lille who had remained loyal to the monarchy during the Hundred Days.[100] However, some of them indicate celebration in less formal settings. A whole repertoire of songs appeared, all associated with the Saint-Louis but not necessarily mentioning Saint Louis himself. Typical verses included:

Friends, friends, with a glass in hand,	*Amis, amis, le verre en main,*
Sing this refrain with me;	*Avec moi chantez ce refrain:*
Long live all the Bourbons!	*Vivent, vivent tous les Bourbons!*
My friends, let us drink to their health.[101]	*A leur santé, mes amis, buvons.*

Many such verses were printed by military units. The fifth legion of the Garde Nationale de Paris, keen to show that its 'monarchist sentiments have never changed', celebrated 25 August with gatherings containing toasts to the royal family and speeches, poems and songs written by officers, all celebrating Louis XVIII as a father figure who had restored order after a period in which France was 'handed over to frightful anarchy'.[102] Other collections of songs to popular tunes were published to broadcast the enthusiasm of loyalists celebrating the monarchy on the feast of Saint-Louis.[103]

Another tradition that developed was that of staging short comic plays *about* the feast of Saint-Louis *on* the feast of Saint-Louis. A typical example was performed in Marseille on 25 August 1816. Set in a nearby village, it is filled with dialogue with obvious political resonances:

Élise (the daughter of Darmont)
I have always heard that France cannot be happy unless it is ruled by a Bourbon.

Mme Darmont
That is a truth

M. Darmont
... that a cruel experience has made us feel and understand well.[104]

Much of the plot revolves around M. Darmont placing obstacles in the way of Élise's desire to marry a young man named Prosper. At one point she is locked away in punishment for disobedience and told she will marry old M. Lecerf. Prosper's father tells Darmont that he cannot be so sad on Saint Louis's day and speaks to him in the king's name, causing Darmont to relent and release his daughter, who does eventually marry Prosper. The characters sing that 'under the happy reign of Louis, Pardon has found its temple', a point reinforced by the appearance on stage of a bust of Louis XVIII and white flags with 'Saint-Louis' written on them.[105] The political resonances of this allegory of pardon are obvious, and it is just one of many similar plays in which the drama resolves around a domestic farce taking place in a small village preparing to celebrate the feast of Saint-Louis.[106] Some were organized by regional officials, such as the prefect of the Haut-Rhin in 1816.[107] The mood was normally one of collective celebration and loyalist sentiment and aimed to show the geographical and social breadth of support for the Restoration. As a character remarks in *La Saint-Louis Villageoise*, performed in Paris in 1816, 'it is the king's feast, it is my feast, it is the feast of us all'.[108]

But did everyone agree? Much of the printed material discussed so far is propagandistic and gives only one side of the story. Manuscript sources give insights into the reality of the celebrations across the kingdom. Prefects sought out information on the festivities in different parts of their *département*. In 1818, Lezay-Marnésia received pleasing reports detailing the enthusiasm on display in several towns, including Belleville, Beaujeu, Quincieux and Oulins. Not all reports, however, were so positive: at Orliénas there was 'no sign of rejoicing'. Even worse was Villefranche, where the celebrations were met with 'a remarkable coldness'. Not only was there 'not a single white flag at the windows and nothing to indicate the least enthusiasm', but, more seriously, the Garde Nationale itself showed considerable disobedience.[109] As Theo Jung has shown, the withholding of acclamation was part of a rhetoric of silence that could be used to display the people's dissatisfaction with their rulers, so such indications of the public mood were not mere trivia.[110]

Having gathered such information, prefects reported back to Paris, often including printed material such as posters to show how effectively the *fête* had been prepared. They wrote from cities as distant as Strasbourg and Bordeaux, Saint-Brieuc and Albi,

Cherbourg and Limoges, indicating that the day was celebrated in each *département*. The vast majority of reports were extremely positive, highlighting the diligence of local authorities in organizing celebrations and the enthusiasm with which the people took part; 25 August was celebrated in Digne in 1822 with every possible solemnity and in Marseille in 1823 'the population threw itself into the festivities with as much order as satisfaction'.[111] The feast was enthusiastically celebrated in the rural villages near Bourges in 1823 (suggesting that the theatrical literature described before was based on a certain reality of rustic celebration).[112] However, the prefects also passed on any information indicating that the population was not quite so enthusiastic. The prefect of Gers reported from Auch in 1816 that he was not as content as he would wish to be with the civil population; some of them participated in the joy of the military celebrations on Saint Louis's day, but 'a more considerable part was cold'.[113] The enthusiasm in the Ardèche in 1823 was not comparable to that of 1814, suggesting that the initial outburst of royalist sentiment that accompanied the Restoration was dying down.[114]

Even more worrying incidents were also reported. Under Napoleon, royalists had occasionally displayed loyalty to the Bourbons on 25 August, as occurred in Tours in 1813.[115] Under the Restoration, Bonapartists sometimes tried to disrupt celebrations by expressing their own loyalties. In Gap in 1821 the prefect wrote of 'an effusion of truly French sentiments' in the main text of his letter but wrote on the outside that just after he had sealed it he heard of an incident of a man disrupting proceedings by crying '*Vive l'Empereur*' (Napoleon having died in May).[116] The culprit had not been caught because there were no gendarmes there at the time, but the prefect presented him as an unrepresentative individual. Still, there were numerous other examples of people similarly disrupting celebrations with cries indicating republican or Bonapartist sentiment, such as person who shouted '*Vive la République*' in Nantes in 1823.[117] More worrying were indications of elites who failed to participate, such as the *premier président de la cour royale* in Dijon, who failed to toast Louis XVIII's health on 25 August 1818: 'it is difficult to believe that this was a mere oversight, and there is general indignation'.[118] There also seemed to be some organized groups actively trying to disrupt celebrations, for example, in Besançon in 1816.[119]

These regular and detailed reports indicate that such information was considered important, probably as a gauge of public support. The minister wrote to the prefect of Doubs in 1822, thanking him for reporting the 'touching unanimity' of the people there on 25 August and expressing his satisfaction 'at a state of things which is moreover not particular to your *département* and which proves that the *fête du Roi* is still the feast of France'.[120] However, there seems to be enough evidence that many people did not accept the identification of Saint Louis's day with France. In 1816, the *commissaire-général de police* of the Haute-Garonne noted that many whose sympathies did not lie with the Bourbons had left Toulouse to avoid the festivities on 25 August. He noted the difficulty of instilling monarchical sentiments in such individuals. 'The most effective means of persuasion is to speak to them often of the goodness and clemency of the king ... We ceaselessly make them hear this language'.[121] The 25 August celebration was often an occasion for such language, with the idea that 'on this solemn day ... may the august blood of the great king Saint Louis' efface the memory of recent division and rebellion.[122] But just as the historical figure of Saint Louis served to deepen divisions between liberals and ultras, celebration of his day also provided a focus for enemies of the Restoration to demonstrate their opposition.

'May God grant Louis XVIII the immortal crown of Saint Louis! May God bless on the head of Charles X the mortal crown of Saint Louis!'[123] So remarked Chateaubriand after Louis XVIII's death in 1824. Saint Louis's importance diminished rapidly during the second reign of the Restoration. His feast was no longer the *fête du roi* and Chateaubriand noted that it passed 'in silence' in 1825.[124] The king's feast was now the day of Saint Charles Borromeo (4 November), an event increasingly marked with demonstrations of anti-Bourbon sentiment.[125] In 1827, it was noted in Brest that fewer white flags than normal were flying and that the 'bad spirit' of the population was on display; 'it is a fact that the liberal opposition has become dominant here'.[126] On the same day, Charles X appeared on the balcony of the Tuileries but was met with cries of 'down with Villèle!' (the prime minister); the attempt of a few guards to drum up acclamations of '*Vive le Roi!*' was ignored by the crowd.[127] If popular participation in the *fête du roi* was indicative of popular support for the monarchy, these were worrying signs that its days were numbered.

The invasion and conquest of Algiers in June 1830 (the beginning of French colonization in Algeria) was motivated in part by the desire to swing public opinion more favourably behind the monarchy. The more positive and patriotic attitude to the crusades that had been developing in the early nineteenth century was now invoked to legitimize modern wars against Muslim powers. In his 1829 panegyric, the Abbé Gaudreau argued that 'the nineteenth century sees the renewal (though not admittedly under the inspiration of the Catholic faith) of these expeditions in the Orient, whose aims recall those of the crusades'; he saw this in the support for the Greeks in their war of independence and in the wish to restrain those people (Muslims) who, according to Gaudreau, had become 'by their customs, their fanaticism, their tyrannical legislation, a danger for their neighbours'. Gaudreau argued that this was what Louis IX had sought to achieve in his crusades.[128] This was quite a change from the attitude of eighteenth-century panegyrists who had criticized the crusades. Saint Louis was cited in nationalistic and propagandistic material celebrating the conquest of Algiers and bishops described the soldiers of the expeditionary army as the 'sons' of Saint Louis and 'new crusaders'; meanwhile the president of the Cour royal in Grenoble declared that the expedition would 'unite . . . the great names of Saint Louis, Louis XIV [who had bombarded Algiers between the 1660s and 1680s] and Charles X'.[129]

Nevertheless, soon after the conquest of Algiers, the July Revolution of 1830 brought down the elder branch of the Bourbons. The new king, Louis-Philippe, was not hostile to the memory of Saint Louis, who was also his ancestor; he commissioned many depictions of him and built a chapel in Tunis, consecrated to Saint Louis on 25 August 1841 to the strains of *Domine salvum fac regem Ludovicum Philippum*.[130] However, the medieval king's associations with the legitimacy of the elder branch and a reactionary model of Catholic kingship were probably what caused Louis-Philippe to celebrate his *fête* on 1 May, the feast of Saint-Philip, signalling a clean break with the previous regime.[131]

Conclusion

Saint Louis and his feast provided an important channel for the expression and consolidation of royalist sentiment that in many instances helped legitimate the Restoration and display a degree of public support. His feast day on 25 August was celebrated during the reign of Louis XVIII far more extensively than it ever had been under the *Ancien Régime*. The ample printed material attests to its importance as a symbol that could be used to highlight loyalty to the crown and the voluminous correspondence that passed between Paris and various levels of the provincial hierarchy every year shows that it held significance for the authorities, who recognized it not just as an opportunity to promote the monarchy but also as a weathervane of popular opinion. The festivities were not overwhelmingly religious and although instances of disruption or lack of participation were numerous they do not seem to have been the norm, contrary to the impression given by Kroen's analysis. However, the secular nature of the celebrations in many towns probably meant that for many people involved the only connection to Saint Louis himself was the name of the day. This was about celebrating the monarchy, not devotion to Saint Louis – hence the abrupt abandonment of 25 August when it ceased to be the reigning king's name day.

What the revival of the cult of Saint Louis could not do was address the underlying political divisions that ran through the period. In a speech of December 1817, the minister of police and future prime minister Élie Decazes – recognizing the danger that Louis XVIII might become the 'king of two peoples' – spoke of the need to 'royalise the nation; nationalise the monarchy . . . to make those in power loved by making them respected'.[132] Saint Louis's memory was unable to contribute to this project for the same reasons that Decazes's ideal of a strong centralized monarchy ensuring the support of the middle classes by guaranteeing the rights of the *Charte* also did not succeed; neither created consensus between liberals and the intransigent traditionalists who increasingly came to dominate the government (if not parliament) under Charles X. Just as the latter group disliked policies of liberal compromise between the Revolution and the *Ancien Régime*, so they resisted attempts to invoke the memory of Saint Louis to legitimate anything other than traditional notions of Christian monarchy (for example by linking his laws to the *Charte*). The role of the church was a source of increasingly acrimonious debate in the later 1820s.[133] Consequently, Saint Louis was a partisan figure rather than a figure of national consensus, ceding that position to Henri IV. From 1814 to 1830 he was too associated with the alliance of throne and altar proposed by traditionalist ultras to inspire more liberal royalists. If Saint Louis's status as an ideal Catholic monarch had ensured his pre-eminence as the historical point of reference for the Bourbons during the period of Catholic Reform in the seventeenth century, the very same factor worked against him in the post-Revolutionary period.

The ode by d'Alissac, quoted earlier, included a section addressing the French people, telling them that in Saint Louis they should 'love a father', 'invoke a protecting saint', and 'see a good king'.[134] Such sentiments did indeed help consolidate loyalty to the monarchy among Catholic royalists, who used Saint Louis and his feast as an opportunity to display and celebrate their political sentiments; however, the same ideas did not inspire many people further to the left. It is crucial to note that the monarchy itself, at least under Louis XVIII, tried to use Saint Louis to legitimize the Restoration settlement by invoking him to support the *Charte*. However, the true custodians of his memory were the traditionalist ultras, who instead used Saint Louis as a symbol around which supporters of old-fashioned Catholic kingship could rally. The more successfully they used this key part of monarchical culture to consolidate their side of the argument, the less that same culture was able to create a broader coalition to support the monarchy. Therefore, instead of inspiring consensus around the restored monarchy the memory of Saint Louis provided material for contestation between different political groups who were not able to find a model of Bourbon monarchy that satisfied them all.

Conclusion

Jean-Marie de Vernon's statement that the kings of France 'consider themselves never more honoured than when they are called the descendants of Saint Louis', the 'perfection' of the royal house, points to the saint-king's pivotal importance as dynastic lynchpin and exemplar of kingship in early modern France.[1] This importance was established at the beginning of the Bourbon period, when the fraught circumstances of Henri IV's accession meant that an appeal to the memory of his saintly ancestor became an important part of a broader strategy of winning over his subjects through a resacralization of the monarchy. The naming of the dauphin in 1606 was crucial in creating an identification between Saint Louis and the soon-to-be Louis XIII who, like all his successors down to the Revolution, would be encouraged to emulate Saint Louis and lauded for inheriting his virtues. The monarchy signalled its commitment by securing the elevation of the feast day in 1618.

The renaissance of Saint Louis's cult occurred at a time when the spirit of Catholic Reform was gaining ground in France. Although controversies remained over his Gallicanism and the wisdom of the Treaty of Paris, the biographies, panegyrics and poems that appeared under Louis XIII cast the saint as a model of idealized Christian kingship. As such, Saint Louis naturally appealed to the *dévots* as a model of political and social behaviour. That this could be potentially harmful for the monarchy was made evident when he was harnessed to oppose government foreign policy. The crusading impulse was still far from dead, and the many invocations of Saint Louis to argue for a renewed attack on the 'infidel' sometimes implied criticism of *raison d'état* policies. The old danger that Saint Louis as the ideal Christian monarch could be used to point out the flaws of his successors and their policies remained a problem into the reign of Louis XIV, as is evident from his use by Frondeurs such as the cardinal de Retz. Contrary to Alain Boureau's argument, Saint Louis was not firmly tied to the cause of royal absolutism in the 1620s but remained a 'site of memory' whose example could be used to critique the present.

Although 'custody of the memory of Saint Louis' was never totally and uniquely the preserve of the monarchy, it certainly became more so during Louis XIV's personal reign, particularly with the institutionalization of the Académie Française's celebrations of the feast day. The panegyrics established a more standardized interpretation of Saint Louis for the rest of the period. That he was a king in the 'absolutist' tradition, for example, would be accepted both by those who praised him for overcoming a rebellious nobility and those such as Boulainvilliers who saw his reign as starting the descent into monarchical despotism. In the panegyric literature, Louis XIV was mostly glorified with reference to his ancestor, and often even held up to be superior. The image of Saint Louis, although more standardized, could be changed to suit the varying circumstances of the reign, so it was his fortitude in the face of military defeat that was the dominant theme by the end of the Sun King's reign. Like his father and grandfather, Louis XIV celebrated his ancestor by founding numerous churches and charitable institutions in his honour, notably the Order of Saint-Louis. For the rest of the *Ancien Régime*, French soldiers and generals would consider it an honour to wear a cross depicting the thirteenth-century royal saint.

The cult drew much of its impetus from corporate groups including trade guilds, provincial academies, *parlementaires* and military elites. As the royal patron saint, celebration of Saint Louis provided an opportunity to demonstrate loyalty to the king. It is notable that, like much of the laudatory 'representational culture' produced under Louis XIV, even the Académie Française's panegyrics were gestures of loyalty rather than top-down propaganda. As such, the cult of Saint Louis became a cultural and religious phenomenon which could serve to bind the monarchy more closely to the kingdom's elites. Celebration of his feast day served to underline the links between church and state, laud the king's virtues and legitimate royal sacrality.

One of the most important bodies to do this was the Society of Jesus, whose precarious position in France necessitated strong statements of loyalty. In churches, paintings, and publications, the Jesuits tried to promote Saint Louis as 'their' saint. They were successful in securing their relationship with the monarchy, and the cult also helped the French Jesuits to develop a particular national identity, adapting to their environment by playing down their supposed loyalty to the papacy. Devotion to Saint Louis was part of the process that made France 'the graveyard of Jesuit internationalism'.[2] However, it was not enough to convince everyone that they were loyal Frenchmen, as the history up to their expulsion in 1764 would prove. Much of this opposition drew its energy from the vicious struggle with the Jansenists, who also tried (less successfully) to appropriate Saint Louis to the legitimation of their cause.

As this dispute showed, the memory of Saint Louis was not under the complete control of the monarchy. In Louis XIV's later decades, the figure of his holy ancestor would feature in the critical literature that flooded from pens hostile to the Sun King. Nevertheless, the cult had reached a certain maturity during his reign. A relatively standardized 'official' interpretation of Saint Louis was being used to glorify the monarchy. By 1700, several annual events such as the meetings of the academies and the Carmelite procession had established the feast as an important date in the Parisian calendar in which religious celebration of the sanctified monarch mixed with secular entertainments. In general, however, it seems that this cult was always centred on Paris. Contrary to expectations in 1618, the feast day was never celebrated across all the dioceses in France. The overwhelmingly regional nature of the 'Gallican church' is seen from the fact that many dioceses preferred to celebrate their own saints rather than 'national' saints such as Louis IX. The attempt to turn a dynastic cult into a national one was never fully realized. Saint Louis's feast was, however, brought to many provincial towns by religious orders and local elites. Although never anything resembling a 'national' day, it provided an occasion for provincial notables of various kinds (noble, military, ecclesiastical and intellectual) to come together and celebrate the king's *fête* under the aegis of his sanctified ancestor, often with a mixture of religious services and secular festivities. Outside France, it provided ambassadors and French residents in foreign cities an opportunity to celebrate their king.

As this suggests, the cult of Saint Louis was a primarily political phenomenon. His relic centres at Saint-Denis and the Sainte-Chapelle did not generate much interest in the early modern period, unlike during the first flourishing of the cult under Philip III and Philip IV. It is striking that the monarchy was so uninterested in his relics. This was partly because a focus on relics and miracles, unlike public celebrations of the feast day and panegyrics, opened a gulf between Saint Louis, as the one king who could perform the intercessory functions of sanctity, and all the other kings who had not been canonized. With the exception of the remote and localized devotion to the relics at Lamontjoie and isolated examples such as the images in Brittany, there is very little evidence that Saint Louis became popular with the vast majority of French people, those below the provincial elites who promoted the feast day. The religious literature of the Catholic Reformation in France cast him as a model of behaviour relevant to the 'great' and wealthy, showing them the compatibility of piety with active life in high society and the imperative of charity to the poor. This, combined with the fact that Saint Louis was not promoted much as a miracle-worker under the Bourbons, probably made him a rather remote and irrelevant saint in the eyes of many French people.

Saint Louis was, therefore, part of a process that tied king and elites together into a culture celebrating the Catholic nature of the French monarchy rather than the centre of a devotion uniting all subjects of the French king. By the early eighteenth century his cult was no longer needed to convince people of Bourbon legitimacy but continued to be celebrated as a routine part of the texture of monarchical representation and religious celebration in France. From the 1750s, however, two factors combined to diminish its efficacy in glorifying the king. The first was the diminishing popularity of Louis XV and the increasing difficulty of praising him alongside Saint Louis, meaning that the panegyrics started to take on a dangerously satirical edge. This was not, however, indicative of overall desacralization of the institution of the monarchy. The dauphin and Madame Louise occupied the space vacated by Louis XV, presenting themselves as devotees and imitators of Saint Louis. Moreover, the awkward disjuncture between reigning king and patron saint was a temporary situation which ended with the accession of Louis XVI.

More problematic was the collapse of the consensus that Saint Louis was a model of ideal kingship. His crusading, so celebrated in the seventeenth century, became a battleground between those with 'philosophical' and 'devout' views in the second half of the eighteenth. The piety that had made him attractive in the era of Catholic Reform was looking increasingly like fanaticism in the Enlightenment. This was not necessarily an indication of dechristianization; much of the disapproval of Louis IX's crusades came from within the church, from 'literary abbés' who argued that crusading was contrary to religion. Moreover, developments in attitudes to Louis's crusading were not linear. On the one hand, criticisms had been frequently voiced in the later middle ages; on the other hand, a more positive appraisal of the crusades as a source of national pride would emerge in the context of nineteenth-century imperialism. Despite the late-eighteenth-century debate on the crusades, Saint Louis continued to be praised up to the Revolution and there was an attempt to bring him more in line with the times by emphasizing his role as lawgiver. Nevertheless, with the Jesuits gone after 1764 and interest in the panegyrics diminishing in the period before the Académie Française finally abandoned the tradition of hearing them in 1785, the cult was in decline.

This suggests that religious symbols of French kingship were losing their power to bind elites into loyalty to Bourbon absolutism, but the concurrent rise of Henri IV shows that royal culture was not moribund. On the contrary, it was able to adapt to changing sensibilities. Henri IV had been an awkward figure under Louis XIV due to his association with the Edict of Nantes; at that point, Saint Louis had reigned supreme as a model for treating heretics, Jews and blasphemers harshly. A century later, however, Henri's reputation for tolerance and pragmatism made him a more attractive model for a less persecutory version of French Catholic monarchy. The relationship between the memory of these two monarchs was complex. If at times Henri came to overshadow Louis in the late eighteenth and early nineteenth centuries, they were also used as a pair, for example, in Heim's image of Louis XVIII. Moreover, in Voltaire's *Henriade* – one of the foundational texts of the 'cult' of Henri IV – the first Bourbon matured into a tolerant and magnanimous king thanks to the guidance of his saintly ancestor.

Of course, the memory of these two idealized kings was unable to save the monarchy in the Revolution. For most of the *Ancien Régime*, however, the cult of the saint-king did serve various purposes. Under Henri IV, it helped the new royal family gain the trust of France's Catholic population after a period of political and religious division and dynastic instability. Under the subsequent kings, the need for Saint Louis to ensure dynastic legitimacy diminished but he served to cast an aura of holiness around the monarchy. The essential problem for the monarchy, never entirely solved, was how to ensure that the individual sanctity of Louis IX served the whole monarchical line rather than emphasizing his unique status among the kings of France. Propagandists and flatterers under successive monarchs tried to do this by establishing a mimetic relationship in which the current king was praised in parallel with Saint Louis. This was probably most effective under Louis XIV, though never entirely so. Louis IX revealed the ambiguities inherent in the cult of a sainted ancestor. He could be used to glorify and even sanctify, but also to criticize and even chastise. The French monarchy derived legitimacy from the past. In this context, Saint Louis was invoked in a vast range of debates, his example recalled to educate, praise or rebuke his successors. This could be a burden, most notably for Louis XVI when confronted with the Civil Constitution of the Clergy. Far from the subsequent collapse of the monarchy being a result of a desacralization dating back to Louis XV's reign, Louis XVI's conception of his role was arguably still too shaped by the traditions of French kingship and the model of Saint Louis – in other words, not desacralized enough – to allow him to adapt successfully to the role of the constitutional monarch in the early 1790s.

In the Revolution, the past lost its unquestionable authority and 'systemic, political, moral, and social change' came to be seen as increasingly possible and desirable.[3] The extraordinary results in the 1790s and 1800s 'divided the French into two irreconcilable camps'.[4] Under Louis XVIII, as under Henri IV, an attempt was made to use Saint Louis to unite the French behind the Bourbon monarchy after periods of chaos and political instability. But the context was very different. Efforts to link Saint Louis to the *Charte* by drawing on the image of the legislator king developed in the late eighteenth century largely failed to prevent his appropriation by those seeking a full restoration of the *Ancien Régime*. The saint-king was not useful in drawing liberals behind the monarchy, serving instead to provide the language for royalists, Catholics and traditionalists to express their loyalty. His feast was celebrated far more extensively than it ever had been before the Revolution, but it became a focus for expressions of alternative allegiances.

The overall arc in Saint Louis's political 'meaning' in this period was from being a symbol of consensus during the Catholic Reformation to one of contestation, a partisan figure in the anticlerical atmosphere of the nineteenth century. The July Revolution of 1830 did not mark the end of his presence in French cultural and political life. Under France's subsequent monarchical and republican regimes, he would remain a symbol around which royalists and Catholic traditionalists could coalesce.[5] The comte de Chambord invoked him in his unsuccessful bid to become 'Henri V' in 1870 and in the 1880s the fervent Catholic Victor de Maumigny regarded it as time for France to choose 'between the monarchy of Saint Louis and the antichristian republic'. There was also a secular view that saw Saint Louis as a patriotic and just king. He appeared in school textbooks, normally depicted dispensing justice under the oak at Vincennes. Saint Louis continued to be instrumentalized in various political contexts and the French government was accused of using his memory to promote an agenda of centralization as late as 1970.[6]

In the twenty-first century, Saint Louis's cult lingers in specific locations associated with him, such as Sète, where canal jousting and fireworks still take place on 25 August. Nevertheless, his star has waned. Despite the conferences, exhibitions and celebrations organized for commemorations such as the 700th anniversary of death in 1970 and 800th of his birth in 2014, opinion polls show that he is decreasingly admired or regarded as a pivotal figure in French history.[7] Instead, he is a hero for the Catholic right, although even there he has been to some extent displaced by Joan of Arc. It is among royalists, particularly supporters of the legitimist Bourbon branch, that the memory of Saint Louis retains most of its potency. In 2014 his statue was carried through the streets of Paris to Notre-Dame to the bemused looks of locals and tourists, followed by 'Louis XX', the Bourbon pretender.[8]

The high point of Saint Louis's cult in France was the period from Henri IV's accession to the Revolution. Under the Bourbon kings he was invoked, praised and honoured as never before or since, becoming an important part of the sacral mystique surrounding Bourbon kingship and the ideological and religious cement that tied crown and elites together. The cult of Saint Louis was restored by the Bourbon monarchy and brought down by its fall. It was a clear manifestation of the frequently fractious but ultimately symbiotic relationship between religion and politics and between church and crown during the tumultuous centuries of Bourbon rule in France.

Notes

Introduction

1   Jean-François Senault, *Le Monarque, ou les Devoirs du Souverain* (Paris, 1661), 24.
2   Baruch Spinoza, *Tractatus theologico-politicus* . . . (Hamburg [Amsterdam], 1670), Præfatio.
3   Nicole Brisch (ed.), *Religion and Power: Divine Kingship in the Ancient World and Beyond* (Chicago, 2008); Paul Kleber Monod, *The Power of Kings: Monarchy and Religion in Europe, 1589-1715* (New Haven and London, 1999), 41.
4   Alain Guéry, 'La dualité de toutes les monarchies et la monarchie chrétienne', in *La royauté sacrée dans le monde chrétien (Colloque de Royaumont, mars 1989)*, eds Alain Boureau and Claudio Sergio Ingerflom (Paris, 1992), 39–51; Marcel Gauchet, 'L'état au miroir de la raison d'état: La France et la chrétienté', in *Raison et déraison d'État: Théoriciens et théories de la raison d'État aux XVIᵉ et XVIIᵉ siècles*, ed. Yves Charles Zarka (Paris, 1994), 211.
5   Gérard Sabatier, 'Imagerie héroïque et sacralité monarchique', in Boureau and Ingerflom, *Royauté*, 115.
6   Martha Edmunds, *Piety and Politics: Imagining Divine Kingship in Louis XIV's Chapel at Versailles* (Newark, 2002).
7   Alexandre Maral, 'Portrait religieux de Louis XIV', *XVIIᵉ Siècle*, 217 (2002): 713–16.
8   Gérard Sabatier, 'Religious Rituals and the Kings of France in the Eighteenth Century', in *Monarchy and Religion: The Transformation of Royal Culture in Eighteenth-Century Europe*, ed. Michael Schaich (Oxford, 2007), 269; Michèle Fogel, *Les cérémonies de l'information dans la France du XVIᵉ au XVIIIᵉ siècle* (Paris, 1989), 443–50.
9   Edmunds, *Piety*, 40.
10 Damien Tricoire, *La Vierge et le Roi: Politique princière et imaginaire catholique dans l'Europe du XVIIᵉ siècle* (Paris, 2017).
11 Jeroen Duindam, *Dynasties: A Global History of Power, 1300-1800* (Cambridge, 2016), 4.
12 Jean-Baptiste Massillon, *Œuvres* . . ., 13 vols (Paris, 1821), VIII, 214.
13 Nicole Reinhardt, *Voices of Conscience: Royal Confessors and Political Counsel in Seventeenth-Century Spain and France* (Oxford, 2016), 5.
14 Teofilo Ruiz, *The City and the Realm: Burgos and Castile, 1080-1492* (Aldershot, 1992), no. XIII: 'Unsacred Monarchy: The Kings of Castile in the Late Middle Ages'.
15 Jacques Le Goff, 'Aspects religieux et sacrés de la monarchie française du Xᵉ au XIIIᵉ siècle', in Boureau and Ingerflom, *Royauté*, 19–28; Joseph Strayer, 'France: The Holy Land, the Chosen People, and the Most Christian King', in *Medieval Statecraft and Perspectives of History: Essays by Joseph Strayer*, ed. John Benton (Princeton, NJ, 1971), 300–14.
16 Alain Boureau, 'Les cérémonies royales françaises entre performance juridique et compétence liturgique', *Annales. Histoire, Sciences Sociales*, 46 (1991): 1253–64;

Richard Jackson, *Vive le Roi! A History of the French Coronation from Charles V to Charles X* (Chapel Hill and London, 1984), 3; Sabatier, 'Religious Rituals', 256.

17 Marc Bloch, *Les rois thaumaturges: étude sur le caractère surnaturel attribué à la puissance royale particulièrement en France et en Angleterre* (Strasbourg, 1924); Frank Barlow, 'The King's Evil', *English Historical Review*, 95 (1980): 3–27; Annette Finley-Croswhite, 'Henry IV and the Diseased Body Politic', in *Princes and Princely Culture, 1450-1650*, eds Martin Gosman, Alasdair MacDonald and Arjo Vanderjagt, 2 vols (Leiden, 2003), I, 131–46.

18 Ernst Kantorowicz, *The King's Two Bodies: A Study in Mediaeval Political Theology*, new edn (Princeton, 2016).

19 Ralph Giesey, *The Royal Funeral Ceremony in Renaissance France* (Geneva, 1960).

20 Alain Boureau, *Le simple corps du roi: l'impossible sacralité des souverains français, XVe-XVIIIe siècle* (Paris, 1988), 8–9, 23–5, 43.

21 Julian Swann, *Exile, Imprisonment, or Death: The Politics of Disgrace in Bourbon France, 1610-1789* (Oxford, 2017), 23.

22 Ronald Asch, *Sacral Kingship between Disenchantment and Re-enchantment: The French and English Monarchies, 1587-1688* (New York and Oxford, 2014), 28–34, 110–18, 157–62.

23 Eric Johnson, 'The Sacred, Secular Regime: Catholic Ritual and Revolutionary Politics in Avignon, 1789-1791', *French Historical Studies*, 30 (2007): 49–50.

24 Dale Van Kley, *The Damiens Affair and the Unravelling of the Ancien Régime, 1750-1770* (Princeton, NJ, 1984), 246–53; idem, 'The religious origins of the French Revolution', in *From deficit to deluge: The origins of the French Revolution*, eds Thomas Kaiser and Dale Van Kley (Stanford, CA, 2011), 104–38; Jeffrey Merrick, *The Desacralization of the French Monarchy in the Eighteenth Century* (Baton Rouge and London, 1990).

25 Roger Chartier, *The Cultural Origins of the French Revolution*, trans. Lydia Cochrane (Durham and London, 1991), 118–19; Robert Darnton, *The Forbidden Bestsellers of pre-Revolutionary France* (New York and London, 1995).

26 Tim Blanning, 'Louis XVI and the Public Sphere', in *Enlightenment and Revolution: Essays in Honour of Norman Hampson*, eds Malcolm Crook, Alan Forrest and William Doyle (Burlington, VT: Ashgate, 2004), 60.

27 John McManners, *Church and Society in Eighteenth-Century France*, 2 vols (Oxford, 1998), I, 13.

28 Reinhardt, *Voices*, 372.

29 Chantal Grell, 'The *sacre* of Louis XVI: The End of a Myth', in Schaich, *Monarchy*, 352; Anne Byrne, *Death and the Crown: Ritual and Politics in France before the Revolution* (Manchester, 2020), chapter 6.

30 Van Kley, *Damiens*, 255.

31 Chartier, *Cultural*, 113, 121–2.

32 William Doyle, *France and the Age of Revolution: Regimes Old and New from Louis XIV to Napoleon Bonaparte* (London, 2013), 95–112.

33 Damien Tricoire, 'Attacking the monarchy's sacrality in late seventeenth-century France: The underground literature against Louis XIV, Jansenism and the Dauphin's court faction', *French History*, 31 (2017): 152–73; Julian Swann, 'Introduction', in *The Crisis of the Absolute Monarchy: France from Old Regime to Revolution*, eds Julian Swann and Joël Félix (Oxford, 2013), 15.

34 Jens Engels, 'Beyond sacral monarchy: A new look at the image of the early modern French monarchy', *French History*, 15 (2001): 139, 143; idem, 'Dénigrer, espérer,

assumer la réalité. Le roi de France perçu par ses sujets', *Revue d'histoire moderne et contemporaine*, 50 (2003): 96–126.

35 Jeroen Deploige and Gita Deneckere (eds), *Mystifying the Monarch: Studies on Discourse, Power and History* (Amsterdam, 2006), 10.

36 William Beik, 'Review article: The Absolutism of Louis XIV as social collaboration', *Past and Present*, 188 (2005): 195–224.

37 Cecilia Gaposchkin, *The Making of Saint Louis; Kingship, Sanctity, and Crusade in the Later Middle Ages* (Ithaca and London, 2008), 3, 19, 123–4.

38 Monod, *Power*, 30–1.

39 Jacques Le Goff, *History and Memory* (New York, 1992), 54.

40 Christian Amalvi, *De l'art et la manière d'accommoder les héros de l'histoire de France: De Vercingétorix à la Révolution* (Paris, 1988); Robert Gildea, *The Past in French History* (New Haven and London, 1994), 10, 340.

41 Judith Pollmann, *Memory in Early Modern Europe, 1500-1800* (Oxford, 2017), 1, 77; Judith Pollmann and Erika Kuijpers, 'Introduction', in *Memory Before Modernity: Practices of Memory in Early Modern Europe*, eds Kuijpers, Pollmann, Johannes Müller and Jasper van der Steen (Leiden and Boston, 2013), 6; Keith Michael Baker, 'Memory and Practice: Politics and the Representation of the Past in Eighteenth-Century France', *Representations*, 11 (1985): 135.

42 Adam Knobler, 'Saint Louis and French Political Culture', in *Medievalism in Europe II*, eds Leslie Workman and Kathleen Verduin (Cambridge, 1997), 156.

43 William Jordan, 'Saint Louis in Epic and Drama', in Workman and Verduin, *Medievalism in Europe II*, 174.

44 David Jordan, 'Introduction', in *Rethinking France: Les Lieux de Mémoire. Volume 1: The State*, ed. Pierre Nora (Chicago and London, 2001), xxv, xxx.

45 Reinhart Koselleck, *Futures Past: On the Semantics of Historical Time* (New York, 2004), 11, 21, 26, 46, 58; Lucian Hölscher, 'Time Gardens: Historical Concepts in Modern Historiography', *History and Theory*, 53 (2014): 578.

46 Pollmann, *Memory*, 72.

47 Nathan Edelman, *Attitudes of Seventeenth-Century France towards the Middle Ages* (Morningside Heights, New York, 1946); René Lanson, *Le Gout du Moyen Age en France au XVIIIᵉ siècle* (Paris and Brussels, 1926); Alicia Montoya, *Medievalist Enlightenment: From Charles Perrault to Jean-Jacques Rousseau* (Cambridge, 2013).

48 Georges Duby, *The Legend of Bouvines: War, Religion and Culture in the Middle Ages* (Berkeley and Los Angeles, 1990).

49 Adrianna Bakos, *Images of Kingship in Early Modern France: Louis XI in Political Thought, 1560-1789* (London and New York, 1997), 24, 177.

50 Philip Benedict, 'Divided Memories? Historical Calendars, Commemorative Processions and the Recollection of the Wars of Religion during the *Ancien Régime*', *French History*, 22 (2008): 381–405.

51 Jean-Marie Le Gall, *Le Mythe de saint Denis entre Renaissance et Révolution* (Seyssel, 2007), 11.

52 Alon Confino, 'Collective Memory and Cultural History: Problems of Method', *American Historical Review*, 102 (1997): 1386–90.

53 Peter Burke, 'How to become a Counter-Reformation Saint', in *The Counter-Reformation: The Essential Readings*, ed. David Luebke (Oxford, 1999), 130; Donald Weinstein and Rudolph Bell, *Saints & Society: The Two Worlds of Western Christendom, 1000-1700* (Chicago and London, 1982), 6; Anne Jacobson Schutte,

Aspiring Saints: Pretence of Holiness, Inquisition, and Gender in the Republic of Venice, 1618-1750 (Baltimore and London, 2001), 73.

54 Simon Ditchfield, 'Tridentine worship and the cult of saints', in *The Cambridge History of Christianity, vol. VI: Reform and Expansion 1500-1660*, ed. R. Po-Chia Hsia (Cambridge, 2007), 207.

55 Moshe Sluhovsky, *Patroness of Paris: Rituals of Devotion in Early Modern France* (Leiden, 1998), 2–8.

56 Robert Bartlett, *Why Can the Dead Do such Great Things? Saints and Worshippers from the Martyrs to the Reformation* (Princeton and Oxford, 2013), 95.

57 Ditchfield, 'Tridentine', 213.

58 Laura Ackerman Smoller, *The Saint & the Chopped-Up Baby: The Cult of Vincent Ferrer in Medieval and Early Modern Europe* (Ithaca and London, 2014), 226–9; Nicolas Balzamo, 'La querelle des reliques au temps de la Renaissance et de la Réforme', *Bibliothèque d'Humanisme et Renaissance*, 77 (2015): 103–31; Andrew Spicer, '(Re)building the Sacred Landscape: Orléans, 1560-1610', *French History*, 21 (2007): 247–68.

59 Albrecht Burkardt, *Les clients des saints: Maladie et quête du miracle à travers les procès de canonisation de la première moitié du XVIIᵉ siècle en France* (Rome, 2004), 1; Éric Suire, *La Sainteté française de la Réforme catholique (XVIᵉ-XVIIIᵉ siècles) d'après les textes hagiographiques et les procès de canonisation* (Bordeaux, 2001), 194–8; Jean de Viguerie, 'Le miracle dans la France du XVIIᵉ siècle', *XVIIᵉ siècle*, 140 (1983): 313–31; Nicolas Balzamo, *Les Miracles dans la France du XVIᵉ siècle: Métamorphoses du surnaturel* (Paris, 2014), 17.

60 Bruno Restif, *La Révolution des paroisses: Culture paroissiale et Réforme catholique en Haute-Bretagne aux XVIᵉ et XVIIᵉ siècles* (Rennes, 2006), chapter 9.

61 Simon Ditchfield, 'Thinking with Saints: Sanctity and Society in the Early Modern World', in *Saints: Faith without Borders*, eds Françoise Meltzer and Jaś Elsner (Chicago and London, 2011), 172; Dominique Julia, 'L'Église post-tridentine et les reliques: Tradition, controverse et critique (XVIᵉ-XVIIIᵉ siècle)', in *Reliques modernes: Cultes et usages chrétiens des corps saints des Réformes aux révolutions*, eds Philippe Boutry, Pierre-Antoine Fabre and Dominique Julia, 2 vols (Paris, 2009), I, 69–120; Nicolas Balzamo, 'L'église au défi du surnaturel: Les enquêtes sur les miracles aux lendemains du Concile de Trente (France, vers 1570 – vers 1620)', in *Dorsale catholique, Jansénisme, Dévotions: XVIᵉ-XVIIIᵉ siècles: Mythe, réalité, actualité historiographique*, eds Gilles Deregnaucourt, Yves Krumenacker, Philippe Martin and Frédéric Meyer (Paris, 2014), 233–42; Balzamo, *Miracles*, 263–81.

62 Joseph Bergin, *Church, Society and Religious Change in France, 1580-1730* (New Haven and London, 2009), 232–41; McManners, *Church*, I, 440–1; Suire, *Sainteté française*, 115–17.

63 Marc Forster, *Catholic Revival in the Age of the Baroque: Religious Identity in southwest Germany, 1550-1750* (Cambridge, 2001), 3, 75, 96.

64 Carlos Eire, 'The Concept of Popular Religion', in *Local Religion in Colonial Mexico*, ed. Martin Nesvig (Albuquerque, 2006), 1–35; Mary Laven, 'Encountering the Counter-Reformation', *Renaissance Quarterly*, 59 (2006): 710.

65 Michel Vovelle, 'Popular Religion', in *Ideologies and Mentalities* (Cambridge, 1990), 113 and *Piété baroque et déchristianisation en Provence au XVIIIᵉ siècle* (Paris, 1978).

66 Viguerie, 'Miracle', 331; Philippe Boutry and Françoise Le Hénand, 'Pèlerins parisiens à l'âge de la monarchie administrative', in *Rendre ses Vœux: Les identités pèlerines dans l'Europe moderne (XVIᵉ-XVIIIᵉ siècle)*, eds Philippe Boutry, Pierre-Antoine Fabre and

Dominique Julia (Paris, 2000), 401, 436; Anne Bonzon and Marc Venard, *La religion dans la France moderne, XVIe-XVIIIe siècle* (Paris, 1998), 156.

67 Georges Provost, *La fête et le sacré: Pardons et pèlerinages en Bretagne aux XVIIe et XVIIIe siècles* (Paris, 1998), 211, 335.

68 Suire, *Sainteté française*, 203–4.

69 Idem, *Sainteté et Lumières: Hagiographie, Spiritualité et propagande religieuse dans la France du XVIIIe siècle* (Paris, 2001), 27–30, 97.

70 McManners, *Church*, II, 442; Swann, *Exile*, 371.

71 Robert Folz, *Les saints rois du moyen âge en occident (VIe-XIIIe siècles)* (Brussels, 1984), 137.

72 Peter Burke, *The Fabrication of Louis XIV* (New Haven, 1992); T. C. W. Blanning, *The Culture of Power and the Power of Culture: Old Regime Europe 1660-1789* (Oxford, 2002); Mathieu da Vinha, Alexandre Maral and Nicolas Milovanovic (eds), *Louis XIV: l'image et le mythe* (Rennes, 2014).

73 Ditchfield, 'Tridentine', 221.

74 Joseph Bergin, *The Politics of Religion in Early Modern France* (New Haven and London, 2014), 5.

75 Nannerl Keohane, *Philosophy and the State in France: The Renaissance to the Enlightenment* (Princeton, NJ, 1980), 124; William Church, 'France', in *National Consciousness, History, and Political Culture in Early-Modern Europe*, ed. Orest Ranum (Baltimore and London, 1975), 43–66.

76 Pollmann, *Memory*, 94–8.

77 Schaich, *Monarchy*, 37.

78 Alain Tallon, *Conscience nationale et sentiment religieux en France au XVIe siècle* (Paris, 2002).

79 Richard Golden, *The Godly Rebellion: Parisian Curés and the Religious Fronde, 1652-1662* (Chapel Hill, 1981), 12–13; Nancy Lyman Roelker, 'The Two Faces of Rome: The Fate of Protestantism in France', in *Politics, Religion, and Diplomacy in Early Modern Europe*, eds Malcolm Thorp and Arthur Slavin (Kirksville, Missouri, 1994), 99–103; J. H. H. Salmon, 'Clovis and Constantine: The Uses of History in Sixteenth-Century Gallicanism', *Journal of Ecclesiastical History*, 41 (1990): 584–605.

80 David Bell, *The Cult of the Nation in France: Inventing Nationalism, 1680-1800* (Cambridge, MA, 2001); Simon Schama, *Citizens: A Chronicle of the French Revolution* (London, 1989); Blanning, *Culture*.

81 Ditchfield, 'Thinking', 181.

82 Jacques Le Goff, *Saint Louis* (Notre Dame, IN, 2009), xxxi.

83 Gaposchkin, *Making*, 20, 237.

84 Collette Beaune, *Naissance de la nation France* (Paris, 1985), 140, 342.

85 Anja Rathmann-Lutz, *'Images' Ludwigs des Heiligen im Kontext dynasticher Konflikte des 14. und 15. Jahrhunderts* (Berlin, 2010).

86 *Exposition: La Renaissance du culte de saint Louis au XVIIe siècle: l'Ordre Militaire; la Maison Royale de Saint-Cyr. Novembre 1970-janvier 1971* (Paris, 1970).

87 Pierre Morel, 'Le culte de saint Louis', *Itineraires, documents* 147 (1970): 127–51.

88 François-Xavier Cuche, 'Le *Panégyrique de saint Louis* de Fléchier', in *Fléchier et les Grands Jours d'Auvergne: Actes d'une journée d'étude, Université Blaise Pascal-Clermont-Ferrard, 3 octobre 1997*, ed. Emmanuèle Lesne-Jaffro (Tübingen, 2000), 93–114; Sean Heath, 'An Ultramontane Jansenist? Charles Hersent's Panegyric of St Louis (1650)', *Journal of Ecclesiastical History*, 70 (2019): 57–76.

89 Pierre Zoberman, 'Généalogie d'une image: L'éloge spéculaire', *XVIIe siècle*, 146 (1985): 80; idem, *Les Panégyriques du Roi prononcés dans l'Académie Française* (Paris, 1991).

90 Jean-Pierre Landry, 'Saint Louis vu par les Prédicateurs de l'Epoque Classique', in *Colloque «L'image du Moyen-Age dans la littérature française de la Renaissance au XXe siècle»* (Poitiers, 1982), 381–404.

91 Guy Degen, 'Autour d'un lit de cendres: l'image de Louis IX et de sa seconde croisade dans les panégyriques de saint Louis aux XVIIe et XVIIIe siècles', in *La littérature et ses avatars: Discrédits, déformations et réhabilitations dans l'histoire de la littérature*, ed. Yvonne Bellenger (Paris, 1991), 127.

92 Bruno Neveu, 'Le Nain de Tillemont et la *Vie de Saint Louis*', in *Septième Centenaire de la Mort de saint Louis: Actes des colloques de Royaumont et de Paris* (Paris, 1976), 315–29.

93 Daniel Weiner, *Constructing the Memory of Saint Louis: The Battling Biographies of 1688* (Saarbrücken, 2010), 12, 18.

94 Manfred Tietz, 'Saint Louis roi chrétien: un mythe de la mission intérieure du XVIIe siècle', in *La Conversion au XVIIe siècle: Actes du XIIe Colloque de Marseille (janvier 1982)* (Marseille, 1983), 59–69.

95 Suire, *Sainteté française*, 141; Tricoire, *Vierge*, 155.

96 Jean Mesnard, 'Port-Royal et Saint Louis', *Chroniques de Port-Royal: Port-Royal et l'Histoire*, 46 (1997): 53–73; Géraldine Lavieille, 'Les Jésuites et la dévotion à saint Louis au XVIIe siècle: la célébration du Roi très chrétien', *Les Cahiers de Framespa* [online].

97 Alain Boureau, 'Les Enseignements Absolutistes de Saint Louis 1610-1630', in *La monarchie absolutiste et l'histoire en France: théories du pouvoir, propagandes monarchiques et mythologies nationales* (Paris, 1986), 79–97.

98 Burke, *Fabrication*, 28, 75, 96, 113–15.

99 Géraldine Lavieille, '«Il ne fesoit point beau voir qu'un Espagnol tournast le dos à St Louys et à un roy de France». Saint Louis au XVIIe siècle, saint dynastique et saint national', in *Saintetés politiques du IXe au XVIIIe siècle. Autour de la Lotharingie-Dorsale catholique*, ed. Sylvène Édouard (Paris, 2020), 201–25.

100 Tietz, 'Saint', 59n, 67.

Chapter 1

1 Michael Lower, *The Tunis Crusade of 1270: A Mediterranean History* (Oxford, 2018).

2 Cecilia Gaposchkin (ed.), *Blessed Louis, the Most Glorious of Kings: Texts Relating to the Cult of Saint Louis of France* (Notre Dame, IN, 2012), 76–81, 136–41; Gaposchkin and Sean Field (eds), *The Sanctity of Louis IX: Early Lives of Saint Louis by Geoffrey of Beaulieu and William of Chartres* (Ithaca and London, 2014), 120–2, 149, 172.

3 Bergin, *Politics*, 34; Michael Wolfe, *The Conversion of Henri IV: Politics, Power, and Religious Belief in Early Modern France* (Cambridge, MA, 1993), 190.

4 The following paragraphs are based on: Le Goff, *Saint*; Jean Richard, *Saint Louis: Crusader King of France* (Cambridge, 1983); William Jordan, *Louis IX and the Challenge of the Crusade: A Study in Rulership* (Princeton, NJ, 1979); Sophie Delmas, *Saint Louis* (Paris, 2017).

5 Cecilia Gaposchkin, 'The Captivity of Louis IX', *Quaestiones Medii Aevi novae*, 18 (2013): 85–114; William Jordan, '*Etiam reges*, Even Kings', *Speculum*, 90 (2015): 613–34.

6 Gaposchkin and Field, *Sanctity*, 79, 109.

7 Ibid., 83–6; David O'Connell, *The Teachings of Saint Louis: A Critical Text* (Chapel Hill, 1972).

8 Jean de Joinville and Geoffroy de Villehardouin, *Chronicles of the Crusades* (London, 1963), 178.

9 Gaposchkin and Field, *Sanctity*, 62.

10 Le Goff, *Saint*, 227–32, 270; Gaposchkin, *Making*, 25–37; Folz, *Saints*, 126.

11 Gaposchkin, *Making*, 48–66.

12 Medard Barth, 'Zum Kult des hl. Königs Ludwig im deutschen Sprachgebiet und in Skandinavien', *Freiburger Diözesan-Archiv*, 82/83 (1962/3): 127–226; Gaposchkin, *Making*, 76–7; Le Goff, *Saint*, 235–6.

13 Delmas, *Saint*, 98–9.

14 Michel Félibien, *Histoire de l'abbaye royale de saint-Denys . . .* (Paris, 1706), 263; Elizabeth Brown, 'Philippe le Bel and the remains of Saint Louis', *Gazette des Beaux-Arts*, 95 (1980): 175–82.

15 Gaposchkin, *Making*, 67–92; Elizabeth Hallam, 'Philip the Fair and the Cult of Saint Louis', *Studies in Church History*, 18 (1982): 201–14; Xavier Hélary, 'Philip of Artois (†1298)'s Last Wishes and the Birth of the Cult of Saint Louis in the Capetian Family', *Le Moyen Age*, 119 (2013): 27–56.

16 Gaposchkin, *Making*, 139–51.

17 William Jordan, 'Honouring Saint Louis in a small town', *Journal of Medieval History*, 30 (2004): 263–77.

18 Beaune, *Naissance*, 153–60; Folz, *Saints*, 189–90, 200–1; Weiner, *Constructing*, 54.

19 Le Goff, *Saint*, 260, 376–98; Gaposchkin, *Making*, 181–96; Delmas, *Saint*, 143–55; Paula Carns, 'The Cult of Saint Louis and Capetian Interests in the *Hours of Jeanne d'Evreux*', *Peregrinations*, 2 (2006): 1–32.

20 Gaposchkin, *Making*, 12–13, 100–24, 155–80; Gaposchkin, *Blessed*, 1, 20–4.

21 Joinville and Villehardouin, *Chronicles*, 351.

22 Beaune, *Naissance*, 127, 140–2, 149; Gaposchkin, *Making*, 84; Folz, *Saints*, 155, 171.

23 Rathmann-Lutz, „*Images*"; Boris Bove, *Le temps de la Guerre de Cent Ans, 1328-1453* (Paris, 2010), 246; Gaposchkin, *Making*, 233–40; Beaune, *Naissance*, 126, 152–7; Jordan, 'Honouring', 269.

24 Alexandre Haran, *Le Lys et le Globe: Messianisme dynastique et rêve impérial en France aux XVIᵉ et XVIIᵉ siècles* (Seyssel, 2000), 45.

25 Beaune, *Naissance*, 81, 126, 144–6, 151, 158; Bove, *Temps*, 169; Delmas, *Saint*, 129–41; Weiner, *Constructing*, 45, 110; Gaposchkin, *Making*, 92; Elizabeth Brown, 'The chapels and cult of Saint Louis at Saint-Denis', *Mediaevalia*, 10 (1984): 299.

26 Pierre Rézeau, *Les Prières aux Saints en Français à la fin du Moyen Âge* (Geneva, 1983), 309–16.

27 Elizabeth Brown and Sanford Zale, 'Louis Le Blanc, Estienne Le Blanc, and the defense of Louis IX's crusades, 1498-1522', *Traditio*, 55 (2000): 235–92.

28 Nathalie Gorochov, 'Entre théologie, humanisme et politique: Les sermons universitaires de la fête de Saint Louis sous le règne de Charles VI (1389-1422)', in *Saint-Denis et la royauté: Études offertes à Bernard Guenée*, eds Françoise Autrand, Claude Gauvard and Jean-Marie Moeglin (Paris, 1999), 51–64.

29 Beaune, *Naissance*, 151; Weiner, *Constructing*, 17, 22, 87–98, 136–50.

30 Weiner, *Constructing*, 90; Jean-Michel Leniaud and Françoise Perrot, *La Sainte-Chapelle* (Paris, 1991), 113–14; Delmas, *Saint*, 153.

31 Robert Sturges, ''The Guise and the Two Jerusalems: Joinville's *Vie de saint Louis* and an Early Modern Family's Medievalism', in *Aspiration, Representation and Memory: The Guise in Europe, 1506-1688*, eds Jessica Munns, Penny Richards and Jonathan Spangler (Farnham, 2015), 25–46.

32 BnF, MS Fr. 25,013, p. 67; François-Timoléon de Choisy, *La vie de Saint Louis* . . . (Paris, 1689), 110–11.

33 Jean Calvin, *Traité des Reliques* . . . (Paris, 1921), 135; Géraud Poumarède, *Pour en finir avec la Croisade: Mythes et réalités de la lutte contre les Turcs aux XVIe et XVIIe siècles* (Paris, 2004), 121–2.

34 Barbara Diefendorf, *Beneath the Cross: Catholics and Huguenots in Sixteenth-Century Paris* (Oxford, 1991), 28; Weiner, *Constructing*, 138; Félibien, *Histoire*, 399, 413, 420; Le Gall, *Mythe*, 86–93; Pierre de l'Estoile, *Registre-Journal du règne de Henri III*, eds Madeleine Lazard and Gilbert Schrenck, 6 vols (Geneva, 1992–2003), VI, 193; Joël Cornette, *Henri IV à Saint-Denis: de l'abjuration à la profanation* (Paris, 2010), 60.

35 Tallon, *Conscience*, 51, 83–4.

36 Denis Hangard, *Dionysii Hangardi, doctoris theologi* . . . (Paris, 1575), unpag.; Claude Nouvelet, *Hymne Trionfal au Roy* . . . (Paris, 1572).

37 *Remonstrance d'un bon Catholique François, aux Trois estats de France, qui s'assembleront à Blois* . . . (s.l., 1576); Mark Greengrass, *Governing Passions: Peace and Reform in the French Kingdom, 1576-1585* (Oxford, 2007), 33–4.

38 Alain Tallon, *La France et le Concile de Trente (1518-1563)* (Rome, 1997), 446.

39 Frederic Baumgartner, *Louis XII* (Basingstoke, 1994), 252–3; idem, 'Le Roi de Bonté: The Image of Louis XII during the French Wars of Religion', in Thorp and Slavin, *Politics*, 113–26.

40 Joaquín Pascual-Barea, 'Quis posset dignos Lodouico dicere uersus? Los tres epigramas en alabanza de San Luis premiados en la justa hispalense del otoño de 1556', *Calamus Renascens*, 10 (2009): 129–49.

41 Martha Hoffman, *Raised to Rule: Educating Royalty at the Court of the Spanish Habsburgs, 1601-1634* (Baton Rouge, 2011), 73.

42 Fabien Montcher, 'L'image et le culte de saint Louis dans la Monarchie hispanique: Le rôle des «reines de paix» (du milieu du XVIe siècle au milieu du XVIIe siècle)', in *«La dame de cœur»: Patronage et mécénat religieux des femmes de pouvoir dans l'Europe des XIVe-XVIIe siècles*, eds Murielle Gaude-Ferragu and Cécile Vincent-Cassy (Rennes, 2016), 167–77, 182.

43 Senault, *Monarque*, 114, 120–1.

44 Norman Ravitch, *The Catholic Church and the French Nation 1589-1989* (London and New York, 1990), 4.

45 Frederic Baumgartner, *Change and Continuity in the French Episcopate: The Bishops and the Wars of Religion, 1547-1610* (Durham, 1986), 157; Michel de Waele, *Réconcilier les Français: la fin des troubles de religion (1589-1598)* (Paris, 2015), 174.

46 Barbara Diefendorf, 'Henri IV, the Dévots and the Making of a French Catholic Reformation', in *Politics and Religion in Early Bourbon France*, eds Alison Forrestal and Eric Nelson (Basingstoke, 2009), 157.

47 Marc Jaffré, 'The Royal Court and Civil War at the founding of the Bourbon Dynasty, 1589-95', *French History*, 31 (2017): 22.

48 Annette Finley-Croswhite, *Henry IV and the Towns: The Pursuit of Legitimacy in French Urban Society, 1589-1610* (Cambridge, 1999), 1–2.

49 Duc de Nevers, *Memoires . . .*, 2 vols (Paris, 1665), I, 768.

50 Ariane Boltanski, *Les ducs de Nevers et l'état royal: Genèse d'un compromis (ca1500-ca1600)* (Geneva, 2006), 467.

51 Delmas, *Saint*, 161.

52 L'Estoile, *Registre-Journal*, VI, 83–4.

53 Wolfe, *Conversion*, 139, 186; Diefendorf, 'Henri IV', 159–60.

54 Simon Vigor, *Sermons Catholiques . . .* (Paris, 1597), 269.

55 Larissa Taylor, 'Dangerous Vocations: Preaching in France in the Late Middle Ages and Reformations', in *Preachers and People in the Reformations and Early Modern Period*, ed. Larissa Taylor (Leiden, 2011), 113–15; Megan Armstrong, *The Politics of Piety: Franciscan Preachers during the Wars of Religion, 1560-1600* (Woodbridge, 2004), 150–7; Larissa Taylor, *Soldiers of Christ: Preaching in Late Medieval and Reformation France* (Oxford, 1992).

56 Jean Boucher, *Sermons de la simulée conversion, et nullité de la pretendue absolution de Henry de Bourbon . . .* (Paris, 1594), 223r, 328v, 373r, 329r-v.

57 Cornette, *Henri IV*, 47.

58 Nevers, *Memoires*, II, 119, 138, 151; Boucher, *Sermons*, 133v.

59 *Procès-verbaux des États Généraux de 1593*, ed. Auguste Bernard (Paris, 1842), 137.

60 Nevers, *Memoires*, II, 485.

61 *Estampe emblêmatique relative à la conduite tenue par les Guise envers la Royauté . . .* Several versions are on BnF Gallica. See also: *Généalogie des descendants de saint Louis* (Michael Snyders, 1619).

62 Christian Jouhaud, 'Readability and Persuasion: Political Handbills', in *The Culture of Print: Power and the Uses of Print in Early Modern Europe*, ed. Roger Chartier (Oxford, 1989), 242–6.

63 Henri de Montagu, *La decente généalogique depuis St Louys de la royale maison de Bourbon* (Paris, 1609).

64 *Discours de la Ioyeuse et Triomphante entrée de tres-haut, tres-puissant et tres magnanime Prince Henry IIII de ce nom, tres-Chrestien Roy de France & de Navarre, faicte en sa ville de Rouën . . .* (Rouen, 1596), 68–70; Finley-Croswhite, *Henry IV*, 47–62; Jaffré, 'Royal', 24; Philip Benedict, *Rouen during the Wars of Religion* (Cambridge, 1981).

65 Bernard Barbiche and Ségolène de Dainville-Barbiche, *Sully: L'homme et ses fidèles* (Paris, 1997), 296–7; Hilary Ballon, *The Paris of Henri IV: Architecture and Urbanism* (Cambridge, MA, 1991), 50–1.

66 Thomas Worcester, 'Saints as Cultural History', in *Exploring Cultural History: Essays in Honour of Peter Burke*, eds Melissa Calaresu, Filippo de Vivo and Joan-Pau Rubiés (Farnham, 2010), 194; Pierre Matthieu, *Histoire de sainct Louys . . .* (Paris, 1618), 489–512; Georges-Étienne Rousselet, *Le lys sacré . . .* (Lyon, 1631), 271–3.

67 Molière, *Le Bourgeois gentilhomme*, Act III, Scene 12.

68 Alain Tallon, 'Henri IV and the Papacy after the League', in Forrestal and Nelson, *Politics*, 32.

69 Hélène Charpentier, 'Sébastien Garnier et la première Henriade', in *Les Lettres au temps de Henri IV: Volume des actes du colloque Agen-Nérac 18-20 mai 1990* (Pau: Association Henri IV, 1989), 146; Delmas, *Saint*, 161–3.

70 Abraham de Vermeil, *Poésies*, ed. Henri Lafay (Paris and Geneva, 1976), xii.

71 Jean Bertaut, *Œuvres Poetiques . . .*, ed. Adolphe Chenevière (Millwood, NY, 1982), xxi–xlvii, 65; Edelman, *Attitudes*, 239.

72 Bertaut, *Œuvres*, 82.

73 Bertaut's poem was translated by Josuah Sylvester and published with a dedication
    to the future Charles I: Josuah Sylvester, *Du Bartas his Divine Weekes* . . . (London,
    1621), 1057–75.
74 Nicolas Rapin, *Œuvres*, ed. Jean Brunel, 3 vols (Paris-Geneva, 1982), II, 191.
75 Matthieu, *Histoire*, 6–8.
76 Ballon, *Paris*, 166–98; Pierre Faure, 'Histoire de l'hôpital Saint-Louis à travers
    l'histoire de ses bâtiments', *Revue d'histoire de la pharmacie*, 324 (1999): 443–8;
    Barbiche and de Dainville-Barbiche, *Sully*, 288–90.
77 *MF*, I (1607), 224.
78 Louis Blond, *La maison professe des Jésuites de la rue saint-Antoine à Paris, 1580-1762*
    (Paris, 1956), 8–9, 23–32, 55–7; E. de Ménorval, *Les Jéuites de la rue Saint-Antoine:
    L'église Saint-Paul-Saint-Louis et le lycée Charlemagne* (Paris, 1872), 23–72; Eric
    Nelson, '*Religion royale* in the sacred landscape of Paris: The Jesuit Church of Saint
    Louis and the resacralization of kingship in early Bourbon France (1590-1650)', in
    Layered Landscapes: Early Modern Religious Space Across Faiths and Cultures, eds Eric
    Nelson and Jonathan Wright (London, 2017), 171–84.
79 Eric Nelson, *The Jesuits and the Monarchy: Catholic Reform and Political Authority
    in France (1590-1615)* (Aldershot, 2005), 24, 32, 51, 77; Robert Descimon, 'Chastel's
    Attempted Regicide (27 December 1594) and its Subsequent Transformation into
    an "Affair"', in Forrestal and Nelson, *Politics*, 86–164; Nicole Reinhardt, 'The King's
    Confessor: Changing Images', in Schaich, *Monarchy*, 159.
80 *MF*, I (1606), 110v.
81 Henri IV, *Recueil des lettres* . . ., 9 vols (Paris, 1843–76), VI, 664.
82 Jean-François Dubost, *Marie de Médicis: La reine dévoilée* (Paris, 2009), 145.
83 BnF MS Fr. 17,876, f. 26v; *G*, 6 October 1634, 423; Henri IV, *Recueil*, V, 491–2.
84 Bartlett, *Why*, 460.
85 Rousselet, *Lys*, 300; Charles Robinet, *Le parfait victorieux* . . . (Paris, 1643), 11.
86 Olivier Chaline, *L'année des quatre dauphins* (Paris, 2009), 77.
87 Henri IV, *Recueil*, VII, 392–3.
88 Lavieille, 'Il', 209n.
89 *MF*, I (1608), 230r.
90 Jacques Salbert, 'La chapelle saint-Louis du collège de Jésuites de La Flèche en Anjou
    (aujourd'hui prytanée militaire)', *Annales de Bretagne et des pays de l'Ouest*, 68 (1961):
    181; Nelson, *Jesuits*, 97–9, 112.
91 Rousselet, *Lys*, 274.
92 Laurence Grove, *Emblematics and 17th-Century French Literature: Descartes, Tristan,
    La Fontaine and Perrault* (Charlottesville, 2000), 5, 11.
93 These cryptic lines are not easy to translate, but the versions offered by Hélène
    Duccini and Laurence Grove take too many liberties with the Latin. They also argue
    that Henri IV says his line after Saint Louis and Louis XIII, but it makes more sense
    if the exchange proceeds from Henri to Saint Louis to Louis XIII. Hélène Duccini,
    Faire voir, faire croire: L'opinion publique sous Louis XIII (Seyssel, 2003), 93–5; Grove,
    Emblematics, 62–7.
94 Jacques Hennequin, *Henri IV dans ses oraisons funèbres, ou la naissance d'une légende*
    (Paris, 1977), 49, 140–8, 201–4.
95 Estienne Binet, *Recueil des oeuvres spirituelles* . . ., 2nd edn (Rouen, 1627), 808.
96 Scipion Dupleix, *Histoire de Louis le Iuste* . . . (Paris, 1635), 1.
97 Louis Richeome, *Consolation envoyee a la royne mere du roy* . . . (Lyon, 1610), 76–8,
    100.

98 *MF*, I (1610), 423r, 425v.

99 Simon-Germain Millet, *Le Tresor sacré* . . ., 4th edn (Paris, 1645), 76.

100 Weiner, *Constructing*, 162.

101 *Recueil des actes, titres et mémoires concernant les affaires du clergé de France* . . . (Paris & Avignon, 1771), 289–90, 294–5.

102 Dubost, *Marie*, 470–1.

103 *Érection de la Paroisse Saint-Louis de Fontainebleau* (Fontainebleau, 1893).

104 Caroline Maillet-Rao, 'Towards a new reading of the political thought of the *dévot* faction: The Opposition to Cardinal Richelieu's Ministériat', *Religions*, 4 (2013): 539–40.

105 Weiner, *Constructing*, 159–62.

106 Clovis Eve, *La vie, legende, et miracles du roy sainct Louys* . . . (Paris, 1610), 3–4.

107 Jean Savaron, *Traicté contre les duels* . . . (Paris, 1610), 67.

108 Idem, *Traicté contre les duels* . . . (Paris, 1614); idem., *Discours abregé, avec l'Ordonnance entiere du Roy sainct Loys, contre les duels* . . . (Paris, 1614). On Savaron, see J. Michael Hayden, *France and the Estates General of 1614* (Cambridge, 1974), 110, 120–2, 142–3, 191n.

109 Weiner, *Constructing*, 163.

110 Mattheus Merian's engraving of the fireworks (*La representation des Artifices de feu, & autres triomphes faits à Paris sur le gué des Celestins & en l'isle Louviers, le Lundy deuxiesme Septembre 1613. en l'honneur de la feste de S. Louys*) is on Gallica.

111 *Discours sur les triomphes qui ont esté faicts le 25, 26 & 27 Aoust 1613 dans la ville de Paris a l'honneur & loüange de la feste S. Louys, & de Louys XIII* . . . (Lyon, 1613).

112 Hayden, *France*, 66; Weiner, *Constructing*, 167.

113 AN, LL 1220, f. 47r-v; Montcher, 'L'image', 178; Félibien, *Histoire*, 440.

114 Duccini, *Faire voir*; Louis Batiffol, *Le roi Louis XIII à vingt ans* (Paris, 1910), 90; Sharon Kettering, 'Political Pamphlets in Early Seventeenth-Century France: The Propaganda War between Louis XIII and His Mother, 1619-20', *The Sixteenth Century Journal*, 42 (2011): 963–4; idem, *Power and reputation at the court of Louis XIII: The career of Charles d'Albret, duc de Luynes (1578-1621)* (Manchester, 2008), chapter 3.

115 Claude Ménard (ed.), *Histoire de S. Loys IX* . . . (Paris, 1617); idem (ed.), *Sancti Ludovici Francorum Regis, vita, conversatio, et miracula* . . . (Paris, 1617).

116 Of the three copies at the Arsenal, they appear as described in 4-H-2687, but not at all in 4-H-2685 and with only the engraving of Saint Louis (in a different place) in 4-H-2686.

117 Ménard, *Histoire*, s.p.

118 Weiner, *Constructing*, 169.

119 Alanson Lloyd Moote, *Louis XIII, the Just* (Berkeley and Los Angeles, 1989), 256–7.

120 AAE, 109CP/25, ff. 83r-84r.

121 Matthieu, *Histoire*, 485–6; Dupleix, *Histoire de Louis le Iuste*, 165.

122 Guido Bentivoglio, *La nunziatura* . . . ed. L. de Steffani (Florence, 1865), II, 395–6.

123 AAE, 109CP/25, ff.183v-184v.

124 *Bref de Nostre S. Père le Pape Paul V. pour la celebration de la feste de Sainct LOVYS iadis Roy de France, par tout ce Royaume. Avec le Mandement de Monseigneur l'Illustrißime & Reverendißime Cardinal de Retz, Evesque de Paris* (Paris, 1618).

125 *MF*, V (1618), 271–6; Bentivoglio, *Nunziatura*, II, 565–6; Paul V, *Bref*, 5–6, 10–12. See the handwritten note at the end of the BnF copy of the *Bref* (BnF E-4720 (1618/07/05)).

126 Étienne Molinier, *Panegyrique du Roy S. Louys* . . . (Paris, 1618), 6, 31, 35–7, 40.

127 Weiner, *Constructing*, 179.
128 *Les Triomphes du très-chretien roy de France et de Navarre, Louys le Juste, Digne Heritier & Successeur du Roy Sainct Louys* (Paris, 1618), 9.
129 Boureau, 'Enseignements', 79. Some historians have ignored the elevation of the cult. It is not mentioned in Kettering's *Power and reputation*, suggesting that she found it unimportant.
130 Montcher, 'L'image', 180.
131 Reinhardt, *Voices*, 6.
132 BnF, MS Clair. 375, f. 182r.
133 Bergin, *Politics*, 6.

Chapter 2

1 Michel Tyvaert, 'L'image du Roi: légitimité et moralité royales dans les Histoires de France au XVIIe siècle', *Revue d'histoire moderne et contemporaine*, 21 (1974): 541–2.
2 Matthieu, *Histoire*, 9.
3 Rousselet, *Lys*, 244–5, 269, 879, 1401.
4 Joseph Filère, *La Devotion à S. Louys . . .* (Lyon, 1641), 25, 229–31, 290–1, 390.
5 Idem, *Le parfait Prince Chretien, Saint Louys . . .* (Lyon, 1654), unpag.
6 Robert Bellarmine, *De Officio Principis Christiani, Libri Tres* (Cologne, 1619), 472–506; Sylvio Hermann De Franceschi, 'Le modèle jésuite du prince chrétien: À propos du *De officio principis Christiani* de Bellarmin', *Dix-septième siècle*, 237 (2007): 713–28.
7 Rousselet, *Lys*, 214, 257–61.
8 Scipion Dupleix, *Histoire Generale de France . . .* 6th edn, 3 vols (Paris, 1658), II, 315.
9 Matthieu, *Histoire*, 99, 480.
10 Boureau, 'Enseignements', 82–3; Adam Théveneau, *Les Preceptes du Roy S. Louys a Philippes III . . .* (Paris, 1627), unpag.
11 O'Connell, *Teachings*, 12–15.
12 *La lettre de Sainct Louys . . .* (Paris, 1617); *Remonstrance de Sainct Louys . . .* (s.l., s.d.).
13 Boureau, 'Enseignements', 91.
14 Théveneau, *Preceptes, Au roy*, 12–14, 196–205, 231–2, 241–8, 251–9, 309.
15 Cardin Le Bret, *De la Souveraineté du Roy . . .* (Paris, 1632), 402.
16 Orest Ranum, *Artisans of Glory: Writers and Historical Thought in Seventeenth-Century France* (Chapel Hill, 1980), 13, 339; Dupleix, *Histoire*, II, 244, 313.
17 François Eudes de Mézeray, *Histoire de France . . .*, 3 vols (Paris, 1643–51), I, 563, 589, 637.
18 Ranum, *Artisans*, 197–9, 265; Edelman, *Attitudes*, 87; John Wolf, 'The Formation of a King', in *Louis XIV and the Craft of Kingship*, ed. John Rule (Columbus, 1969), 107.
19 André-Hercule de Fleury, *L'Abrégé de l'Histoire de France écrit pour le jeune Louis XV* (Bonnières-sur-Seine, 2004), 27; Hugh Gaston Hall, *Richelieu's Desmarets and the Century of Louis XIV* (Oxford, 1990), 230–6.
20 Senault, *Monarque*, 117–18.
21 Louis Maimbourg, *Les Histoires du sieur Maimbourg, cy-devant Jesuite*, 12 vols (Paris, 1686), VI, 477; Jean-Pascal Gay, 'Le «cas Maimbourg». La possibilité d'un gallicanisme jésuite au XVIIᵉ siècle', *Revue historique*, 316 (2014): 785.

22 Senault, *Monarque*, 123, 139, 337.

23 Maimbourg, *Histoires*, VI, 477–9.

24 Jean-Marie de Vernon, *Le Roy Très-Chrestien, ou la Vie de St Louis* . . . (Paris, 1662), *Au roy*, 60–9, 74–7, 420–8, 454–7, 469, 484–9, 628–9, 636, 732–3. The idea that Louis IX was a Third Order Franciscan went back to the fourteenth century: Delmas, *Saint*, 108, 124; Gaposchkin, *Making*, 155n.

25 Vernon, *Roy*, 2, 11, 96, 110, 140, 155, 612.

26 Charles du Fresne du Cange, *Histoire de S. Louis...* (Paris, 1668).

27 Matthieu, *Histoire*, 249–60; John Considine, *Dictionaries in Early Modern Europe: Lexicography and the Making of Heritage* (Cambridge, 2008), 261–87.

28 Agnes of Harcourt, *The Writings of Anne of Harcourt: The Life of Isabelle of France & the Letter on Louis IX and Longchamp*, ed. Sean Field (Notre Dame, Indiana, 2003), 24–9; Vyon d'Hérouval, 'Notes de Vyon d'Hérouval sur les baptisés et les convers et sur les enquêteurs royaux au temps de saint Louis et de ses successeurs (1234-1334)', *Bibliothèque de l'école des chartes*, 28 (1867): 609–21; Edelman, *Attitudes*, 64–75; Neveu, 'Nain', 315; Vernon, *Roy*, *Preface*; Cange, *Histoire*, Préface.

29 [C. H. Le Fèbvre de Saint Marc and A. de la Chassagne] *Vie de Monsieur Pavillon* . . . (Saint Miel, 1738), 131; Pierre Blet, *Le Clergé du Grand Siècle en ses Assemblées (1615-1715)* (Paris, 1995), 247.

30 Angélique Arnauld, *Lettres* . . ., 3 vols (Utrecht, 1742–1744), II, 116, 135, 177–8, 195, 324, 420–1, 507, 563–4; Weiner, *Constructing*, 192–4, 258; Mesnard, 'Port-Royal', 54–6.

31 Neveu, 'Nain', 321–2.

32 Martin McGuire, 'Louis-Sebastien le Nain de Tillemont', *Catholic Historical Review*, 52 (1966): 186–200.

33 Louis-Sébastien Le Nain de Tillemont, *Vie de Saint Louis* . . ., ed. J. de Gaulle, 6 vols (Paris, 1847–1851).

34 Mesnard, 'Port-Royal', 64–5.

35 Nicolas Filleau de la Chaise, *Histoire de S. Louis* . . ., 2 vols (Paris, 1688), I, *Epître* (unpag.), 4–6, 207, 421–2; II, 208–9, 295–6, 383–5, 601–2.

36 Blet, *Clergé*, 299.

37 Filleau, *Histoire*, I, 24, 104, 116, 133–4, 162–3, 630–1; II, 93–4.

38 Ibid., II, 518.

39 Filère, *Parfait Prince Chretien*, 277–8.

40 Weiner, *Constructing*, 210; Mesnard, 'Port-Royal', 69.

41 Madame de Sévigné, *Correspondance*, ed. Roger Duchêne, 3 vols (Paris, 1978), III, 377 (lettre 1014), 458 (lettre 1051), 535 (lettre 1081), 622–3 (lettre 1120).

42 Weiner, *Constructing*, 212–13.

43 Ibid., 7, 14, 207, 221, 231, 249, 251; Paul Scott, 'Authenticity and Textual Transvestism in the Memoirs of the Abbé de Choisy', *French Studies*, 69 (2015): 15–18.

44 Choisy, *Vie, Avertissement* (unpag.), (livres I-III) 1–2, 85–6.

45 Choisy, *Vie, Au roy* (unpag.), (livres I-III) 17, 34–5, 43–4, 99–102, 125, 142, 171, (livres IV-VI) 14–15, 27.

46 *MG*, September 1707, 2; Abbé de Saint-Vincent, *Panégyrique de saint Louis* . . . (Paris, 1739), 7; Nicolas-Jérôme Le Cousturier, *Panégyrique de Saint Louis* . . . (Paris, 1769), 20; Jacques-François de la Tour du Pin de La Charce, *Panégyrique de Saint Louis* . . . (Paris, 1751), 10, 29.

47 Weiner, *Constructing*, 260.

48 Louis-Pierre Manuel, *Coup d'œil philosophique sur le règne de Saint-Louis* (Damietta [Paris], 1788), 3–5. The work was first published in 1786.

49 BnF, MS Fr. 25,013, pp. 1–6; AD Seine-Maritime, Montbret MSS 27 (1811), ff. 1–19; Antoine Varillas, *La Minorité de Saint Louis . . .* (The Hague, 1685).

50 Jean Boizard, *Traité des monoyes . . .* (Paris, 1692), 17–18.

51 Thomas Worcester, 'The Catholic Sermon', in Taylor, *Preachers and People*, 26–7.

52 Suire, *Sainteté et Lumières*, 276–7.

53 Charles Hersent, *L'empire de Dieu dans les saincts, ou bien l'éloge de sainct Louis . . .* (Rome, 1651), 9, 12.

54 Heath, 'Ultramontane', 57–76.

55 G, 18 April 1671, 387–8; *MG*, September 1681, 154–7; *MG*, September 1683, 34; *Les Registres de l'Académie Françoise, 1672-1793*, 4 vols (Paris, 1895–1906), I, 71, 198–9; II, 299; Pierre Zoberman, *Les Panégyriques du Roi prononcés dans l'Académie Française* (Paris, 1991), 9–15.

56 *MG*, September 1699, 213; August 1701, 324.

57 Abbé Anselme, *Panegyrique de S. Louis . . .* (Paris, 1681), 30; *MG*, September 1688, 32.

58 Zoberman, *Panégyriques*, 10.

59 Vincent Houdry, *La Bibliotheque des Prédicateurs. Troisième Partie . . .* (Lyon, 1781), III, 343.

60 Leon de Saint Ian, *Saint Louys, le Snt. des Roys, & le Roy des Saints . . .* (Rome, 1648), 4.

61 Worcester, 'Catholic Sermon', 3.

62 *MG*, August 1703, 389–90.

63 *MG*, September 1705, 16.

64 *MG*, September 1706, 20–1.

65 Anselme, *Panegyrique*, 3.

66 *Les Panégyristes de saint Louis . . .*, 2 vols (Paris, 1814), I, 222–3.

67 Pierre Cureau de la Chambre, *Panégyrique de Saint Louis . . .* (Paris, 1681), 13.

68 Abbé du Buisson, *Panegyrique de saint Louis . . .* (Paris, 1710), 34–5.

69 Antoine de Bretagne, *Panégyrique de Saint Louys . . .* (Rome, 1674), 10.

70 Anselme, *Panegyrique*, 12–18.

71 Abbé de Montelet, *Panégyrique de Saint Louis. . . .* (Paris, 1691), 15.

72 Pierre Robert Le Prévost, *Panégyrique de saint Louis . . .* (Paris, 1705), 4.

73 *MG*, September 1707, 21.

74 Chambre, *Panégyrique*, 12–15.

75 *Panégyristes*, I, 25.

76 Chambre, *Panégyrique*, 7–9.

77 Edme Mongin, *Panégyrique de Saint Louis . . .* (Paris, 1701), 24–30.

78 *Panégyristes*, I, 42.

79 Ibid., I, 181–2.

80 Ibid., I, 21.

81 Le Prévost, *Panégyrique*, 18.

82 Buisson, *Panegyrique*, 7–8, 17.

83 Zoberman, *Panégyriques*, 48, 264n.

84 Abbé Estor, *Panégyrique de Saint Louis . . .* (Paris, 1694), 58.

85 *MG*, September 1705, 17.

86 Abbé Bion, *Panégyrique de saint Louis . . .* (Paris, 1715), 6; *NMG*, August 1715, 172–3.

87 Laurent Juillard du Jarry, *Panegyrique de S. Louis . . .* (Paris, 1689), 53–4.

88 Montelet, *Panégyrique*, 13.

89 Bretagne, *Panégyrique*, 11; Chambre, *Panégyrique*, 22; *NMG*, August 1715, 177.

90 *Panégyristes*, I, 12; Le Prévost, *Panégyrique*, 19.

91 *MG*, September 1707, 14–15.

92 Abbé de Lopis de la Fare, *Panégyrique de saint Louis . . .* (Paris, 1709), 7.

93 Buisson, *Panégyrique*, 29–31.

94 *Panégyristes*, I, 30.

95 Abbé de Pézène, *Panégyrique de Saint Louis . . .* (Paris, 1690), 11.

96 *MG*, September 1707, 26.

97 Montelet, *Panégyrique*, 18–19; *MG*, September 1707, 38.

98 *Panégyristes*, I, 17; Jean-Pascal Gay, 'Voués à quel royaume? Les Jésuites entre vœux de religion et fidélité monarchique. À propos d'un mémoire inédit du P. de La Chaize', *Dix-septième siècle*, 227 (2005): 285–314.

99 Bretagne, *Panégyrique*, 12; Anselme, *Panégyrique*, 30; *Panégyristes*, I, 52.

100 Estor, *Panégyrique*, 8.

101 Montelet, *Panégyrique*, 5.

102 Pézène, *Panégyrique*, 9.

103 *MG*, August 1692, 218.

104 *Panégyristes*, I, 46–7.

105 de Saint Ian, *Saint Louys*, 11–12.

106 Zoberman, *Panégyriques*, 49; Landry, 'Saint Louis', 393.

107 Houdry, *Bibliotheque*, 354–413.

108 Degen, 'Autour', 129.

109 Heath, 'Ultramontane', 67.

110 Monique Vincent, *Le Mercure Galant; Présentation de la première revue feminine d'information et de culture, 1672-1710* (Paris, 2005).

111 *MG*, September 1707, 5–95.

112 *MG*, September 1706, 7–9, 23–4.

113 *Gazette*, 28 August 1706, 419; 1 September 1708, 420; 31 August 1709, 419; 30 August 1710, 420; 27 August 1712, 444; 26 August 1713, 408.

114 Maximilien de Béthune de Sully, *Mémoires . . .*, 8 vols (London, 1747), VIII, 222–3.

115 *MF*, V (1619), 225–32; Brian Sandberg, 'Going Off to the War in Hungary: French Nobles and Crusading Culture in the Sixteenth Century', *The Hungarian Historical Review*, 4 (2015): 346–83.

116 Christine Isom-Verhaaren, *Allies with the Infidel: The Ottoman and French Alliance in the Sixteenth Century* (London, 2011); Alphonse Dupront, *Le mythe de croisade* (Paris, 1997); Poumarède, *Pour*, 12, 104–7, 118–22, 404–6, 432–4, 532; Faruk Bilici, *Louis XIV et son projet de conquête d'Istanbul* (Ankara, 2004), 1–3, 13–14; Haran, *Lys*, 14–16.

117 Poumarède, *Pour*, 53, 283; Hubert Carrier, *Le Labyrinthe de l'État: Essai sur le débat politique en France au temps de la Fronde (1648-1653)* (Paris, 2004), 370.

118 I am grateful to Megan Armstrong for sharing with me chapters from her forthcoming book, *Going to the Source: The Holy Land, the Friars and the Reinvention of the Catholic Tradition 1517-1700*.

119 Matthieu, *Histoire*, 135, 234, 241, 269–70.

120 Rousselet, *Lys*, 1094–100.

121 *MG*, September 1707, 47–8.

122 *Panégyristes*, I, 185–90; Le Prévost, *Panégyrique*, 6; Buisson, *Panégyrique*, 35.

123 Bretagne, *Panégyrique*, 27–8.

124 Estor, *Panégyrique*, 43–6.

125 Mongin, *Panégyrique*, 33; Chambre, *Panégyrique*, 28–9; Le Prévost, *Panégyrique*, 23.

126 Filère, *Parfait Prince*, 247, 258.

127 *Panégyristes*, I, 187.

128 Pierre Corneille, *Œuvres*, ed. M. Ch. Marty-Laveaux, 12 vols (Paris, 1862–1868), X, 192–3, 211.

129 BMaz, MS 3914, 626–39; Nicolas de Bonnécamp, *Sonnets . . .* (Vennes, 1687), 65.

130 Yvan Loskoutoff, *L'armorial de Calliope: L'œuvre du Père Le Moyne S.J. (1602-1671): littérature, héraldique, spiritualité* (Tübingen, 2000), 49–50.

131 Gilles Banderier, 'Du *Saint Louis* à la *Louisiade*: note sur la réception du P. Le Moyne au XVIIIᵉ siècle', *Papers on French Seventeenth Century Literature*, 25 (1998): 597.

132 William Calin, *Crown, Cross, and "Fleur-de-Lis": An Essay on Pierre Le Moyne's baroque epic "Saint Louis"* (Saratoga, 1977), 14–15, 21; Jordan, 'Saint', 175; Edelman, *Attitudes*, 239; Véronique Meyer, 'L'illustration du *Saint Louis* du Père Le Moyne', *Cahiers de l'Association internationale des études françaises*, 57 (2005): 47–73.

133 Pierre Le Moyne, *Œuvres poetiques . . .* (Paris, 1671), unpag.

134 *Panégyristes*, I, 5.

135 Pierre Le Moyne, *Les Poesies . . .* (Paris, 1651), unpag.

136 Le Moyne, *Œuvres*, unpag.

137 Pierre Le Moyne, *Saint Louys . . .* (Paris, 1653), 1, 21, 37, 62, 127, 155, 179, 221; Calin, 'Crown', 26–7, 55; Jordan, 'Saint', 176.

138 Le Moyne, *Saint Louys*, 2, 4, 15, 40, 70, 76, 86, 172, 204, 214.

139 Ibid., 125–6, 140–2; Le Moyne, *Œuvres*, 85, 96.

140 Le Moyne, *Saint Louys*, 231, 242; Le Moyne, *Œuvres*, 131; Edelman, *Attitudes*, 242.

141 Le Moyne, *Œuvres*, 223.

142 Joël Cornette, *Le roi de guerre: essai sur la souveraineté dans la France du Grand Siècle* (Paris, 1993); Gérard Sabatier, 'La gloire du roi: Iconographie de Louis XIV de 1661 à 1672', *Histoire, Économie et Société*, 19 (2000): 527–60.

143 BnF, MS Fr. 25,460, ff. 31v-32r; Pierre Perrin, *Cantica pro Capella regis* (Paris, 1665), 58–9; Henri du Mont, *Motets pour la Chapelle du Roy . . .* (Paris, 1686), no. 18. Laurence Decobert, *Henry du Mont (1610-1684): Maistre et compositeur de la Musique de la Chapelle du Roy et de la Reyne* (Wavre, 2011), 121–2, 305, 456.

144 Marc-Antoine Charpentier, *Œuvres complètes, I: Meslanges autographes . . .* (Paris, 1990-2004), III, 14 (cah. 17, f. 7v); III, 92–7 (cah. 22, ff. 104r-107r); VI, 13–21 (cah. 38, ff. 7r-11r). Catherine Cessac, Jane Gosine, Laurent Guillo and Patricia Ranum, 'Chronologie raisonnée des manuscrits autographes de Charpentier. Essai de bibliographie matérielle', *Bulletin Charpentier*, 3 (2013).

145 H. Wiley Hitchcock, 'The Latin Oratorios of Marc-Antoine Charpentier', *The Musical Quarterly*, 41 (1955): 58.

146 Haran, *Lys*, 300.

147 Ménard, *Histoire*, unpag.

148 Benoist Pierre, *Le père Joseph: l'Éminence grise de Richelieu* (Paris, 2007), 129–35, 141–8, 207–9.

149 Liborio Siniscalchi, *Panegirici sacri . . .*, 4th edn (Venice, 1769), 79.

150 Sandberg, 'Going', 375–6.

151 Abbé Puyol, *Louis XIII et le Béarn, ou le rétablissement du Catholicisime en Béarn et réunion du Béarn et de la Navarre a la France* (Paris, 1872), 340.

152 François Langlois, *Le Miroir du temps passé, à l'usage du present . . .* (Paris, 1625), 45.

153 Zoberman, *Panégyriques*, 52.

154 Carrier, *Labyrinthe*, 371–4.

155 Poumarède, *Pour*, 139–42, 149–50.

156 Haran, *Lys*, 300.
157 Carrier, *Labyrinthe*, 373.
158 Cange, *Histoire*, unpag.
159 Poumarède, *Pour*, 151–2, 162–5, 171; Bilici, *Louis XIV*, 63, 68, 90–4, 103, 175–6; Henri Auguste Omont, 'Projets de prise de Constantinople et de fondation d'un empire français d'orient sous Louis XIV', *Revue d'histoire diplomatique*, 7 (1893): 195–246; Édouard, sieur de La Croix, *Mémoires . . .*, 2 vols (Paris, 1684), I, *Epistre au Roy*; idem, *Etat Present des Nations et Eglises Grecque, Armenienne, et Maronite en Turquie* (Paris, 1695), *Au Roi*.
160 Nicholas Jolley (ed.), *The Cambridge Companion to Leibniz* (Cambride, 1995), 20–4.
161 Willhelm Gottfried Leibniz, *Œuvres*, ed. A. Foucher de Careil, 7 vols (Paris, 1859–75), V, 6–12, 25–9, 34–8, 41–6, 249–50, 262–5, 298.
162 Paul Sonnino, *Louis XIV's View of the Papacy, 1661-1667* (Berkeley and Los Angeles, 1966), 15–16, 24, 28.
163 Louis XIV, *Mémoires for the Instruction of the Dauphin*, ed. Paul Sonnino (London, 1970), 54, 183; Paul Sonnino, *Louis XIV and the origins of the Dutch War* (Cambridge, 1988), 12, 51–5, 78–82; Bilici, *Louis XIV*, 30–8.
164 Philip McCluskey, '"Les ennemis du nom Chrestien": Echoes of the crusade in Louis XIV's France', *French History*, 29 (2015): 56.
165 Idem, 'Commerce before crusade? France, the Ottoman Empire and the Barbary Pirates (1661-1669)', *French History*, 23 (2009): 1–21.
166 Leibniz, *Œuvres*, V, xli.
167 Ahmed Youssef, *La Fascination de l'Égypte: Du Rêve au Projet. Avec "Consilium Aegyptiacum", le texte inédit que Leibniz présenta à Louis XIV* (Paris, 1998), 39–40.
168 Leibniz, *Œuvres*, V, 359.
169 Philippe Roy, *Louis XIV et le Second siège de Vienne (1683)* (Paris, 1999); Burke, *Fabrication*, 144.
170 Charpentier, *Œuvres*: V, 1–9 (cah. 63, ff. 1r-5r); XXIV, 64–78 (cah. LXIII, ff. 34v-41v); Cessac, 'Chronologie', 23, 35–6.
171 *MG*, August 1692, 220.
172 Patricia Ranum, *Portraits around Marc-Antoine Charpentier* (Baltimore, 2004), 315; Patrick Bergin, 'M.-A. Charpentier's *In honorem Sancti Ludovici Regis Galliae Canticum* (H. 365): A Case Study in Chronology and Rhetoric' (MA diss., Ohio State University, 2012).
173 Herman Teule, 'Saint Louis and the East Syrians, the Dream of a Terrestrial Empire: East Syrian Attitudes to the West', in *East and West in the Crusader States; Context-Contacts-Confrontations*, eds Krijnie Ciggaar and Herman Teule (Leuven, 2003), 101–22.
174 Le Moyne, *Saint Louys*, 128.

Chapter 3

1 Daniel Weiner has labelled this process 'preconstruction': *Constructing*, 11.
2 Oded Rabinovitch, *The Perraults: A Family of Letters in Early Modern France* (Ithaca and London, 2018), 104–5, 117–19.
3 BnF, MS Fr. 3708, ff. 45v, 47r.

4 *Remonstrance salutaire aux rebelles de Montauban* . . . (Paris, 1621), 4; Pierre Bernard and Pierre Soulier, *L'Explication de l'édit de Nantes* . . . (Paris, 1683), 548–53.

5 *Les ceremonies faictes dans la Nouvelle Chappelle du Chasteau de Bissestre* . . . (Paris, 1634); *G*, 26 August 1634, 356; 30 September 1634, 420; 6 October 1634, 423–4.

6 Jean Loret, *La Muze Historique*, 1664, letter 39, 27 September (vol. XV, pp. 153–4); *MG*, October/November 1703, 355–7; *MdF*, August 1726, 1787–96; Jean Lebeuf, *Histoire de la ville et de tout le diocese de Paris*, 7 vols (Paris, 1883–93), I, 224–6.

7 *NM*, August 1717, unpag; *MdF*, September 1728, 2064.

8 Blond, *Maison professe*, 58; Barbara Gaehtgens, 'A toutes les gloires de l'État: Richelieu, les Jésuites et le maître-autel de Saint-Louis à Paris', in *Richelieu, patron des arts*, eds Jean-Claude Boyer, Barbara Gaehtgens and Bénédicte Gady (Paris, [2009]), 216–49; Ménorval, *Jésuites*, 54–8; *G*, 11 May 1641, 262–4; Le Moyne, *Poesies*, 552; Vernon, *Roy*, 770; Nelson, 'Religion'.

9 *Les couleurs du ciel: Peintures des églises de Paris au XVIIe siècle* (Paris, 2012), 130–1.

10 Tricoire, *Vierge*, 155–83, 218–26; idem, 'What was the Catholic Reformation? Marian Piety and the Universalization of Divine Love', *Catholic Historical Review*, 103 (2017): 20–49.

11 François de Sales, *Œuvres* . . . 10 vols (Annecy, 1892–1910), VII, 462; Rousselet, *Lys*, 392.

12 Bruno Maës, *Le Roi, La Vierge et La Nation: Pèlerinages et identité nationale entre guerre de Cent Ans et Révolution* (Paris, 2002), 306; Sabatier, 'Religious', 266.

13 Tricoire, *Vierge*, 199–203.

14 Matthieu, *Histoire*, 4; François de Sarcé, *La vie du bien-heureux sainct Louys roy de France* . . . (Paris, 1619), 1.

15 Dominique de Iesus Maria, *Les Poincts principaux* . . . (Paris, 1621), 7; Tricoire, *Vierge*, 174–7.

16 *Les royalles vertus qui ont illustré la vie et le trespas de S. Louys* . . . (Rouen, [s.d.]), 3–4, 15.

17 P. Le Comte, *Paraphrase sur le Gaude Mater ecclesia* . . . (Paris, 1628).

18 Bergin, *Politics*, 103; Eric Nelson, 'Royal Authority and the Pursuit of a Lasting Religious Settlement: Henri IV and the Emergence of the Bourbon Monarchy', in Forrestal and Nelson, *Politics*, 107–31.

19 Kettering, *Power*, 204–11; Reinhardt, *Voices*, 315–6.

20 Anthony Wright, *The Divisions of French Catholicism, 1629-1645: 'The Parting of the Ways'* (Farnham, 2011), 115–18.

21 *Mysteria politica* . . . (Naples, 1625), 12.

22 *MF*, XI (1625): 94–103; William Church, *Richelieu and Reason of State* (Princeton, NJ, 1972), 121–2.

23 *Collectio judiciorum de novis erroribus* . . . (Paris, 1728), 190-2.

24 Barbara Diefendorf, 'Henri IV', 158; Monod, *Power*, 110–1; Keohane, *Philosophy*, 176; Bergin, *Politics*, 97–8.

25 Damien Tricoire, 'La Fronde, un soulèvement areligieux au XVIIe siècle? De l'opposition «dévote» sous Richelieu aux Mazarinades de 1649', *Dix-septième siècle*, 257 (2012): 710–11; Maillet-Rao, 'Towards', 529–49.

26 Pierre de Bérulle, *Œuvres* . . . (Paris, 1644), 137, 433.

27 Ibid., 428; Wright, *Divisions*, 62, 116–21; Bergin, *Politics*, 176–7.

28 Nicolas Caussin, *La Cour Sainte* . . ., 3 vols (Paris, 1643), I, 11; II, 81–3; III, 180–1. Caussin also regarded Louis IX's holy sister Isabelle as a model of piety 'in the world': Nicolas Caussin, *La vie de Ste. Isabelle Soeur du roy Saint Louis* . . . (Paris, 1644);

Thomas Worcester, '"Neither Married nor Cloistered": Blessed Isabelle in Catholic Reformation France', *Sixteenth-Century Journal*, 30 (1999): 457–72.

29 Joseph Bergin, 'The Royal Confessor and his rivals in Seventeenth-Century France', *French History*, 21 (2007): 189; Reinhardt, *Voices*, 235–41.

30 Asch, *Sacral*, 79.

31 *La voix gemissante du peuple Chrestien et Catholique* . . . (Paris, 1640), 66, 97–8.

32 *G*, 30 August 1635, 490.

33 Jean-Jacques Bouchard, *Sermon Panegyrique sur Saint Louis* . . . (Rome, 1640), 4, 8–9, 12–13, 23–4.

34 Alexandre Haran, 'Louis le Juste à travers les oraisons funèbres. Roi-Sauveur et monarque providentiel', in *Pouvoirs, contestations et comportements dans l'Europe moderne. Mélanges en l'honneur du professeur Yves-Marie Bercé*, eds Bernard Barbiche, Jean-Pierre Poussou and Alain Tallon (Paris, 2005), 248.

35 Daniel Aznar, 'Louis (XIII) II de Catalogne: La construction d'un mythe royal (1641-1643)', in *La Paix des Pyrénées (1659) ou le triomphe de la raison politique*, eds Lucien Bély, Bertrand Haan and Stéphane Jettot (Paris, 2015), 279–81.

36 Bernard Guyard, *Oraison Funebre* . . . (Paris, 1643), 17.

37 Lavieille, 'II', 221–2.

38 Charles Teisseyre, 'Le prince chrétien aux XVᵉ et XVIᵉ siècle, à travers les représentations de Charlemagne et de Saint Louis', *Actes des congrès de la Société des historiens médiévalistes de l'enseignement supérieur public*, 8 (1977): 412; *La voye de laict, ou le chemin des heros au palais de la gloire...* (Avignon, 1623), 252–3; Geneviève Bresc-Bautier, 'Richelieu et l'effigie royale sculptée', in Boyer, *Richelieu*, 132.

39 Saint Louis Art Museum (Saint Louis, Missouri – Object number 719:1961).

40 Clotilde Feuilloy, Jannie Long and Catherine de Maupeou, 'Représentations de Saint Louis sous l'aspect des rois de France', *Les Monuments Historiques de la France*, 16 (1970): 49–51; Burke, *Fabrication*, 193.

41 Edmunds, *Piety*, 60.

42 *G*, 22 April 1643, 317; Olivier Lefèvre d'Ormesson, *Journal*, 2 vols (Paris, 1860–1), I, 31.

43 Charles de Combault Auteuil, *Blanche, infante de Castille* . . . (Paris, 1644).

44 Mézeray, *Histoire*, I, unpag., 560–5.

45 Weiner, *Constructing*, 188.

46 Jean-François-Paul de Gondi, cardinal de Retz, *Œuvres* . . ., 9 vols (Paris, 1870-87), I, 271–2; *Collection des Procès-verbaux des Assemblées-générales du Clergé de France*, 8 vols (Paris, 1767–78), III, 433–5.

47 Golden, *Godly*, 38.

48 Gondi, *Œuvres*, IX, 123–4.

49 Edelman, *Attitudes*, 237.

50 Retz, *Œuvres*, IX, 129–31.

51 *G*, 29 August 1648, 1160.

52 Orest Ranum, *The Fronde: A French Revolution* (New York, 1993), 152–60; Alanson Lloyd Moote, *The Revolt of the Judges: The Parlement of Paris and the Fronde, 1643-1652* (Princeton, 1970), 149–53.

53 Guy Joly, *Memoirs* . . ., trans. Edward Taylor, 3 vols (London, 1775), I, 20; III, 3; Retz, *Œuvres*, II, 11.

54 Retz, *Œuvres*, III, 242.

55 *La source glorieuse du sang de l'auguste maison de Bourbon* . . . (Paris, 1687), 1, 6–7; Joly, *Memoirs*, I, 208.

56 Retz, *Œuvres*, IX, 119–20.

57 Ibid., IV, 345; Michel Pernot, *La Fronde* (Paris, 1994), 317–8.

58 Claude Joly, *Recueil de maximes veritables et importantes pour l'institution du Roy . . .* (Paris, 1653), 197–8.

59 Reinhardt, *Voices*, 60–2.

60 *G*, 29 August 1643, 748; 26 August 1645, 792; 30 August 1653, 887.

61 *G*, 27 August 1649, 698.

62 *Relation curieuse et remarquable de la pompe royale du jour de la saint Louis . . .* (Paris, 1649), 11; Omer Talon, *Mémoires*, 6 vols (The Hague, 1732), VI, 161.

63 *G*, 27 August 1649, 701–4; *Suite des Triolets Royaux . . .* (Paris, 1649), 3.

64 Joly, *Memoirs*, I, 78; François-Annibal d'Estrées, *Mémoires . . .*, ed. Paul Bonnefon (Paris, 1910), 287.

65 Le Gall, *Mythe*, 103.

66 *Gazette*, 9 September 1651, 969–70.

67 Françoise Le Hénand, 'Les translations des reliques en France au XVIIᵉ siècle', in Boutry, Fabre and Julia, *Reliques modernes*, 335–6.

68 Lavieille, 'Il', 205–6.

69 Kettering, 'Pamphlet', 966.

70 Dale Van Kley, *The Religious Origins of the French Revolution: From Calvin to the Civil Constitution, 1560-1791* (New Haven, 1996), 46–7; Golden, *Godly*.

71 Tricoire, 'Fronde', 716–17.

72 Moshe Sluhovsky, 'La mobilisation des saints dans la Fronde parisienne d'après les mazarinades', *Annales. Histoire, Sciences Sociales*, 54 (1999): 355, 358.

73 *L'entrée triomphante de Leurs Maiestez Louis XIV . . .* (Paris, 1662), 19–21.

74 Cange, *Histoire*, unpag.

75 Rabinovitch, *Perraults*, 86.

76 Jean-Baptiste Colbert, *Lettres, instructions et mémoires . . .*, 9 vols (Paris, 1861–73), V, 487, 496. Mézeray, d'Hérouval and Varillas also received *gratifications*.

77 *Recueil des Harangues prononcées par Messieurs de l'Académie Françoise...* (Amsterdam, 1709), I, 502–8.

78 Le Prévost, *Panégyrique*, 21.

79 *MG*, September 1698, 8.

80 Montelet, *Panégyrique*, 33–4.

81 *MG*, October 1689, 194; September 1699, 194; September 1708, 13–14.

82 *MG*, September 1685, 220–1; September 1703, 273.

83 *MG*, August 1686, 297–8.

84 BnF Musique MS Rés Vm¹ 117, pp. 17–31; Claire Fontijn, *Desperate Measures: The Life and Music of Antonia Padoani Bembo* (New York, 2006), 96.

85 *MG*, October 1689, 91–3.

86 Zoberman, 'Généalogie', 80–7.

87 *MG*, September 1687, I, 237–40.

88 *MG*, September 1688, 23–4.

89 *MG*, September 1707, 60.

90 *MG*, October 1707, 30.

91 Edmunds, *Piety*, 216; *MG*, August 1709, 338.

92 Jarry, *Panegyrique*, 103.

93 *MG*, September 1693, 213–14.

94 Buisson, *Panegyrique*, 41; *MG*, June/July/August 1710, 281.

95 *MG*, September 1707, 7.

96 Jacques-Bénigne Bossuet, *Politics Drawn from the Very Words of Holy Scripture*, ed. Patrick Riley (Cambridge, 1990), liii–liv.

97 Jacques-Bénigne Bossuet, *Œuvres*, 4 vols (Paris, 1866-70), II, 160.

98 Schaich, *Monarchy*, 15.

99 François Bluche, *Louis XIV* (Oxford, 1990), 387.

100 Esprit Fléchier, *Œuvres complètes . . .*, 10 vols (Nîmes, 1782), V, 205.

101 Ibid., V, 207–16.

102 Cuche, 'Panégyrique', 98–9.

103 Fléchier, *Œuvres*, V, 222.

104 Bluche, *Louis XIV*, 387.

105 Cuche, 'Panégyrique', 102, 114.

106 BnF, MS Fr. 12,839, ff. 150v, 160v.

107 Bossuet, *Œuvres*, I, 1, 8.

108 François de Fénelon, *Œuvres*, ed. Jacques Le Brun, 2 vols (Paris, 1983), I, 547.

109 Ibid., II, 980–1, 1672n.

110 Louis XIV, *Mémoires; suivis de, Manière de visiter les jardins de Versailles*, ed. Joël Cornette (Paris, 2007).

111 Fleury, *L'Abrégé*, 44–5.

112 Louis de Rouvroy, duc de Saint-Simon, *Mémoires*, ed. A. de Boislisle, 45 vols (Paris: Hachette, 1879–1931), XX, 180.

113 Fénelon, *Œuvres*, I, 543; Nicole Ferrier-Caverivière, *L'image de Louis XIV dans la littérature française de 1660 à 1715* (Paris, 1981), 304.

114 P. J. W. van Malssen, *Louis XIV d'après les pamphlets répandus en Hollande* (Amsterdam, 1937), 41–2.

115 Ibid., 152; Ferrier-Caverivière, *L'image*, 331.

116 Gatien de Courtilz de Sandras, *L'Alcoran de Louis XIV . . .* (Rome, 1695), 28–40, 44, 49, 125, 152–5, 173–4.

117 BnF, MS Fr. 12,645, pp. 231–8; MS Fr. 12,796, ff. 7v-12r;

118 Reinhardt, *Voices*, 334–5.

119 Francis Assaf, *La Mort du roi: Une thanatographie de Louis XIV* (Tübingen, 1999), 165–6.

120 Massillon, *Œuvres*, VIII, 239.

121 Assaf, *Mort*, 113.

122 G, 6 September 1659, 879–80.

123 *MG,* September 1699, 220–3.

124 Zoberman, *Panégyriques*, 15.

125 F. N. Lefèvre d'Ormesson, *Panégyrique de saint Louis. Au Roy* (s.l., s.d.).

126 René Rapin, *Mémoires . . .*, 3 vols (Paris, 1865), III, 449.

127 G, 14 September 1663, 869–70.

128 G, 22 February 1659, 192.

129 G, 31 August 1658, 835–6; 30 August 1664, 864.

130 G, 18 July 1671, 691.

131 G, 2 September 1673, 843.

132 BnF (musique), Rés Vm⁶ 5, ff. 347r-348v.

133 Primi Visconti, *Mémoires sur la cour de Louis XIV* (Paris, 2015), 82.

134 BnF, MS Lat. 8828.

135 Alexandre Maral, *La Chapelle Royale de Versailles sous Louis XIV: cérémonial, liturgie et musique* (Sprimont, 2002), 38, 132, 153.

136 Christine Gouzi, 'Louis XIV en Saint Louis: une autre image de la figure royale?', in da Vinha, Maral and Milovanovic, *Louis XIV*, 58.

137 Lebeuf, *Histoire*, III, 200; Edmunds, *Piety*, 100, 132, 169–80, 204–9.

138 *Comtes des Bâtiments du Roi sous le règne de Louis XIV*, 4 vols (Paris, 1881), II, cols. 620, 653, 1130.

139 Lucien Pfleger, 'Le culte de saint Louis en Alsace', *Revue des sciences religieuses*, 1 (1921): 222–7.

140 Cédric Andriot, 'La paroisse Saint-Louis de Strasbourg administrée par les chanoines réguliers lorrains', *Revue d'Alsace*, 138 (2012): 61; M. Th. de Bussièrre, *Culte et pèlerinages de la Très-Sainte Vierge en Alsace* (Paris, 1862), 151; P. J. Fargès-Méricourt, *Description de la ville de Strasbourg . . .* (Strasbourg, 1825), 76–7.

141 The next church was built between 1732 and 1736, consecrated and dedicated to Saint Louis in 1777.

142 *G*, 23 May 1671, 508; *M*, February 1722, 25–6.

143 ASM, Collection de Montbret, MSS 513 (1684).

144 Gouzi, 'Louis XIV', 58; *Comtes des Bâtiments*, III, cols. 555, 557, 558.

145 Sabatier, 'Religious', 251.

146 *Comtes des Bâtiments*, IV, cols. 728, 846, 955, 1066.

147 Sabatier, 'Religious', 251n.

148 *Couleurs du ciel*, 312–5.

149 *Edit du Roy portant Creation et Institution d'un Ordre Militaire sous le Nom de S. Loüis . . .* (Paris, 1693); Greengrass, *Governing*, 64; *Exposition*, 14–21.

150 *Declaration du Roy en interpretation de l'Edit du mois de Mars 1693 concernant la desunion des biens de l'Ordre de Notre-Dame de Montcarmel & de Saint Lazare . . .* (Paris, 1693); Angelo Ranuzzi, *Correspondance . . .*, ed. Bruno Neveu, 2 vols (Rome, 1973), II, 114–15.

151 *MG*, April 1693, 92–4.

152 SHD, GR A1, 2251, n. 12, n. 15.

153 BnF, MS Fr. 8210, f. 33r.

154 *MG*, May 1693, 250.

155 *MG*, April 1693, 98–108; BnF, MS Fr. 8210, ff. 8r, 21r.

156 Alexandre Mazas, *Histoire de l'Ordre Militaire de Saint-Louis . . .* (Paris, 1855), 55–64, 75–6.

157 Ambrogio Caiani, *Louis XVI and the French Revolution, 1789-1792* (Cambridge, 2012), 171–2.

158 Mazas, *Histoire*, 139.

159 BnF, MS Fr. 8210, f. 190r.

160 Burke, *Fabrication*, 113.

161 Asch, *Sacral*, 152.

162 Byrne, *Death*, 172.

163 H.C. Barnard, *Madame de Maintenon and Saint-Cyr* (London, 1934).

164 Bruno Neveu, 'Du culte de Saint Louis à la glorification de Louis XIV: la maison royale de Saint-Cyr', *Journal des savants*, 3 (1988): , 284–6.

165 *MG*, September 1686 I, 37-8.

166 McManners, *Church*, I, 537–8.

167 AN, L 853 no. 28.

168 Jarry, *Panegyrique*, 4–7, 61.

169 BnF Richelieu (musique) Rés-1562, pp. 144–5; Rés-2271, pp. 172–6; *Chants et motets à l'usage de l'Eglise et Communauté des Dames de la Royale Maison de St. Loüis à St.*

Cyr (Paris, 1733), 168–72. Deborah Kauffman, 'Performance Traditions and Motet Composition at the Convent School at Saint-Cyr', *Early Music*, 29 (2001): 234–49.

170 Maral, 'Portrait', 710, 723; Weiner, *Constructing*, 33, 106.

171 Jean Chapelain, *Lettres . . .*, 2 vols (Paris, 1880–83), II, 509n.

172 *MG*, October 1708, 6–7.

173 Saint-Simon, *Mémoires*, XXVII, 258.

174 Bernard Hours, 'De la piété personnelle de Louis XIV', in Gérard Sabatier and Margarita Torrione (eds.) *¿Louis XIV espagnol?* (Versailles, 2009), 250.

175 Bossuet, *Politics*, 409–10, 257–8.

Chapter 4

1 Johnson, 'Sacred', 65.

2 Loret, *Muze historique*, 1653 – letter 31, 30 August (vol. IV, p. 99).

3 *Comptes des Bâtiments*, I, cols. 1084, 1231, 1342–3; II, cols. 102, 237, 538, 780, 1010, 1204; III, cols. 125, 305, 441; *MG*, September 1698, 11; September 1706, 6.

4 *MG*, August 1680, 189–90.

5 *Motet chanté le jour de S. Louis, dans l'église de l'Oratoire . . .* (Paris, 1707).

6 Chambre, *Panégyrique*; BnF, MS Fr. 20,064, ff. 247–72; *MG*, August 1692, 219; *NMG*, July 1714, 190–1; *Panégyrique de saint Louis, prononcé . . . par Monseigneur l'évêque d'Olimpe* (Paris, 1748); AN, L 674, no. 17, LL 520, p. 176; LL 824, ff. 215r, 394–414; *MdF*, September 1726, 2075–6; Theophile Létour, *Panegyrique de saint Louis . . .* (Paris, 1730); *NMG*, August 1717, 163; BnF, 4-LB18-195; 4-LB18-156.

7 *NE*, January 1743, 11–12; *MdF*, August 1739, 1878; *G*, 29 August 1739, 420.

8 Abbé de Rosné, 'Une cause de la décadence de la chaire au XVIIIᵉ siècle: Les prédicateurs du panégyrique de saint Louis devant l'Académie Française', *Revue du clergé français*, 62 (1897): 113.

9 *Statuts et reglemens pour la communauté des Barbiers . . .* (Paris, 1746), 15; *Dictionnaire portatif du commerce* (Paris, 1777), 431–3. Louis Mercier, *Tableau de Paris*, ed. Jean-Claude Bonnet, 2 vols (Paris, 1994), I, 95, 1343.

10 *Dictionnaire portatif*, 224–5, 247, 258, 276, 295–7, 377, 469–71; Beaune, *Naissance*, 155–6.

11 Nicholas de La Mare, *Traité de la Police . . .*, 4 vols (Paris, 1705–38), II, 127–36.

12 *Permission de monseigneur l'archevêque de Paris . . .* (Paris, 1677); Clare Haru Crowston, *Fabricating Women: The Seamstresses of Old Regime France, 1675-1791* (Durham and London, 2001), 275–7.

13 *L'Office de S. Louis . . .* (Paris, 1688); *L'Office de saint Louis . . .* (Paris, 1711); *L'Office de Saint Louis . . .* (Paris, 1733); *L'Office de Saint Louis . . .* (Paris, 1749); Louis Le Blanc, *La sainte vie, et les hauts faits de Monseigneur saint Louis . . .* (Paris, 1666).

14 *Office* (1688), unpag.

15 Edmunds, *Piety*, 211.

16 Monod, *Power*, 248–50.

17 Loret, *Muze Historique*, 1655 – letter 34, 28 August (vol. VI, p. 131).

18 *MG*, September 1679, 55–7.

19 Patricia Ranum, *Vers une chronologie des œuvres de Marc-Antoine Charpentier* (Baltimore, 1994), 40; idem, *Portraits*, 270–1, 466–71, 555. Ranum argues the motet was H323, but Cessac shows that this and H332 are on paper from the early 1680s. It could have been H320: Cessac, 'Chronologie'.

20 *Journal de santé de Louis XIV*, ed. Stanis Perez (Grenoble, 2004), 115–38, 427.

21 *G*, 1 September 1668, 913–14; 1 September 1685, 523; 28 August 1688, 432; 29 August 1716, 419; *MG*, September 1685, 210–19; September 1708, 140–2; AN, K 1009, nos. 59, 175, 210; K 1010, nos. 57–8; K 1011, no. 18; K 1012, nos. 35, 115, 185 bis, 212, 253; K 1013, nos. 32, 132, 195; K 1014, nos. 58, 61, 89, 125, 139, 192, 211–12; K 1015, nos. 68, 100, 134–5, 180; K 1016, nos. 29, 128, 174, 324–5, 395; K 1017, nos. 23, 45, 121, 147, 173; K 1018, no. 19, 76, 141, 156.

22 AN K 1010, no. 87.

23 Joseph Dulaurent, *Discours . . .* (Paris, 1732); Cyrille Gouneaud, *Discours . . .* (Paris?, 1735?).

24 Noah Shusterman, *Religion and the Politics of Time: Holidays in France from Louis XIV through Napoleon* (Washington, DC, 2010), 23–4.

25 Rousselet, *Lys*, 685–6; Choisy, *Vie*, 68–9.

26 *MG*, August 1715, 192; *MdF*, August 1734, 1874–5; *G*, 28 August 1769, 282.

27 *G*, 29 August 1716, 419; 28 August 1717, 419–20; 27 August 1718, 408; 26 August 1719, 419; 31 August 1720, 420; 30 August 1721, 434; *Description du concert et du feu d'artifice de la veille de S. Louis . . .* (Paris, 1719).

28 *NM*, August 1719, 168.

29 *MdF*, August 1742, 1887.

30 *Anecdotes curieuses et plaisantes, relatives à la Révolution de France* (Paris, 1791), 199–200.

31 *M*, August 1721, 200–7; *Explication du feu d'artifice, qui sera tiré dans le Jardin des Tuilleries . . .* (Paris, 1721).

32 *MdF*, September 1741, 2111–12; *Brevet exclusif qui permet aux sieurs Guérin, Testard, & autres Artificiers . . .* (Paris, 1741); AN, K 1006, no. 63; *Description Historique de l'Edifice que les sieurs Guérin . . .* (Paris, 1741).

33 *G*, 29 August 1682, 513–14. Louis-François du Bouschet, marquis de Sourches, *Mémoires . . .*, 13 vols (Paris, 1882–93), I, 138.

34 *G*, 10 September 1682, 556–61; *Les Rejouissances du College de Clermont . . .* (Paris, 1682).

35 *G*, 30 August 1704, 419–20; AN, K 1016, nos. 377–80, 392, 412.

36 Byrne, *Death*, 99; Swann, *Exile*, 317–19; BnF MS Fr. 13,735, ff. 90–1.

37 Schama, *Citizens*, 238–9.

38 *MG*, September 1699, 224; *MdF*, August 1725, 1831; August 1735, 1850–1; August 1737, 1842; September 1739, II, 2246; August 1742, 1843; September 1768, 192; *G*, 28 August 1769, 282; McManners, *Church*, I, 527.

39 Paul V, *Bref*, 6; *Collection des Procès-verbaux*, II, 341; BMaz MS 2516.

40 *Les royalles vertus . . .*, 5.

41 *MF*, V (1618), 276; Weiner, *Constructing*, 177n.

42 Folz, *Saints*, 201; Ravitch, *Catholic*, 3.

43 Mathieu Marais, *Journal de Paris*, 2 vols (Saint-Étienne, 2004), II, 552.

44 *Arrest de la Cour de Parlement . . .* (Paris, 1666), 10; ACDF, G 4-C, f. 1; *Mandement de Monseigneur l'archevêque de Paris . . .* (Paris, 1778), 13.

45 BnF MS Fr. 11,681, p. 38.

46 Shusterman, *Religion*, 255–63.

47 *Rituale Carnotense . . .* (Paris, 1640), unpag. (*festa*); Abbé Lalore, *Les Fêtes chômées dans le diocèse de Troyes . . .* (Troyes, 1869), 27; *Ordonnances et decrets synodaulx du dioceze de Maillezais . . .* (Fontenay le Comte, 1623), 19v; *Statuts synodaux du diocese*

de Rieux . . . (Toulouse, 1624), 87; *Statuts et Reglemens du diocese de Cahors* . . . (Paris, 1640), 37.

48 *Statuts et Ordonnances faittes en diverses assemblées* . . . (Langres, 1629), 22 (BSG, Z 284/Inv. 5487).

49 *Ordonnances Synodales d'Illustrissime et Reverendissime Père en Dieu Messire Iean de Lingendes* . . .. (Mâcon, s.d. [1659?]), 85.

50 *G*, 3 September 1633, 364.

51 Aznar, 'Louis (XIII)', 280.

52 *Statuts synodaux, pour la diocese de Sainct Malo* . . . (Saint Malo, 1620), 40; *Canons synodaux statuez* . . . (Clermont, 1620), 131; *Ordonnances et Constitutions synodales* . . . (Bordeaux, 1621), 50; *Statuts et Reglements du Diocese de Limoges...* (Limoges, 1629), 251; *Manuale Bellovacense* (s.l., s.d. [1637?]), *festa*; *Sacerdotale seu Manuale Ecclesiae Rothomagensis* . . . (Rouen, 1640), *festa*; *Rituale Aurelianese...* (Orléans, 1642), catalogus festorum; *Ordonnances de Monseigneur l'evesque de Perigueux...* (Périgueux, 1649), 101.

53 *Ordonnances et constitutions synodales* . . . (Bordeaux, 1686), 64.

54 *Ordonnances synodales* . . . (Mâcon, 1668), 3; *Statuts du diocese d'Angers* (Angers, 1680), 228; *Ordonnances Synodales* . . . (Vannes, 1695), 102; *Recueil des Ordonnances synodales du diocèse du Chalon* . . . (Lyon, 1700), 231.

55 *Recueil des Ordonnances Synodales* . . . (Nîmes, s.d. [1670?]), unpag.; *Les Ordonnances synodales* . . . (Aix, 1672), 45; *Statuts et Reglemens* . . . (Tulle, 1692), 69; *Ordonnances Synodalles* . . . (Toulon, 1704), 101.

56 *Statuta seu decreta synodalia Bisuntinæ Diocesis* . . . (Besançon, 1680), 157.

57 Shusterman, *Religion*, 42–3; *Les Festes qui se doivent chommer dans le Diocese de Saintes* . . . (Saintes, 1667); *Ordonnance de Monseigneur l'evesque de Luçon* . . . (La Rochelle, 1668).

58 *Ordonnance de Monseigneur l'Evesque* . . . (Angers, 1693).

59 *Statuts synodaux de nos seigneurs François Rouxel de Medavy, Philippes Cospean et Leonor de Matignon, Evesques et comtes de Lisieux* . . . (Caen, [1651]), 45; *Ordonnances synodales pour le diocese d'Uzès* . . . (Montpellier, 1654), 138; *Ordonnances publiées au synode* . . . (Narbonne, 1667), 41; *Recueil des ordonnances synodales* . . . (Toulouse, 1669), 945; *Statuts synodaux du diocese d'Alet* . . . (Toulouse, 1670); *Ordonnances et instructions synodales par Antoine Godeau, evesque de Grasse, & de Vence*, 5th edn (Brussels, 1672), 239; *Ordonnances synodalles* . . . (Rodez, 1674), 90; *Rituel de la province de Reims* . . . (Paris, 1677), *festes*; *Ordonnances et Constitutions Synodales pour le Diocese de Digne* . . . (Aix, 1680), 158; *Ordonnances synodales du diocèse de Grenoble* . . . (Paris, 1690), 210; *Rituel du diocèse de Sens* . . . (Sens, 1694), *festes*; *Statuts synodaux* . . . (Albi, 1695), 93; *Ordonnances* . . . (Lisieux, 1696), 57; *Ordonnances synodales* . . . 2nd edn (Toulouse, 1696), 163; *Ordonnances synodales pour le diocèse de Pamiers* . . . (Toulouse, 1702), 223; *Ordonnances synodales* . . . (Autun, 1706), 40; *Ordonnances et Réglemens synodaux du diocèse de La Rochelle* . . . (Paris, 1780), 300; *Statuts synodaux du diocese de Sisteron* . . . (Aix, 1711), 162; *Recueil des anciennes et nouvelles ordonnances du diocèse d'Oleron* . . . (Pau, 1712), 123; *Ordonnances synodales* . . . (Toulouse, 1713), 284; *Statuts sinodaux* . . . (Autun, 1715), 40.

60 *Rituel Romain du Pape Paul V à l'usage du diocèse d'Alet*, 3rd edn (Paris, 1677), unpag.

61 *Mandement de Monseigneur l'evêque comte de Noyon* . . . (s.l., 1705), 5–6.

62 *Rituel du diocèse de Blois* . . . (Blois, 1730), *festes*; *Statuts synodaux, publiés dans le Synode de 1702* . . . (Vienne, 1730), 217; *Ordonnances synodales* . . . (Dijon, 1744), 56.

63 *Rituel Romain à l'usage de la Province ecclesiastique d'Auch.* (Paris, 1701), *calendrier des festes*; *Ordonnances synodales du diocèse de Soissons* (Soissons, 1701), 127; *Statuts synodaux* . . . (Troyes, 1706), 115; *Ordonnances synodales du diocese de Lavaur* . . . (Toulouse, 1729), 167; *Rituel du diocèse de Bourges* . . . (Bourges, 1746), xviii.

64 *Statuta diocesis Carnotensis* (Chartres, 1742), 138, 141; *Ordonnance de Monseigneur l'évêque de Metz* . . . (Metz, 1744), 6.

65 Shusterman, *Religion*, 251; *Mandement de Monsieur l'évêque* . . . (Poitiers, 1766), 7.

66 *Statuts synodaux* . . . (Boulogne, [1746]), 65; *Mandement de Monseigneur l'évêque de Boulogne* . . . (Boulogne, 1778), 6.

67 *Rituel du diocèse de Luçon* . . . (Luçon, 1768), unpag.

68 Suire, *Sainteté et Lumières*, 27–8.

69 *Statuts et reglemens synodaux* . . . (Quimper, 1717), 43–4; *Statuts du diocese de Saint Brieuc* . . . (Rennes, 1723), 43; *Ordonnances Synodales* . . . (Valence, 1728), 387; *Manuel pour les ecclésiastiques du diocese de Belley* . . . (Saint-Claude, 1759), 222; *Statuts synodaux du diocese de Comenges* . . . (Toulouse, 1752), 88; *Ordonnances Synodales du diocèse de Fréjus* . . . (Paris, 1779), 130; *Rituel* . . . (Amiens, 1784), unpag.

70 *Ordonnances synodales* . . . (St-Malo, 1769), 32; *Mandement de Monseigneur l'Archevêque de Rouen* . . . (Rouen, 1767), 9–10; *Lettres-patentes du roi, sur un Mandement de M. l'Archevêque de Trêves* . . . (Nancy, 1773), 6; *Mandement de Monseigneur l'évêque d'Évreux* . . . (Évreux, 1775), 7–8.

71 *Rituale Aurelianese* . . . (Orléans, 1726), *catalogus festorum*; *Rituel du diocèse de Meaux* . . . (Paris, 1734), *festes*; *Rituel* . . . (Lyon, 1788), lxxxv.

72 *Mandement de Monseigneur l'archevêque de Tours* . . . (Tours, 1781); *Mandement de Nosseigneurs les archevêque et évêques de la province ecclésiastique de Tours* . . . (Vannes, 1781), 9, 14; *Lettres patentes portant confirmation d'un Mandement de M. l'Evêque du Mans* . . . (Paris, 1782).

73 *Lettres-patentes du roi, qui confirment des Mandemens par lesquels les Evêques de Toul, de Saint-Dié & de Nancy, ont réduit le nombre des Fêtes* . . . (Nancy, 1781), 8, 13, 17–18.

74 Restif, *Révolution*, 302.

75 *Collection des Procès-verbaux*, IV, 776, 1044.

76 Roland Gauthier, *Louis XIV et saint Joseph* (Montréal, 1999).

77 Colbert, *Lettres*, VI, 433–5.

78 Shusterman, *Religion*, 1–2, 41; BnF, MS Fr. 20,728, ff. 21r–24v.

79 Nicolas Travers, *Histoire civile, politique et religieuse de la ville et du comté de Nantes* . . ., 3 vols (Nantes, 1836–41), III, 448–50, 485.

80 Decobert, *Henry*, 93–5.

81 Jean-Yves Grenier, 'Temps de travail et fêtes religieuses au XVIIIᵉ siècle', *Revue historique*, 663 (2012): 609–41.

82 *Bulle de Nostre S. Pere le pape Urbain VIII* . . . (Paris, 1646), 5.

83 *Statuts synodaux, pour la diocese de Sainct Malo*, 37; *Mandement de Monseigneur l'archevêque de Tours*; *Lettres-patentes du roi, qui confirment des Mandemens par lesquels les Evêques de Toul* . . ., 8, 13, 17–18.

84 Bartlett, *Why*, 129, 227; Spicer, '(Re)building', 264–8.

85 *Saint Marc ne peut souffrir ces abus inouis/Il veut être festé comme on fait Saint Louis.* BnF, MS Fr. 12,618, pp. 47–8; Shusterman, *Religion*, 45–7.

86 ACDF, G 4-C, ff. 365, 375, 377, 444.

87 *Ordonnance de Monsieur le Prevost de Paris* . . . (Paris, 1667); *Ordonnance de police* . . . (Paris, 1731).

88 Shusterman, *Religion*, 225; Venard and Bonzon, *Religion*, p. 66.

89 *L'Ecclésiastique citoyen* . . . (Paris, 1787), 380.

90 *MG*, October 1681, 16–17; September 1688, 237–8; *MdF*, September 1740, 2052; October 1741, 2267–8; October 1742, 2262; April 1760, I, 130, November 1772, 152; January 1774, II, 155; April 1776, II, 154.

91 *MdF*, September 1724, 1923–4; September 1726, 2042; December 1728, I, 2687; November 1729, 2670; October 1748, 70.

92 Representative examples: September 1742, 2052; September 1747, 149; November 1753, 73, 79, 139; October 1758, II, 160; October 1760, II, 143; May 1764, 152–3; October 1764, II, 137; January 1767, I, 158; October 1767, II, 133; November 1767, 121; October 1772, I, 144; October 1773, II, 164; March 1776, 161, 169; January 1778, II, 161; March 1778, 159; 5 October 1778, 55.

93 *MdF*, January 1778, II, 121–3; April 1778, II, 153; M. Journu, *Éloge de Saint Louis* . . . (Bordeaux, 1743).

94 John Hajdu Heyer, *The Lure and Legacy of Music at Versailles: Louis XIV and the Aix School* (Cambridge, 2014), 113; *MdF*, September 1724, 1923–4; ASM, MS Bachelet 048-2.

95 Daniel Roche, *Le siècle des lumières en province: académies et académiciens provinciaux, 1680-1789*, 2 vols (Paris, 1978).

96 *MG*, September 1687, 226–7.

97 *G*, 6 September 1687, 484.

98 *G*, 9 September 1758, 437.

99 BmG, Bb. 5404.

100 *MG*, October 1689, 81–96.

101 *G*, 3 September 1661, 934; 20 September 1776, 342; *MG*, October 1689, 77–80.

102 *MG*, September 1711, IV, 20–3.

103 *Relation d'une Fête donnée à Bar-le-Duc* . . . (Bar-le-Duc, 1757).

104 *G*, 9 September 1778, 329; 21 September 1778, 347–8.

105 *G*, 12 January 1779, 16.

106 *G*, 8 September 1657, 921–2.

107 *G*, 2 September 1673, 843; 9 September 1673, 875.

108 *G*, 29 August 1648, 1159.

109 *G*, 7 September 1658, 865.

110 *G*, 1 September 1668, 911–12.

111 *M*, September 1721, 189–90, 209–10; October 1721, 165–70; January 1722, 31–2.

112 *G*, 29 August 1665, 831.

113 *G*, 9 September 1785, 306.

114 *Bouquet de la St. Louis* . . . (Bordeaux, 1785); *Le Triple Mariage, Comedie en un Acte et en Vers libres, Analogue à la Fête du Roi* . . . (Bouillon, 1774).

115 *Relation de ce qui s'est passé le 25 août 1776 & le Dimanche suivant, à la Fête des Mœurs établie à Saint Ferjeux* . . . (Besançon, [1776]).

116 Bluche, *Louis XIV*, 386; Maral, *Chapelle*, 153n; Delmas, *Saint*, 178.

117 Pierre Delattre, et al., *Les établissements des Jésuites en France…*, 5 vols (Enghien, 1949–57), I, 473–4, 698–9; Antonin Soucaille, *État monastique de Béziers avant 1789: Notices sur les anciens couvents d'hommes & de femmes d'après des documents originaux* (Béziers, 1889), 72.

118 Delattre, *Établissements*, IV, 523–4; François Lemoine and Jacques Tanguy, *Rouen aux 100 clochers: Dictionnaire des églises et chapelles de Rouen (avant 1789)* (Rouen, 2004), 136.

119 Delattre, *Établissements*, I, 258–9; *MF*, XII (1626): 148–50.

120 Lavieille, 'Jésuites', par. 1n.

121 Annie Cosperec, *Blois, la forme d'une ville* (Paris, 1994), 238–42; Yves Denis, *Histoire de Blois et de sa région* (Toulouse, 1988), 15.

122 *G*, 26 September 1643, 830.

123 Delattre, *Établissements*, II, 1449, 1489; Joseph Dehergne, 'Note sur les Jésuites et l'enseignement supérieur dans la France d'Ancien Régime', *Revue d'histoire de l'Église de France*, 158 (1971): 74.

124 Delattre, *Établissements*, III, 253–5.

125 Louis Viansson-Ponté, *Les Jésuites à Metz* (Strasbourg, 1897), 46; Eugène Volz, 'L'église Notre-Dame de Metz', *Mémoires de l'Académie de Metz* (1967–1969): 181.

126 Abbé Prégnon, *Histoire du pays et de la ville de Sedan depuis les temps les plus reculés jusqu'à nos jours*, 3 vols (Charleville, 1856), III, 16–35, 109–10; *G*, 6 September 1664, 886–7; Bernard and Soulier, *L'Explication*, 500–2.

127 Lavieille, 'Jésuites', par. 1n, 4; Delmas, *Saint*, 172.

128 Delattre, *Établissements*, IV, 1334–6.

129 BIC, Collection Peiresc MS. 1816, f. 484r-v; Delattre, *Établissements*, I, 53–6; Lavieille, 'II', 201–2.

130 *G*, 1 September 1657, 885; Prégnon, *Histoire*, III, 104–5.

131 *G*, 5 September 1665, 875.

132 AN: S4613, liasse 1; Lebeuf, *Histoire*, IV, 597–8.

133 Cédric Andriot, 'Le college Saint-Louis de Metz: un prestigieux établissement scolaire d'Ancien Régime', *Le pays Lorrain*, 97 (2016): 55–62; *MdF*, September 1760, 181–2.

134 Louis Clément de Ris, *Histoire et description de l'église de Saint-Louis d'Antin* (Paris, 1883); McManners, *Church*, II, 60; Louis Petit de Bachaumont (attr.), *Mémoires secrets, pour servir à l'histoire de la République des Lettres en France, depuis 1762 jusqu'à nos jours* . . ., 21 vols (London, 1777–83), XXI, 201–2; *District des capucins de Saint-Louis de la Chaussée d'Antin* . . . (Paris, 1790).

135 Morel, 'Culte', 138; Jean-Joseph-Antoine Pilot de Thorey, *Histoire municipale de Grenoble* (Grenoble, 1851), 41.

136 Camille Gabet, *La naissance de Rochefort sous Louis XIV, 1666-1715* (Rochefort, 1985), 27; Théodore de Blois, *Histoire de Rochefort* (Paris, 1733), 74.

137 *Relation du port de Saint Loüis au Cap de Sète en Languedoc* . . . (Pézenas, 1666); Jean Sagnes, *Histoire de Sète* (Toulouse, 1987), 49–81.

138 Morel, 'Culte', 141.

139 Michel Vergé-Franceschi, *Toulon: Port royal, 1481-1789* (Paris, 2002), 128, 155; *G*, 18 July 1777, 275; 25 July 1777, 285.

140 Vergé-Franceschi, *Toulon*, 120, 177, 226; Jean-Marie-Yves Calvé, *Les ports militaires de la France: Toulon* (Paris, 186?), 20–1.

141 Prosper Levot, *Histoire de la ville et du port de Brest*, 3 vols (Brest and Paris, 1864–6), I, 251–318, 345–6; Delattre, *Établissements*, I, 903–4; 'Affaire des Jésuites de Brest, au sujet de l'Eglise Paroissiale de Saint Louis de la même Ville', a polemical work fiercely opposed to the Jesuits: *Procès pour la succession d'Ambroise Guys* . . . (Brest, s.d.), 128–65.

142 Lebeuf, *Histoire*, II, 559.

143 Delmas, *Saint*, 186.

144 Jules Gallerand, 'L'érection de l'évêché de Blois (1697)', *Revue d'histoire de l'Église de France*, 42 (1956): 175–228; Eric Nelson, *The Legacy of Iconoclasm: Religious War and the Relic Landscape of Tours, Blois and Vendôme, 1550-1750* (St Andrews, 2013), 27; *G*, 13 July 1784, 232.

145 Wright, *Divisions*, 94; Morel, 'Culte', 139; McManners, *Church*, I, 201, 294; Lemoine and Tanguy, *Rouen*, 138; Lebeuf, *Histoire*, I, 283.

146 Lemoine and Tanguy, *Rouen*, 161.

147 Yannick Marec, *Les hôpitaux de Rouen du Moyen Âge à nos jours: Dix siècles de protection sociale* (Rouen, 2005), 19–20, 130–9.

148 Abbé E. Bavard, *Histoire de l'Hôtel-Dieu de Beaune* (Beaune, 1881), 212–13.

149 *L'Hospital general de Paris* (Paris, 1676), 17; *Declaration du roy portant reglement pour l'hospital general de Toulouse* (Toulouse, 1687), 3; Daniel Hickey, *Local Hospitals in Ancien Régime France: Rationalization, Resistance, Renewal 1530-1789* (Montreal and Kingston, 1997); Olivier Chaline, *Le règne de Louis XIV* (Paris, 2005), 545–51.

150 Philip Riley, *A Lust for Virtue: Louis XIV's Attack on Sin in Seventeenth-Century France* (Westport, CT, 2001), 41–4; Georges Guillain and Pierre Mathieu, *La Salpêtrière* (Paris, 1925), 23–7.

151 Alain Michaud, *Histoire de Saintes* (Toulouse, 1989), 154; *Recueil de la commission des arts et monuments historiques de la Charente-Inférieure . . .*, vol. XVIII (La Rochelle, 1908), 412–15; *Lettres patentes du roy, portant établissement d'un Hôpital . . .* (Bordeaux, [1714]); *Statuts de l'hôpital saint Loüis . . .* (Bordeaux, 1721).

152 McManners, *Church*, I, 568.

153 Gerard Ingold, *Saint Louis de 1586 à nos jours: de l'art du verre à l'art du cristal* (Paris, 1986), 23–5.

154 Claude d'Abbeville, *Histoire de la mission des pères capucins en l'isle de Maragnan et terres circonvoysines . . .* (Paris, 1614), ff. 65v-66r.

155 James Searing, *West African Slavery and Atlantic Commerce: The Senegal River Valley, 1700-1860* (Cambridge, 1993).

156 *G*, 24 September 1666, 979–80.

157 *Rituel du diocèse de Quebec . . .* (Paris, 1703), unpag.; Morel, 'Culte', 138–9.

158 Auguste Chouteau, 'Narrative of the Settlement of St. Louis', in *Seeking St. Louis; Voices from a River City, 1670-2000*, ed. Lee Ann Sandweiss (Saint Louis, 2000), 13–19; Carl Ekberg and Sharon Person, *St. Louis Rising: The French Regime of Louis St. Ange de Bellerive* (Urbana, Chicago and Springfield, 2015), 107–8.

159 *ADPAA*, 28 August 1765, 4 December 1765.

160 *M*, April 1722, 177; *MdF*, November 1754, 197; *G*, 5 March 1757, 119.

161 *NM*, September 1717, 128–32; February 1718, 112–15; *MdF*, March 1751, 155.

162 Morel, 'Culte', 136; *MG*, April 1712, 17–18; *Les voyages de la nouvelle France occidentale . . .* (Paris, 1632), 6–10, 40, 82, 187, 306; *Relations des Jésuites . . .*, 3 vols. (Quebec, 1858), I, 2, 34, 42; III, 7; Alan Greer, *The Jesuit Relations: Natives and Missionaries in Seventeenth-Century North America* (Boston and New York, 2000), 146–54.

163 *Relations*, I, 14; II, 11; III, 10, 50; Greer, *Jesuit*, 112; Alan Greer, 'Colonial Saints: Gender, Race, and Hagiography in New France', *The William and Mary Quarterly*, 3rd series, 57 (2000): 333.

164 Heath, 'Ultramontane', 65–8; J.-M. Vidal, *Les Oratoriens à Saint-Louis des Français* (Paris, 1928); Catherine de Médicis, *Lettres . . .*, 9 vols (Paris, 1905), IX, 493–4.

165 Florian Bassani Grampp, 'On a Roman Polychoral Performance in August 1665', *Early Music*, 36 (2008): 415.

166 AAE, 109CP/119, f. 266r.

167 *G*, 27 September 1698, 468; 20 September 1732, 452; 19 September 1739, 465.

168 *G*, 26 September 1648, 1322.

169 *MG*, September 1703, 266–73.

170 *G*, 26 September 1665, 943; Grampp, 'On', 415–29; Retz, *Œuvres*, VII, 52–3, 479.

171 Representative examples: *G*, 17 September 1661, 1008; 17 September 1664, 956;
25 September 1688, 478; 18 September 1700, 474; 27 September 1732, 466;
24 September 1740, 469; 27 September 1749, 489; 22 September 1753, 451;
14 September 1767, 320; 22 September 1775, 340; 23 September 1785, 313.

172 *G*, 19 September 1705, 460–1; 27 September 1727, 466; 14 September 1729,
469; 29 September 1731, 463; 24 September 1735, 461; 19 September 1739, 468;
18 September 1769, 305; 21 September 1779, 367; *MdF*, September 1725, II, 2302;
September 1739, I, 2036.

173 Representative examples: (Frankfurt) *MdF*, September 1741, 2081–2; (The Hague) *G*,
7 September 1720, 431; 6 September 1727, 430; 8 September 1736, 430; 10 September
1757, 441; (Copenhagen) *G*, 20 September 1727, 447; 18 September 1772, 345;
(Warsaw) *G*, 27 September 1732, 458; (Bonn) *G*, 12 September 1761, 449; *MdF*,
October 1761 I, 200; (Lisbon) *G*, 24 October 1648, 1437; 2 October 1700, 494;
4 October 1721, 489; 2 October 1728, 474; 21 September 1764, 305; 30 September
1776, 355.

174 *G*, 4 October 1698, 473.

175 *G*, 20 September 1749, 472–3.

176 *G*, 22 September 1777, 380.

177 *Ordonnance . . . concernant les droits à percevoir par la Nation françoise à Lisbonne,
relativement à l'administration de l'église et confrairie nationale de Saint-Louis* (Paris,
1782).

178 *MdF*, September 1726, 2143.

179 *G*, 18 October 1642, 970; 29 August 1643, 789; 13 October 1646, 895.

180 *G*, 3 October 1750, 470; 4 October 1771, 322.

181 *G*, 26 September 1665, 942; 25 September 1666, 990; 6 September 1698, 426;
18 September 1728, 449.

182 *NM*, August 1717, 117; September 1718, 153–4.

183 *G*, 20 September 1679, 478; 5 October 1680, 527; 18 September 1683, 536;
15 September 1685, 555; *G*, 29 September 1685, 587–8.

184 Representative examples: *G*, 22 September 1703, 459; 13 September 1704, 436;
24 September 1712, 485; 18 September 1717, 449; 14 September 1720, 438;
18 September 1723, 450; 14 September 1729, 464–5; 14 September 1737, 438;
15 September 1742, 422; 16 September 1747, 444; 19 September 1750, 452;
16 September 1763, 329; 21 September 1772, 351.

185 *G*, 1 October 1701, 463–4.

186 *MdF*, February 1724, 239–40.

187 *MG*, October and November 1703, 9–13.

188 *MG*, November 1711, 90–6.

Chapter 5

1 *Breviarium Parisiense . . .* (Paris, 1640), 1048–52; BnF, MS Fr. 13,171, pp. 48–9, 62–5,
106–7, 116–17, 146–9; MS Lat. 9476, p. 130; MS Lat. 9477, p. 158; *Office* (1688),
16–17, 34, 49; *Office de saint Louis roi de France . . .* (Paris, 1697), 10, 71, 89–91, 109;
Office (1711), 13–14, 89, 113–16; *L'Office de l'église à l'usage du diocèse de Rouen . . .*,
2 vols (Rouen, 1719), II, 496; BMaz, MS 463, pp. 224–5; *Breviarium Parisiense . . .*

(Paris, 1736), 519, 524; *L'Office de saint Louis, roi de France* . . . (Paris, 1742), 4–5, 104; *Office* (1749), 62, 105–6; *Offices divins, à l'usage des dames et demoiselles de la maison de Saint Louis à Saint Cyr* (Paris, 1754), 174; *L'Office de Saint Louis, Roy de France, à l'usage de la Chapelle du Roy à Versailles* . . . (Paris, 1760), 12, 71, 91, 107, 116; *L'Office de saint Louis, roi de France, le vingt-cinq Août; A l'usage de la maison de la Salpétrière de l'Hôpital-Général.* (Paris, 1767), 5.

2 Rousselet, *Lys*, 1391.

3 AN LL 1223/A, pp. 103–4; LL 1229/C, f. 33r; LL 1223/B, pp. 267–8; Lebeuf, *Histoire*, I, 500. Joseph Clemens was then resident in Lille, where he consecrated two churches to Saint Louis in August 1707 (Saint-Louis de la Citadelle and Saint-Louis du Fort Saint-Sauveur); the gift of the relic was probably related to these ceremonies. Edmond Leclair, *Joseph Clément, Électeur de Cologne: Son séjour à Lille de 1704 à 1708* (Dunkirk, 1933), 27.

4 Millet, *Tresor*, 76–7; Félibien, *Histoire*, 259–60, 306–7, 335, 393–4, 540–5 (engravings of the reliquaries); Brown, 'Chapels', 279–331; AN L 863 no. 2, f. 6v; LL 1327, ff. 9r-13v, 72v-75r, 239r-242r; *Inventaire du trésor de S. Denis*, 9–15.

5 AN, LL 638, ff. 10v-11r, 17v, 24r, 75r.

6 Gaehtgens, 'A toutes', 238; *Office* (1760), 141.

7 AN, L 620, nos. 27, 35; LL 638, ff. 63v-71v; Cange, *Histoire* (frontispiece engraving of the reliquary).

8 Diefendorf, 'Henri IV', 159–60; Leniaud and Perrot, *Sainte-Chapelle*, 78; Nelson, 'Religion', 171.

9 AN, LL 602, ff. 12r-14r.

10 *Gazette*, 6 Dec. 1664, 1205; Le Gall, *Mythe*, 425; BnF, MS Fr. 11,681, pp. 48–9.

11 AN, LL 602, f. 15r; LL 604, f. 253v; LL 605, ff. 13r, 89v; LL 612, f. 171v; LL 617, ff. 15v, 59v, 70r, 105v.

12 AN, LL 607, pp. 114–15; 341; Pierre-Jacques Brillon, *Dictionnaire des arrêts* . . ., 6 vols (Paris, 1727), II, 341.

13 AN, LL 604, f. 230v.

14 AN, LL 605, ff. 43r, 64v-66r.

15 AN, LL 607, p. 114.

16 AN, LL 609, ff. 66r-67r.

17 AN LL 605, f. 80r.

18 AN, LL 605, ff. 36v-38r; AN, L 620, no. 25.

19 Leniaud and Perrot, *Sainte-Chapelle*, 74–5; McManners, *Church*, II, 127–30.

20 AN, LL 610, ff. 105v-106r; McManners, *Church*, I, 16.

21 *G*, 30 August 1653, 887–8; Delmas, *Saint*, 177; Félibien, *Histoire*, 496–500.

22 *M*, November 1722, II, 120–1; Le Gall, *Mythe*, 105–8.

23 Jannic Durand and Marie-Pierre Laffitte, *Le trésor de la Sainte-Chapelle* (Paris, 2001), 113–22, 176; Leniaud and Perrot, *Sainte-Chapelle*, 58–60.

24 Millet, *Trésor*, 80; Cornette, *Henri IV*, 54.

25 AN, L 863, no. 9, f. 1r.

26 AN, K 153–156, liasse III no. 1.

27 J.-J. Guiffrey, 'Les tombes royales de saint-Denis à la fin du XVIIIe siècle', *Le Cabinet Historique*, 22 (1876): 3–4.

28 Asch, *Sacral*, 96; Nelson, 'Religion', 180.

29 Le Gall, *Mythe*, 101–12, 143, 424; idem, 'Vieux saint et grande noblesse à l'époque moderne: Saint Denis, les Montmorency et les Guise', *Revue d'histoire moderne et contemporaine*, 50 (2003): 7–33.

30 AN, L 835 (liasse 3), no. 58; AN, L 853 no. 17; *Actes concernans l'union de l'Abbaye de S. Denys à la maison royale de Saint Louis à Saint Cyr* (Paris, 1694); *Lettres patentes de confirmation d'establissement de la Maison de saint Loüis, establie à saint Cyr* (Paris, 1719).

31 Cange, *Histoire*, II, 315.

32 Vernon, *Roy*, 597–8.

33 *Office* (1697), 181–6.

34 Vernon, *Roy*, 596.

35 *Procès-verbaux des Etats Généraux de 1593*, 452.

36 Lavieille, 'Il', 213.

37 The painting was criticized for Saint Louis's feminine pose. *Couleurs du ciel*, 122–3.

38 Gaehtgens, 'A toutes', 238–40.

39 Gaposchkin and Field, *Sanctity*, 150–9.

40 Menard, *Sancti Ludovici*, 136.

41 François Duchêne (ed.), *Historiæ Francorum Scriptores . . .* (Paris, 1649), V.

42 Anicet Melot, abbé Sallier and Jean Capperonier (eds), *Histoire de saint Louis . . .* (Paris, 1761), 391–522.

43 Gaposchkin and Field, *Sanctity*, 150.

44 *Conversion du seigneur de Moissac* (Paris and Toulouse, 1620).

45 Rousselet, *Lys*, 271–3, 1360–92.

46 Vernon, *Roy*, 749–52.

47 Lavieille, 'Il', 214.

48 ALG, E SUP 2695, ff. 1r, 9r, 11r-12r.

49 ALG, E SUP 2696, f. 1r.

50 ALG, E SUP 2699/1; E SUP 2695, f. 19r.

51 ALG, E SUP 2696, ff. 3r, 5v, 24v, 27v; E SUP 2697, ff. 8r, 9r, 19v, 20v, 21r, 37r.

52 *Notice sur les reliques de Saint Louis à Lamontjoie* (Agen, 1855), 2.

53 ALG, E SUP 2696, f. 1r; E SUP 2691/1, ff. 18r-v, 93v; *La Montjoie de Saint-Louis: La Bastide et ses Environs* (Lamontjoie, 1970), 67–9; Catherine Petit-Aupert, Ézéchiel Jean-Courret and Isabelle Cartron, *Une bastide pour le roi; autour des reliques de saint Louis à Lamontjoie* (Pessac, 2014).

54 *Notice sur les reliques*, 11; ALG, E SUP 2698/1, no. 4, ff. 1v, 2r.

55 ALG, E SUP 2696, f. 1r; E SUP 2688/1, ff. 91r-v; E SUP 2691/3, ff. 21r, 22r-v, 23r, 29r-v, 34r; E SUP 2692/1, ff. 3r-v, 8v-9r, 15v; E SUP 2692/2, f. 25r; E SUP 2693, ff. 20v-21r.

56 ALG, E SUP 2695, f. 12v.

57 Choisy, *Vie*, 33; Vernon, *Roy*, 53; Henri Parguez, *Saint Louis et Poissy: Sa Naissance, son Baptême, ses Charités, ses Miracles, son Culte à Poissy 1214-1914* (Saint-Germain-en-Laye, 1914).

58 Jean-Aimar Piganiol de la Force, *Nouvelle Description de la France . . .* 3rd edn (Paris, 1753), I, 216–17.

59 Parguez, *Saint Louis*, 27.

60 Piganiol de la Force, *Nouvelle Description*, I, 269–70.

61 *MG*, August 1695, 167–73.

62 *MdF*, February 1735, 283–90; November 1735, 2400–21; June 1736, II, 1327–37; December 1736, I, 2595–606; March 1737, 412–51; June 1737, II, 1338–50; *JT*, October 1736, 1894–1903; Natalis de Wailly, *Mémoire sur la date et le lieu de naissance de Saint Louis* (Paris, 1867).

63 *Breviarum Parisiense* (1640), 1049–50.

64 *Office* (1697), 37–43.
65 BnF MS Fr. 13,171, pp. 28–39.
66 BMaz MS 463, pp. 72–102; *Office* (1742), 24–31; *Office* (1760), 32–9.
67 *Office* (1697), 134–7; *Office* (1742), 125–31; *Office* (1760), 141–4, 149–53, 158–62.
68 *Breviarium Parisiense* (1640), 1048; BnF, MS Lat. 8828, pp. 216–8; BnF, MS Lat. 9477, pp. 154–5; *Office* (1688), 12–14; *Office* (1697), 23–4; BMaz MS 463, pp. 10–17; *Breviarium Parisiense* (1736), 519; *Office* (1742), 3–4; *Office* (1749), 57–9; *Office* (1760), 9–10.
69 *Office* (1749), 58.
70 *O qui*: *Office* (1697), 7–9; *Office* (1711), 9–11. *Templa*: *Office* (1742), 8–9.
71 *Breviarium Parisiense* (1640), 1052; *Office* (1697), 68–9; BMaz, MS 463, pp. 210–17; *Breviarium Parisiense* (1736), 525–6; *Office* (1760), 67–8.
72 BnF, MS Fr. 24,323, pp. 78–9.
73 BnF, MS Fr. 13,171, unpag.
74 *Office* (1688), 3–4, 6–8.
75 BnF, MS Lat. 8828, pp. 213–16.
76 BnF, MS Fr. 13,171, pp. 126–7.
77 *Office* (1697), 101–2; *Office* (1711), 11, 125–6; *Office* (1742), 80–1; *Office* (1749), 86–7; *Office* (1767), 11.
78 *Office* (1688), 44–5; BnF, MS Lat. 9476, p. 134; *Office* (1760), 97.
79 *Office* (1711), 118–22.
80 *Office* (1749), 73.
81 *Office* (1767), 6–14.
82 *Office* (1697), BMaz MS 463; *Office* (1742).
83 BnF MS Fr. 13,171; MS Lat 8828, 9476–7; *Office* (1760).
84 *Office* (1742).
85 *Office* (1767).
86 *Office* (1688); *Office* (1711); *Office* (1733); *Office* (1749).
87 BnF MS Lat. 8831.
88 BMaz MS 463, unpag.
89 Alison Forrestal, *Fathers, Pastors and Kings: Visions of Episcopacy in Seventeenth-Century France* (Manchester, 2004), 183, 198, 204; de Sales, *Œuvres*, III, xviii–xix, xxvii; Bergin, *Church*, 194.
90 François de Sales, *Introduction à la vie dévote* (Paris, 1651), 13, 16, 19, 83, 178, 215, 326–8, 397–8, 405–6, 440, 476–7, 608, 645–50.
91 De Sales, *Œuvres*, IV, 19; V, 126; XII, 367–8.
92 Ibid., XIV, 380.
93 Pierre Le Moyne, *La Devotion aisée*, 2nd edn (Paris, 1668), 71.
94 *Panégyristes*, I, 6, 53.
95 A. J. Krailsheimer, *Armand-Jean de Rancé, abbot of La Trappe: His Influence in the Cloister and the World* (Oxford, 1974), 266.
96 Rousselet, *Lys*, 945.
97 BnF MS Fr. 20,064, ff. 248r-v, 250–1.
98 *Panégyristes*, I, 220–1.
99 Alain Tallon, *La Compagnie du Saint-Sacrement (1629-1667): Spiritualité et société* (Paris, 1990).
100 F. Laurent, *Le palais de l'amour divin . . .* (Paris, 1614), 756.
101 Alison Forrestal, *Vincent de Paul, the Lazarist Mission, and French Catholic Reform* (Oxford, 2017).

102 Vincent de Paul, *Correspondance, entretiens, documents*, ed. Pierre Coste, 12 vols (Paris, 1920–5), I, 113, 135; IX, 13, 119–20; XI, 301–3; XIII, 546.

103 Bérulle, *Œuvres*, XVI.

104 Sarcé, *Vie*, 6, 11.

105 Louis Forget, *Le Monarque sainct et glorieux . . .* (Tours, 1645), 1–2, 16, 23, 52, 92, 112.

106 Jacques Vignier, *La pratique de la paix de l'ame dans la vie de sainct Louis . . .* (Autun, 1642), 6–7.

107 Estor, *Panégyrique*, 69–70.

108 *MG*, September 1688, 26–7.

109 Eve, *Vie*, 45.

110 Zoberman, *Panégyriques*, 62.

111 de Saint Ian, *Saint Louys*, 25–6.

112 Montelet, *Panégyrique*, 50.

113 Tricoire, 'What'; Tricoire, *Vierge*, 64–6.

114 Hersent, *Empire*, 30.

115 Mesnard, 'Port-Royal', 54–6.

116 Arnauld, *Lettres*, I, 296–7; II, 175–8, 349–50, 367–8; III, 59, 119–22.

117 Robert Mandrou, *De la culture populaire aux XVIIe et XVIIIe siècles: La Bibliothèque bleue de Troyes* (Paris, 1964), 91–7, 145–8.

118 *Exercice de dévotion . . .* (Troyes, [1758]), 29.

119 Diefendorf, *Beneath*, 42–3.

120 Pierre Chaunu, *La mort à Paris, XVIe, XVIIe, XVIIIe siècles* (Paris, 1978), 311.

121 AN, L 675, no. 31; L 676, no. 4.

122 AN, L 675, no. 2.

123 Vovelle, *Piété*, 167.

124 *MdF*, October 1730, 2325; October 1757, I, 59–60; 13 November 1784, 52.

125 *MdF*, October 1748, 115.

126 Jean-Philippe Rameau, *Cantate Pour le jour de la saint Louis*, introd. Mary Cyr (Bias, 1985); Graham Sadler, *The Rameau Compendium* (Woodbridge, 2014), 51, 104.

127 Vovelle, *Piété* 175–80; McManners, *Church*, II, 105.

128 Guilhelm Scherf, 'L'image sculptée de saint Louis au XVIIIe siècle', in *Le plaisir de l'art du Moyen Âge: Commande, production et réception de l'œuvre d'art. Mélanges en hommage à Xavier Barral i Altet*, various eds (Paris, 2012), 1013–22.

129 'Cantique spirituel; Oraison à St Louis': Musée des Civilisations de l'Europe et de la Méditerranée, Marseilles.

130 Pierre-Marie Auzas, 'Essai d'un répertoire iconographique de saint Louis', *Septième Centenaire*, 3–56.

131 Géraldine Lavieille, 'Le Rosaire de La Forêt-Fouesnant (Basse-Bretagne): jeux de pouvoir et création collective de l'image religieuse royale sous Louis XIV', *Revue d'histoire moderne et contemporaine*, 61 (2014): 89–119.

132 Lavieille, 'Il', 216–8.

133 Alain Mérot, *Eustache Le Sueur (1616-1655)* (Paris, 1987), 75, 99, 320–3.

134 Guillaume de Saint-Martin, *Panégyriques des saints . . .*, 2 vols (Paris, 1683–4), II, 99–100.

135 Alexandre Gady, 'Charité bien ordonnée . . .: Richelieu et l'architecture hospitalière', in Boyer, *Richelieu*, 98–106.

136 Edmunds, *Piety*, 58.

137 *L'hospital general*, 8–9, 18.

138 *MG*, September 1690, 163.

139 Binet, *Recueil*, 471.
140 Vignier, *Pratique*, 40, 51–4.
141 Vincent de Paul, *Correspondance*, X, 560–1.
142 Sluhovsky, *Patroness*, 212; Balzamo, *Miracles*, 20.
143 Asch, *Sacral*, 157.
144 Edmunds, *Piety*, 210.
145 Burkardt, *Clients*, 181–336.

Chapter 6

1 J. C. D. Clark, 'The Re-Enchantment of the World? Religion and Monarchy in Eighteenth-Century Europe', in Schaich, *Monarchy*, 63.
2 Olivier Ferret, *La Fureur de nuire: échanges pamphlétaires entre philosophes et antiphilosophes (1750-1770)* (Oxford, 2007); Mark Curran, '*Mettons toujours Londres*: Enlightened Christianity and the Public in Pre-Revolutionary Francophone Europe', *French History*, 24 (2009): 40–59.
3 Voltaire, *La Henriade . . .* (Geneva, 1768), 114 (Chant VI, 339–44).
4 Ibid., 120, 128 (Chant VII, 31–2, 276).
5 Ibid., 133 (Chant VII, 423–4).
6 Fleury, *L'Abrégé*, 113–14; Pascale Mormiche, 'Éduquer un roi ou l'histoire d'une modification progressive du projet pédagogique pour Louis XV (1715-1722)', *Histoire de l'éducation*, 132 (2011): 17–47.
7 BnF,.MS Fr. 2324, ff. 2r-v, 347v-348v.
8 *M*, September 1721, 42.
9 *M*, August 1722, 147.
10 *M*, November 1722, 149–50.
11 *MdF*, April 1726, 749–51.
12 *MdF*, September 1726, 2061.
13 Létour, *Punegyrique*, 20.
14 *MdF*, October 1736, 2303–4; September 1736, 2082–3.
15 Pierre-Barthélemy Carrelet de Rosay, *Panégyrique de saint Louis . . .* (Paris, 1735), 10.
16 Abbé Josset, *Compliment, fait à la Reine . . .* (Metz, [1744]), 3–4.
17 Paul-François Velly, *Histoire de France . . .*, 30 vols (Paris, 1755–86), IV, 311.
18 Lisa Jane Graham, 'Fiction, Kingship, and the Politics of Character in Eighteenth-Century France', in Deploige and Deneckere, *Mystifying*, 142.
19 Abbé Josset, *Panégyrique de saint Louis . . .* (Paris, 1747); *Panégyrique* (Paris, 1748); Abbé Le Cren, *Panégyrique de Saint Louis . . .* (Saint Brieuc, 1765); Abbé de Cambacérès, *Panegyrique de Saint Louis . . .* (Paris, 1768).
20 Tour du Pin de La Charce, *Panégyrique*, 12, 32.
21 Christophe de Beaumont, *Mandement de Monseigneur l'Archevêque de Paris* (Paris, 1751), 5–6.
22 Émile Régnault, *Christophe de Beaumont, archevêque de Paris (1703-1781)*, 2 vols (Paris, 1882), I, 201.
23 M. Le Cousturier, *Panégyrique de saint Louis . . .* (Paris, 1746), 20; Nicolas-Louis Poulle, *Panégyrique de saint Louis . . .* (Paris, 1748), 27; Nicolas Thyrel de Boismont, *Panégyrique de Saint Louis . . .* (Paris, 1750), 17; Antoine-Auguste-Lambert Gayet de Sansale, *Panégyrique de Saint Louis . . .* (Paris, 1767), 28–9.

24 *MdF*, October 1736, 2299; Guillaume-Germain Guyot, *Panégyrique de Saint Louis* . . . (Paris, 1758), 23.

25 McManners, *Church*, I, 38.

26 P. Bernard, *Panégyrique de Saint Louis* . . . (Paris, 1756), 56, 63–4.

27 François-Xavier Talbert, *Panégyrique de Saint Louis* . . . (Paris, 1779), 9–10.

28 Asch, *Sacral*, 7.

29 *M*, September 1722, 97–100; *Bouquet au Roy* . . . (Paris, 1726); *MdF*, October 1725, I, 2485; October 1726, 2309–10; December 1729, I, 2915; September 1730, 2022–31; October 1749, 196–8.

30 *MdF*, October 1755, 52–3.

31 *MdF*, August 1722, 208; August 1728, 1888; September 1732, 2068; August 1741, 1905; October 1752, 194; *G*, 28 August 1717, 419–20; 30 August 1721, 434–5; 30 August 1732, 420.

32 *G*, 28 August 1767, 301; 28 August 1769, 281; 31 August 1770, 286; 28 August 1772, 316; 30 August 1773, 314.

33 Melot et al., *Histoire*, i; *G*, 16 May 1761, 246–7; *JT*, August 1761, 1965–73; AN, LL 1223 B, p. 267.

34 Hannah Williams, 'Saint Geneviève's Miracles: Art and Religion in Eighteenth-Century Paris', *French History*, 30 (2016): 338–40.

35 AN, L 613, nos. 1, 3; LL 520, pp. 51–2, 103–4, 112, 131–3; *MdF*, February 1743, 400; September 1744, 2085–6; *G*, 5 September 1744, 431–2.

36 *MdF*, August 1727, 1848.

37 *MdF*, June 1743, II, 1429–32; October 1754, 207.

38 *MdF*, October 1773, I, 152–65.

39 *MdF*, December 1729, II, 3228–9; April 1730, 655–73.

40 Liévin-Bonaventure Proyart, *Vie du Dauphin* . . . (Lyon, 1788), 31, 274–5.

41 *Office* (1760), V, XXXII–XXXVI, LII–LVII.

42 *MdF*, June 1773, II, 92.

43 Jacques-Olivier Pleuvri, *Panegyrique de Saint Louis* . . . (Paris, 1772), 37.

44 Louise de France, *Méditations eucharistiques* . . . (Lyon, 1810), 121, 161–2, 217–26; Bernard Hours, *Madame Louise; Princesse au Carmel, 1737-1787* (Paris, 1987), 52–5, 86–7, 96, 105–9, 123, 184, 200, 298–9, 353–4.

45 Harold Ellis, *Boulainvilliers and the French Monarchy: Aristocratic Politics in Early Eighteenth-Century France* (Ithaca and London, 1988), ix, 5, 57–63, 93, 153, 165, 192–6; Keohane, *Philosophy*, 346–9.

46 Ars, MS 6335, ff. 7r–12r, 18r, 30v–31r, 64r, 69r; BMaz, MS 2014, f. 7r.

47 Marais, *Journal*, I, 450; II, 561–2.

48 BnF, MS Fr. 7575; Swann, *Exile*, 170–6, 191–8. Saint Louis did not feature in the *Conférences sur le droit public* (BnF, MSS Fr. 7565–7).

49 Baker, 'Memory', 139–44; Julian Swann, *Politics and the Parlement of Paris under Louis XV, 1754-1774* (Cambridge, 1995), 164.

50 Louis-Adrien Le Paige, *Lettres historiques, sur les fonctions essentielles du Parlement* . . ., 2 vols (Amsterdam, 1753–4), I, 60, 274, 320–2; II, 168–71, 325–7.

51 *JT*, October 1763, I, 2423–49; *MdF*, November 1775, 119–21; Richard de Bury, *Histoire de saint Louis* . . . (Paris, 1775); Jordan, 'Saint', 191n.

52 Velly, *Histoire*, IV, 80, 93, 150.

53 Paul-César de Ciceri, *Panégyrique de Saint Louis* . . . (Paris, 1721), 18–20; Cl. Guichon, *Panégyrique de saint Louis* . . . (s.l., 1727), 105–6.

54 *Panégyrique* (Olimpe), 19.

55 Poulle, *Panégyrique*, 9.
56 Guillaume Plantavit de la Pause, *Panégyrique de saint Louis . . .* (Paris, 1728), 12.
57 *MdF*, October 1736, 2298.
58 Antoine Brès de Vammalle, *Panégyrique de saint Louis . . .* (Paris, 1766), 18.
59 Saint-Vincent, *Panégyrique*, 11.
60 Ciceri, *Panégyrique*, 17; Poncet de la Rivière, *Panégyrique de saint Louis . . .* (Paris, 1734), 12, 23; *MdF*, September 1725, 2149; December 1741, II, 2807.
61 Le Cousturier, *Panégyrique* (1746), 6.
62 Pierre-Mathurin de l'Ecluse Desloges, *Panégyrique de saint Louis . . .* (Paris, 1744), 14.
63 *NE*, September 1724, 122–3; 1748, 4.
64 The treatise by François Pinsson des Riolles provoked a spirited rebuttal calling it an attack on 'one of the most famous ordinances of the kingdom': Riolles, *Sancti Ludovici Francorum regis Christianissimi Pragmatica Sanctio . . .* (Paris, 1663); *La Deffense de la Pragmatique de Saint Louis...* (s.l., 1663), 32. Choisy also rebutted those who had questioned the Pragmatic's authenticity: Choisy, *Vie*, 105–6.
65 *JT*, November 1743, 2765–7; August 1757, 1653.
66 Abbé Boulogne, *Panégyrique de Saint Louis . . .* (Paris, 1782), 57; *NE*, March 1789, 37–8; November 1789, 185–6.
67 Boismont, *Panégyrique*, 13; Guyot, *Panégyrique*, 18; Jean-Baptiste-Charles-Marie de Beauvais, *Panégyrique de Saint Louis . . .* (Paris, 1761), 41; Guillaume Planchot, *Panégyrique de saint Louis . . .* (Paris, 1766), 9; Jean-Sifrain Maury, *Panégyrique de Saint Louis . . .* (Paris, 1772), 28; *G*, 14 September 1772, 341.
68 Beauvais, *Panégyrique*, 1.
69 Velly, *Histoire*, IV, 385–7.
70 Delmas, *Saint*, 196.
71 *L'Esprit des Lois*, book 28 chapters 29, 37–9.
72 *Du contrat social*, book 1 chapter 4.
73 Bernard, *Panégyrique*, 28; Simon-Jérôme Bourlet de Vauxcelles, *Panégyrique de Saint Louis . . .* (Paris, 1762), 29; Le Cren, *Panégyrique*, 44.
74 Maury, *Panégyrique*, 44.
75 J. Mackrell, *The Attack on 'Feudalism' in Eighteenth-Century France* (Abingdon, 1973).
76 Abbé Bon, *Panégyrique de Saint Louis* (Paris, 1753), 3.
77 Vammalle, *Panégyrique*, 4–5, 28–30, 38–40.
78 Le Cousturier, *Panégyrique* (1769), 34.
79 Durand Echeverria, *The Maupeou Revolution: A Study in the History of Libertarianism, France, 1770-1774* (Baton Rouge and London, 1985); Swann, *Politics*, chapters 9–11; Swann, *Exile*, 394–403.
80 Bachaumont, *Mémoires*, XIX, 226–32.
81 Jules Flammermont (ed.), *Remontrances du Parlement de Paris au XVIIIᵉ siècle*, 3 vols (Paris, 1888–1898), I, 429–30, 534, 555–6; II, 537–8.
82 *MdF*, October 1736, 2299.
83 Poulle, *Panégyrique*, 20.
84 *JT*, March 1745, 381.
85 Joseph du Baudory, *Œuvres . . .* (Paris, 1750), 467–542; *Louis IX, roi de France . . .* (Dijon, [1746]); Jordan, 'Saint', 192n; *NE*, October 1759, 167–8.
86 Velly, *Histoire*, IV, 221.
87 Beauvais, *Panégyrique*, 26.
88 Gayet de Sansale, *Panégyrique*, 16–19.
89 *MdF*, February 1751, 58.

90 Voltaire, *La Pucelle d'Orléans*, new edn (London, 1780), 75–6 (Chant V).

91 Bachaumont, *Mémoires*, III, 220–1.

92 Alexandre-Joseph de Bassinet, *Panegyrique de Saint Louis* . . . (Paris, 1768), vi–vii, 26, 34.

93 Le Cousturier, *Panégyrique* (1769), 38–40.

94 Bachaumont, *Mémoires*, IV, 354–5; V, 5–6; XX, 279.

95 Degen, 'Autour', 133–9.

96 Bernard, *Panegyrique*, 20–1.

97 Nigel Aston, 'The Abbé Sieyès before 1789: The Progress of a Clerical Careerist', *Renaissance and Modern Studies*, 32 (1989): 43.

98 Rosné, 'Une', 121.

99 Ibid., 133–4.

100 Françoise de Graffigny, *Correspondance*, ed. J. A. Dainard, 14 vols (Oxford, 1985–2013), X, 224.

101 Abbé d'Arty, *Panégyrique de saint Louis* . . . (Paris, 1749), 13–14; Voltaire, *Œuvres Complètes* . . ., various eds, 203 vols (Geneva and Oxford, 1968–2020), XXXI B, 473–519.

102 *MdF*, October 1774, II, 132.

103 Henri Griffet, *Panégyrique de saint Louis* . . . (Paris, 1743), 10, 17.

104 Claude Fauchet, *Panégyrique de Saint Louis* . . . (Paris, 1774), 44–5.

105 Maury, *Panégyrique*, 54–5.

106 Voltaire, *Œuvres*, LXXIV B, 101, 109.

107 Rosné, 'Une', 114–15.

108 *Registres de l'Académie*, II, 543; *MdF*, October 1771, II, 106.

109 BmB, MS 828/020 (065).

110 McManners, *Church*, II, 526.

111 *NM*, March 1717, 180.

112 McManners, *Church*, II, 59.

113 *Registres de l'Académie*, II, 277–8, III, 318–19.

114 *MdF*, September 1748, 196.

115 Rosné, 'Une', 118.

116 Ciceri, *Panégyrique*, 6; Guichon, *Panégyrique*, 85; Carrelet de Rosay, *Panégyrique*, 5; Maury, *Panégyrique*, 30–1.

117 *MdF*, September 1724, 1923; November 1729, 2651; October 1735, 2216; December 1741, II, 2798–800.

118 *MdF*, October 1748, 148.

119 *MdF*, October 1774, II, 134–5.

120 Graffigny, *Correspondance*, XI, 124; XIII, 10.

121 BnF MS Fr. 10,479, f. 156r.

122 Bachaumont, *Mémoires*, XXI, 150–1.

123 *Lettres persanes*, lettre LXXIII.

124 BnF MS Fr. 13,659, pp. 254–5.

125 Roch-Ambroise Sicard (ed.), *Vie de Madame la Dauphine* . . . (Paris, 1817), 111.

126 Ars MS 2324, ff. 128r-159v.

127 Bernard Hours, 'Moureau et Proyart, pédagogues en attente du prince et éducateurs de la nation', *Histoire de l'éducation*, 132 (2011): 162–3.

128 Doyle, *France*, 108–9; Nigel Aston, *Religion and Revolution in France, 1780-1804* (Basingstoke, 2000).

129 Fauchet, *Panégyrique*, 73–5; M. de Gery, *Panégyrique de saint Louis* . . . (Châlons, 1777), 38; Hugues du Temps, *Panégyrique de Saint Louis* . . . (Paris, 1781), 62; Boulogne, *Panégyrique* (1782), 75.

130 Louis-Pierre de Saint-Martin, *Panégyrique de Saint Louis* . . .. (Paris, 1785), 59.

131 *MdF*, 9 September 1786, 84–6; *G*, 29 August 1786, 288–9.

132 Abbé de Véri, *Journal*, 2 vols (Paris, 1928–30), II, 192–3; *NM*, August 1719, 56–60; *MdF*, June 1730, 1259–61; 22 July 1780, 171–2; *G*, 9 August 1749, 407–8; BMaz, MS 2846.

133 *MdF*, 24 July 1779, 278.

134 *MdF*, February 1753, 85.

135 Caiani, *Louis XVI*, 172.

136 Du Temps, *Panégyrique*, 15–16, 23.

137 P. Mandar, *Panégyrique de S. Louis* . . . (Paris, 1774), 30, 34, 41, 58.

138 *NMG*, August 1715, 189–90.

139 *MdF*, October 1736, 2293; October 1769, I, 120; October 1772, I, 123; *JT*, October 1761, II, 2520; October 1765, I, 869.

140 *MdF*, January 1778, II, 122.

141 Mackrell, *Attack*, 93; Christopher Todd, 'La Rédaction du *Mercure de France* (1721–1744): Dufresny, Fuzelier, La Roque', *Revue d'Histoire littéraire de la France*, 83 (1983): 439–41.

142 *MdF*, October 1764, I, 148.

143 *Registres de l'Académie*, III, 551.

144 *MdF*, 11 June 1785, 75; 3 September 1785, 40.

145 Gery, *Panégyrique*, 4.

146 *MdF*, July 1770, I, 13–17, 83–90, 102–6; December 1770, 57–70; April 1773, II, 23; June 1774, 224–5; July 1774, I, 183; January 1775, I, 62–6, 183; January 1775, II, 5–21; January 1776, I, 22–5.

147 Bachaumont, *Mémoires*, XIV, 169 (29 August 1779).

148 *MdF*, May 1775, 80–3; 4 September 1784, 29–33; 1 November 1788, 29–38; Baumgartner, *Louis XII*, 253.

149 *MdF*, October 1772, II, 144–5.

150 *Relation de la fête célébrée dans la Chapelle Royale de Messieurs les Pénitens Bleus de Toulouse, le 25 Août 1775* . . . (Toulouse, 1775), 5–8, 37, 44–6, 51.

151 Abbé Lambert, *Panégyrique de Saint Louis* . . . (Lyon and Paris, [s.d.]), 37–9.

152 *MdF*, 19 July 1788, 146–7.

153 *MdF*, 15 June 1779, 144–5. Another *Louisiade*, an anonymous prose version of Le Moyne, had been published a few years earlier: *Les quatre premiers chants de la Louisiade* . . . (Avranches and Paris, 1774); Banderier, 'Du *Saint Louis*'; Jordan, 'Saint', 177.

154 Saint-Martin, *Panégyrique*, 6–7.

155 Louis-Pierre de Saint-Martin, *Les Établissemens de Saint Louis* . . . (Paris, 1786), 1–2, 18, 243, 273, 507n.

156 Manuel, *Coup*, 1–2, 34, 46, 64, 92–3, 156; Degen, 'Autour', 132.

157 *Saint Louis à Louis XVI. Ode* (Rennes, 1788).

158 *Cahiers de Doléances de la Sénéchaussée de Montauban* . . . (Montauban, 1925), 9; Chartier, *Cultural*, 111–12.

159 *Cahiers du Bailliage d'Arques* . . . (Lille, 1922), xiii; *Cahiers de Doléances du bailliage de Contentin* . . . (Paris, 1908), II, 544; *Les Élections et les Cahiers de Paris en 1789*,

I, 75, 311; Gilbert Shapiro and John Markoff, *Revolutionary Demands: A Content Analysis of the Cahiers de Doléances of 1789* (Stanford, 1998), 374.

160 *La fête du Louisée, 25 Août 1789* . . . ([Le Havre], 1789).

161 Galart de Montjoye, *L'ami du roi, des François* . . . (Paris, 1791), 16.

162 *MdF*, 5 September 1789, 36; *G*, 1 September 1789, 347–8; Caiani, *Louis XVI*, 174; Stanislas de Clermont-Tonnerre, *Du 24 Août 1789. Réponse de Monsieur le Président de l'Assemblée nationale à la Députation de la Garde nationale de Versailles* . . . (Versailles, 1789).

163 *MU*, LXXV: 15–20 October 1789, 71.

164 Pierre-Samuel Dupont de Nemours, *Discours au Roi* . . . (Paris, 1790); *MdF*, 4 September 1790, 39; *AR*, 26 August 1790, 356; *G*, 31 August 1790, 349–50.

165 *AP*, 26 August 1790.

166 *MU*, CLXXI: 20 June 1790, 672.

167 *AR*, 11 July 1790, 168; Mark Darlow, *Staging the French Revolution: Cultural Politics and the Paris Opéra, 1789-1794* (Oxford, 2012), 204.

168 Many regarded the story of Louis IX being offered the Egyptian crown to be ridiculous: Voltaire, *Œuvres*, IV, 570–1; Manuel, *Coup*, 6.

169 Nicolas-François Guillard and François-Guillaume-Jean-Stanislas Andrieux, *Louis IX en Égypte* . . . (Avignon, 1790), 3, 9, 24–5, 31.

170 Darlow, *Staging*, 251–62.

171 *RdP*, l: 19–26 June 1790, 643.

172 *MdF*, 26 June 1790, 153.

173 Abbé Vigneras, *Discours sur l'Amour de la Patrie* (Paris, 1790), 5.

174 Louis XVI, *Lettres de Louis XVI* . . . ed. B. Chauvelot (Paris, 1862), 112, 124.

175 Caiani, *Louis XVI*, 7, 163, 174–6.

176 Timothy Tackett, *When the King Took Flight* (Cambridge, MA, 2003).

177 *G*, 30 August 1791, 306.

178 Johnson, 'Sacred', 69–70.

179 Marquis de Sade, *Aline et Valcour, ou Le roman philosophique* . . . 4 vols (Paris, 1795), II, 366–7n.

180 Louis La Vicomterie, *Les crimes des rois de France* . . . (Paris, 1792), 10–11, 201–11.

181 *Archives Parlementaires de 1787 à 1860: recueil complet des débats législatifs et politiques des chambres françaises*, 96 vols (Paris, 1867–1990), LX, 237.

182 *GNF*, 16 October 1792, 830; *Archives Parlementaires*, LII, 505.

183 *Archives Parlementaires*, LXIX, 608–9; LXXIX, 238.

184 Ibid., LXXII, 681–2.

185 Fabien Oppermann, 'Le remeublement du château de Versailles au XXᵉ siècle: Entre action scientifique et manœuvres politiques', *Bibliothèque de l'École de chartes*, 170 (2012): 210.

186 *Archives Parlementaires*, LXXIX, 614.

187 Ernest Delamont, *Histoire de la Ville de Cette pendant la Révolution 1789-1796 (an V)* (Gap, 1989), 68; Abbé Collignon, *Histoire de la paroisse Saint-Louis-en-l'Ile* (Paris, 1888), 242.

188 Edmunds, *Piety*, 214.

189 Richard Clay, 'Signs of Power: Iconoclasm in Paris, 1789-1795' (PhD thesis, University College London, September 1999), 169, 210.

190 Levot, *Histoire*, 309–11.

191 [Nicolas-Pierre-Christophe Rogue], *Souvenirs et journal d'un bourgeois d'Évreux, 1740-1830* (Évreux, 1850), 68.

192 Boureau, *Simple*, 7–8, 71–90; Philippe Boiry, *Le Mystère du cœur de Saint Louis* (Paris, 2008), 55; Durand and Lafitte, *Trésor*, 240, 262–3.

193 Brown, 'Chapels', 300.

194 *Archives Parlementaires*, LXXIX, 84–5.

195 Boiry, *Mystère*, 50, 245–57; *Notice sur les reliques*, 12. The Musée Tavet-Delacour in Pontoise holds teeth and fragments of Saint Louis's skull, apparently saved from St-Denis in 1793.

196 *VC*, No. 5: Quintidi Nivose, 1ère Décade, an II, 57–8.

Chapter 7

1 An earlier version of this chapter appeared as 'Consensus or Contestation? The Memory of Saint Louis during the Restoration, 1814-30', *French History*, 33 (2019): 44–64. I am grateful to Oxford University Press for allowing me to publish this revised and expanded version.

2 Marie-Antoine de Reiset, *Souvenirs . . .*, 3 vols (Paris, 1900–2), III, 36–8.

3 *G*, 26 August 1814, 946.

4 Reiset, *Souvenirs*, III, 269–70.

5 A contemporary print (*Fête de S.M. Louis Dix-huit au jardin des Tuileries le 24 août 1815*, visible on Gallica) shows the scene.

6 Mazas, *Histoire*, II, 448.

7 Bettina Frederking, '"Il ne faut pas être le roi de deux peuples": Strategies of national reconciliation in Restoration France', *French History*, 22 (2008): 447.

8 Emmanuel de Waresquiel, *C'est la Révolution qui continue! La Restauration, 1814-1830* (Paris, 2015), 78.

9 Olivier Tort, 'Le mythe du retour à l'Ancien Régime sous la Restauration', in *Rien appris, rien oublié? Les Restaurations dans l'Europe postnapoléonienne (1814-1830)*, eds Jean-Claude Caron and Jean-Philippe Luis (Rennes, 2015), 244; Francis Démier, *La France de la Restauration (1814-1830): L'impossible retour du passé* (Paris, 2012), 17.

10 Sheryl Kroen, *Politics and Theater: The Crisis of Legitimacy in Restoration France, 1815-1830* (Berkeley and Los Angeles, 2000), xi, 7–9, 96–101.

11 Françoise Waquet, *Les Fêtes Royales sous la Restauration ou l'Ancien Régime retrouvé* (Paris, 1981), 2.

12 James McMillan, 'Catholic Christianity in France from the Restoration to the separation of church and state, 1815-1905', in *The Cambridge History of Christianity, vol. 8: World Christianities, c.1815-c.1914*, eds Sheridan Gilley and Brian Stanley (Cambridge, 2005), 217.

13 Fabien Rausch, 'The impossible *gouvernement représentatif*: Constitutional culture in Restoration France, 1814-30', *French History*, 27 (2013): 242, 247.

14 Jacques Necker, *De la Révolution française*, 4 vols (Paris, V [1797]), III, 327–32.

15 *GNF*, 27 August 1792, 619.

16 *GNF*, 6 September 1792, 658.

17 *GNF*, 16 September 1792, 697.

18 Another version is 'go, son of Saint Louis, Heaven expects you': John Hardman, *Louis XVI: The Silent King* (London, 2000), 177.

19 C. Sneyd Edgeworth (ed.), *Memoirs of the Abbé Edgeworth . . .* (London, 1815), 87–8.

20 *Discours Funèbre sur la mort du Roi-Martyr Louis XVI* (Lille, 1816), 4.

21 *Déclaration des Français fidèles au roi, réunis sous les ordres de M. de Gaston . . .* (Brussels, 1793), 4.

22 *Collection des mémoires relatifs à la Révolution Française . . . Guerres des Vendéens . . .*, 6 vols (Paris, 1824–7), IV, 17.

23 Ibid., I, 381; VI, 230.

24 Ibid., VI, 156.

25 Ibid., IV, 128, 181–2; VI, 130, 175–7; Philip Mansel, *Louis XVIII* (London, 1981), 92.

26 Michael Ross, *Banners of the King: The War of the Vendée, 1793-4* (London, 1975), 140.

27 André Montagnon, *Les Guerres de Vendée, 1793-1832* (Paris, 1974), 257–8.

28 *Collection des mémoires*, IV, 331–2.

29 Ibid., V, 327.

30 Ibid., VI, 147.

31 Louis-Antoine-Henri de Bourbon, duc d'Enghein, *Correspondance*, ed. Comte Boulay de la Meurthe, 4 vols (Paris, 1904–13), I, 217.

32 Philip Mansel, 'From Exile to the Throne: The Europeanization of Louis XVIII', in Philip Mansel and Torsten Riotte (eds.), *Monarchy and Exile: The Politics of Legitimacy from Marie de Médicis to Wilhelm II* (Basingstoke, 2011), 188–9.

33 Enghein, *Correspondance*, I, 278.

34 Emmanuel de Waresquiel, 'L'obstination d'un roi: Louis XVIII en exil, 1791-1814', *Napoleonica. La Revue*, 22 (2015): 38.

35 Enghein, *Correspondance*, II, 53–4.

36 Ibid., I, 365.

37 *Le Bouquet de la Saint Louis* (s.l., s.d.).

38 Jean-Paul Clément, 'L'utilisation du mythe de Saint-Louis par Chateaubriand dans les controverses politiques de l'Empire et de la Restauration', *Revue d'Histoire littéraire de la France*, 98 (1998): 1059–72.

39 François-René de Chateaubriand, *Le Génie du Christianisme*, 2 vols (Paris, 1847), I, 2, 166, 365.

40 Idem, *Itinéraire de Paris à Jerusalem et de Jérusalem à Paris* (Paris, 1867), 372; Khalid Chaouch, 'Chateaubriand's time travel in Tunis and Carthage: An archaeology of mappings', *Nineteenth-Century French Studies*, 46 (2018): 254–69.

41 See the emphasis on dynastic descent from Saint Louis in the *Mémoires sur le duc de Berry* (1820): François-René de Chateaubriand, *Œuvres complètes . . .*, 5 vols (Paris, 1839–40), II, 3–4.

42 Vincent Petit, 'Religion du souverain, souverain de la religion: l'invention de saint Napoléon', *Revue Historique*, 314 (2012): 643–58.

43 Sudhir Hazareesingh, *The Saint-Napoleon: Celebrations of Sovereignty in Nineteenth-Century France* (Cambridge, MA, 2004), 3–4.

44 Clément-Joseph Pays d'Alissac, *Ode pour la Fête de la St.-Louis . . .* (Paris, 1814), 10.

45 Waquet, *Fêtes*, 92; Morel, 'Culte', 142.

46 Mansel, *Louis XVIII*, 285.

47 Regnaud de Paris, *Bouquet adressé au Roi . . .* (Paris, 1815), 3.

48 Jordan, 'Saint', 177; P. Le Moyne, *Saint Louis . . .* (Paris, 1816), ix–x.

49 *Historie de St Louis* (Paris, 1819); *Histoire de saint Louis . . ., édition dédiée à la jeunesse française par M. Paul Gervais* (Paris, 1822); *Histoire de saint Louis . . .* (Paris, 1826). The interest in Joinville is also attested by the publication in 1824 of Charles du Cange's dissertations in a publication that also included excerpts from Arabic

manuscripts relating to the reign of Saint Louis: Claude-Bernard Petitot, *Collection complete des mémoires relatifs à l'histoire de France*, vol. III (Paris, 1824).

50 Joseph-François Michaud, *Histoire des Croisades, Quatrième Édition*, 5 vols (Paris, 1825–9). The accounts of Louis IX's crusades are in vols 4 and 5 (books 14–17).

51 Corinne Legoy, 'La figure du souverain médiéval sur les scènes parisiennes de la Restauration', *Revue Historique*, 293 (1995): 321–65.

52 Jacques-François Ancelot, *Louis IX, Tragédie en cinq actes . . .*, 3rd edn (Paris, 1819), *A Sa Majesté Louis XVIII*.

53 Jordan, 'Saint', 178–80.

54 Legoy, 'Figure', 358.

55 *Panégyristes*; Étienne-Antoine de Boulogne, *Panégyrique de Saint-Louis, Roi de France, prononcé devant les deux Académies Royales des Belles-Lettres et des Sciences, en 1782 . . .* (Paris, 1814).

56 Corinne Legoy, 'De la célébration au combat politique: l'adversaire dans les éloges de la Restauration', *Annales historiques de la Révolution française*, 334 (2003): 23–43.

57 Marie-Nicolas-Silvestre Guillon, *Panégyrique de S. Louis . . .* (Paris, 1818), 4–6, 11, 22, 34, 39–42.

58 Abbé Béraud, *Panégyrique de S. Louis . . .* (Paris, 1823), 8.

59 Jean-François Montès, *Panégyrique de Saint-Louis . . .* ([Paris], [1819]), 2.

60 Versailles MV 19. Rouget had already painted three depictions of Saint Louis for the Conseil d'État from 1817-20: Knobler, 'Saint', 158.

61 *Panégyrique de Saint-Louis, prononcé dans la Cathédrale de Rennes, en présence de Mgr. l'Evêque et des Autorités constituées, le 25 août 1816, par M. A. D. L . . .* (Rennes, 1816), 10, 18–19.

62 Béraud, *Panégyrique*, 25–7.

63 Pierre-Paul Castelli, *Discours prononcé le jour de Saint-Louis . . .* (Ajaccio, 1825), 13–14.

64 Jean-Paul Clément, *Charles X: Le dernier Bourbon* (Paris, 2015), 231; Waresquiel, *C'est*, 198.

65 Louis Gaudreau, *Panégyrique de Saint Louis, prêché dans l'église de Saint-Germain-l'Auxerrois, en présence de l'Académie Française, le 25 Aout 1829...* (Paris, 1854), 5, 22–5.

66 *Panégyristes*, v–vi.

67 Germaine de Staël, *Considérations sur les principaux événements de la Révolution française*, ed. Lucia Omacini, 2 vols (Paris, 2017), 24–5, 816.

68 Jacques-Pierre de Barrin, *La Fête de Saint-Louis, 25 auguste 1817. Ode* (Grenoble, 1817), 2, 9. The flower brought back by Saint Louis was the buttercup and the allusion to 'son fils' in Holland refers to the comte de Provence's (Louis XVIII's) proclamation of 1 January 1814.

69 Jean Labouderie, *Panégyrique de Saint Louis . . .* (Paris, 1824), 16.

70 David Higgs, *Ultraroyalism in Toulouse: From Its Origins to the Revolution of 1830* (Baltimore and London, 1973), 156.

71 *ARR*, XLII, 401–7.

72 Labouderie, *Panégyrique*, 36, 40.

73 *JD*, 26 August 1824, 3.

74 *C*, 26/27 August 1824, 2.

75 *C*, 15 January 1825, 3–4.

76 Jordan, 'Saint', 179; *C*, 6 August 1821, 3.

77 *MinF*, August 1818, III, 204–7.

78 Natalie Scholz, *Die imaginierte Restauration: Repräsentationen der Monarchie im Frankreich Ludwigs XVIII* (Darmstadt, 2006), 155–69; idem, 'La monarchie sentimentale: un remède aux crises politiques de la Restauration?' in *Représentation et pouvoir: La politique symbolique en France (1789-1830)*, eds Scholz and Christina Schröer (Rennes, 2007), 188; Waquet, *Fêtes*, 136; Waresquiel, *C'est*, 279–99; Rausch, 'Impossible', 229; Martin Wrede, 'Le portrait du roi restauré, ou la fabrication de Louis XVIII', *Revue d'histoire moderne et contemporaine (1954-)*, 53 (2006): 116–18, 129–32; Démier, *France*, 180. All apart from Démier assign Henri IV a more important place in the Restoration pantheon.

79 Victoria Thompson, 'The Creation, Destruction and Recreation of Henri IV: Seeing Popular Sovereignty in the Statue of a King', *History and Memory*, 24 (2012) 5–540; Casimir-Ménestrier and P. Ledoux, *La statue de Henri IV. nouveau Pont-Neuf . . .* (Paris, 1818).

80 *Couplets en l'honneur de la fête de Sa Majesté Louis XVIII, chantés le 25 août 1816, aux Champs-Élysées, par Bobêche, Bouffon des fêtes de Gouvernement* (Paris, 1816); *Cantate chantée à Belfort en 1823, à l'occasion de la fête de Saint Louis* (Belfort, [1823]).

81 Démier, *France*, 942.

82 Jean-Baptiste Robert Lindet, *Correspondance politique de brumaire an IV à 1823*, ed. François Pascal (Paris, 2011), 153.

83 *Discours prononcé dans l'église des Ménages, le jour de la célébration de la fête de Saint Louis . . .* (Paris, 1819), 4.

84 For the use of civic festivals as tools of nation building, see Mona Ozouf, *Festivals and the French Revolution* (Cambridge, MA, 1988).

85 Démier, *France*, 176–7.

86 Kroen, *Politics*, 166–9.

87 Hazareesingh, *Saint-Napoleon*, 4.

88 BmL, MS Coste 698: (6111) Adjoint de la Commune de Savigny to Préfet du Rhône, 29 August 1820; (6111), Maire de Savigny to Préfet du Rhône, 31 August 1818.

89 *Discours prononcé le jour de Saint Louis . . .* (Rouen, 1816), 15; *Discours prononcé le 25 Août 1824 . . .* (Colmar, 1824), 7.

90 *Programme des Fêtes, Cérémonies et Réjouissances publiques municipales qui auront lieu dans la Ville de Paris le mardi 25 août 1818, jour de la Saint-Louis* (Paris, 1818); Wrede, 'Portrait', 122; AN, AJ/19/19, pp. 55, 234–7; AJ/19/577, fos 27v-28r, 48v-49r, 85r-86r; *Programme des Cérémonies, Fêtes et Réjouissances publiques et Municipales, qui auront lieu dans la Ville de Paris, le Vendredi 25 Août 1820, jour de la Saint-Louis* (Paris, 1820); *Programme des Cérémonies, Fêtes et Réjouissances Publiques Municipales, qui auront lieu dans la ville de Paris, Dimanche prochain 25 Août, jour de la Fête de Sa Majesté* (Paris, 1822).

91 *G*, 26 August 1814, 946.

92 *Q*, 25 August 1818, 1–2; 1 September 1821, 2–3; *DB*, 24 August 1824, 1–2.

93 *JD*, 5 Sept. 1820, 2–3.

94 Shusterman, *Religion*, 10, 135–6, 216, 231.

95 BmL, MS Coste 668: (6113) Lezay to Rambaud, 12 August 1818; (6113) Rambaud to Lezay, 13 August 1818; (6113) Lezay to Rambaud, 19 August 1818; (6114) *État des dépenses*, 16 August 1819.

96 BmL, MS Coste 700.

97 *Mairie d'Orléans. Fête de Saint-Louis* (Orléans, 1822).

98 *Précis de ce qui s'est passé dans la Ville de Rheims, le 25 Août 1816, jour de Saint Louis, à l'occasion de la Fête de Sa Majesté* . . . (Reims, 1816), 5; *Procès-Verbal et Relation de la Fête de Saint Louis, le 25 Aout 1816, à Morlaix* (Morlaix, 1816). Cf. *Mairie de Valenciennes. Fête de Saint Louis, du 25 Août 1816* (Valenciennes, 1816).

99 *Fête de Sa Majesté Louis XVIII, le 25 Août dix-huit cent seize* (Cambrai, 1816).

100 BmA, MS 2998/35; see also *Épitre semi-historique, pour la fête de Saint-Louis, à Stanislas-Xavier, roi de France; dédiée à la Garde Nationale...* (Versailles, 1817).

101 *Fête de la Saint-Louis, Quatrième réunion. 24 Août 1818* (s.l., [1818]), 5.

102 *Fête de Saint Louis, 25 Août 1824. Onzième Banquet. 5ᵉ Légion de la Garde Nationale* (Paris, 1824), 3; *Garde Nationale de Paris, Cinquième Légion. Fête de la Saint-Louis* (Paris, 1822), 7.

103 Père Laquille, *La Saint-Louis aux Invalides, 25 Août 1824* (Paris, 1824); J. P. Vitelly d'Orsal, *Le Bouquet de Saint-Louis, pour la Fête du Roi...* (Paris, 1816); Alexandre Denuelle, *Fête de la Saint-Louis, 25 Août 1824. Hommage à S.A.R. Mademoiselle* and *Hommage à Son Altesse Royale M. le Duc d'Angoulême* (Paris, 1824).

104 *La Saint-Louis, ou la Fête d'un Bon Roi, comédie en un acte...* (Marseille, 1816), 7.

105 Ibid., 14, 17–18.

106 Antoine-Marie Coupart and Emmanuel-François Varez. *Un Trait de Bienfaisance, ou la Fête d'un Bon Maire, à-propos en un Acte, mêlé de couplets, à l'occasion de la Saint-Louis...* (Paris, 1822); Jean-Toussaint Merle, Antoine Jean-Baptiste Simonnin and Ferdinand Laloue, *La Sᵗ-Louis des Artistes, ou La Fête du Salon, vaudeville en un acte, en l'honneur de la Fête du Roi...* (Paris, 1824); C, 26/27 August 1824, 4.

107 *Le Garde Nationale, ou la Fête d'un Bon Roi, Vaudeville en un acte, joué à l'orangerie de la Pépinière, dans la fête donnée par M. de Comte de Castéja, Préfet du Haut-Rhin, à l'occasion de la Saint-Louis...* (Colmar, 1816).

108 Jean-Toussaint Merle, Nicolas Brazier and Michel-Nicolas Balisson de Rougemont, *La Saint-Louis Villageoise, Comédie en un acte...* (Paris, 1816), 7.

109 BmL, MS Coste 698: (6113) Lezay to maire de Belleville, 31 August 1818; (6113) maire de Beaujeu to Lezay, 27 August 1818; (6111) maire de Quincieux to Lezay, 26 August 1818; (6111) maire d'Oulins to Lezay, 30 August 1818; (6113) adjoint du maire d'Orliénas to Lezay, 26 August 1818; (6113) sous-préfet du 1 arrondissement to Lezay, 26 August 1818.

110 Theo Jung, '*Le silence du peuple:* The rhetoric of silence during the French Revolution', *French History*, 31 (2017): 468.

111 AN, F/7/9897, Basses-Alpes: Préfet to Ministre de l'Intérieur, 3 September 1822; Bouches-du-Rhône: Préfet to Ministre de l'Intérieur, 28 August 1823.

112 AN, F/7/9897, Cher: Préfet to Ministre de l'Intérieur, 24 September 1823.

113 AN, F/7/9897, Gers: Préfet to Ministre de la Police, 26 August 1816.

114 AN, F/7/9897, Ardèche: Préfet to Ministre de l'Intérieur, 3 September 1823.

115 Mansel, *Louis XVIII*, 160.

116 AN, F/7/9897, Hautes-Alpes: Préfet to Directeur Général de la Police, 31 August 1821.

117 AN, F/7/9897, Loire-Inférieure: Préfet to Ministre de l'Intérieur, 26 August 1823. Kroen gives other examples: *Politics*, 166–9.

118 AN, F/7/9897, Côte d'Or: Commissaire general de Police to Ministre de la Police Générale, 12 September 1818.

119 AN, F/7/9897, Doubs: Préfet to Ministre de l'Intérieur, 26 August 1816.

120 AN, F/7/9897, Doubs: Ministre de l'Intérieur to Préfet, 5 September 1822.

121 AN, F/7/9897, Haute-Garonne: Commissaire-général de police to Ministre de la Police Générale, 27 August 1816.

122 M. Poujol, *Élan d'un cœur Français. Cantate pour la Fête de Saint Louis* (Montpellier, 1816).

123 Chateaubriand, *Œuvres*, II, 62.

124 Ibid., II, 659.

125 AN, AJ/19/804, pp. 201–7; F/7/9898; *Fête de S.M. Charles Dix, célébrée par la Douzième Légion de la Garde Nationale* (Paris, 1824); Auguste Hus, *Bouquet de Pensées Bourbonniennes pour la S^t. Charles, Fête de S.M. Charles X...* (Paris, 1826); *Henri-Quatre Second. Couplets pour la Fête de S.M. Charles X* (Paris, 1827); *Vive le Roi! Couplet à l'occasion de la Saint-Charles, Fête de S.M. Charles X* (Paris, 1828).

126 AN, F/7/9898, Finistère: Sous-Préfet to Ministre de l'Intérieur, 5 November 1827.

127 Esprit Victor Élisabeth Boniface, comte de Castellane, *Journal du Maréchal de Castellane, 1804-1862*, 5 vols (Paris, 1895–7), II, 198.

128 Gaudreau, *Panégyrique*, 25–6.

129 *La Conquête d'Alger...* (Paris, 1832), 26; Christopher Tyerman, *The Debate on the Crusades* (Manchester, 2011); Jennifer Sessions, *By Sword and Plow: France and the Conquest of Algeria* (Ithaca and London, 2011), 38–40.

130 Grégoire Franconie, 'Louis-Philippe et la sacralité royale après 1830', in *La dignité de roi: Regards sur la royauté en France au premier XIX siècle*, eds Hélène Becquet and Bettina Frederking (Rennes, 2009), 97–115.

131 Gabriel Vauthier, 'Le Clergé et la Fête de Louis-Philippe en 1831', *Revue d'Histoire du XIXe siècle*, 71 (1917): 17–23.

132 Waresquiel, *C'est*, 185; Frederking, 'Il', 463.

133 Pamela Pilbeam, 'The growth of liberalism and the crisis of the Bourbon Restoration, 1827-1830', *The Historical Journal*, 25 (1982): 354, 364–5.

134 d'Alissac, *Ode*, 13.

Conclusion

1 Vernon, *Roy*, 45.

2 Henry Phillips, *Church and Culture in Seventeenth-Century France* (Cambridge, 1997), 114.

3 Pollmann, *Memory*, 196.

4 Robert Gildea, *Children of the Revolution: The French. 1799-1914* (London, 2008), 1.

5 Knobler, 'Saint'; Tietz, 'Saint', 60.

6 Delmas, *Saint*, 216–25; José Dupré, 'L'année "Saint-Louis": La propagande continue . . ', *Cahiers d'études cathares*, 21 (1970): 46–54.

7 Delmas, *Saint Louis*, 241.

8 'Louis, duc d'Anjou et Henri, comte de Paris, célèbrent Saint Louis', YouTube (posted by L'Avenir Royal).

Bibliography

Manuscripts

Archives des Affaires Étrangères, Paris

CP 26/57-8, 27/2 (Cologne)
CP 109/25, 109/119 (Rome)

Archives départementales de Lot-et-Garonne, Agen

E SUP 2688-2699

Archives départementales de Seine-Maritime, Rouen

Collection Coquebert de Montbret
MSS 27; 513; 775
MS Bachelet 048-2

Archives nationales de France, Paris

AJ/19/19; AJ/19/577; AJ/19/804
F/7/9897; F/7/9898
K 153-156, liasse III
K 1006–1018
L 613; 620; 674–6; 835; 853; 863
LL 520; 602–18; 633; 638; 824; 1220; 1223/A; 1223/B; 1229/C; 1327
S 4613

Archivio della Congregazione per la Dottrina della Fede, Rome

G 4-C

Bibliothèque de l'Arsenal, Paris (BnF)

MSS 2324; 6335

Bibliothèque Inguimbertine, Carpentras

Collection Peiresc
MS 1816

Bibliothèque François-Mitterand, Paris (BnF)

4-LB18-156; 4-LB18-195
8-Z Le Senne- 8887

Bibliothèque Mazarine, Paris

MSS 463; 2014; 2516; 2846; 3914

Bibliothèque municipale d'Avignon

MS 2998/35

Bibliothèque municipale de Bordeaux

MSS 828/020 (065); 4117

Bibliothèque municipale de Grenoble

Bb. 5404

Bibliothèque municipale de Lyon

MSS Coste 698, 700

Bibliothèque nationale de France, Paris

MS Clairambault 375
MSS Français 1803; 2324; 3708; 7565-7; 7575; 8210; 10479; 11681; 12,616-12,659; 12,796;
    12,839; 13,171; 13,659; 13,735; 17,876; 20,064; 20,728; 24,323; 25,460; 25,013
MSS Latin 8828; 8831; 9476-7
MS Nouvelles acquisitions français 22,144

Bibliothèque Richelieu (musique), Paris (BnF)

Rés-1562; Rés-2271
Rés Vm1 117; Rés Vm6 5

Service historique de la Défense, Vincennes (Paris)

GR A 1: 1457; 2251; 3186.

Primary sources printed before 1830

Abbeville, Claude d'. *Histoire de la mission des pères capucins en l'isle de Maragnan* . . .
    Paris: François Huby, 1614.

Actes concernans l'union de l'Abbaye de S. Denys à la maison royale de Saint Louis à Saint Cyr. Paris: François Muguet, 1694.

Alissac, Clément-Joseph Pays d'. *Ode pour la Fête de la St.-Louis . . .* Paris: C.-F. Patris, 1814.

Ancelot, Jacques-François. *Louis IX, Tragédie en cinq actes . . .*, 3rd edn. Paris: Huet, 1819.

Anecdotes curieuses et plaisantes, relatives à la Révolution de France. Paris: s.p., 1791.

Anselme, abbé. *Panegyrique de S. Louis . . .* Paris: Pierre le Petit, 1681.

Arnauld, Marie-Angélique. *Lettres . . .*, 3 vols. Utrecht: Aux Depens de la Compagnie, 1742–4.

Arrest de la Cour de Parlement du 1. Decembre 1666. qui ordonne le Registrement & Execution de la Lettre du Roy du vingt-sept Novembre audit an: Et de l'Ordonnance de Monsieur l'Archevéque de Paris; Portant Reglement General des Festes à chomer dans le Diocese. Paris: Imprimeurs ordinaires du Roy, 1666.

Artaud, abbé. *Panégyrique de saint Louis . . .* Paris: Jean-Baptiste Coignard, 1741.

Arty, abbé d'. *Panégyrique de saint Louis . . .* Paris: Bernard Brunet, 1749.

Auteuil, Charles de Combault. *Blanche, infante de Castille, mère de saint Louis, reine et régente de France.* Paris: Antoine de Sommaville, 1644.

Avertissement politique au Roi. Paris: s.p., 1649.

Bachaumont, Louis Petit de (attr.). *Mémoires secrets, pour servir à l'histoire de la République des Lettres en France, depuis 1762 jusqu'à nos jours . . .*, 21 vols. London: John Adamson, 1777–83.

Barral, abbé de. *Éloge du roi Saint Louis . . .* Paris: Imprimerie de Monsieur, 1785.

Barrin, Jacques-Pierre de. *La Fête de Saint-Louis, 25 août 1817. Ode.* Grenoble: veuve Pevronard, 1817.

Bassinet, Alexandre-Joseph de. *Panégyrique de Saint Louis . . .* Paris: v[euve] Regnard, 1768.

Baudory, Joseph du. *Œuvres diverses . . .* Paris: Marc Bordelet, 1750.

Beaumont, Christophe de. *Mandement de Monseigneur l'Archevêque de Paris, qui ordonne que le* Te Deum *sera chanté dans toutes les Eglises de son Diocèse, en actions de grâces de l'heureux Accouchement de Madame La Dauphine, & de la Naissance d'un Duc de Bourgogne.* Paris: Claude Simon, 1751.

Beauvais, Jean-Baptiste-Charles-Marie de. *Panégyrique de Saint Louis . . .* Paris: veuve de Bernard Brunet, 1761.

Bellarmine, Robert. *De Officio Principis Christiani . . .* Cologne: Ioannem Kinchium, 1619.

Béraud, abbé. *Panégyrique de S. Louis . . .* Paris: Firmin Didot, 1823.

Bernard, P. *Panégyrique de Saint Louis . . .* Paris: Chaubert et Herissant, 1756.

Bernard, Pierre and Pierre Soulier. *L'Explication de l'édit de Nantes . . .* Paris: A. Dezallier, 1683.

Bérulle, Pierre de. *Œuvres . . .* Paris: Antoine Estiene and Sebastien Hure, 1644.

Billiard, M. *Panégyrique de saint Louis . . .* Paris: Jean-Baptiste Coignard, 1736.

Binet, Estienne. *Recueil des oeuvres spirituelles . . .*, 2nd edn. Rouen: Richard l'Allemant, 1627.

Bion, abbé. *Panégyrique de saint Louis . . .* Paris: Jean-Baptiste Coignard, 1715.

Le Blanc, Louis. *La sainte vie, et les hauts faits de Monseigneur saint Louis . . .* Paris: Robert Ballard, 1666.

Blois, Théodore de. *Histoire de Rochefort . . .* Paris: Briasson, 1733.

Boismont, Nicolas Thyrel de. *Panégyrique de Saint Louis . . .* Paris: Bernard Brunet, 1750.

Boizard, Jean. *Traité des monoyes, de leurs circonstances & dépendances.* Paris: veuve Jean-Baptiste Coignard and Jean-Baptiste Coignard, 1692.

Bon, abbé. *Panégyrique de Saint Louis . . .* Paris: Brunet, 1753.

Bonnécamp, Nicolas de. *Sonnets . . .* Vennes: Guillaume le Sieur, 1687.

Bouchard, Jean-Jacques. *Sermon Panegyrique sur Saint Louis* . . . Rome: Ioseph Lune, 1640.

Boucher, Jean. *Sermons de la simulée conversion, et nullité de la pretendue absolution de Henry de Bourbon* . . . Paris: G. Chavdiere, R. Nicelle & R. Thierry, 1594.

Boulogne, Étienne-Antoine de. *Panégyrique de Saint Louis* . . . Paris: Merigot le jeune, 1782.

Boulogne, Étienne-Antoine de. *Panégyrique de Saint-Louis, roi de France, prononcé devant les deux Académies Royales des Belles-Lettres et des Sciences, en 1782* . . . Paris: Adrien le Clere, 1814.

Bouquet au Roy, pour le jour de saint Louis de la presente année 1726. Paris: V[euve] de Nicolas Oudot, 1726.

Le Bouquet de la Saint Louis. s.l.: s.p., s.d.

Bouquet de la St. Louis, intermède, en un acte et en prose, mêlée de chants et de danse. Représenté, pour la premiere fois, sur le Théâre des Variétés, à Bordeaux, ce 24 Août 1785, par un Amateur de cette Ville. Bordeaux: J.B. Séjourné, 1785.

Bourlet de Vauxcelles, Simon-Jérôme. *Panégyrique de Saint Louis* . . . Paris: V[euve] Bernard Brunet, 1762.

Le Bret, Cardin. *De la Souveraineté du Roy* . . . Paris: Toussaincts du Bray, 1632.

Bretagne, Antoine de. *Panégyrique de Saint Louys* . . . Rome: Iaques Dragondelli, 1674.

Brevet exclusif qui permet aux sieurs Guérin, Testard, & autres Artificiers, de faire & exécuter, pendant 12 ans, un Feu d'Artifice sur la Riviere de Seine, la veille de la Fête de S. Louis. Du dix-neuf May 1741. Paris: Le Breton, 1741.

Breviarium Parisiense . . . Paris: Apud Sebastianum & Gabrielem Cramoisy, Stephanum Richer, & Gabrielem Clopejav, 1640.

Breviarium Parisiense . . . Paris: Sumptibus suis ediderunt Bibliopolæ, 1736.

Brillon, Pierre-Jacques. *Dictionnaire des arrêts, ou Jurisprudence universelle des Parlemens de France* . . ., New edn, 6 vols. Paris: G. Cavelier, 1727.

Buisson, abbé du. *Panegyrique de saint Louis* . . . Paris: Jean-Baptiste Coignard, 1710.

Bury, Richard de. *Histoire de saint Louis* . . . Paris: veuve Desaint, 1775.

Cambacérès, abbé de. *Panégyrique de Saint Louis* . . . Paris: Dessain, 1768.

Cange, Charles du Fresne, sieur du (ed.). *Histoire de S. Louis* . . . Paris: Sebastien Mabre-Cramoisy, 1668.

Canons synodaux statuez par Reverend Père en Dieu Messire Ioachim Destaing Evesque de Clairmont . . . Clermont: Bertrand Durand, 1620.

Cantate chantée à Belfort en 1823, à l'occasion de la fête de Saint Louis. Belfort: J.P. Clerc, [1823].

Carrelet de Rosay, Pierre-Barthélemy. *Panégyrique de saint Louis* . . . Paris: Jean-Baptiste Coignard, 1735.

Castelli, Pierre-Paul. *Discours prononcé le jour de Saint-Louis* . . . Ajaccio: Marc Marchi, 1825.

Caussin, Nicolas. *La Cour Sainte* . . ., 3 vols. Paris: Denis Bechet, 1643.

Caussin, Nicolas. *La vie de Ste. Isabelle Soeur du roy Saint Louis* . . . Paris: Claude Sonnius, Denis Bechet & Iean du Bray, 1644.

Les ceremonies faictes dans la Nouvelle Chappelle du Chasteau de Bissestre, suivant l'Ordonnance de Monseigneur l'Archevesque de Paris, a l'Establissement de la Pieté & Charité du Roy, en la Commenderie de S. Louis, soubs la conduitte de Monseigneur l'Eminentissime Cardinal, Duc de Richelieu, Pair de France, le iour & Feste de Sainct Louis, le 25. Aoust 1634. Paris: Iean Brunet, 1634.

Chambre, Pierre Cureau de la. *Panégyrique de Saint Louis* . . . Paris: Gabriel Martin, 1681.

Charaud, abbé. *Panégyrique de saint Louis* . . . Paris: Jean-Baptiste Coignard, 1723.

Chéret, Louis-Nicolas. *Panégyrique de saint Louis* . . . Paris: Jean-Baptiste Coignard, 1718.

Choisy, François-Timoléon de. *La vie de Saint Louis* . . . Paris: Claude Barbin et Daniel Horthemels, 1689.

Ciceri, Paul César de. *Panégyrique de Saint Louis* . . . Paris: Jean-Baptiste Coignard, 1721.

Clermont-Tonnerre, Stanislas de. *Du 24 Août 1789. Réponse de Monsieur le Président de l'Assemblée nationale à la Députation de la Garde nationale de Versailles* . . . Versailles: Imprimerie Royale, 1789.

Collectio judiciorum de novis erroribus qui ab initio duodecimi seculi post Incarnationem Verbi, usque ad annum 1632. in Ecclesia proscripti sunt & notati . . ., vol. II. Paris: Apud Andream Cailleau, 1728.

Collection des mémoires relatifs à la Révolution Française, avec des notices sur leurs auteurs. Guerres des Vendéens et des Chouans contre la République Française, 6 vols. Paris: Baudouin Frères, 1824–7.

Collection des Procès-verbaux des Assemblées-générales du Clergé de France . . ., 8 vols. Paris: Guillaume Desprez, 1767–78.

Le Comte, P. *Paraphrase sur le Gaude Mater ecclesia, &c. pour la feste de Sainct Louys* . . . Paris: s.p., 1628.

La Conversion du seigneur de Moissac, sur la preuve des Miracles de Sainct Louys Roy de France . . . Paris and Toulouse: Pierre Quiesac, 1620.

Coupart, Antoine-Marie and Emmanuel-François Varez. *Un Trait de Bienfaisance, ou la Fête d'un Bon Maire, à-propos en un Acte, mêlé de couplets, à l'occasion de la Saint-Louis* . . . Paris: Duvernois, 1822.

Couplets en l'honneur de la fête de Sa Majesté Louis XVIII, chantés le 25 août 1816, aux Champs-Élysées, par Bobêche, Bouffon des fêtes de Gouvernement. Paris: L-E Herhan, 1816.

Le Cousturier, M. *Panégyrique de saint Louis* . . . Paris: G. F. Quillau, 1746.

Le Cousturier, Nicolas-Jérôme. *Panégyrique de Saint Louis* . . . Paris: veuve Regnard & Demonville, 1769.

Le Cren, abbé. *Panégyrique de Saint Louis* . . . Saint Brieuc: J. L. Mahé, 1765.

La Croix, Édouard sieur de. *Etat Present des Nations et Eglises Grecque, Armenienne, et Maronite en Turquie.* Paris: Pierre Herissant, 1695.

La Croix, Édouard sieur de. *Mémoires . . .*, 2 vols. Paris: veuve A. Cellier, 1684.

Déclaration des Français fidèles au roi, réunis sous les ordres de M. de Gaston, dans les Départemens de la Vendée, de Maine & Loire, & de la Loire inférieure, publiée par un Emigré français, qui vient de la recevoir dans une Lettre de M. de Gaston. Brussels: Chez Emm. Flon, 1793.

Declaration du Roy en interpretation de l'Edit du mois de Mars 1693 concernant la desunion des biens de l'Ordre de Notre-Dame de Montcarmel & de Saint Lazare. Donnée à Versailles le 15. Avril 1693. Paris: Estienne Michallet, 1693.

Declaration du Roy portant reglement pour l'hospital general de Toulouse. Toulouse: Jean Boude, 1687.

La Deffense de la Pragmatique de Saint Louis contre les erreurs du Commentaire que l'on y a fait & publié depuis peu de temps. s.l.: s.p., 1663.

Denuelle, Alexandre. *Fête de la Saint-Louis, 25 Août 1824. Hommage à S.A.R. Mademoiselle* and *Hommage à Son Altesse Royale M. le Duc d'Angoulême.* Paris: Jules Didot Ainé, 1824.

Description du concert et du feu d'artifice de la veille de S. Louis, aux Tuilleries . . . Paris: Guillaume Valleyre, 1719.

Description Historique de l'Edifice que les sieurs Guerin père & fils, Testard & Dodenard Artificiers du Roy, auront l'honneur de présenter pour Bouquet à Sa Majesté à la Fête de la Saint Louis 1741. Paris: Gonichon, 1741.

Dictionnaire portatif du commerce. Paris: Jean-Francois Bastien, 1777.

Discours de la Ioyeuse et Triomphante entrée de tres-haut, tres-puissant et tres magnanime Prince Henry IIII de ce nom, tres-Chrestien Roy de France & de Navarre, faicte en sa ville de Rouën . . . Rouen: Iean Crevel, 1596.

Discours Funèbre, sur la mort du Roi-Martyr Louis XVI, Prononcé le 21 Janvier 1816, par la Société Rhétoricienne de Commines. Lille: Veuve Dumortier, 1816.

Discours prononcé le 25 Août 1824, jour de la Saint-Louis, Fête du Roi, par un pasteur du culte protestant, du département du Haut-Rhin. Traduit de l'Allemand. Colmar: J.-H. Decker, 1824.

Discours prononcé dans l'église des Ménages, le jour de la célébration de la fête de Saint Louis . . . Paris: De Renaudière, 1819.

Discours prononcé le jour de Saint Louis, Fête de Sa Majesté Louis Dix-huit, par M. L........, Prêtre du Diocèse et de l'Arrondissement de Rouen. Rouen: Mégard, 1816.

Discours sur les triomphes qui ont esté faicts le 25, 26 & 27 Aoust 1613 dans la ville de Paris a l'honneur & loüange de la feste S. Louys . . . Lyon: Iean Poyet, 1613.

District des capucins de Saint-Louis de la Chaussée d'Antin. Rapport fait en l'Assemblée générale du 18 mars 1790 . . . Paris: Prault, 1790.

Dominique de Iesus Maria, F. *Les Poincts principaux* . . . Paris: Iean de Bordeaux, 1621.

Duchêne, François (ed.). *Historiæ Francorum Scriptores* . . ., vol. V. Paris: Sumptibus Sebastiani Cramoisy et Gabrielis Cramoisy, 1649.

Dulaurent, Joseph. *Discours a Monsieur le Prevôt des Marchands, & à Messieurs les Echevins de la Ville de Paris, pour les inviter à la Procession qui se fait tous les ans à la Chapelle des Thuileries le jour de S. Loüis* . . . Paris: Louis-Denis Delatour, 1732.

Du Mont, Henri. *Motets pour la Chapelle du Roy* . . . Paris: Christophe Ballard, 1686.

Dupleix, Scipion. *Histoire de Louis le Iuste* . . . Paris: Claude Sonnius, 1635.

Dupleix, Scipion. *Histoire Generale de France* . . ., 6th edn, 3 vols. Paris: Denys Bechet & Louis Billaine, 1658.

Dupont de Nemours, Pierre-Samuel. *Discours au Roi, à l'occasion de sa fête* . . . Paris: Baudouin, 1790.

Du Temps, Hugues. *Panégyrique de Saint Louis* . . . Paris: Demonville, 1781.

Edgeworth de Firmont, Henry Essex. *Memoirs* . . ., ed. C. Sneyd Edgeworth. London: Rowland Hunter, 1815.

Edit du Roy portant Creation et Institution d'un Ordre Militaire sous le Nom de S. Loüis . . . Paris: Guillaume Desprez, 1693.

Épitre semi-historique, pour la fête de Saint-Louis, à Stanislas-Xavier, roi de France; dédiée à la Garde Nationale de Versailles et de tous les Départements du Royaume, par Edmond de B.e, de la Garde Nationale à cheval. Versailles: J. Jacob, 1817.

Estor, abbé. *Panégyrique de Saint Louis* . . . Paris: veuve Jacques Langlois, 1694.

Eve, Clovis. *La vie, legende, et miracles du roy sainct Louys* . . . Paris: Clovis Eve, 1610.

Exercice de dévotion . . . Troyes: P. Garnier, [1758].

Explication du feu d'artifice, qui sera tiré dans le Jardin des Tuilleries, le jour de Saint Louis . . . Paris: veuve Le Febvre, 1721.

Fargès-Méricourt, P. J. *Description de la ville de Strasbourg* . . . Strasbourg: F.G. Levrault, 1825.

Fauchet, Claude. *Panégyrique de Saint Louis* . . . Paris: Dorez, 1774.

[Le Fèbvre de Saint-Marc, C. H. and A. de la Chassagne]. *Vie de Monsieur Pavillon, evêque d'Alet* . . . Saint Miel: [s.p.], 1738.

Félibien, Michel. *Histoire de l'abbaye royale de saint-Denys en France* . . . Paris: Frederic Leonard, 1706.

Les Festes qui se doivent chommer dans le Diocese de Saintes . . . Saintes: Estienne Bichon, 1667.

Fête de Sa Majesté Louis XVIII, le 25 Août dix-huit cent seize. Cambrai: Defrémery-Dehollain, 1816.

Fête de la Saint-Louis, Quatrième réunion. 24 Août 1818. s.l.: s.p., [1818].

Fête de Saint Louis, 25 Août 1824. Onzième Banquet. 5e Légion de la Garde Nationale. Paris: Pillet ainé, 1824.

Fête de S.M. Charles Dix, célébrée par la Douzième Légion de la Garde Nationale. Paris: Lebègue, 1824.

La fête du Louisée, 25 Août 1789 . . . [Le Havre]: s.p., 1789.

Filère, Joseph. *La Devotion à S. Louys pour honnorer ses Merites* . . . Lyon: Philippe Borde, 1641.

Filère, Joseph. *Le parfait Prince Chretien, Saint Louys, et l'obligation des François à honorer ses merites* . . . Lyon: Iacques Canier, 1654.

[Filleau de la Chaise, Nicolas]. *Histoire de S. Louis* . . ., 2 vols. Paris: Jean Baptiste Coignard, 1688.

Fléchier, Esprit. *Œuvres complettes* . . ., 10 vols. Nîmes: Pierre Beaume, 1782.

Forget, Louis. *Le Monarque sainct et glorieux, ou les Vertus et les Triomphes de Sainct Louis*. Tours: Iacques Poinsot, 1645.

Garde Nationale de Paris, Cinquième Légion. Fête de la Saint-Louis. Paris: Éverat, 1822.

Le Garde Nationale, ou la Fête d'un Bon Roi, Vaudeville en un acte, joué à l'orangerie de la Pépinière, dans la fête donnée par M. de Comte de Castéja, Préfet du Haut-Rhin, à l'occasion de la Saint-Louis . . . Colmar: J.H. Decker, 1816.

Gayet de Sansale, Antoine-Auguste-Lambert. *Panégyrique de Saint Louis* . . . Paris: Cuissar, Librarie, 1767.

Gery, M. de. *Panégyrique de saint Louis* . . . Châlons: Seneuze, 1777.

Gouneaud, Cyrille. *Discours prononcé à Messieurs les Prevôt des Marchands & Échevins de la Ville de Paris en 1735. Pour les inviter à la Procession qui se fait tous ans au Louvre le jour de Saint Loüis* . . . [Paris]: [s.p.], [1735].

Griffet, Henri. *Panégyrique de saint Louis* . . . Paris: Jean-Baptiste Coignard, 1743.

Guichon, Cl. *Panégyrique de saint Louis* . . . s.l.: s.p., 1727.

Guillard, Nicolas-François and François-Guillaume-Jean-Stanislas Andrieux. *Louis IX en Égypte, Opéra en Trois actes* . . . Avignon: Jacques Garrignan, 1790.

Guillon, Marie-Nicolas-Silvestre. *Panégyrique de S. Louis* . . . Paris: Firmin Didot, 1818.

Guyard, Bernard. *Oraison funèbre prononcée à Paris en l'église de la Magdelaine au service de Louis le Iuste* . . . Paris: Arnould Cotinet, 1643.

Guyot, Guillaume-Germain. *Panégyrique de Saint Louis* . . . Paris: Bernard Brunet, 1758.

Hangard, Denis. *Dionysii Hangardi, doctoris theologi, Parisiensis, Cameracensis diocoesis, de divi Ludovici laudibus, oratio* . . . Paris: Ioannis d'Ongoys, 1575.

Henri-Quatre Second. Couplets pour la Fête de S.M. Charles X. Paris: Ballard, 1827.

Hersent, Charles. *L'empire de Dieu dans les saincts, ou bien l'éloge de sainct Louis roy de France, prononcé à Rome le iour de sa Feste* . . . Rome: Mascardy, 1651.

L'Hospital general de Paris. Paris: François Muguet, 1676.

Houdry, Vincent. *La Bibliotheque des Prédicateurs. Troisième Partie. Contenant des materiaux pour les Panegyriques de quelques Saints que l'on prêche plus ordinairement. Tome Troisième. Suite des Materiaux pour les Fêtes de quelques Saints* . . . Lyon: Les Frères Bruyset, 1781.

Hus, Auguste. *Bouquet de Pensées Bourbonniennes pour la S^t. Charles, Fête de S.M. Charles X* . . . Paris: Beauchamp, 1826.

Jarry, Laurent Juillard du. *Panegyrique de S. Louis* . . . Paris: Jean Villette and Daniel Horthemels, 1689.

Joinville, Jean de. *Histoire de saint Louis* . . . Paris: A. Désuages, 1826.

Joinville, Jean de. *Histoire de saint Louis* . . . *édition dédiée à la jeunesse française par M. Paul Gervais.* Paris: Gervais, 1822.

Joinville, Jean de. *Histoire de St Louis.* Paris: Foucault, 1819.

[Joly, Claude]. *Recueil de Maximes Veritables et Importantes pour l'institution du Roy. Contre la fausse & pernicieuse Politique du Cardinal Mazarin* . . . Paris: [s.p.], 1653.

Joly, Guy. *Memoirs of Guy Joli, Counsellor of the Châtelet, Private Secretary to Cardinal de Retz; Claude Joli, Canon of Notre-Dame; and the Dutchess de Nemours* . . ., trans. Edward Taylor, 3 vols. London: T Davies, 1775.

Josset, abbé. *Compliment, fait à la Reine, par Mr. l'Abbé Josset, Chanoine de la Cathédrale de Metz, lorsqu'il a prononcé devant Sa Majesté le Panégyrique de Saint Louïs* . . . Metz: Jean Antoine, [1744].

Josset, abbé. *Panégyrique de saint Louis* . . . Paris: Jean-Baptiste Coignard, 1747.

Journu, M. *Éloge de Saint Louis* . . . Bordeaux: Raymond Labottiere, 1743.

Labouderie, Jean. *Panégyrique de Saint Louis* . . . Paris: Rignoux, 1824.

Lambert, abbé. *Panégyrique de Saint Louis* . . . Lyon and Paris: [s.p.], [s.d.].

Laquille, Père. *La Saint-Louis aux Invalides, 25 Août 1824.* Paris: veuve Porthmann, 1824.

Laurent, F. *Le palais de l'amour divin entre Iesus et l'ame Chrestienne* . . ., vol. I. Paris: Denys de la Noüe et Charles Chastellan, 1614.

L'Ecclésiastique citoyen, ou lettres sur les moyens de rendre les personnes, les établissemens & les biens de l'Eglise encore plus utiles à l'Etat & même à la Religion. Paris: s.p., 1787.

L'Ecluse Desloges, Pierre-Mathurin de. *Panégyrique de saint Louis* . . . Paris: G. F. Quillau, 1744.

Lefèvre d'Ormesson, F. Nicolas. *Panégyrique de saint Louis. Au Roy.* s.l.: s.p., s.d.

L'entrée triomphante de Leurs Maiestez Louis XIV. Roy de France et de Navarre, et Marie Therese d'Austriche son espouse, dans la ville de Paris . . . Paris: Pierre le Petit, Thomas Ioly, Louis Bilaine, 1662.

Leon de Saint Ian. *Saint Louys, le Snt. des Roys, & le Roy des Saints. Sermon Panegyrique* . . . Rome: Bernardin Tani, 1648.

Létour, Theophile. *Panegyrique de saint Louis* . . . Paris: C.L. Thiboust, 1730.

La lettre de Sainct Louys Roy de France addressée à son fils aisné Philippe le Bel [sic] . . . Paris: Sebastien Lescuyer, 1617.

Lettres patentes de confirmation d'establissement de la Maison de saint Loüis, establie à saint Cyr . . . Paris: veuve de François Muguet, Hubert Muguet, & Louis Denis de la Tour, 1719.

Lettres patentes du roy, portant établissement d'un Hôpital pour les Enfans trouvez de la ville de Bordeaux . . . Bordeaux: Guillaume Boudé-Boé, [1714].

Lettres-patentes du roi, qui confirment des Mandemens par lesquels les Evêques de Toul, de Saint-Dié & de Nancy, ont réduit le nombre des Fêtes dans leurs Diocèses . . . Nancy: veuve Charlot, 1781.

Lettres-patentes du roi, sur un Mandement de M. l'Archevêque de Trêves, qui supprime plusieurs Fêtes, & règle celles qui seront chômées à l'avenir dans son Diocèse . . . Nancy: veuve Charlot, 1773.

Lettres patentes portant confirmation d'un Mandement de M. l'Evêque du Mans, pour suppression de Fêtes. Paris: P.G. Simon, 1782.

Lezeau, Simon-François de. *Panégyrique de saint Louis* . . . Paris: veuve Knapen, 1735.

Lopis de la Fare, abbé de. *Panégyrique de saint Louis* . . . Paris: Jean-Baptiste Coignard, 1709.

Loret, Jean. *La Muze Historique* . . ., 16 vols. Paris: Charles Chenault, 1650–65.

Louis IX, roi de France, captive en Egypte, tragédie en latin . . . Dijon: P. de Saint, [1746].

Louise de France. *Méditations eucharistiques* . . . Lyon: Théodore Pitraut, 1810.

Maimbourg, Louis. *Les Histoires du sieur Maimbourg, cy-devant Jesuite*, 12 vols. Paris: Sebastien Mabre-Cramoisy, 1686.

Mairie de Valenciennes. Fête de Saint Louis, du 25 Août 1816. Valenciennes: J.B. Henry, 1816.

Mairie d'Orléans. Fête de Saint-Louis. Orléans: Rouzeau-Montant, 1822.

Mandar, Jean-François. *Panégyrique de S. Louis* . . . Paris: Lottin et Onfroy, 1774.

Mandement de Monseigneur l'archevêque de Paris portant suppression de quelques Fêtes. Paris: Cl. Simon, 1778.

Mandement de Monseigneur l'archevêque de Rouen, Primat de Normandie, portant suppression de quelques fêtes. Rouen: J.J. Le Boullenger, 1767.

Mandement de Monseigneur l'archevêque de Tours, concernant les fêtes. Tours: L.M.F. Legier, 1781.

Mandement de Monseigneur l'evêque comte de Noyon, pair de France, et lettres patentes enregistrées au Parlement, pour la Réduction des Fêtes. s.l.: s.p., 1705.

Mandement de Monseigneur l'évêque de Boulogne, portant suppression de plusieurs Fêtes de son Diocese. Boulogne: Ch. Battut, 1778.

Mandement de Monseigneur l'évêque d'Évreux, portant suppression de quelques festes. Évreux: veuve Malassis, 1775.

Mandement de Monsieur l'évêque de Poitiers, portant suppression de plusieurs Fêtes, & de quelques Jeûnes. Poitiers: Jean-Felix Faulcon, 1766.

Mandement de Nosseigneurs les archevêque et évêques de la province ecclésiastique de Tours, concernant les fêtes. Vannes: veuve de Jean-Nicolas Galles, 1781.

Mandement de Son Altesse Monseigneur l'Eveque de Basle, pour la suppression d'un certain nombre de Fêtes . . . Basel: s.p., 1773.

Manuale Bellovacense. s.l.: s.p., s.d. [1637?].

Manuel, Louis-Pierre. *Coup d'œil philosophique sur le règne de Saint-Louis*. Damietta [Paris]: Chez les Marchands qui vendent les Nouveautés, 1788.

Manuel pour les ecclésiastiques du diocese de Belley . . . Saint-Claude: Pierre Delhorme, 1759.

La Mare, Nicolas de. *Traité de la Police* . . ., 4 vols. Paris: J. et P. Cot/M. Brunet/J.-F. Hérissant, 1705–38.

Marquet de Villefonds, M. *Panégyrique de saint Louis* . . . Paris: Jean-Baptiste Coignard, 1738.

Massillon, Jean-Baptiste. *Œuvres* . . ., 13 vols. Paris: Raymond, 1821.

Matthieu, Pierre. *Histoire de sainct Louys* . . . Paris: Bértrand Martin, 1618.

Maury, Jean-Sifrain. *Panégyrique de Saint Louis* . . . Paris: Le Jay, 1772.

Melot, Anicet, abbé Sallier and Jean Capperonier (eds). *Histoire de saint Louis, par Jehan sire de Joinville* . . . Paris: Imprimerie Royale, 1761.

Ménard, Claude (ed.). *Histoire de S. Loys IX. du nom, Roy de France. Par Messire Iean Sire de Ionville* . . . Paris: Sebastien Cramoisy, 1617.

Ménard, Claude (ed.). *Sancti Ludovici Francorum Regis, vita, conversatio, et miracula* . . . Paris: Sumptibus Sebastiani Cramoisy, 1617.

Ménestrier, Casimir and P. Ledoux. *La statue de Henri IV. nouveau Pont-Neuf* . . . Paris: Pillet, 1818.

Merle, Jean-Toussaint, Antoine Jean-Baptiste Simonnin and Ferdinand Laloue. *La St-Louis des Artistes, ou La Fête du Salon, vaudeville en un acte, en l'honneur de la Fête du Roi . . . . Paris: Pollet, 1824.*

Merle, Jean-Toussaint, Nicolas Brazier and Michel-Nicolas Balisson de Rougemont. *La Saint-Louis Villageoise, Comédie en un acte . . . Paris: J.N. Barba, 1816.*

Mézeray, François Eudes de. *Histoire de France...*, 3 vols. Paris: Mathieu Guillemont, 1643–51.

Michaud, Joseph-François. *Histoire de Croisades, Quatrième Édition*, 5 vols. Paris: Michaud, 1825–9.

Millet, Simon-Germain. *Le Tresor sacré, ou inventaire des sainctes reliques et autres precieux ioyaux qui se voyent en l'Eglise, & au Tresor de l'Abbaye Royale de S. Denis en France . . .*, 4th edn. Paris: Jean Billaine, 1645.

Molinier, Étienne. *Panegyrique du Roy S. Louys . . .* Paris: René Gissart, 1618.

Mongin, Edme. *Panégyrique de Saint Louis . . .* Paris: Jean Baptiste Coignard, 1701.

Montagu, Henri de. *La decente généalogique depuis St Louys de la royale maison de Bourbon . . .* Paris: Claude Rigaud, 1609.

Montelet, abbé de. *Panégyrique de Saint Louis . . .* Paris: Edme Couterot, 1691.

Montès, Jean-François. *Panégyrique de Saint-Louis . . .* [Paris]: s.p., [1819].

Montjoye, Galart de. *L'ami du roi, des François, de l'ordre et sur-tout de la vérité, ou Histoire de la Révolution de France . . .* Paris: Crapart, 1791.

Motet chanté le jour de S. Louis, dans l'église de l'Oratoire . . . Paris: Christophe Ballard, 1707.

Le Moyne, Pierre. *Œuvres poetiques . . .* Paris: Thomas Jolly, 1671.

Le Moyne, Pierre. *La Devotion aisée*, 2nd edn. Paris: Iacques Cottin, 1668.

Le Moyne, Pierre. *Poesies . . .* Paris: Augustin Courbé, 1651.

Le Moyne, Pierre. *Saint Louis, poëme héroique et chrétien, publié par E.-T. Simon, . . . suivi de deux odes du même auteur.* Paris: Brunot-Labbé, 1816.

Le Moyne, Pierre. *Saint Louys, ou le Heros Chrestien . . .* Paris: Charles du Mesnil, 1653.

Mysteria politica... Naples: s.p., 1625.

Necker, Jacques. *De la Révolution française*, 4 vols. Paris: Drisonnier, V [1797].

Nevers, Louis de Gonzague, duc de. *Mémoires . . .*, 2 vols. Paris: Thomas Iolly, 1665.

Nivers, Guillaume-Gabriel and Louis-Nicolas Clérambault. *Chants et motets a l'usage de l'Eglise et Communauté des Dames de la Royale Maison de St. Loüis a St. Cyr*, vol. I. Paris: Colin, 1733.

Nouvelet, Claude. *Hymne Trionfal au Roy, sus l'equitable iustice que sa Maiesté feit des rebelles la veille & iour de Sainct Loys . . .* Paris: Robert Granjon, 1572.

L'Office de l'église à l'usage du diocèse de Rouen . . ., 2 vols. Rouen: Imprimeurs de l'Archevêché, 1719.

L'Office de Saint Louis, Roy de France, à l'usage de la Chapelle du Roy à Versailles . . . Paris: G. Desprez, 1760.

L'Office de saint Louis roy de France et confesseur. A l'usage de Messieurs les Marchands Merciers, Grossiers, & Joüailliers de la Ville de Paris. Paris: veuve Chardon, 1711.

L'Office de Saint Louis roy de France et confesseur. A l'usage de Messieurs les Marchands Merciers, Grossiers, & Joüailliers de la Ville de Paris. Paris: J. Chardon, 1733.

L'Office de Saint Louis, Roy de France, et Confesseur. A l'usage de Messieurs les Marchands Merciers, Grossiers, & Jouailliers de la Ville de Paris. Paris: Jacques Chardon, 1749.

L'Office de S. Louis roy de France, et confesseur. Tant pour le jour de sa Fête que pour la Translation de son Chef . . . Paris: s.p., 1688.

L'Office de saint Louis, roi de France, le vingt-cinq Août; A l'usage de la maison de la Salpétrière de l'Hôpital-Général. Paris: veuve Thiboust, 1767.

L'Office de saint Louis, roi de France, pour le jour et l'octave de sa feste, en Latin et en François, à l'usage de l'église paroissiale de saint Louis de l'Hotel Royal des Invalides . . . Paris: J.B. Herissant, 1742.

Office de saint Louis roi de France, pour le jour, l'octave de sa feste, et pour la Translation de son Chef, suivant l'usage de Paris . . . Paris: Jacques Villery, 1697.

Offices divins, à l'usage des dames et demoiselles de la maison de Saint Louis à Saint Cyr. Paris: Gissey, 1754.

Ordonnance . . . *concernant les droits à percevoir par la Nation françoise à Lisbonne, relativement à l'administration de l'église et confrairie nationale de Saint-Louis.* Paris: Imprimerie royale, 1782.

Ordonnance de Monseigneur l'evêque de Metz, pour la Fixation des Fêtes qui se célébreront dorénavant dans le Diocese. Metz: Dominique Antoine, 1744.

Ordonnance de Monseigneur l'Evesque d'Angers touchant les Festes. Angers: Olivier Avril, 1693.

Ordonnance de Monseigneur l'evesque de Luçon, touchant les festes qui doivent estre observées dans son Diocese. La Rochelle: Bathelemy Blanchet, 1668.

Ordonnance de Monsieur le Prevost de Paris ou son Lieutenant de Police; Portant tres-expresses deffenses, sous les peines portées par les Ordonnances, à tous Marchands & Artisans de cette Ville, Prevosté & Vicomté de Paris, d'ouvrir leurs boutiques & magazins, & de faire aucun commerce & debit de marchandises les Dimanches & autres jours de Festes de Commandement . . . Paris: Imprimeurs & Libraires ordinaires du Roy, 1667.

Ordonnance de police qui renouvelle les deffenses de vendre ni étaller aucunes Marchandises sur les Ponts, Quais, Trotoirs & sous les Portes de la Ville de Paris les Festes & Dimanches . . . Paris: P.J. Mariette, 1731.

Ordonnances de Monseigneur l'evesque de Perigueux faictes en son premier synode tenu le 13.14. & 15. d'Avil dans son Eglise Cathedrale. Périgueux: P. Dalvy, 1649.

Ordonnances de Monseigneur l'Illustrissime et Reverendissime Leonor de Matignon, Evesque et Comte de Lisieux. Lisieux: Remy le Boullenger, 1696.

Ordonnances et Constitutions synodales, decrets, & reglements, donnez au dioceze de Bourdeaus . . . Bordeaux: Iac. Millanges & Cl. Mongiroud, 1621.

Ordonnances et constitutions synodales. Decrets & Reglemens, donnés au Dioceze de Bordeaux . . . Bordeaux: veuve de G. de la Court & N. de la Court, 1686.

Ordonnances et Constitutions Synodales pour le Diocese de Digne . . . Aix: Charles David, 1680.

Ordonnances et decrets synodaulx du dioceze de Maillezais . . . Fontenay le Comte: Pierre Petit, 1623.

Ordonnances et instructions synodales par Antoine Godeau, evesque de Grasse, & de Vence, 5th edn. Brussels: Lambart Marchant, 1672.

Ordonnances et Réglemens synodaux du diocèse de La Rochelle . . . Paris: P.G. Simon, 1780.

Ordonnances publiées au synode du diocese de Narbonne . . . Narbonne: Guillaume Besse, 1667.

Ordonnances synodales de Monseigneur l'Illustrissime & Reverendissime Evêque d'Autun. Autun: Antoine Chervau, 1706.

Ordonnances synodales de Monseigneur l'Illustrissime & Reverendissime Messire Louis-Joseph-Adheimar de Monteil de Grignan, evêque de Carcassonne . . . Toulouse: Claude-Gilles Lecamus, 1713.

Ordonnances synodales de Monseigneur l'Illustrissime et Reverendissime, Messire Michel Colbert eveque de Mascon. Mâcon: Simon Bonard, 1668.

Ordonnances Synodales d'Illustrissime et Reverendissime Père en Dieu Messire Iean de Lingendes Evesque de Mascon. Mâcon: Simon Bonard, [1659?].

Ordonnances synodales du diocése de Dijon. Dijon: Pierre de Saint, 1744.

Ordonnances synodales du diocèse de Fréjus . . . Paris: Cl. Simon, 1779.

Ordonnances synodales du diocèse de Grenoble . . . Paris: André Pralard, 1690.

Ordonnances synodales du diocese de Lavaur . . . Toulouse: Claude Gilles Licamus, 1729.

Ordonnances synodales du diocèse de S. Malo . . . St-Malo: Julien Valais, 1769.

Ordonnances synodales du diocèse de Soissons. Soissons: veuve de N. Hanisset, 1701.

Ordonnances synodales du diocèse de Toulouse . . . Toulouse: J. Boude, 1696.

Ordonnances Synodales du diocèse de Valence . . . Valence: J. Gilibert, 1728.

Ordonnances Synodales du diocèse de Vannes . . . Vannes: Jacques de Heuqueville, 1695.

Ordonnances synodalles du dioceze de Rodez . . . Rodez: Nicolas le Roux, 1674.

Ordonnances Synodalles du dioceze de Toulon . . . Toulon: veuve de Pierre-Louis Mallard, 1704.

Les Ordonnances synodales pour le diocese d'Aix . . . Aix: Charles David, 1672.

Ordonnances synodales pour le diocèse de Pamiers... Toulouse: veuve de J.J. Boude, 1702.

Ordonnances synodales pour le diocese d'Uzès . . . Montpellier: Daniel Pech, 1654.

Le Paige, Louis-Adrien. *Lettres historiques, sur les fonctions essentielles du Parlement . . .*, 2 vols. Amsterdam: Aux dépens de la Compagnie, 1753–4.

Panégyrique de Saint-Louis, prononcé dans la Cathédrale de Rennes, en présence de Mgr. l'Evêque et des Autorités constituées, le 25 août 1816, par M. A. D. L . . . Rennes: veuve Vatar et Bruté, 1816.

Panégyrique de saint Louis, prononcé dans l'église des RR. PP. Jésuites de la Maison Professe le 25. Août 1748. par Monseigneur l'évêque d'Olimpe. Paris: J.B. Coignard, 1748.

Les Panégyristes de saint Louis . . ., 2 vols. Paris: Mame Frères, 1814.

Paul V, Pope. *Bref de Nostre S. Père le Pape Paul V. pour la celebration de la feste de Sainct LOVYS iadis Roy de France, par tout ce Royaume. Avec le Mandement de Monseigneur l'Illustriβime & Reverendiβime Cardinal de Retz, Evesque de Paris.* Paris: François Iulliot, 1618.

Permission de monseigneur l'archevêque de Paris pour ériger une confrérie en l'honneur de saint Louis en l'église paroissiale de Saint-Gervais et de Saint-Protais, pour les maîtresses couturières de ladite ville et faubourgs de Paris (10 août 1677). [Paris]: s.p., [1677].

Perrin, Pierre. *Cantica pro Capella regis...* Paris: Robert Ballard, 1665.

Perussault, Sylvain. *Panégyrique de saint Louis . . .* Paris: Jean-Baptiste Coignard, 1737.

Petitot, Claude-Bernard (ed.). *Collection complete des mémoires relatifs à l'histoire de France . . .*, vol. III. Paris: Foucault, 1824.

Pézène, abbé de. *Panégyrique de Saint Louis . . .* Paris: veuve de Jean-Baptiste Coignard & Jean-Baptiste Coignard fils, 1690.

Piganiol de la Force, Jean-Aimar. *Nouvelle Description de la France . . .*, 3rd edn, vol. I. Paris: Theodore Legras, 1753.

Pinsson des Riolles, François. *Sancti Ludovici Francorum regis Christianissimi Pragmatica Sanctio, et in eam Historica Præfatio et commentarius . . .* Paris: Apud Franciscum Muguet, 1663.

Planchot, Guillaume. *Panégyrique de saint Louis . . .* Paris: Panckoucke, 1766.

Plantavit de La Pause, Guillaume. *Panégyrique de saint Louis . . .* Paris: Jean-Baptiste Coignard fils, 1728.

Pleuvri, Jacques-Olivier. *Panégyrique de Saint Louis . . .* Paris: Le Clerc, 1772.

Poncet de la Rivière. *Panégyrique de saint Louis . . .* Paris: Jean-Baptiste Coignard fils, 1734.

Poujol, M. *Élan d'un cœur Français. Cantate pour la Fête de Saint Louis.* Montpellier: J.-G. Tournel, 1816.

Poulle, Nicolas-Louis. *Panégyrique de saint Louis* . . . Paris: Jean-Baptiste Coignard, 1748.

Précis de ce qui s'est passé dans la Ville de Rheims, le 25 Août 1816, jour de Saint Louis, à l'occasion de la Fête de Sa Majesté . . . Reims: Le Batard, 1816.

Prevost, Jean. *Panégyrique de Saint Louis* . . . Paris: Jean-Baptiste Coignard, 1717.

Le Prévost, Pierre Robert. *Panégyrique de saint Louis* . . . Paris: Christophe Ballard, 1705.

Procès pour la succession d'Ambroise Guys; on y a joint les affaires des Jésuites de Liège, de Fontenay-le-Comte, de Châlons, de Muneau, de Brest, de Bruxelles, avec la prophétie de Georges Bronsuel. Brest: s.p., s.d.

Procès-Verbal et Relation de la Fête de Saint Louis, le 25 Aout 1816, à Morlaix. Morlaix: Guilmer, 1816.

Programme de l'Académie Royale des Sciences, Belles-Lettres et Arts de Bordeaux du 25 Août 1790. Bordeaux: Michel Rade, 1790.

Programme des Cérémonies, Fêtes et Réjouissances publiques et Municipales, qui auront lieu dans la Ville de Paris, le Vendredi 25 Août 1820, jour de la Saint-Louis. Paris: Gretschy, 1820.

Programme des Cérémonies, Fêtes et Réjouissances Publiques Municipales, qui auront lieu dans la ville de Paris, Dimanche prochain 25 Août, jour de la Fête de Sa Majesté. Paris: F.-P. Mardy, 1822.

Programme des Fêtes, Cérémonies et Réjouissances publiques municipales qui auront lieu dans la Ville de Paris le mardi 25 août 1818, jour de la Saint-Louis. Paris: J. Moronval, 1818.

Proyart, Liévin-Bonaventure. *Vie du Dauphin, père de Louis XVI* . . ., 5th edn. Lyon: Pierre Bruyset-Ponthus, 1788.

Les quatre premiers chants de la Louisiade, poême héroique, proposés aux amateurs. Avranches and Paris: Couturier, 1774.

Ragon, Jean-Baptiste. *Panégyrique de saint Louis* . . . Paris: Jean-Baptiste Coignard fils, 1730.

Recueil des actes, titres et mémoires concernant les affaires du clergé de France . . . Paris: Guillaume Desprez; Avignon: Jacques Garrigan, 1771.

Recueil des anciennes et nouvelles ordonnances du diocèse d'Oleron . . . Pau: Jerôme Dupoux, 1712.

Recueil des Harangues prononcées par Messieurs de l'Académie Françoise . . ., 2 vols. Amsterdam: Aux dépens de La Compagnie, 1709.

Recueil des Ordonnances Synodales du diocèse de Nismes . . . Nîmes: Jean Plasses, [1670?].

Recueil des Ordonnances Synodales du diocèse du Chalon . . . Lyon: Jean Certe, 1700.

Recueil des ordonnances synodales et autres, faites en divers temps par Nos seigneurs les Illustrissimes & Reverendissimes Archevesques de Tolose . . . Toulouse: veuve A.R. Colomiez, 1669.

Regnaud de Paris. *Bouquet adressé au Roi, pour le jour de sa fête* . . . Paris: Michaud, 1815.

Les Rejouissances du College de Clermont de la Compagnie de Jesus pour la Naißance de Monseigneur Duc de Bourgogne. Paris: s.p., 1682.

Relation curieuse et remarquable de la pompe royale du jour de la saint Louis . . . Paris: veuve Iean Remy, 1649.

Relation de la fête célébrée dans la Chapelle Royale de Messieurs les Pénitens Bleus de Toulouse, le 25 Août 1775 à l'occasion du Sacre & du Couronnement de Sa Majesté Louis XVI . . . Toulouse: Joseph Dalles, 1775.

Relation de ce qui s'est passé le 25 août 1776, & le Dimanche suivant, à la Fête des Mœurs établie à Saint Ferjeux près Besançon, en l'honneur de Louis XVI. Besançon: Lépagnez, [1776].

Relation du port de Saint Loüis au Cap de Sète en Languedoc . . . Pézenas: Jean Martel, 1666.

Relation d'une Fête donnée à Bar-le-Duc, le 25. Août 1757, en l'honneur du Roy. Bar-le-Duc: Richard Briflot, 1757.

Remonstrance de Sainct Louys faite à son Fils. s.l.: s.p., s.d.

Remonstrance d'un bon Catholique François, aux Trois estats de France, qui s'assembleront à Blois . . . s.l.: s.p., 1576.

Remonstrance salutaire aux rebelles de Montauban, & de la Rochelle, par les Eschevins iadis de S. Iean d'Angely, & à present nommé le Bourg S. Louys, sur leur desobeyssance & Resistance au Roy. Paris: Iean Chrestien, 1621.

Resnel du Bellay, Jean-François du. *Panégyrique de saint Louis* . . . Paris: Jean-Baptiste Coignard fils, 1732.

Richeome, Louis. *Consolation envoyée à la royne mere du roy* . . . Lyon: Pierre Rigaud, 1610.

Rituale Aurelianese . . . Orléans: Typis Mariae Paris, 1642.

Rituale Aurelianese... Orléans: Sumptibus Francisci Rouzeau, 1726.

Rituale Carnotense... Paris: Apud Iosephum Cottereau, 1640.

Rituel de la province de Reims . . . Paris: Frederic Leonard, 1677.

Rituel du diocèse d'Amiens . . . Amiens: Louis-Charles Caron père, 1784.

Rituel du diocèse de Blois . . . Blois: Philbert-Joseph Masson, 1730.

Rituel du diocèse de Bourges . . . Bourges: Jean-Baptiste Cristo, 1746.

Rituel du diocèse de Luçon . . . Luçon: Gibert, 1768.

Rituel du diocèse de Lyon . . . Lyon: Ailé de la Roche, 1788.

Rituel du diocèse de Meaux . . . Paris: Jean-Baptiste Coignard fils & Antoine Boudet, 1734.

Rituel du diocèse de Quebec . . . Paris: Simon Langlois, 1703.

Rituel du diocèse de Sens . . . Sens: Claude Auguste Prussurot & Laurent Raveneau, 1694.

Rituel Romain à l'usage de la Province ecclesiastique d'Auch. Paris: Antoine Dezallier, 1701.

Rituel Romain du Pape Paul V à l'usage du diocèse d'Alet, 3rd edn. Paris: Guillaume Desprez, 1677.

Robinet, Charles. *Le parfait victorieux, discours funebre sur la mort de Louis le Iuste.* Paris: Michel Brunet, 1643.

Rousselet, Georges-Étienne. *Le lys sacré, iustifiant le bon-heur de la pieté par divers Parangons du Lys avec les vertus, & les miracles du Roy S. Louys, & des autres Monarques de France* . . . Lyon: Louys Muguet, 1631.

Roy, Pierre-Charles. *Au Roy, le jour de Saint-Louis.* Paris: J-B-C. B[allard], 1722.

Les royalles vertus qui ont illustré la vie et le trespas de S. Louys Roy de France, & incitent les François de solemniser sa feste . . . Rouen: Abraham Cousturier, [s.d.].

Sacerdotale seu Manuale Ecclesiae Rothomagensis . . . Rouen: Apud Societatem Typographicam, 1640.

Sade, Donatien Alphonse François, marquis de. *Aline et Valcour, ou Le roman philosophique* . . . 4 vols. Paris: veuve Girouard, 1795.

Saint Jacques, R. P. de. *Panégyrique de saint Louis* . . . Paris: Barthelemi Girin, 1706.

Saint Louis à Louis XVI. Ode. Rennes: s.p., 1788.

La Saint-Louis, ou la Fête d'un Bon Roi, comédie en un acte . . . Marseilles: Antoine Ricard, 1816.

Saint-Martin, Guillaume de. *Panégyriques des saints* . . ., 2 vols. Paris: Edme Couterot, 1683–4.

Saint-Martin, Louis-Pierre de. *Les Établissemens de Saint Louis* . . . Paris: Nyon l'aîné, 1786.

Saint-Martin, Louis-Pierre de. *Panégyrique de Saint Louis* . . . Paris: Nyon l'aîné, 1785.

Saint Vincent, abbé de. *Panégyrique de saint Louis* . . . Paris: Jean-Baptiste Coignard, 1739.

Sales, François de. *Introduction à la vie dévote* . . . Paris: Imprimerie Royale, 1651.

Saluces-Boisseau, M. de. *Panégyrique de St. Louis* . . . s.l.: s.p., s.d.

Sandras, Gatien de Courtilz, sieur de [attrib.]. *L'Alcoran de Louis XIV* . . . Rome: Antonio Maurino Stampatore, 1695.

Sarcé, François de. *La vie du bien-heureux sainct Louys roy de France* . . . Paris: Toussainct du Bray, 1619.

Savaron, Jean. *Discours abregé, avec l'Ordonnance entiere du Roy sainct Loys, contre les duels* . . . Paris: Pierre Chevalier, 1614.

Savaron, Jean. *Traicté contre les duels* . . . Paris: Adrian Perier, 1610.

Savaron, Jean. *Traicté contre les duels. Avec les Ordonnances & Arrests du Roy Sainct Loys* . . . Paris: Pierre Chevalier, 1614.

Segui, Joseph. *Panégyrique de saint Louis* . . . Paris: Jean-Baptiste Coignard fils, 1730.

Senault, Jean-François. *Le Monarque, ou les Devoirs du Souverain* . . . Paris: Pierre le Petit, 1661.

Sicard, Roch-Ambroise (ed.). *Vie de Madame la Dauphine, mère de S.M. Louis XVIII* . . . Paris: Audot, 1817.

Siniscalchi, Liborio. *Panegirici sacri* . . ., 4th edn. Venice: Lorenzio Baseggio, 1769.

La source glorieuse du sang de l'auguste maison de Bourbon dans le coeur de saint Louis roy de France suiet de l'appareil funèbre pour l'inhumation du cœur de tres-haut, tres-puissant, tres-illustre et magnanime prince Louis de Bourbon, prince de Condé, premier Prince du sang. Paris: Estienne Michallet, 1687.

[Spinoza, Baruch]. *Tractatus theologico-politicus* . . . Hamburg [Amsterdam]: Apud Henricum Künrath [Jan Rieuwertsz], 1670.

Statuta diocesis Carnotensis. Chartres: Apud Jacobum Roux, 1742.

Statuta seu decreta synodalia Bisuntinæ Diocesis... Besançon: Apud Ludovicum Rigoine, 1680.

Statuta synodi Dioecesanæ Metensis... Metz: Apud Claudium Felix, 1629.

Statuts de l'hôpital saint Loüis . . . Bordeaux: Guillaume Boudé-Boé, 1721.

Statuts du diocese d'Angers. Angers: Olivier Avril, 1680.

Statuts du diocese de Saint Brieuc . . . Rennes: Pierre-André Garnier, 1723.

Statuts et Ordonnances faittes en diverses assemblées synodales . . . Langres: Iehan Chauvetet, 1629.

Statuts et Reglemens du diocese de Cahors . . . Paris: Denis Moreau, 1640.

Statuts et Reglements du Diocese de Limoges . . . Limoges: A. Barbou, 1629.

Statuts et Reglemens du diocese de Tulle . . . Tulle: Jean Seb. Dalvy, 1692.

Statuts et reglemens pour la communauté des Barbiers, Perruquiers, Baigneurs & Etuvistes de la Ville, Faubourgs & Banlieue de Paris . . . Paris: Valleyre, 1746.

Statuts et reglemens synodaux du diocése de Quimper . . ., 2nd edn. Quimper: Jean Perier, 1717.

Statuts sinodaux du diocèse d'Autun . . . Autun: Pierre Laymeré, 1715.

Statuts synodaux de nos seigneurs François Rouxel de Medavy, Philippes Cospean et Leonor de Matignon, Evesques et comtes de Lisieux . . . Caen: Pierre Poisson, [1651].

Statuts synodaux du diocese d'Alby . . . Albi: Jean & G. Pech, 1695.

Statuts synodaux du diocese d'Alet . . . Toulouse: Raymond Bosc, 1670.

Statuts synodaux du diocése de Boulogne. Boulogne: P. Battut, [1746].

Statuts synodaux du diocese de Comenges . . . Toulouse: N. Caranove, 1752.

Statuts synodaux du diocese de Rieux . . . Toulouse: Raimond Colomiez, 1624.

Statuts synodaux du diocese de Sisteron . . . Aix: Jean Adibert, 1711.

Status synodaux, ordonnances, et reglemens pour le diocèse de Troyes . . . Troyes: Charles Briden & Jaque Oudot, 1706.

Statuts synodaux, pour la diocese de Sainct Malo . . . Saint-Malo: Pierre Marcigay, 1620.

Statuts synodaux, publiés dans le Synode de 1702 . . . Vienne: Ant. Mazinier, 1730.

Suite des Triolets Royaux, sur ce qui s'est passé de plus remarquable depuis le retour de leurs Maiestez à Paris, tant le iour de la Feste de S. Louys qu'autres iours. Paris: Alexandre Lesselin, 1649.

Sully, Maximilien de Béthune de. *Mémoires* . . ., new edn, 8 vols. London: s.p., 1747.

Sylvester, Josuah. *Du Bartas his Divine Weekes* . . . London: Humphrey Lownes, 1621.

Talbert, François-Xavier. *Panégyrique de Saint Louis* . . . Paris: Demonville, 1779.

Talon, Omer. *Mémoires* . . ., 6 vols. The Hague: Gosse & Neaulme, 1732.

Théveneau, Adam. *Les Preceptes du Roy S. Louys a Philippes III* . . . Paris: Iean Petit-Pas, 1627.

Tour du Pin de La Charce, Jacques-François-René de la. *Panégyrique de saint Louis* . . . Paris: Brunet, 1751.

Le Triple Mariage, Comedie en un Acte et en Vers Libres, Analogue à la Fête du Roi . . . Bouillon: Imprimerie de la Société Typographique, 1774.

Les Triomphes du très-chretien roy de France et de Navarre, Louys le Juste, Digne Heritier & Successeur du Roy Sainct Louys. Paris: Nicolas Alexandre, 1618.

Urban VIII, Pope. *Bulle de Nostre S. Pere le pape Urbain VIII. contenant les Festes qui doivent estre gardées de commandement* . . . Paris: Sebastien Mabre-Cramoisy, 1646.

Vammalle, Antoine Brès de. *Panégyrique de S. Louis* . . . Paris: Desaint, 1766.

Varillas, Antoine. *La Minorité de Saint Louis* . . . La Haye: Adrian Moetjens, 1685.

Velly, Paul-François. *Histoire de France* . . ., 30 vols. Paris: Desaint & Saillant, 1755–86.

Vernon, Jean-Marie de. *Le Roy Très-Chrestien, ou la Vie de St Louis Roy de France* . . . Paris: George Iosse, 1662.

La Vicomterie, Louis. *Les crimes des rois de France, depuis Clovis jusqu'à Louis Seize*, new edn. Paris: Bureau des Révolutions de Paris, 1792.

Vigneras, abbé. *Discours sur l'Amour de la Patrie* . . . Paris: J.B.N. Crapart, 1790.

Vignier, Jacques. *La pratique de la paix de l'ame dans la vie de sainct Louis. Par un père de la Compagnie de Iesus.* Autun: Blaise Simonnot, 1642.

Vigor, Simon. *Sermons Catholiques* . . . Paris: veuve de Gabriel Buon, 1597.

Vitelly d'Orsal, J. P. *Le Bouquet de Saint-Louis, pour la Fête du Roi* . . . Paris: Beraud, 1816.

Vive le Roi! Couplet à l'occasion de la Saint-Charles, Fête de S.M. Charles X. Paris: Duverger, 1828.

La voix gemissante du peuple Chrestien et Catholique . . . Paris: s.p., 1640.

Voltaire, *La Henriade* . . . Geneva: [Cramer], 1768.

Voltaire, *La Pucelle d'Orléans*, new edn. London: s.p., 1780.

Les voyages de la nouvelle France occidentale, dicte Canada, faits par le Sr de Champlain Xainctongeois . . . Paris: Claude Collet, 1632.

Les voyages du sieur de Champlain, Xaintongeois, capitaine ordinaire pour le Roy en la marine . . . Paris: Iean Berjon, 1613.

La voye de laict, ou le chemin des heros au palais de la gloire, ouvert a l'entrée triomphante de Louys XIII. Roy de France & de Navarre en la Cité d'Avignon le 16. de Novembre 1622 . . . Avignon: I. Bramereau, 1623.

Primary sources printed after 1830

Agnes of Harcourt. *The Writings of Agnes of Harcourt: The Life of Isabelle of France & the Letter on Louis IX and Longchamp*, ed. Sean Field. Notre Dame: University of Notre Dame Press, 2003.

Archives Parlementaires de 1787 à 1860 . . ., 96 vols. Paris: Dupont, 1867–1990.

Bentivoglio, Guido. *La nunziatura di Francia...*, ed. L. de Steffani, vol. II. Florence: Felice le Monnier, 1865.

Bertaut, Jean. *Œuvres Poetiques* . . ., ed. Adolphe Chenevière. Millwood: Kraus Reprint & Co., 1982.

Bossuet, Jacques-Bénigne. *Œuvres*, 4 vols. Paris: Firmin Didot frères, 1866–70.

Bossuet, Jacques-Bénigne. *Politics drawn from the Very Words of Holy Scripture*, ed. Patrick Riley. Cambridge: Cambridge University Press, 1990.

Cahiers de Doléances de la Sénéchaussée de Montauban et du Pays et Jugerie de Rivière-Verdun pour les États Généraux de 1789, ed. Victor Malrieu. Montauban: Barrier, 1925.

Cahiers de Doléances du bailliage de Contentin (Coutances et secondaires) pour les États Généraux de 1789, ed. Emile Bridrey. Paris: Imprimerie Nationale, 1908.

Cahiers du Bailliage d'Arques (Secondaire de Caudebec) pour les États Généraux de 1789, ed. E. Le Parquier. Lille: Camille Robbe, 1922.

Calvin, Jean. *Traité des reliques* . . ., ed. Albert Autin. Paris: Bossard, 1921.

Castellane, Esprit Victor Élisabeth Boniface comte de. *Journal du Maréchal de Castellane, 1804–1862*, 5 vols. Paris: E. Plon, Nourrit et Cie, 1895–7.

Chapelain, Jean. *Lettres*, ed. Ph. Tamizey de Larroque, 2 vols. Paris: Imprimerie Nationale, 1880–83.

Charpentier, Marc-Antoine. *Œuvres complètes, I: Meslanges autographes*, ed. H. Wiley Hitchcock, 28 vols. Paris: Minkoff, 1990–2004.

Chateaubriand, François-René de. *Œuvres complètes* . . ., 5 vols. Paris: Firmin Didot frères, 1839–40.

Chateaubriand, François-René de. *Itinéraire de Paris à Jérusalem et de Jérusalem à Paris*. Paris: Bernardin-Béchet, 1867.

Chateaubriand, François-René de. *Le Génie du Christianisme*, 2 vols. Paris: Firmin Didot frères, 1847.

Chouteau, Auguste. 'Narrative of the Settlement of St. Louis'. In *Seeking St. Louis; Voices from a River City, 1670–2000*, ed. Lee Ann Sandweiss, 13–19. Saint Louis: Missouri Historical Society Press, 2000.

Colbert, Jean-Baptiste. *Lettres, instructions et mémoires*, ed. Pierre Clément, 9 vols. Paris: Imprimerie impériale, 1861–73.

Comptes des Bâtiments du Roi sous le règne de Louis XIV, 4 vols. Paris: Imprimerie Nationale, 1881.

La Conquête d'Alger en 1830. Poëme en trois chants par un jeune Breton. Paris: Dentu, 1832.

Corneille, Pierre. *Œuvres*, ed. M. Ch. Marty-Laveaux, 12 vols. Paris: Hachette, 1862–8.

Les Élections et les Cahiers de Paris en 1789, ed. C. H.-L. Chassin, 3 vols. Paris: Jouaust et Sigaux, Charles Noblet, 1889.

Enghien, Louis-Antoine-Henri de Bourbon, duc d'. *Correspondance du duc d'Enghien (1801–1804) et documents sur son enlèvement et sa mort*, ed. Comte Boulay de la Meurthe, 4 vols. Paris: Alphonse Picard et fils, 1904–13.

L'Estoile, Pierre de. *Registre-Journal du règne de Henri III*, eds Madeleine Lazard and Gilbert Schrenck, 6 vols. Geneva: Droz, 1992–2003.

Estrées, François-Annibal, maréchal d'. *Mémoires* . . ., ed. Paul Bonnefon. Paris: Renouard, 1910.

Fénelon, François de. *Œuvres*, ed. Jacques Le Brun, 2 vols. Paris: Gallimard, 1983.

Flammermont, Jules (ed.). *Remontrances du Parlement de Paris au XVIIIe siècle*, 3 vols. Paris: Imprimerie Nationale, 1888–1898.

Fleury, André-Hercule. *L'Abrégé de l'Histoire de France écrit pour le jeune Louis XV*, ed. Chantal Grell. Bonnières-sur-Seine: Archives départementales des Yvelines, 2004.

Gaposchkin, Cecilia (ed.). *Blessed Louis, the most glorious of kings: Texts relating to the Cult of Saint Louis of France*, translations with Phyllis Katz. Notre Dame: University of Notre Dame Press, 2012.

Gaposchkin, Cecilia and Sean Field (eds). *The Sanctity of Louis IX: Early Lives of Saint Louis by Geoffrey of Beaulieu and William of Chartres*, trans. Larry Field. Ithaca and London: Cornell University Press, 2014.

Gaudreau, Louis. *Panegyrique de Saint Louis, prêché dans l'église de Saint-Germain-l'Auxerrois, en présence de l'Académie Française, le 25 Aout 1829* . . . Paris: F. Malteste, 1854.

Graffigny, Françoise de. *Correspondance de Madame de Graffigny*, ed. J. A. Dainard inter al., 14 vols. Oxford: Alden Press, 1985-.

Henri IV. *Recueil des lettres* . . ., ed. M. Berger de Xivrey, 9 vols. Paris: Imprimerie Royale/Impériale, 1843–76.

Hérouval, Antoine Vyon d'. 'Notes de Vyon d'Hérouval sur les baptisés et les convers et sur les enquêteurs royaux au temps de saint Louis et de ses successeurs (1234-1334)', ed. Alexandre Bruel. *Bibliothèque de l'école des chartes*, 28 (1867): 609–21.

Joinville, Jean de and Geoffroy de Villehardouin. *Chronicles of the Crusades*, trans. M. R. B. Shaw. London: Penguin, 1963.

Journal de santé de Louis XIV, ed. Stanis Perez. Grenoble: Jérôme Millon, 2004.

Lefèvre d'Ormesson, Olivier. *Journal d'Olivier Lefèvre d'Ormesson, et extraits des mémoires d'André Lefèvre d'Ormesson*, ed. M. Chéruel, 2 vols. Paris: Imprimerie Impériale, 1860–1.

Leibniz, Gottfried Willhelm. *Œuvres* . . ., ed. A. Foucher de Careil, 7 vols. Paris: Firmin Didot frères, 1859–75.

Lindet, Jean-Baptiste Robert. *Correspondance politique de brumaire an IV à 1823*, ed. François Pascal. Paris: SPM, 2011.

Louis XIV. *Mémoires for the Instruction of the Dauphin*, ed. Paul Sonnino. London: Collier-Macmillan, 1970.

Louis XIV. *Mémoires; suivis de, Manière de visiter les jardins de Versailles*, ed. Joël Cornette. Paris: Tallandier, 2007.

Marais, Mathieu. *Journal de Paris*, eds Henri Duranton and Robert Granderoute, 2 vols. Saint-Étienne: Université de Saint-Étienne, 2004.

Médicis, Catherine de. *Lettres*, ed. le Cte Baguenault de Puchesse, 9 vols. Paris: Imprimerie Nationale, 1905.

Mercier, Louis Sébastien. *Tableau de Paris*, ed. Jean-Claude Bonnet, 2 vols. Paris: Mercure de France, 1994.

Procès-verbaux des États Généraux de 1593, ed. Auguste Bernard. Paris: Imprimerie Royale, 1842.

Rameau, Jean-Philippe. *Cantate pour le jour de la saint Louis*, introd. Mary Cyr. Bias: Edition Opéra de Guyenne, 1985.

Ranuzzi, Angelo. *Correspondance* . . ., ed. Bruno Neveu, 2 vols. Rome: École Française de Rome and Université Pontificale Grégorienne, 1973.

Rapin, Nicolas. *Œuvres*, ed. Jean Brunel, 3 vols. Paris and Geneva: Droz, 1982.

Rapin, René. *Mémoires* . . ., ed. Léon Aubineau, 3 vols. Paris: Gaum Frères et J. Duprey, 1865.

Les Registres de l'Académie Françoise, 1672–1793, 4 vols. Paris: Firmin-Didot, 1895–1906.

Reiset, Marie-Antoine de. *Souvenirs du Lieutenant Général Vicomte de Reiset, 1814–1836*, 3 vols. Paris: L.G. Michaud, 1900–2.

Relations des Jésuites contenant ce qui s'est passé de plus remarquable dans les Missions des Pères de la Compagnie de Jésus dans la Nouvelle-France, 3 vols. Quebec: Augustin Coté, 1858.

Retz, Jean-François-Paul de Gondi, cardinal de. *Œuvres . . .*, 9 vols. Paris: Hachette, 1870–87.

[Rogue, Nicolas-Pierre-Christophe]. *Souvenirs et journal d'un bourgeois d'Évreux, 1740–1830*. Évreux: A. Hérissey, 1850.

Saint-Simon, Louis de Rouvroy duc de. *Mémoires*, ed. A. de Boislisle, 45 vols. Paris: Hachette, 1879–1931.

Sales, François de. *Œuvres . . .*, 10 vols. Annecy: J. Niérat, 1892–1910.

Sévigné, Marie de Rabutin Chantal, marquise de. *Correspondance*, ed. Roger Duchêne, 3 vols. Paris: Gallimard, 1978.

Sourches, Louis-François du Bouschet, marquis de. *Mémoires . . .*, 13 vols. Paris: Hachette, 1882–93.

Staël, Germaine de. *Considérations sur les principaux événements de la Révolution française*, ed. Lucia Omacini, 2 vols. Paris: Honoré Champion, 2017.

Tillemont, Louis-Sebastien le Nain de, *Vie de Saint Louis . . .*, ed. J. de Gaulle, 6 vols. Paris: Jules Renouard, 1847–51.

Travers, Nicolas. *Histoire civile, politique et religieuse de la ville et du comté de Nantes . . .*, ed. Aug. Savagner, 3 vols. Nantes: Forest, 1836–41.

Véri, Joseph-Alphonse de, *Journal . . .*, ed. Jehan de Witte, 2 vols. Paris: Jules Tallendier, 1928–30.

Vermeil, Abraham de, *Poésies*, ed. Henri Lafay. Paris and Geneva: Droz, 1976.

Vincent de Paul. *Correspondance, entretiens, documents*, ed. Pierre Coste, 12 vols. Paris: Lecoffre, 1920–5.

Visconti, Primi. *Mémoires sur la cour de Louis XIV*. Paris: Perrin, 2015.

Voltaire. *Œuvres Complètes*, various eds, 203 vols. Geneva: L'Institut et Musée Voltaire, 1968–71; Oxford: Alden Press, 1971–2020.

Secondary sources

Amalvi, Christian. *De l'art et la manière d'accommoder les héros de l'histoire de France; De Vercingétorix à la Révolution. Essais de mythologie nationale*. Paris: Albin Michel, 1988.

Andriot, Cédric. 'La paroisse Saint-Louis de Strasbourg administrée par les chanoines réguliers lorrains'. *Revue d'Alsace*, 138 (2012): 61–82.

Andriot, Cédric. 'Le collège Saint-Louis de Metz: un prestigieux établissement scolaire d'Ancien Régime'. *Le pays Lorrain*, 97 (2016): 55–62.

Armstrong, Megan. *The Politics of Piety: Franciscan Preachers during the Wars of Religion, 1560–1600*. Woodbridge: Boydell & Brewer, 2004.

Asch, Ronald. *Sacral Kingship between Disenchantment and Re-enchantment: The French and English Monarchies, 1587–1688*. New York and Oxford: Berghahn, 2014.

Assaf, Francis. *La Mort du roi: Une thanatographie de Louis XIV*. Tübingen: Narr, 1999.

Aston, Nigel. 'The Abbé Sieyès before 1789: The Progress of a Clerical Careerist'. *Renaissance and Modern Studies*, 32 (1989): 41–52.

Aston, Nigel. *Religion and Revolution in France, 1780-1804*. Basingstoke: Macmillan, 2000.

Auzas, Pierre-Marie. 'Essai d'un répertoire iconographique de saint Louis'. In *Septième Centenaire de la Mort de saint Louis: Actes des colloques de Royaumont et de Paris*, ed. Louis Carolus-Barré, 3–56. Paris: Société d'Édition «Les Belles Lettres», 1976.

Aznar, Daniel. 'Louis (XIII) II de Catalogne: La construction d'un mythe royal (1641–1643)'. In *La Paix des Pyrénées (1659) ou le triomphe de la raison politique*, eds Lucien Bély, Bertrand Haan and Stéphane Jettot, 253–88. Paris: Classiques Garnier, 2015.

Baker, Keith Michael. 'Memory and Practice: Politics and the Representation of the Past in Eighteenth-Century France'. *Representations*, 11 (1985): 134–64.

Bakos, Adrianna. *Images of Kingship in Early Modern France: Louis XI in Political Thought, 1560-1789*. London and New York: Routledge, 1997.

Ballon, Hilary. *The Paris of Henri IV: Architecture and Urbanism*. Cambridge, MA: MIT Press, 1991.

Balzamo, Nicolas. 'La querelle des reliques au temps de la Renaissance et de la Réforme'. *Bibliothèque d'Humanisme et Renaissance*, 77 (2015): 103–31.

Balzamo, Nicolas. *Les Miracles dans la France du XVIe siècle: Métamorphoses du surnaturel*. Paris: Société d'Édition Les Belles Lettres, 2014.

Banderier, Gilles. 'Du *Saint Louis* à la *Louisiade*: note sur la réception du P. Le Moyne au XVIIIᵉ siècle'. *Papers on French Seventeenth-Century Literature*, 25 (1998): 595–9.

Barbiche, Bernard, Jean-Pierre Poussou and Alain Tallon (eds). *Pouvoirs, contestations et comportements dans l'Europe moderne. Mélanges en l'honneur du professeur Yves-Marie Bercé*. Paris: Presses de l'Université Paris-Sorbonne, 2005.

Barbiche, Bernard and Ségolène de Dainville-Barbiche. *Sully: L'homme et ses fidèles*. Paris: Fayard, 1997.

Barlow, Frank. 'The King's Evil'. *English Historical Review*, 95 (1980): 3–27.

Barnard, H. C. *Madame de Maintenon and Saint-Cyr*. London: A. & C. Black, 1934.

Barth, Medard. 'Zum Kult des hl. Königs Ludwig im deutschen Sprachgebiet und in Skandinavien'. *Freiburger Diözesan-Archiv*, 82/83 (1962/3): 127–226.

Bartlett, Robert. *Why Can the Dead Do Such Great Things? Saints and Worshippers from the Martyrs to the Reformation*. Princeton: Princeton University Press, 2013.

Batiffol, Louis. *Le roi Louis XIII à vingt ans*. Paris: Calmann-Lévy, 1910.

Baumgartner, Frederic. *Change and Continuity in the French Episcopate: The Bishops and the Wars of Religion, 1547-1610*. Durham: Duke University Press, 1986.

Baumgartner, Frederic. *Louis XII*. Basingstoke: Macmillan, 1994.

Bavard, Abbé E. *Histoire de l'Hôtel-Dieu de Beaune*. Beaune: Batault-Morot, 1881.

Beaune, Collette. *Naissance de la nation France*. Paris: Gallimard, 1985.

Becquet, Hélène and Bettina Frederking (eds). *La dignité de roi: Regards sur la royauté en France au premier XIXᵉ siècle*. Rennes: Presses universitaires de Rennes, 2009.

Beik, William. 'Review article: The Absolutism of Louis XIV as Social Collaboration'. *Past and Present*, 188 (2005): 195–224.

Bell, David. *The Cult of the Nation in France: Inventing Nationalism, 1680-1800*. Cambridge, MA: Harvard University Press, 2001.

Benedict, Philip. 'Divided Memories? Historical Calendars, Commemorative Processions and the Recollection of the Wars of Religion during the *Ancien Régime*'. *French History*, 22 (2008): 381–405.

Benedict, Philip. *Rouen during the Wars of Religion*. Cambridge: Cambridge University Press, 1981.

Bergin, Joseph. *Church, Society and Religious Change in France, 1580–1730*. New Haven and London: Yale University Press, 2009.

Bergin, Joseph. *The Politics of Religion in Early Modern France*. New Haven and London: Yale University Press, 2014.

Bergin, Joseph. 'The Royal Confessor and His Rivals in Seventeenth-Century France'. *French History*, 21 (2007): 187–204.

Bilici, Faruk. *Louis XIV et son projet de conquête d'Istanbul*. Ankara: Société d'Histoire Turque, 2004.

Blanning, T. C. W. *The Culture of Power and the Power of Culture: Old Regime Europe 1660–1789*. Oxford: Oxford University Press, 2002.

Blet, Pierre. *Le Clergé du Grand Siècle en ses Assemblées (1615–1715)*. Paris: Éditions du Cerf, 1995.

Bloch, Marc. *Les rois thaumaturges: étude sur le caractère surnaturel attribué à la puissance royale particulièrement en France et en Angleterre*. Strasbourg: Istra 1924.

Blond, Louis. *La maison professe des Jésuites de la rue saint-Antoine à Paris, 1580–1762*. Paris: Éditions Franciscaines, 1956.

Bluche, François. *Louis XIV*, trans. Mark Greengrass. Oxford: Blackwell, 1990.

Boiry, Philippe. *Le mystère du cœur de Saint Louis*. Paris: Diffusion International Édition, 2008.

Boltanski, Ariane. *Les ducs de Nevers et l'état royal: Genèse d'un compromis (ca1500-ca1600)*. Geneva: Droz, 2006.

Bonzon, Anne and Marc Venard. *La religion dans la France moderne, XVIe-XVIIIe siècle*. Paris: Hachette, 1998.

Boureau, Alain. *Le simple corps du roi: l'impossible sacralité des souverains français, XVe-XVIIIe siècle*. Paris: Éd. de Paris, 1988.

Boureau, Alain. 'Les cérémonies royales françaises entre performance juridique et compétence liturgique'. *Annales. Histoire, Sciences Sociales*, 46 (1991): 1253–64.

Boureau, Alain. 'Les Enseignements Absolutistes de Saint Louis 1610–1630'. In *La monarchie absolutiste et l'histoire en France: théories du pouvoir, propagandes monarchiques et mythologies nationales*, 79–97. Paris: Université de Paris-Sorbonne, 1986.

Boureau, Alain and Claudio Sergio Ingerflom (eds). *La royauté sacrée dans le monde chrétien (Colloque de Royaumont, mars 1989)*. Paris: École des Hauts Études en Sciences Sociales, 1992.

Boutry, Philippe, Pierre-Antoine Fabre and Dominique Julia (eds). *Reliques modernes: Cultes et usages chrétiens des corps saints des Réformes aux révolutions*. Paris: École des Hautes Études en Sciences Sociales, 2009.

Boutry, Philippe, Pierre-Antoine Fabre and Dominique Julia (eds). *Rendre ses Vœux: Les identités pèlerines dans l'Europe moderne (XVIe-XVIIIe siècle)*. Paris: École des Hautes Études en Sciences Sociales, 2000.

Bove, Boris. *Le temps de la Guerre de Cent Ans, 1328–1453*. Paris: Belin, 2010.

Boyer, Jean-Claude, Barbara Gaehtgens and Bénédicte Gady (eds). *Richelieu, patron des arts*. Paris: Éditions de la Maison des sciences de l'homme, [2009].

Brisch, Nicole (ed.). *Religion and Power: Divine Kingship in the Ancient World and Beyond*. Chicago: Oriental Institute, 2008.

Brown, Elizabeth. 'The Chapels and Cult of Saint Louis at Saint-Denis'. *Mediaevalia*, 10 (1984): 279–331.

Brown, Elizabeth. 'Philippe le Bel and the remains of Saint Louis'. *Gazette des Beaux-Arts*, 95 (1980): 175–82.

Brown, Elizabeth and Sanford Zale. 'Louis Le Blanc, Estienne Le Blanc, and the defense of Louis IX's crusades, 1498-1522'. *Traditio*, 55 (2000): 235–92.

Burkardt, Albrecht. *Les clients des saints: Maladie et quête du miracle à travers les procès de canonisation de la première moitié du XVIIe siècle en France*. Rome: École Française de Rome, 2004.

Burke, Peter. *The Fabrication of Louis XIV*. New Haven: Yale University Press, 1992.

Bussièrre, M. T. de. *Culte et pèlerinages de la Très-Sainte Vierge en Alsace*. Paris: Henri Plon, 1862.

Byrne, Anne. *Death and the Crown: Ritual and Politics in France before the Revolution*. Manchester: Manchester University Press, 2020.

Caiani, Ambrogio. *Louis XVI and the French Revolution, 1789–1792*. Cambridge: Cambridge University Press, 2012.

Calin, William. *Crown, Cross, and "Fleur-de-Lis": An essay on Pierre Le Moyne's baroque epic "Saint Louis"*. Saratoga: Anma Libri, 1977.

Calvé, Jean-Marie-Yves. *Les ports militaires de la France: Toulon*. Paris: Paul Dupont, 1867.

Campbell, Peter. *Power and Politics in Old Regime France, 1720–1745*. London and New York: Palgrave, 1996.

Carns, Paula. 'The Cult of Saint Louis and Capetian Interests in the *Hours of Jeanne d'Evreux*'. *Peregrinations*, 2 (2006): 1–32.

Carrier, Hubert. *Le Labyrinthe de l'État; Essai sur le débat politique en France au temps de la Fronde (1648–1653)*. Paris: Honoré Champion, 2004.

Cessac, Catherine, Jane Gosine, Laurent Guillo and Patricia Ranum. 'Chronologie raisonnée des manuscrits autographes de Charpentier. Essai de bibliographie matérielle'. *Bulletin Charpentier*, 3 (2013): 1–43.

Chaline, Olivier. *L'année des quatre dauphins*. Paris: Flammarion, 2009.

Chaline, Olivier. *Le règne de Louis XIV*. Paris: Flammarion, 2005.

Chaouch, Khalid. 'Chateaubriand's Time Travel in Tunis and Carthage: An Archaeology of Mappings'. *Nineteenth-Century French Studies*, 46 (2018): 254–69.

Chartier, Roger. *The Cultural Origins of the French Revolution*, trans. Lydia Cochrane. Durham and London: Duke University Press, 1991.

Chartier, Roger (ed.). *The Culture of Print: Power and the Uses of print in Early Modern Europe*, trans. Lydia Cochrane. Oxford: Polity Press, 1989.

Chaunu, Pierre. *La mort à Paris, XVIe, XVIIe, XVIIIe siècles*. Paris: Fayard, 1978.

Church, William. 'France'. In *National Consciousness, History, and Political Culture in Early-Modern Europe*, ed. Orest Ranum, 43–66. Baltimore and London: John Hopkins University Press, 1975.

Church, William. *Richelieu and Reason of State*. Princeton: Princeton University Press, 1972.

Clément, Jean-Paul. *Charles X: Le dernier Bourbon*. Paris: Perrin, 2015.

Clément, Jean-Paul. 'L'utilisation du mythe de Saint-Louis par Chateaubriand dans les controverses politiques de l'Empire et de la Restauration'. *Revue d'Histoire littéraire de la France*, 98 (1998): 1059–72.

Clément de Ris, Louis. *Histoire et description de l'église de Saint-Louis d'Antin*. Paris: Plon, 1883.

Collignon, abbé. *Histoire de la paroisse Saint-Louis-en-l'Ile: ses origines, son développement, description de son église*. Paris: Soye et fils, 1888.

Confino, Alon. 'Collective Memory and Cultural History: Problems of Method'. *American Historical Review*, 102 (1997): 1386–403.

Considine, John. *Dictionaries in Early Modern Europe: Lexicography and the Making of Heritage*. Cambridge: Cambridge University Press, 2008.

Cornette, Joël. *Henri IV à Saint-Denis: De l'abjuration à la profanation*. Paris: Belin, 2010.

Cornette, Joël. *Le roi de guerre: essai sur la souveraineté dans la France du Grand Siècle*. Paris: Payot et Rivages, 1993.

Cosperec, Annie. *Blois, la forme d'une ville*. Paris: Imprimerie Nationale, 1994.

Crook, Malcolm, Alan Forrest and William Doyle (eds). *Enlightenment and Revolution: Essays in Honour of Norman Hampson*. Burlington: Ashgate, 2004.

Crowston, Clare Haru. *Fabricating Women: The Seamstresses of Old Regime France, 1675–1791*. Durham and London: Duke University Press, 2001.

Cuche, François-Xavier. 'Le *Panégyrique de saint Louis* de Fléchier'. In *Fléchier et les Grands Jours d'Auvergne; Actes d'une Journée d'étude, Université Blaise Pascal-Clermont-Ferrard, 3 octobre 1997*, ed. Emmanuèle Lesne-Jaffro, 93–114. Tübingen: Narr, 2000.

Curran, Mark. '*Mettons toujours Londres*: Enlightened Christianity and the Public in Pre-Revolutionary Francophone Europe'. *French History*, 24 (2009): 40–59.

Darlow, Mark. *Staging the French Revolution: Cultural Politics and the Paris Opéra, 1789–1794*. Oxford: Oxford University Press, 2012.

Darnton, Robert. *The Forbidden Bestsellers of pre-Revolutionary France*. New York and London: Norton, 1995.

Decobert, Laurence. *Henry du Mont (1610–1684): Maistre et compositeur de la Musique de la Chapelle du Roy et de la Reyne*. Wavre: Mardaga, 2011.

Degen, Guy. 'Autour d'un lit de centres: l'image de Louis IX et de sa seconde croisade dans les panégyriques de saint Louis aux XVIIe et XVIIIe siècles'. In *La littérature et ses avatars: Discrédits, déformations et réhabilitations dans l'histoire de la littérature*, ed. Yvonne Bellenger, 125–49. Paris: Klincksieck, 1991.

Dehergne, Joseph. 'Note sur les Jésuites et l'enseignement supérieur dans la France d'Ancien Régime'. *Revue d'histoire de l'Église de France*, 158 (1971): 73–82.

Delamont, Ernest. *Histoire de la Ville de Cette pendant la Révolution 1789–1796 (an V)*. Gap: Louis-Jean, 1989.

Delattre, Pierre. *Les établissements des Jésuites en France depuis quatre siècles. Répertoire Topo-bibliographique publié à l'occasion du quatrième centenaire de la fondation de la compagnie de Jésus, 1540–1940*, 5 vols. Enghien: Institut Supérieur de Théologie, 1949–57.

Delmas, Sophie. *Saint Louis*. Paris: Ellipses, 2017.

Demier, Francis. *La France de la Restauration (1814–1830): L'impossible retour du passé*. Paris: Gallimard, 2012.

Denis, Yves. *Histoire de Blois et de sa région*. Toulouse: Privat, 1988.

Deploige, Jeroen and Gita Deneckere (eds). *Mystifying the Monarch: Studies on Discourse, Power, and History*. Amsterdam: Amsterdam University Press, 2006.

Deregnaucourt, Gilles, Yves Krumenacker, Philippe Martin and Frédéric Meyer (eds). *Dorsale catholique, Jansénisme, Dévotions: XVIe-XVIIIe siècles: Mythe, réalité, actualité historiographique*. Paris: Riveneuve, 2014.

Diefendorf, Barbara. *Beneath the Cross; Catholics and Huguenots in Sixteenth-Century Paris*. Oxford: Oxford University Press, 1991.

Doyle, William. *France and the Age of Revolution: Regimes Old and New from Louis XIV to Napoleon Bonaparte*. London: Tauris, 2013.

Dubost, Jean-François. *Marie de Médicis: La reine dévoilée*. Paris: Payot, 2009.

Duby, Georges. *The Legend of Bouvines: War, Religion and Culture in the Middle Ages*, trans. Catherine Tihanyi. Berkeley and Los Angeles: University of California Press, 1990.

Duccini, Hélène. *Faire voir, faire croire: l'opinion publique sous Louis XIII*. Seyssel: Champ Vallon, 2003.

Duindam, Jeroen. *Dynasties: A Global History of Power, 1300–1800*. Cambridge: Cambridge University Press, 2006.

Dupré, José. 'L'année "Saint-Louis": La propagande continue . . .'. *Cahiers d'études cathares*, 21 (1970): 46–54.

Dupront, Alphonse. *Le mythe de croisade*. Paris: Gallimard, 1997.

Echeverria, Durand. *The Maupeou Revolution: A Study in the History of Libertarianism, France, 1770–1774*. Baton Rouge and London: Louisiana State University Press, 1985.

Edelman, Nathan. *Attitudes of Seventeenth-Century France towards the Middle Ages*. Morningside Heights: King's Crown Press, 1946.

Edmunds, Martha Mel Stumberg. *Piety and Politics: Imagining Divine Kingship in Louis XIV's Chapel at Versailles*. Newark: University of Delaware Press, 2002.

Eire, Carlos. 'The Concept of Popular Religion'. In *Local Religion in Colonial Mexico*, ed. Martin Nesvig, 1–35. Albuquerque: University of New Mexico Press, 2006.

Ekberg, Carl and Sharon Person. *St. Louis Rising: The French Regime of Louis St. Ange de Bellerive*. Urbana, Chicago and Springfield: University of Illinois Press, 2015.

Ellis, Harold. *Boulainvilliers and the French Monarchy: Aristocratic Politics in Early Eighteenth-Century France*. Ithaca and London: Cornell University Press, 1988.

Engels, Jens. 'Beyond Sacral Monarchy: A New Look at the Image of the Early Modern French Monarchy'. *French History*, 15 (2001): 139–58.

Engels, Jens. 'Dénigrer, espérer, assumer la réalité. Le roi de France perçu par ses sujets'. *Revue d'histoire moderne et contemporaine*, 50 (2003): 96–126.

Érection de la Paroisse Saint-Louis de Fontainebleau: Une Lettre Inédite de Louis XIV. Fontainebleau: Ernest Bourges, 1893.

Exposition: La Renaissance du culte de saint Louis au XVIIᵉ siècle: l'Ordre Militaire; la Maison Royale de Saint-Cyr, novembre 1970-janvier 1971 (Année Saint Louis, 1270-1970). Paris: Musée national de la légion d'Honneur et des Ordres de Chevalerie, 1970.

Faure, Pierre. 'Histoire de l'hôpital Saint-Louis à travers l'histoire de ses bâtiments'. *Revue d'histoire de la pharmacie*, 324 (1999): 443–8.

Ferret, Olivier. *La Fureur de nuire: échanges pamphlétaires entre philosophes et antiphilosophes (1750–1770)*. Oxford: Voltaire Foundation, 2007.

Ferrier-Caverivière, Nicole. *L'image de Louis XIV dans la littérature française de 1660 à 1715*. Paris: Presses Universitaires de France, 1981.

Feuilloy, Clotilde, Jannie Long and Catherine de Maupeou. 'Représentations de Saint Louis sous l'aspect des rois de France'. *Les Monuments Historiques de la France*, 16 (1970): 47–52.

Finley-Croswhite, Annette. *Henry IV and the Towns: The Pursuit of Legitimacy in French Urban Society, 1589–1610*. Cambridge: Cambridge University Press, 1999.

Fogel, Michèle. *Les cérémonies de l'information dans la France du XVIe au XVIIIe siècle*. Paris: Fayard, 1989.

Folz, Robert. *Les saints rois du moyen âge en Occident (VIᵉ – XIIIᵉ siècles)*. Brussels: Société des Bollandistes, 1984.

Fontijn, Claire. *Desperate Measures: The Life and Music of Antonia Padoani Bembo*. New York: Oxford University Press, 2006.

Forrestal, Alison. *Fathers, Pastors and Kings: Visions of Episcopacy in Seventeenth-Century France*. Manchester: Manchester University Press, 2004.

Forrestal, Alison. *Vincent de Paul, the Lazarist Mission, and French Catholic Reform*. Oxford: Oxford University Press, 2017.

Forrestal, Alison and Eric Nelson (eds). *Politics and Religion in Early Bourbon France*. Basingstoke: Palgrave Macmillan, 2009.

Forster, Marc. *Catholic Revival in the Age of the Baroque: Religious Identity in southwest Germany, 1550–1750*. Cambridge: Cambridge University Press, 2001.

Franceschi, Sylvio Hermann De. 'Le modèle jésuite du prince chrétien: À propos du *De officio principis Christiani* de Bellarmin'. *Dix-septième siècle*, 237 (2007): 713–28.

Frederking, Bettina. 'Il ne faut pas être le roi de deux peuples': Strategies of National Reconciliation in Restoration France'. *French History*, 22 (2008): 446–68.

Gabet, Camille. *La naissance de Rochefort sous Louis XIV, 1666–1715: une ville nouvelle et ses habitants au Grand Siècle*. Rochefort: Centre d'Animation Lyrique et Culturel de Rochefort, 1985.

Gallerand, Jules. 'L'érection de l'évêché de Blois (1697)'. *Revue d'histoire de l'Église de France*, 42 (1956): 175–228.

Gaposchkin, Cecilia. 'The Captivity of Louis IX'. *Quaestiones Medii Aevi novae*, 18 (2013): 85–114.

Gaposchkin, Cecilia. *The Making of Saint Louis: Kingship, Sanctity, and Crusade in the Later Middle Ages*. Ithaca and London: Cornell University Press, 2008.

Gauchet, Marcel. 'L'état au miroir de la raison d'état: La France et la chrétienté'. In *Raison et déraison d'État: Théoriciens et théories de la raison d'État aux XVIe et XVIIe siècles*, ed. Yves Charles Zarka, 193–244. Paris: Presses Universitaires de France, 1994.

Gauthier, Roland. *Louis XIV et saint Joseph*. Montréal: Publié à compte d'auteur, 1999.

Gay, Jean-Pascal. 'Le «cas Maimbourg». La possibilité d'un gallicanisme jésuite au XVIIe siècle'. *Revue historique*, 316 (2014): 783–831.

Gay, Jean-Pascal. 'Voués à quel royaume? Les Jésuites entre vœux de religion et fidélité monarchique. À propos d'un mémoire inédit du P. de La Chaize'. *Dix-septième siècle*, 227 (2005): 285–314.

Giesey, Ralph. *The Royal Funeral Ceremony in Renaissance France*. Geneva: Droz, 1960.

Gildea, Robert. *Children of the Revolution: The French, 1799–1914*. London: Penguin, 2008.

Gildea, Robert. *The Past in French History*. New Haven and London: Yale University Press, 1994.

Golden, Richard. *The Godly Rebellion; Parisian Curés and the Religious Fronde, 1652–1662*. Chapel Hill: The University of North Carolina Press, 1981.

Gorochov, Nathalie. 'Entre théologie, humanisme et politique: Les sermons universitaires de la fête de Saint Louis sous le règne de Charles VI (1389–1422)'. In *Saint-Denis et la royauté: Études offertes à Bernard Guenée*, eds Françoise Autrand, Claude Gauvard and Jean-Marie Moeglin, 51–64. Paris: La Sorbonne, 1999.

Gosman, Martin, Alasdair MacDonald and Arjo Vanderjagt (eds). *Princes and Princely Culture, 1450–1650*, 2 vols. Leiden: Brill, 2003.

Grampp, Florian Bassani. 'On a Roman Polychoral Performance in August 1665'. *Early Music*, 36 (2008): 415–33.

Greengrass, Mark. *Governing Passions: Peace and Reform in the French Kingdom, 1576–1585*. Oxford: Oxford University Press, 2007.

Greer, Alan. 'Colonial Saints: Gender, Race, and Hagiography in New France'. *The William and Mary Quarterly*, 3rd series, 57 (2000): 323–48.

Greer, Alan. *The Jesuit Relations: Natives and Missionaries in Seventeenth-Century North America*. Boston/New York: Bedford/St Martin's, 2000.

Grenier, Jean-Yves. 'Temps de travail et fêtes religieuses au XVIIIe siècle'. *Revue historique*, 663 (2012): 609–41.

Grove, Laurence. *Emblematics and 17th-Century French Literature: Descartes, Tristan, La Fontaine and Perrault*. Charlottesville: Rookwood Press, 2000.

Guiffrey, J.-J. 'Les tombes royales de saint-Denis à la fin du XVIIIe siècle'. *Le Cabinet Historique*, 22 (1876): 1–31.

Guillain, Georges and Paul Mathieu. *La Salpêtrière*. Paris: Masson, 1925.

Hall, Hugh Gaston. *Richelieu's Desmarets and the Century of Louis XIV*. Oxford: Oxford University Press, 1990.

Hallam, Elizabeth. 'Philip the Fair and the cult of Saint Louis'. In *Studies in Church History 18 – Religion and National Identity: Papers Read at the Nineteenth Summer Meeting and the Twentieth Winter Meeting of the Ecclesiastical History Society*, ed. Stuart Mews, 201–14. Oxford: Blackwell, 1982.

Haran, Alexandre. *Le Lys et le Globe: Messianisme dynastique et rêve impérial en France aux XVIe et XVIIe siècles*. Seyssel: Champ Vallon, 2000.

Hardman, John. *Louis XVI: The Silent King*. London: Arnold, 2000.

Hayden, J. Michael. *France and the Estates General of 1614*. Cambridge: Cambridge University Press, 1974.

Hazareesingh, Sudhir. *The Saint-Napoleon: Celebrations of Sovereignty in Nineteenth-Century France*. Cambridge, MA: Harvard University Press, 2004.

Heath, Sean. 'An Ultramontane Jansenist? Charles Hersent's Panegyric of Saint Louis (1650)'. *Journal of Ecclesiastical History*, 70 (2019): 57–76.

Hélary, Xavier. 'Philip of Artois (†1298)'s Last Wishes and the Birth of the Cult of Saint Louis in the Capetian Family'. *Le Moyen Age*, 119 (2013): 27–56.

Hennequin, Jacques. *Henri IV dans ses oraisons funèbres, ou la naissance d'une légende*. Paris: Klincksieck, 1977.

Heyer, John Hajdu. *The Lure and Legacy of Music at Versailles: Louis XIV and the Aix School*. Cambridge: Cambridge University Press, 2014.

Hickey, Daniel. *Local Hospitals in Ancien Régime France: Rationalization, Resistance, Renewal 1530–1789*. Montreal and Kingston: McGill-Queen's University Press, 1997.

Higgs, David. *Ultraroyalism in Toulouse: From Its Origins to the Revolution of 1830*. Baltimore and London: The John Hopkins University Press, 1973.

Hitchcock, H. W. 'The Latin Oratorios of Marc-Antoine Charpentier'. *Musical Quarterly*, 41 (1955): 41–65.

Hoffman, Martha. *Raised to Rule: Educating Royalty at the Court of the Spanish Habsburgs, 1601–1634*. Baton Rouge: Louisiana State University Press, 2011.

Hölscher, Lucian. 'Time Gardens: Historical Concepts in Modern Historiography'. *History and Theory*, 53 (2014): 577–91.

Hours, Bernard. *Madame Louise: Princesse au Carmel, 1737–1787*. Paris: Éditions du Cerf, 1987.

Hours, Bernard. 'Moureau et Proyart, pédagogues en attente du prince et éducateurs de la nation'. *Histoire de l'éducation*, 132 (2011): 153–76.

Hsia, Ronnie Po-Chia (ed.). *The Cambridge History of Christianity, vol. VI: Reform and Expansion 1500–1660*. Cambridge: Cambridge University Press 2007.

Ingold, Gerard. *Saint Louis de 1586 à nos jours: de l'art du verre à l'art du cristal*. Paris: Denoël, 1986.

Isom-Verhaaren, Christine. *Allies with the Infidel: The Ottoman and French alliance in the Sixteenth Century*. London: Tauris, 2011.

Jackson, Richard. *Vive le Roi! A History of the French Coronation from Charles V to Charles X*. Chapel Hill and London: University of North Carolina Press, 1984.

Jaffré, Marc. 'The Royal Court and Civil War at the founding of the Bourbon Dynasty, 1589–95'. *French History*, 31 (2017): 20–38.

Johnson, Eric. 'The Sacred, Secular Regime: Catholic Ritual and Revolutionary Politics in Avignon, 1789–1791'. *French Historical Studies*, 30 (2007): 49–76.

Jolley, Nicholas (ed.). *The Cambridge Companion to Leibniz*. Cambridge: Cambridge University Press, 1995.

Jordan, William. '*Etiam reges*, Even Kings'. *Speculum*, 90 (2015): 613–34.

Jordan, William. 'Honouring Saint Louis in a small town'. *Journal of Medieval History*, 30 (2004): 263–77.

Jordan, William. *Louis IX and the Challenge of the Crusade: A Study in Rulership*. Princeton: Princeton University Press, 1979.

Jordan, William. 'Saint Louis in French Epic and Drama'. In *Medievalism in Europe II*, eds Leslie Workman and Kathleen Verduin, 174–94. Cambridge: Brewer, 1997.

Jung, Theo. '*Le silence du peuple*: The Rhetoric of Silence during the French Revolution'. *French History*, 31 (2017): 440–69.

Kantorowicz, Ernst. *The King's Two Bodies: A Study in Mediaeval Political Theology*, new edn. Princeton: Princeton University Press, 2016.

Kauffman, Deborah. 'Performance Traditions and Motet Composition at the Convent School at Saint-Cyr'. *Early Music*, 29 (2001): 234–49.

Keohane, Nannerl. *Philosophy and the State in France: The Renaissance to the Enlightenment*. Princeton: Princeton University Press, 1980.

Kettering, Sharon. 'Political Pamphlets in Early Seventeenth-Century France: The Propaganda War between Louis XIII and His Mother, 1619–20'. *Sixteenth Century Journal*, 42 (2011): 963–80.

Kettering, Sharon. *Power and Reputation at the Court of Louis XIII: The Career of Charles d'Albret, duc de Luynes (1578–1621)*. Manchester: Manchester University Press, 2008.

Knobler, Adam. 'Saint Louis and French Political Culture'. In *Medievalism in Europe II*, eds Leslie Workman and Kathleen Verduin, 156–73. Cambridge: Brewer, 1997.

Koselleck, Reinhart. *Futures Past: On the Semantics of Historical Time*, trans. Keith Tribe. New York: Columbia University Press, 2004.

Krailsheimer, A. J. *Armand-Jean de Rancé, abbot of La Trappe: His Influence in the Cloister and the World*. Oxford: Clarendon Press, 1974.

Kroen, Sheryl. *Politics and Theater: The Crisis of Legitimacy in Restoration France, 1815–1830*. Berkeley and Los Angeles: University of California Press, 2000.

Kuijpers, Erika, Judith Pollmann, Johannes Müller and Jasper van der Steen (eds). *Memory Before Modernity: Practices of Memory in Early Modern Europe*. Leiden: Brill, 2013.

Lalore, abbé Ch. *Les Fêtes chômées dans le diocèse de Troyes, depuis l'origine du Christianisme jusques en 1802*. Troyes: E. Caffé, 1869.

Landry, Jean-Pierre. 'Saint Louis vu par les Prédicateurs de l'Epoque classique'. In *Colloque «L'image du Moyen-âge dans la littérature française de la Renaissance au XXe siècle», 1981*, 381–404. Poitiers: Faculté des lettres et des langues, 1982.

Lanson, René. *Le Gout du Moyen Age en France au XVIIIe siècle*. Paris and Brussels: G. Van Oest, 1926.

Laven, Mary. 'Encountering the Counter-Reformation'. *Renaissance Quarterly*, 59 (2006): 706–20.

Lavieille, Géraldine. '«Il ne fesoit point beau voir qu'un Espagnol tournast le dos à St Louys et à un roy de France». Saint Louis au XVIIe siècle, saint dynastique et saint national'. In *Saintetés politiques du IXe au XVIIIe siècle. Autour de la Lotharingie-Dorsale catholique*, ed. Sylvène Édouard, 201–25. Paris: Garnier, 2020.

Lavieille, Géraldine. 'Le Rosaire de La Forêt-Fouesnant (Basse-Bretagne): jeux de pouvoir et création collective de l'image religieuse royale sous Louis XIV'. *Revue d'histoire moderne et contemporaine*, 61 (2014): 89–119.

Lavieille, Géraldine. 'Les Jésuites et la dévotion à saint Louis au XVIIᵉ siècle: la célébration du Roi très chrétien'. *Les Cahiers de Framespa*, put online on 23 November 2012, accessed on 16 September 2014. URL: http://framespa.revues.org/2025

Lebeuf, Jean. *Histoire de la ville et de tout le diocese de Paris*, 7 vols. Paris: Féchoz, 1883–93.

Le Gall, Jean-Marie. *Le Mythe de saint Denis entre Renaissance et Révolution*. Seyssel: Champ Vallon, 2007.

Le Gall, Jean-Marie. 'Vieux saint et grande noblesse à l'époque moderne: Saint Denis, les Montmorency et les Guise'. *Revue d'histoire moderne et contemporaine*, 50 (2003): 7–33.

Le Goff, Jacques. *History and Memory*, trans. Steven Rendall and Elizabeth Claman. New York: Columbia University Press, 1992.

Le Goff, Jacques. *Saint Louis*, trans. Gareth Evan Gollrad. Notre Dame: University of Notre Dame Press, 2009.

Legoy, Corinne. 'De la célébration au combat politique: l'adversaire dans les éloges de la Restauration'. *Annales historiques de la Révolution française*, 334 (2003): 23–43.

Legoy, Corinne. 'La figure du souverain médiéval sur les scènes parisiennes de la Restauration'. *Revue Historique*, 293 (1995): 321–65.

Lemoine, François and Jacques Tanguy. *Rouen aux 100 clochers: Dictionnaire des églises et chapelles de Rouen (avant 1789)*. Rouen: PTC, 2004.

Leniaud, Jean-Michel and Françoise Perrot. *La Sainte-Chapelle*. Paris: Nathan/CNMHS, 1991.

Les Lettres au temps de Henri IV: Volume des actes du colloque Agen-Nérac 18–20 mai 1990. Pau: Association Henri IV, 1989.

Levot, Prosper. *Histoire de la ville et du port de Brest*, 3 vols. Brest and Paris: l'auteur & Mme Bachelin-Deflorenne, 1864–6.

Loskoutoff, Yvan. *L'armorial de Calliope: L'œuvre du Père Le Moyne S.J. (1602–1671): littérature, héraldique, spiritualité*. Tübingen: Narr, 2000.

Lower, Michael. *The Tunis Crusade of 1270: A Mediterranean History*. Oxford: Oxford University Press, 2018.

Luebke, David (ed.). *The Counter-Reformation: The Essential Readings*. Oxford: Blackwell, 1999.

Mackrell, J. Q. C. *The Attack on 'Feudalism' in Eighteenth-Century France*. Abingdon: Routledge, 1973.

Maës, Bruno. *Le Roi, La Vierge et La Nation: Pèlerinages et identité nationale entre guerre de Cent Ans et Révolution*. Paris: Publisud, 2002.

Maillet-Rao, Caroline. 'Towards a new reading of the political thought of the *dévot* faction: The Opposition to Cardinal Richelieu's Ministériat'. *Religions*, 4 (2013): 529–49.

Malssen, P. J. W. van. *Louis XIV d'après les pamphlets répandus en Hollande*. Amsterdam and Paris: H.J. Paris, A. Nizet and M. Bastard, 1937.

Mandrou, Robert. *De la culture populaire aux XVIIᵉ et XVIIIᵉ siècles: La Bibliothèque bleue de Troyes*. Paris: Stock, 1964.

Mansel, Philip. 'From Exile to the Throne: The Europeanization of Louis XVIII'. In *Monarchy and Exile: The Politics of Legitimacy from Marie de Médicis to Wilhelm II*, eds Philip Mansel and Torsten Riotte, 181–213. Basingstoke: Palgrave Macmillan, 2011.

Mansel, Philip. *Louis XVIII*. London: Blond & Briggs, 1981.

Maral, Alexandre. *La Chapelle Royale de Versailles sous Louis XIV: cérémonial, liturgie et musique*. Sprimont: Mardaga, 2002.

Maral, Alexandre. 'Portrait religieux de Louis XIV'. *XVIIe Siècle*, 217 (2002): 627–723.

Marec, Yannick. *Les hôpitaux de Rouen du Moyen Âge à nos jours: Dix siècles de protection sociale*. Rouen: PTC, 2005.

Mazas, Alexandre. *Histoire de l'Ordre Militaire de Saint-Louis depuis son institution en 1693 jusqu'en 1830*. Paris: Dentu, 1855.

McCluskey, Philip. 'Commerce before crusade? France, the Ottoman Empire and the Barbary Pirates (1661–1669)'. *French History*, 23 (2009): 1–21.

McCluskey, Philip. '"Les ennemis du nom Chrestien": Echoes of the crusade in Louis XIV's France'. *French History*, 29 (2015): 46–61.

McGuire, Martin. 'Louis-Sebastien le Nain de Tillemont'. *Catholic Historical Review*, 52 (1966): 186–200.

McManners, John. *Church and Society in Eighteenth-Century France*, 2 vols. Oxford: Clarendon Press, 1998.

McMillan, James. 'Catholic Christianity in France from the Restoration to the Separation of Church and State, 1815–1905'. In *The Cambridge History of Christianity, vol. 8: World Christianities, c.1815–c.1914*, eds Sheridan Gilley and Brian Stanley, 215–32. Cambridge: Cambridge University Press, 2005.

Meltzer, Françoise and Jaś Elsner (eds). *Saints: Faith without Borders*. Chicago and London: University of Chicago Press, 2011.

Ménorval, E. de. *Les Jésuites de la rue Saint-Antoine: L'église Saint-Paul-Saint-Louis et le lycée Charlemagne*. Paris: Auguste Aubry, 1872.

Mérot, Alain. *Eustache Le Sueur (1616–1655)*. Paris: Arthena, 1987.

Merrick, Jeffrey. *The Desacralization of the French Monarchy in the Eighteenth Century*. Baton Rouge and London: Louisiana State University Press, 1990.

Mesnard, Jean. 'Port-Royal et Saint Louis'. *Chroniques de Port-Royal: Port-Royal et l'Histoire*, 46 (1997): 53–73.

Meyer, Véronique. 'L'illustration du *Saint Louis* du Père Le Moyne'. *Cahiers de l'Association internationale des études françaises*, 57 (2005): 47–73.

Michaud, Alain. *Histoire de Saintes*. Toulouse: Privat, 1989.

Monod, Paul Kleber. *The Power of Kings: Monarchy and Religion in Europe, 1589–1715*. New Haven and London: Yale University Press, 1999.

Montagnon, André. *Les Guerres de Vendée, 1793–1832*. Paris: Perrin, 1974.

Montcher, Fabien. 'L'image et le culte de saint Louis dans la Monarchie hispanique: Le rôle des «reines de paix» (du milieu du XVIe siècle au milieu du XVIIe siècle)'. In *«La dame de cœur»: Patronage et mécénat religieux des femmes de pouvoir dans l'Europe des XIVe-XVIIe siècles*, eds Murielle Gaude-Ferragu and Cécile Vincent-Cassy, 167–91. Rennes: Presses Universitaires de Rennes, 2016.

La Montjoie de Saint-Louis: La Bastide et ses Environs. Lamontjoie: Comité d'organisation pour le VIIe centenaire de la mort de saint Louis, 1970.

Montoya, Alicia. *Medievalist Enlightenment: From Charles Perrault to Jean-Jacques Rousseau*. Cambridge: Brewer, 2013.

Moote, Alanson Lloyd. *Louis XIII, the Just*. Berkeley and Los Angeles: University of California Press, 1989.

Moote, Alanson Lloyd. *The Revolt of the Judges: The Parlement of Paris and the Fronde, 1643–1652*. Princeton: Princeton University Press, 1970.

Morel, Pierre. 'Le culte de saint Louis'. *Itinéraires, documents* 147 (1970): 127–51.

Mormiche, Pascale. 'Éduquer un roi ou l'histoire d'une modification progressive du projet pédagogique pour Louis XV (1715–1722)'. *Histoire de l'éducation*, 132 (2011): 17–47.

Nelson, Eric. *The Jesuits and the Monarchy: Catholic Reform and Political Authority in France (1590–1615)*. Aldershot: Ashgate, 2005.

Nelson, Eric. *The Legacy of Iconoclasm: Religious War and the Relic Landscape of Tours, Blois and Vendôme, 1550–1750*. St Andrews: St Andrews Studies in French History and Culture, 2013.

Nelson, Eric. '*Religion royale* in the sacred landscape of Paris: The Jesuit Church of Saint Louis and the re-sacralization of kingship in early Bourbon France (1590–1650).' In *Layered Landscapes: Early Modern Religious Space Across Faiths and Cultures*, eds Eric Nelson and Jonathan Wright, 171–84. London: Routledge, 2017.

Neveu, Bruno. 'Du culte de Saint Louis à la glorification de Louis XIV: la maison royale de Saint-Cyr'. *Journal des savants*, 3 (1988): 277–90.

Neveu, Bruno. 'Le Nain de Tillemont et la *Vie de Saint Louis*.' In *Septième Centenaire de la Mort de saint Louis: Actes des colloques de Royaumont et de Paris*, ed. Louis Carolus-Barré, 315–29. Paris: Société d'Édition «Les Belles Lettres», 1976.

Nora, Pierre (ed.). *Rethinking France: Les Lieux de Mémoire. Volume 1: The State*, trans. Mary Trouille. Chicago and London: University of Chicago Press, 2001.

Notice sur les reliques de Saint Louis à Lamontjoie. Agen: Imprimerie de Prosper Noubel, 1855.

O'Connell, David. *The Teachings of Saint Louis: A Critical Text*. Chapel Hill: University of North Carolina Press, 1972.

Omont, Henri Auguste. 'Projets de prise de Constantinople et de fondation d'un empire français d'orient sous Louis XIV'. *Revue d'histoire diplomatique*, 7 (1893): 195–246.

Oppermann, Fabien. 'Le remeublement du château de Versailles au XXᵉ siècle: Entre action scientifique et manœuvres politiques'. *Bibliothèque de l'École de chartes*, 170 (2012): 209–32.

Ozouf, Mona. *Festivals and the French Revolution*, trans. Alan Sheridan. Cambridge, MA: Harvard University Press, 1988.

Parguez, Henri. *Saint Louis et Poissy: Sa Naissance, son Baptême, ses Charités, ses Miracles, son Culte à Poissy 1214–1914*. Saint-Germain-en-Laye: Mirvault, 1914.

Pascual-Barea, Joaquín. 'Quis posset dignos Lodouico dicere uersus? Los tres epigramas en alabanza de San Luis premiados en la justa hispalense del otoño de 1556'. *Calamus Renascens*, 10 (2009): 129–49.

Pernot, Michel. *La Fronde*. Paris: Éditions de Fallois, 1994.

Petit, Vincent. 'Religion du souverain, souverain de la religion: l'invention de saint Napoléon'. *Revue Historique*, 314 (2012): 643–58.

Petit-Aupert, Catherine, Ézéchiel Jean-Courret and Isabelle Cartron. *Une bastide pour le roi; autour des reliques de saint Louis à Lamontjoie*. Pessac: Ausonius, 2014.

Pfleger, Lucien. 'Le culte de saint Louis en Alsace'. *Revue des sciences religieuses*, 1 (1921): 222–7.

Phillips, Henry. *Church and Culture in Seventeenth-Century France*. Cambridge: Cambridge University Press, 1997.

Pierre, Benoist. *Le père Joseph: l'Éminence grise de Richelieu*. Paris: Perrin, 2007.

Pilbeam, Pamela. 'The Growth of Liberalism and the Crisis of the Bourbon Restoration, 1827–1830'. *Historical Journal*, 25 (1982): 351–66.

Pilot de Thorey, Jean-Joseph-Antoine. *Histoire municipale de Grenoble*. Grenoble: N. Maisonville, 1851.

Pollmann, Judith. *Memory in Early Modern Europe, 1500–1800*. Oxford: Oxford University Press, 2017.

Poumarède, Géraud. *Pour en finir avec la Croisade: Mythes et réalités de la lutte contre les Turcs aux XVIᵉ et XVIIᵉ siècles*. Paris: Presses Universitaires de France, 2004.

Prégnon, abbé. *Histoire du pays et de la ville de Sedan depuis les temps les plus reculés jusqu'à nos jours*, 3 vols. Charleville: Pouillard, 1856.

Provost, Georges. *La fête et le sacré: Pardons et pèlerinages en Bretagne aux XVIIᵉ et XVIIIᵉ siècles*. Paris: Cerf, 1998.

Puyol, abbé. *Louis XIII et le Béarn, ou le rétablissement du Catholicisime en Béarn et réunion du Béarn et de la Navarre à la France*. Paris: Soye et fils, 1872.

Quantin, Jean-Louis. 'A Godly Fronde? Jansenism and the Mid-Seventeenth-Century Crisis of the French Monarchy'. *French History*, 25 (2011): 473–91.

Rabinovitch, Oded. *The Perraults: A Family of Letters in Early Modern France*. Ithaca and London: Cornell University Press, 2018.

Ranum, Orest. *Artisans of Glory: Writers and Historical Thought in Seventeenth-Century France*. Chapel Hill: University of North Carolina Press, 1980.

Ranum, Orest. *The Fronde: A French Revolution*. New York: Norton, 1993.

Ranum, Patricia. *Portraits around Marc-Antoine Charpentier*. Baltimore: Dux Femina Facti, 2004.

Ranum, Patricia. *Vers une chronologie des œuvres de Marc-Antoine Charpentier. Les papiers employés par le compositeur: un outil pour l'étude de sa production et de sa vie*. Baltimore: Dux Femina Facti, 1994.

Rathmann-Lutz, Anja. „*Images" Ludwigs des Heiligen im Kontext dynasticher Konflikte des 14. und 15. Jahrhunderts*. Berlin: Akademie Verlag, 2010.

Rausch, Fabian. 'The Impossible *Gouvernement Représentatif*: Constitutional Culture in Restoration France, 1814–30'. *French History*, 27 (2013): 223–48.

Ravitch, Norman. *The Catholic Church and the French Nation 1589–1989*. London and New York: Routledge, 1990.

Régnault, Émile. *Christophe de Beaumont, archevêque de Paris (1703–1781)*, 2 vols. Paris: Victor Lecoffre, 1882.

Reinhardt, Nicole. *Voices of Conscience: Royal Confessors and Political Counsel in Seventeenth-Century Spain and France*. Oxford: Oxford University Press, 2016.

Restif, Bruno. *La Révolution des paroisses: Culture paroissiale et Réforme catholique en Haute-Bretagne aux XVIᵉ et XVIIᵉ siècles*. Rennes: Presses universitaires de Rennes, 2006.

Rézeau, Pierre. *Les Prières aux Saints en Français à la fin du Moyen-Âge*. Geneva: Droz, 1983.

Richard, Jean. *Saint Louis: Crusader King of France*, ed. Simon Lloyd, trans. Jean Birrell. Cambridge: Cambridge University Press, 1983.

Riley, Philip. *A Lust for Virtue: Louis XIV's Attack on Sin in Seventeenth-Century France*. Westport, CT: Greenwood Press, 2001.

Roche, Daniel. *Le siècle des lumières en province: académies et académiciens provinciaux, 1680–1789*, 2 vols. Paris: Mouton, 1978.

Rosné, abbé de. 'Une cause de la décadence de la chaire au XVIIIᵉ siècle: Les prédicateurs du panégyrique de saint Louis devant l'Académie Française'. *Revue du clergé français*, 62 (1897): 113–34.

Ross, Michael. *Banners of the King: The War of the Vendée, 1793–4*. London: Seeley, 1975.

Roy, Philippe. *Louis XIV et le Second siège de Vienne (1683)*. Paris: Honoré Champion, 1999.

Ruiz, Teofilo. *The City and the Realm: Burgos and Castile, 1080–1492*. Ashgate: Variorum, 1992.

Rule, John (ed.). *Louis XIV and the Craft of Kingship*. Columbus: Ohio State University Press, 1969.

Sabatier, Gérard. 'La gloire du roi: Iconographie de Louis XIV de 1661 à 1672'. *Histoire, Économie et Société*, 19 (2000): 527–60.

Sabatier, Gérard and Margarita Torrione (eds). *¿Louis XIV espagnol?* Versailles: Aulica, 2009.

Sadler, Graham. *The Rameau Compendium*. Woodbridge: Boydel, 2014.

Sagnes, Jean. *Histoire de Sète*. Toulouse: Privat, 1987.

Salbert, Jacques. 'La chapelle saint-Louis du collège de Jésuites de La Flèche en Anjou (aujourd'hui prytanée militaire)'. *Annales de Bretagne et des pays de l'Ouest*, 68 (1961): 163–87.

Salmon, J. H. M. 'Clovis and Constantine: The Uses of History in Sixteenth-Century Gallicanism'. *Journal of Ecclesiastical History*, 41 (1990): 584–605.

Sandberg, Brian. 'Going Off to the War in Hungary: French Nobles and Crusading Culture in the Sixteenth Century'. *The Hungarian Historical Review*, 4 (2015): 346–83.

Schaich, Michael (ed.). *Monarchy and Religion: The Transformation of Royal Culture in Eighteenth-Century Europe*. Oxford: Oxford University Press, 2007.

Schama, Simon. *Citizens: A Chronicle of the French Revolution*. London: Penguin, 1989.

Scherf, Guilhelm. 'L'image sculptée de saint Louis au XVIIIe siècle'. In *Le plaisir de l'art du Moyen Âge: Commande, production et réception de l'œuvre d'art. Mélanges en hommage à Xavier Barral i Altet*, various eds, 1013–22. Paris: Picard, 2012.

Scholz, Natalie. *Die imaginierte Restauration: Repräsentationen der Monarchie im Frankreich Ludwigs XVIII*. Darmstadt: WBG, 2006.

Scholz, Natalie. 'La monarchie sentimentale: un remède aux crises politiques de la Restauration?' In *Représentation et pouvoir: La politique symbolique en France (1789-1830)*, eds Natalie Scholz and Christina Schröer, 185–98. Rennes: Presses Universitaires de Rennes, 2007.

Schutte, Anne Jacobson. *Aspiring Saints: Pretense of Holiness, Inquisition, and Gender in the Republic of Venice, 1618-1750*. Baltimore and London: John Hopkins University Press, 2001.

Scott, Paul. 'Authenticity and Textual Transvestism in the Memoirs of the Abbé de Choisy'. *French Studies*, 69 (2015): 14–29.

Searing, James. *West African Slavery and Atlantic Commerce: The Senegal River Valley, 1700-1860*. Cambridge: Cambridge University Press, 1993.

Sessions, Jennifer. *By Sword and Plow: France and the Conquest of Algeria*. Ithaca and London: Cornell University Press, 2011.

Shapiro, Gilbert and John Markoff. *Revolutionary Demands: A Content Analysis of the Cahiers de Doléances of 1789*. Stanford: Stanford University Press, 1998.

Shusterman, Noah. *Religion and the Politics of Time: Holidays in France from Louis XIV through Napoleon*. Washington, DC: Catholic University of America Press, 2010.

Sluhovsky, Moshe. 'La mobilisation des saints dans la Fronde parisienne d'après les mazarinades'. *Annales. Histoire, Sciences Sociales*, 54 (1999): 353–74.

Sluhovsky, Moshe. *Patroness of Paris: Rituals of Devotion in Early Modern France*. Leiden: Brill, 1998.

Smoller, Laura Ackerman. *The Saint & the Chopped-Up Baby: The Cult of Vincent Ferrer in Medieval and Early Modern Europe*. Ithaca and London: Cornell University Press, 2014.

Sonnino, Paul. *Louis XIV and the Origins of the Dutch War*. Cambridge: Cambridge University Press, 1988.

Sonnino, Paul. *Louis XIV's View of the Papacy (1661-1667)*. Berkely and Los Angeles: University of California Press, 1966.

Soucaille, Antonin. *État monastique de Béziers avant 1789: Notices sur les anciens couvents d'hommes & de femmes d'après des documents originaux*. Béziers: Sapte et Chavardès, 1889.

Spicer, Andrew. '(Re)building the Sacred Landscape: Orléans, 1560-1610'. *French History*, 21 (2007): 247–68.

Strayer, Joseph. *Medieval Statecraft and Perspectives of History: Essays by Joseph Strayer*, ed. John Benton. Princeton: Princeton University Press, 1971.

Sturges, Robert. 'The Guise and the Two Jerusalems: Joinville's *Vie de saint Louis* and an Early Modern Family's Medievalism'. In *Aspiration, Representation and Memory: The Guise in Europe, 1506–1688*, eds Jessica Munns, Penny Richards and Jonathan Spangler, 25–46. Farnham: Ashgate, 2015.

Suire, Éric. *La Sainteté française de la Réforme catholique (XVIᵉ-XVIIIᵉ siècles) d'après les textes hagiographiques et les procès de canonisation*. Bordeaux: Presses Universitaires de Bordeaux, 2001.

Suire, Éric. *Sainteté et Lumières: Hagiographie, Spiritualité et propagande religieuse dans la France du XVIIIᵉ siècle*. Paris: Honoré Champion, 2001.

Swann, Julian. *Exile, Imprisonment, or Death: The Politics of Disgrace in Bourbon France, 1610–1789*. Oxford: Oxford University Press, 2017.

Swann, Julian. *Politics and the Parlement of Paris under Louis XV, 1754–1774*. Cambridge: Cambridge University Press, 1995.

Swann, Julian and Joël Félix (eds). *The Crisis of the Absolute Monarchy: France from Old Regime to Revolution*. Oxford: British Academy, 2013.

Tackett, Timothy. *When the King took flight*. Cambridge, MA: Harvard University Press, 2003.

Tallon, Alain. *Conscience nationale et sentiment religieux en France au XVIᵉ siècle*. Paris: Presses Universitaires de France, 2002.

Tallon, Alain. *La Compagnie du Saint-Sacrement (1629–1667). Spiritualité et société*. Paris: Éditions du Cerf, 1990.

Tallon, Alain. *La France et le Concile de Trente (1518–1563)*. Rome: École Française de Rome, 1997.

Taylor, Larissa (ed.). *Preachers and People in the Reformations and Early Modern Period*. Leiden: Brill, 2001.

Taylor, Larissa. *Soldiers of Christ: Preaching in Late Medieval and Reformation France*. Oxford: Oxford University Press, 1992.

Teisseyre, Charles. 'Le prince chrétien aux XVᵉ et XVIᵉ siècle, à travers les représentations de Charlemagne et de Saint Louis'. *Actes de congrès de la Société des historiens médiévalistes de l'enseignement supérieur public*, 8 (1977): 409–14.

Teule, Herman. 'Saint Louis and the East Syrians, the Dream of a Terrestrial Empire: East Syrian Attitudes to the West'. In *East and West in the Crusader States: Context-Contacts-Confrontations*, eds Krijnie Ciggaar and Herman Teule, 101–22. Leuven: Peeters, 2003.

Thompson, Victoria. 'The Creation, Destruction and Recreation of Henri IV: Seeing Popular Sovereignty in the Statue of a King'. *History and Memory*, 24 (2012): 5–40.

Thorp, Malcolm and Arthur Slavin (eds). *Politics, Religion, and Diplomacy in Early Modern Europe*. Kirksville: Sixteenth Century Journal Publishers, 1994.

Tietz, Manfred. 'Saint Louis roi chrétien: un mythe de la mission intérieure du XVIIᵉ siècle'. In *La Conversion au XVIIᵉ siècle: Actes du XIIe Colloque de Marseille (janvier 1982)*, eds Louise Godard de Donville, 59–69. Marseille: Centre Méridional de Rencontres sur le XVIIᵉ siècle, 1983.

Todd, Christopher. 'La Rédaction du *Mercure de France* (1721–1744): Dufresny, Fuzelier, La Roque'. *Revue d'Histoire littéraire de la France*, 83 (1983): 439–41.

Tort, Olivier. 'Le mythe du retour à l'Ancien Régime sous la Restauration'. In *Rien appris, rien oublié? Les Restaurations dans l'Europe postnapoléonienne (1814–1830)*, eds Jean-Claude Caron and Jean-Philippe Luis, 243–54. Rennes: Presses Universitaires de Rennes, 2015.

Tricoire, Damien. 'Attacking the Monarchy's Sacrality in Late Seventeenth-Century France: The Underground Literature against Louis XIV, Jansenism and the Dauphin's Court Faction'. *French History*, 31 (2017): 152–73.

Tricoire, Damien. 'La Fronde, un soulèvement areligieux au XVIIᵉ siècle? De l'opposition «dévote» sous Richelieu aux Mazarinades de 1649'. *Dix-septième siècle*, 257 (2012): 705–17.

Tricoire, Damien. *La Vierge et le Roi: Politique princière et imaginaire catholique dans l'Europe du XVIIᵉ siècle*. Paris: Presses de l'université Paris-Sorbonne, 2017.

Tricoire, Damien. 'What was the Catholic Reformation? Marian Piety and the Universalization of Divine Love'. *The Catholic Historical Review*, 103 (2017): 20–49.

Tyerman, Christopher. *The Debate on the Crusades*. Manchester: Manchester University Press, 2011.

Tyvaert, Michel. 'L'image du Roi: légitimité et moralité royales dans les Histoires de France au XVIIᵉ siècle'. *Revue d'histoire moderne et contemporaine (1954-)*, 21 (1974): 521–47.

Van Kley, Dale. *The Damiens Affair and the Unravelling of the Ancien Régime, 1750-1770*. Princeton: Princeton University Press, 1984.

Van Kley, Dale. 'The Religious Origins of the French Revolution'. In *From Deficit to Deluge: The Origins of the French Revolution*, eds Thomas Kaiser and Dale Van Kley, 104–38. Stanford: Stanford University Press, 2011.

Van Kley, Dale. *The Religious Origins of the French Revolution: From Calvin to the Civil Constitution, 1560–1791*. New Haven: Yale University Press, 1996.

Vauthier, Gabriel. 'Le Clergé et la Fête de Louis-Philippe en 1831'. *Revue d'Histoire du XIXᵉ siècle*, 71 (1917): 17–23.

Vergé-Franceschi, Michel. *Toulon: Port royal, 1481–1789*. Paris: Tallandier, 2002.

Viansson-Ponté, Louis. *Les Jésuites à Metz*. Strasbourg: F.X. Le Roux, 1897.

Vidal, J.-M. *Les Oratoriens à Saint-Louis des Français: Établissement du pouvoir de l'ambassadeur de France sur l'église nationale (1617-1629)*. Paris: Auguste Picard, 1928.

Viguerie, Jean de. 'Le miracle dans la France du XVIIᵉ siècle'. *XVIIᵉ siècle*, 140 (1983): 313–31.

Vincent, Monique. *Le Mercure Galant: Présentation de la première revue féminine d'information et de culture, 1672-1710*. Paris: Honoré Champion, 2005.

Vinha, Mathieu da, Alexandre Maral and Nicolas Milovanovic (eds). *Louis XIV: l'image et le mythe*. Rennes and Versailles: Presses Universitaires de Rennes and Centre de Recherche du Château de Versailles, 2014.

Volz, Eugène. 'L'église Notre-Dame de Metz'. *Mémoires de l'Académie de Metz*, 13 (1967–1969): 175–200.

Vovelle, Michel. *Ideologies and Mentalities*, trans. E. O'Flaherty. Cambridge: Cambridge University Press, 1990.

Vovelle, Michel. *Piété baroque et déchristianisation en Provence au XVIIIᵉ siècle*. Paris: Seuil, 1978.

Waele, Michel de. *Réconcilier les Français: La fin des troubles de religion (1589-1598)*. Paris: Hermann, 2015.

Wailly, Natalis de. *Mémoire sur la date et le lieu de naissance de Saint Louis.* Paris: Imprimerie impériale, 1867.

Waquet, Françoise. *Les Fêtes Royales sous la Restauration ou l'Ancien Régime retrouvé.* Paris: Arts et Métiers Graphiques, 1981.

Waresquiel, Emmanuel de. *C'est la Révolution qui continue! La Restauration, 1814–1830.* Paris: Tallandier, 2015.

Waresquiel, Emmanuel de. 'L'obstination d'un roi: Louis XVIII en exil, 1791–1814'. *Napoleonica. La Revue,* 22 (2015): 32–43.

Weiner, Daniel. *Constructing the Memory of Saint Louis: The Battling Biographies of 1688.* Saarbrücken: Lambert, 2010.

Weinstein, Donald and Rudolph Bell. *Saints & Society: The Two Worlds of Western Christendom, 1000–1700.* Chicago and London: University of Chicago Press, 1982.

Williams, Hannah. 'Saint Geneviève's Miracles: Art and Religion in Eighteenth-Century Paris'. *French History,* 30 (2016): 322–53.

Wolfe, Michael. *The Conversion of Henri IV: Politics, Power, and Religious Belief in Early Modern France.* Cambridge, MA: Harvard University Press, 1993.

Worcester, Thomas. '"Neither Married nor Cloistered: Blessed Isabelle in Catholic Reformation France"'. *Sixteenth-Century Journal,* 30 (1999): 457–72.

Worcester, Thomas. 'Saints as Cultural History'. In *Exploring Cultural History; Essays in Honour of Peter Burke,* eds Melissa Calaresu, Filippo de Vivo and Joan-Pau Rubiés, 191–205. Farnham: Ashgate, 2010.

Wrede, Martin. 'Le portrait du roi restauré, ou la fabrication de Louis XVIII'. *Revue d'histoire moderne et contemporaine (1954-),* 53 (2006): 112–38.

Wright, Anthony. *The Divisions of French Catholicism, 1629–1645: 'The Parting of the Ways'.* Farnham: Ashgate, 2011.

Youssef, Ahmed. *La Fascination de l'Égypte; Du Rêve au Projet. Avec "Consilium Aegyptiacum", le texte inédit que Leibniz présenta à Louis XIV.* Paris: L'Harmattan, 1998.

Zoberman, Pierre. 'Généalogie d'une image: l'éloge spéculaire'. *XVIIᵉ siècle,* 146 (1985): 79–91.

Zoberman, Pierre. *Les Panégyriques du Roi prononcés dans l'Académie Française.* Paris: Presses de l'Université de Paris-Sorbonne, 1991.

Theses

Bergin, Patrick. 'M.-A. Charpentier's *In honorem Sancti Ludovici Regis Galliae Canticum* (H. 365): A Case Study in Chronology and Rhetoric'. MA diss., Ohio State University, Columbus, 2012.

Clay, Richard Simon. 'Signs of Power: Iconoclasm in Paris, 1789–1795'. PhD thesis, University College London, London, 1999.

Index

Lightning Source UK Ltd.
Milton Keynes UK
UKHW050034260421
382350UK00018B/80